The Changing American Family

The Changing American Family

Sociological and Demographic Perspectives

EDITED BY

Scott J. South
and Stewart E. Tolnay

Westview Press
BOULDER • SAN FRANCISCO • OXFORD

Published in 1992 in the United States of America by Westview Press, Inc., 5500 Central Avenue, Boulder, Colorado 80301-2847, and in the United Kingdom by Westview Press, 36 Lonsdale Road, Summertown, Oxford OX2 7EW

Library of Congress Cataloging-in-Publication Data
The Changing American family : sociological and demographic
perspectives / edited by Scott J. South and Stewart E. Tolnay.
p. cm.
Papers from a conference held in Albany, N.Y., April 6–7, 1990,
sponsored by the Department of Sociology at the State University of
New York at Albany.
Includes bibliographical references.
ISBN 0-8133-1100-4
1. Family demography—United States—Congresses. 2. Family—
United States—Congresses. I. South, Scott J. II. Tolnay,
Stewart Emory. III. State University of New York at Albany. Dept.
of Sociology.
HQ759.98.C45 1992
306.85′0973—dc20 91-39295
CIP

Printed and bound in the United States of America

The paper used in this publication meets the requirements of the American National Standard for Permanence of Paper for Printed Library Materials Z39.48-1984.

10 9 8 7 6 5 4 3 2 1

Contents

Acknowledgments

Several individuals and organizations were instrumental in making the conference for which most of these chapters were prepared a success. Still others have helped push this project toward its completion in the form of this edited volume. We wish to acknowledge here our sincere appreciation of their contributions.

Louise Tornatore, assistant to the chair of the Department of Sociology at SUNY-Albany, performed the herculean tasks of making all of the conference arrangements and seeing that things ran smoothly. They did, but only because of her tireless efforts. Joan Cipperly, administrative assistant in the Department of Sociology, also worked long and hard to ensure an effective conference. We appreciate the support of our colleagues in the sociology department, especially John Logan, chair of the department, and Richard Alba. The thoughtful comments and reactions of all of the conference participants generated a constructive exchange of ideas, and we thank them for their attendance. Dean Birkenkamp, senior editor at Westview Press, deserves our gratitude for encouraging us to publish these chapters as a collection and for tolerating the ever-changing composition of the book.

Financial support for the conference was provided by the American Sociological Association, the National Science Foundation, and SUNY-Albany's Office for Research, College of Social and Behavioral Sciences, Center for Social and Demographic Analysis, and Department of Sociology. Of course, these organizations bear no responsibility for views expressed herein. Finally, we are grateful to the editors and publishers of the *American Sociological Review* and *Population and Development Review* for permission to reprint Chapters 3 and 7, respectively.

Scott J. South
Stewart E. Tolnay

1

Current Themes in the Social Demography of the American Family

Stewart E. Tolnay and Scott J. South

The chapters contained in this volume are drawn from a conference held in Albany, New York, on April 6 and 7, 1990, under the title, Demographic Perspectives on the American Family: Patterns and Prospects. The tenth in a series of conferences sponsored by the Department of Sociology at the State University of New York at Albany, the Albany Conference brought together some of the most prominent sociologists, demographers, and social-historians currently studying the complex issues surrounding the changing American family. The papers presented at the conference were uniformly excellent, often provoking thoughtful debates and unusually productive exchanges of ideas and data. A unique feature of the conference was the blending of historical and contemporary perspectives on family organization and change.

Collectively, the chapters in this volume tackle a wide range of issues central to the social demography of the family. Given the myriad manifestations of change in the American family, this inclusiveness is not merely desirable but necessary. The issues receiving attention include past and current racial differences in family and household structure; the rise in and consequences of nonmarital cohabitation; the role of divorced fathers in the financial and emotional well-being of their children; changing attitudes toward marriage and family life, and the frequently conflictive division of household labor. Although these chapters have not been drafted with the explicit intention of influencing public policy (cf. Cherlin 1988), with their focus on such crucial and enduring concerns they cannot help but inform civic debate.

Our original intent in gathering together the current chapters within a single edited volume was, quite simply, to provide a forum for some of the most insightful and knowledgeable social scientists currently working in the area of family research. Of course, given space limitations it would be foolish to claim that the work represented here is exhaustive of all excellent work in the field. Nevertheless, we believe that we have been successful in achieving our primary objective. In addition, however, this collection enjoys additional benefits of our decision to spotlight the work of this particular group of scholars. As the following chapters will clearly demonstrate, the work represented here is extremely innovative in the questions posed, the data exploited, and the techniques employed. Further, there is a strong multidisciplinary flavor to the volume, with perspectives ranging from strictly demographic to the primarily social-psychological. Finally, this collection of scholarship not only provides answers to many important questions within the field of family studies but also helps to identify potentially fruitful avenues for future research. We have no doubt that much family research conducted in coming years will pursue issues that have been raised by the chapters in this book.

Second, our own interest in the subject matter of this book, as well as our choice of these specific chapters, must also be considered the result of two palpable trends in family research during the past two decades. During that period, scholarly interest and productivity in *family demography* and *family history* have grown phenomenally.

The Growth of Family Demography

Recent shifts in the composition of session topics at the annual meetings of the Population Association of America (PAA) provide revealing evidence of the extent of growth of family demography in recent years. Between the late 1960s and the late 1980s, the number of paper and panel sessions at the PAA meetings grew from about 5 percent to about 15 percent of the total sessions (Presser 1991). By the late 1980s, more paper and panel sessions were devoted to family and household demography than to any other topic, and the total number of sessions on family demography (including roundtables and workshops) was second only to fertility.

What lies behind this rapid growth in social-demographic approaches to the family? Certainly changing demographic realities—the decline in marriage rates and the rise in divorce, the alarming expansion of female-headed households, important changes in household composition, the reallocation of tasks within households, among others—account for some of this recent curiosity. That these demographic shifts are linked so closely to issues of poverty, inequality, and well-being undoubtedly increases our motivation to know more about these changes.

But as Cherlin (1981) points out, demographic change has been a constant throughout this century, so these trends and their correlates can probably not account for all of the contemporary interest in family demography. Rather, we suspect that two other forces have played important roles in the growth of this field. The first of these is a greater willingness among demographers to look outside the demographic system, strictly defined, for explanations of demographic change. More purely demographic approaches to family issues are still taken (e.g., Bongaarts et al. 1987), but the general trend, we sense, is away from insular designs and toward multidisciplinary perspectives. Facilitating the mutual embrace of demography, sociology, and history illustrated in this collection of chapters is the growing number of researchers with expertise in two or more of these fields (Sweet 1977). As one example of this disciplinary catholicism we can point to the joint sponsorship of conference sessions by the Family and Population Sections of the American Sociological Association.

A second and, in our opinion, equally salutary development behind the growth of family demography is the availability of large-scale, nationally representative data sets with which to examine key issues. Given their penchant for accurate description, demographers have traditionally been loath to use small nonrandom samples of the population, although these have been a staple of more general family sociology. Consequently, most of the early work in the demography of the American family relied extensively on census and vital statistics data (Glick 1959). With the advent of large social surveys—including the National Longitudinal Surveys of Men, Women, and Youth, the Panel Study of Income Dynamics, the National Longitudinal Studies of the High School Classes of 1972 and 1980 (the latter more popularly referred to as High School and Beyond), the Survey of Income and Program Participation, and the National Survey of Families and Households, to name a few—demographers were free to engage issues that could not be treated with the customary data sources. Although these data were not always collected with the explicit purpose of monitoring and explaining demographic change, demographers have nevertheless put them to good use.

These twin developments in the study of family demography—the broadened scope and the use of social surveys—both find expression in the chapters in this volume. The chapters go well beyond a narrow concern with marriage and divorce rates, trends, and differentials to consider a wide range of family issues. Moreover, most of the studies rely on one of the large social surveys mentioned previously. Two of them make use of public-use samples from historical U.S. censuses. Perhaps most telling, none of the chapters relies solely on data from the 1980 census or from vital statistics. This is a far cry from Paul Glick's discussion of data sources in his contribution to Hauser and Duncan's classic *The Study of Population* (1959), which focused almost exclusively on census and vital statistics data.

The Growth of Family History

The past two decades have also witnessed explosive growth in the study of family history (see, e.g., Stone 1981). Originally, family historians seemed to have greater curiosity about the family in Western European societies, particularly England and France, than about the American family. Path-breaking studies appeared that considered widely divergent issues pertaining to aspects of family organization and change. For instance, Laslett (1965) exploded the myth that extended families necessarily prevailed in preindustrial times. And Levine (1977) demonstrated how shifts in the organization of production in society could shape the timing of marriage and the pace of marital reproduction. An important impetus for these and other explorations into the Western European family was growing sophistication in the use of surviving documents such as household censuses and parish registries. Much like skilled detectives, family historians have been able to use techniques like family reconstitution to piece together important events in the life course of individual families including marriage, birth, death, and migration. As a result, a much clearer picture has emerged of the Western European family in the past.

Though of slightly more recent origin, studies of American family history have also grown markedly during the past several years. Although not a perfect milepost, the introduction of *The Journal of Family History* in 1976 by the National Council on Family Relations does symbolize the growing interest in the field during the past two decades. Although also publishing work on the European family, this journal has served as a major outlet for research on American family history. This rapidly expanding literature has examined a number of important issues concerning historical patterns and change in the American family including household structure, marriage, childbearing, and the family economy (see, e.g., Gordon 1973; Hareven and Vinovskis 1978; Ruggles 1987; Stern 1987).

Explorations into the American family of the past have benefited enormously from the availability of microfilmed copies of the original U.S. census enumerator's manuscripts. Especially useful have been the nationally representative public-use samples that were created from the 1900 and 1910 censuses. Researchers using these data sources have offered compelling accounts of how American families around the turn of the twentieth century were formed, how they worked, and how they differed by race, ethnicity, and social class. Soon a public-use sample will also be available for the 1880 census, and there are plans to create a public-use sample for the 1920 census as well. In addition to the rich information on families available in federal census data, other data sources of information have been explored by students of American family history—an excellent example being the work of the Mormon Historical Demography Project based on family genealogies maintained by the Mormon church (see, e.g., Bean et al. 1978).

Family scholars in general cannot help but be pleased by the increasing attention paid to family patterns and change in the past. As in other disciplines and specialties, there appears to be a growing awareness in the field of family studies that a comprehensive understanding of present conditions and problems really requires an appreciation of what transpired before.

As with the growth of family demography, the expansion of family history has been distinctly multidisciplinary in nature. Historians, sociologists, political scientists, and anthropologists have collaborated to produce important work (see, e.g., Kertzer and Hogan 1989) or have worked separately, contributing to an incremental growth of knowledge in the field. Seemingly impenetrable barriers that traditionally divided social scientists interested in the family have begun to disintegrate—much to the benefit of scholars from all disciplines and theoretical persuasions.

Interlocking Themes

The diversity of topics addressed in this collection implies that no single explanatory framework can encompass all of the chapters. As noted above, the chapters were selected more on the basis of their contribution to knowledge than their ability to form a coherent and unified whole. Still, although the strength of the collection rests primarily on the quality of the individual chapters, certain recurring themes can be discerned, and these are worth discussing here.

A central concern for many family scholars is racial and ethnic differences in family formation, composition, and cohesion. Recent research shows clearly that not all racial or ethnic groups behave identically as they form new households, or dissolve existing ones. Are such differences merely the result of group differences in access to society's social and economic rewards? Or is part of this racial and ethnic variation in family patterns due to persistent and substantial cultural differences among groups? As a vigorous debate over these questions rages in scholarly circles, policymakers also struggle with the practical implications of group differences in such arenas as teenage childbearing and female-headed households.

Several of the chapters in this volume tackle, in one fashion or another, the thorny issue of racial differences. Two chapters (Schoen and Owens, and Sweet and Bumpass) include race in their consideration of marriage and cohabitation in contemporary American society. Although racial differences are observed, they are not the focus of those chapters, and little interpretative effort is made. Racial differences and their etiology play a central role in the chapters by Ruggles and Goeken; Landale and Tolnay;

South; and Bennett, Bloom, and Craig. Those authors infer strong effects of race at two distinct stages of the life course—the transition to marriage and living arrangements of the elderly.

Other focal concerns of several of these chapters are the behaviors and life circumstances of two actors not often considered in social-demographic research, namely, fathers and children. Two of the chapters (Furstenberg and Harris; Teachman) examine patterns of contact between divorced fathers and their children and the exchange of emotional affect and nonmonetary support between them. Another chapter (Waite and Goldscheider) looks at the contribution of husbands and children to household labor. In his chapter, Thornton gauges the degree to which familial attitudes are transmitted from parents to children. These chapters continue and extend prior efforts to bring these social actors into the social-demographic purview (e.g., Furstenberg 1988; Hernandez 1986; Preston 1984). The inclusion of fathers and children as participants (and perhaps targets) of demographic change does not, of course, deny the predominant roles played by wives and mothers; it does, however, expand the demographic framework to include individuals whose presence (or, in the case of divorced fathers, absence) is too often ignored. We view this as a welcome corrective to much prior research.

There is also a strong undercurrent of historical change in many of the chapters in this collection. This is quite obvious among the chapters in Part 1 (Family Patterns: The Historical Dimension), but also implicit in many of the chapters in the remainder of the volume. As with other social institutions, the American family must be somewhat malleable and able to evolve in response to other societal transformations. Although the connections are not always drawn explicitly, there can be little doubt that two central concerns of some of these chapters—the role of absent fathers (Furstenberg and Harris; Teachman) and the rise of nonmarital cohabitation (Rindfuss and VandenHeuvel; Schoen and Owens; Sweet and Bumpass) would not have been present if this collection had been published fifty years ago. Similarly, an examination of the division of household labor (Waite and Goldscheider) is made much more salient by the astounding rise of female labor-force participation during the past fifty years. One can only wonder how a collection of chapters on the changing American family published fifty years from now will differ from this volume.

One theme crosscutting several of the chapters is a recognition of the importance for demographic behavior of norms, attitudes, perceptions, and emotions, subjects that if not previously anathema to most demographers have not been accorded much prominence. Traditionally, social demographers have been more concerned with actual behavior than with the cultural supports and psychological predispositions that underlie that behavior. In contrast, these chapters examine such nonbehavioral matters as affective relations between divorced fathers and their children, attitudes toward sex roles and family life, and the perceptions of marriage and cohabitation.

This new emphasis on norms and attitudes has the potential to add significantly to our theoretical explanations of demographic behavior. For example, one plausible implication of Arland Thornton's chapter is that the transmission of attitudes from parents to their children serves as a mechanism for the perpetuation of cultural differences in family behavior and structure. If, as some have suggested (e.g., Morgan et al. 1990), racial differences in family structure are attributable more to culture than to sociodemographic background, then the intergenerational transmission of values and beliefs explains how those cultural differences persist through time. It would be unwise, of course, to overplay these types of explanations. The demographic armamentarium is probably not well equipped to explain how and why these cultural variations arose in the first place; this task is perhaps best left to other social scientists. And, as Steven Ruggles and Ron Goeken point out, norms and attitudes are to some extent part of the behaviors themselves and are thus equally deserving of explanation. Nevertheless, the further incorporation of norms, culture, attitudes, and values into social-demographic studies has considerable potential to enrich both descriptive and explanatory research.

Organization and Content of the Book

The chapters are grouped into three sections reflecting their general overall focus. However, as suggested previously, there will also be obvious linkages across the three sections. Here we offer a very brief description of the book's three sections and the chapters included in each.

Part 1. Family Patterns: The Historical Dimension

Increasingly, social scientists are acknowledging that an appreciation of historical patterns is essential for a complete understanding of present conditions. At the very least, we cannot be sure whether the present is truly different unless we know what the past was like. Of potentially greater value, however, is the possibility that a historical appreciation can inform us of the etiology of the present status quo. In light of this perspective, Part 1 examines some key issues related to the American family of the past.

Two chapters in Part 1 examine racial differences in family formation or household structure in the historical context. Ruggles and Goeken take a long view and describe trends in the prevalence of multigenerational families among whites and blacks from 1900 to 1980. Their evidence reveals intriguing differences in the level of and trend in multigenerational families during the past century. Although they acknowledge the role of structural changes that differentially affected blacks and whites during this era, they also suggest that underlying cultural differences between blacks and whites may help to explain the divergent patterns.

Landale and Tolnay also examine racial variation in family behavior in a historical context but shift our attention to the timing of marriage and establishment of independent households in the rural South in 1910. They contend that racial stratification (i.e., the southern caste system) helps to determine the structure of economic opportunities available to young adults. In turn, economic opportunity is an important determinant of the feasibility of marriage. As a result, blacks and whites are found to exhibit different patterns of family formation and to respond differently to the prevailing socioeconomic climate.

In a somewhat different vein, Holmes and Vinovskis provide an interesting description of the origins of the Federal Pension Program for Civil War Widows and its influence on the living arrangements of war widows. This program was one of the first social welfare policies to attempt to alleviate the negative consequences of family disruption and may be valuable for understanding the implications of modern programs that have proliferated during the past half-century. This chapter also illustrates the potentially paramount impact of unpredictable events (such as wars) on demographic structure and behaviors.

Part 2. Marriage and Cohabitation: Current Issues

The chapters in Part 2 move us into the present and shift out attention to the apparently increasing reluctance of Americans to enter marital unions and their growing willingness to enter into alternative lifestyles such as nonmarital cohabitation. This set of chapters examines in some depth recent attitudes and behaviors related to the timing of and desirability of marriage, as well as alternatives to it.

Bennett, Bloom, and Craig describe recent trends for American women in the timing of marriage and the propensity to ever marry. Significant racial differences emerge from their analyses. On average, black women marry somewhat later than white women and are considerably more likely to never marry—28 percent and 11 percent for blacks and whites, respectively. They emphasize, however, that marriage patterns for blacks *and* whites are complex and vary markedly by educational attainment and economic status. Schoen and Owens show that as the popularity of early marriage has declined, the incidence of nonmarital cohabitation has increased sharply. Moreover, a shrinking percentage of first cohabitations are ending with marriage of the couple. The findings by Schoen and Owens are generally consistent with the provocative argument made by Rindfuss and VandenHeuvel that nonmarital cohabitation is really an "extension of singlehood" rather than an alternative to marriage. They find that cohabiters are more similar to single persons than to married persons along a range of social and demographic dimensions.

A somewhat different viewpoint is represented by Sweet and Bumpass, who examine a wide variety of attitudes about marriage and cohabitation held by young adults. According to Sweet and Bumpass, although cohabitation is widely accepted, the overwhelming majority of cohabiting couples (80 percent) expect to marry their current partner. And most Americans firmly intend to marry at some point in their lifetimes. The chapter by South continues this focus on the subjective aspects of marital entry by examining sociodemographic differentials in the expected benefits from marriage. His key finding is that the expected benefits from marriage vary sharply by age, race, sex, and socioeconomic resources but that complex interactions among these variables defy any simple interpretation. One striking result is that compared to other sociodemographic groups, young black men see the least benefit to marriage, implying that the reticence of black males, along with other factors described by Bennett, Bloom, and Craig, may help account for the low marriage rates of black women.

Part 3. Families, Parents, and Children

If the increasing popularity of nonmarital cohabitation and the increasing reluctance to enter marital unions suggest the decline of American marriages, so too does the impressive likelihood of marital dissolution and the weakening attachments between absent parents and their biological children. The chapters in Part 3 focus our attention on these and other issues dealing with relationships among family members—especially across generations.

Among the many concerns associated with the increasing prevalence of divorce in American society is the possibility of deteriorating attachments between children and absent parents. Not only does this threaten the availability of appropriate parental role models, but certain sociological theories tell us that the absence of such attachments is a key antecedent of nonnormative behavior. Two chapters in this section explore a specific dimension to this problem—the failure of absent fathers to maintain contact or to provide assistance for their biological children. Furstenberg and Harris provide sobering evidence of the deterioration of father-child relations after divorce and note that the fusion of biological and sociological fatherhood is being radically transformed as the institution of marriage declines. Reinforcing the picture sketched by Furstenberg and Harris, Teachman documents a disturbing infrequency of financial *and* nonmonetary assistance from divorced fathers to their biological children. When combined, these chapters raise important and timely questions about the future of fatherhood in a society in which marriage is perhaps an all-too-fleeting phenomenon.

The second two chapters in this section shift our focus from disrupted families to relationships within intact families. One of the key functions of families is the transmission of attitudes, knowledge, and values across generations. Thornton's chapter describes the similarities and differences in behavior and beliefs between parental and children's generations. He demonstrates interesting intergenerational continuity in some behaviors—especially early marriage and premarital pregnancy. Waite and Goldscheider's examination of work in the home shows an overwhelming share of the burden falling on women. Although the share of work performed by husbands has increased, it is largely a substitution for the remarkably shrinking involvement of children in work around the home. Thus, not only are fathers (divorced ones) becoming estranged from their biological children but children are increasingly withdrawing from the routine tasks required in the home.

References

Bean, L. L., D. L. May, and M. Skolnick. 1978. "The Mormon Historical Demography Project." *Historical Methods* 11: 45–53.

Bongaarts, John, Thomas K. Burch, and Kenneth Wachter (eds.). 1987. *Family Demography: Methods and Their Applications.* Oxford: Clarendon Press.

Cherlin, Andrew J. 1981. *Marriage, Divorce, Remarriage.* Cambridge, MA: Harvard University Press.

——— (ed.). 1988. *The Changing American Family and Public Policy.* Washington, DC: Urban Institute Press.

Furstenberg, Frank F., Jr. 1988. "Good Dads-Bad Dads: The Two Faces of Fatherhood." Pp. 193–218 in Andrew J. Cherlin (ed.), *The Changing American Family and Public Policy.* Washington, DC: Urban Institute Press.

Glick, Paul C. 1959. "Family Statistics." Pp. 576–603 in Philip M. Hauser and Otis Dudley Duncan (eds.), *The Study of Population: An Inventory and Appraisal.* Chicago: University of Chicago Press.

Gordon, Michael (ed.). 1973. *The American Family in Social-Historial Perspective.* New York: St. Martin's Press.

Hareven, Tamara, and Maris Vinovskis (eds.). 1978. *Family and Population in Nineteenth-Century America.* Princeton, NJ: Princeton University Press.

Hernandez, Donald J. 1986. "Childhood in Sociodemographic Perspective." *Annual Review of Sociology* 12: 159–180.

Kertzer, David I., and Dennis P. Hogan. 1989. *Family, Political Economy, and Demographic Change: The Transformation of Life in Casalecchio, Italy, 1861–1921.* Madison, WI: University of Wisconsin Press.

Laslett, Peter. 1965. *The World We Have Lost.* New York: Charles Scribner's Sons.

Levine, David. 1977. *Family Formation in an Age of Nascent Capitalism.* New York: Academic Press.

Morgan, S. Philip, Antonio McDaniel, Andrew Miller, and Samuel H. Preston. 1990. "Racial Differences in Household and Family Structure at the Turn of the Century." Paper presented at the Albany Conference on Demographic Perspectives on the American Family: Patterns and Prospects, Albany, NY, April 6–7.

Presser, Harriet B. 1991. "Changes in the PAA Program: Late 1960s vs. Late 1980s." *PAA Affairs* (Spring): 2–3.

Preston, Samuel H. 1984. "Children and the Elderly: Divergent Paths for America's Dependents." *Demography* 21: 435–457.

Ruggles, Steven. 1987. *Prolonged Connections: The Rise of the Extended Family in Nineteenth Century England and America.* Madison, WI: University of Wisconsin Press.

Stern, Mark. 1987. *Family and Society: Erie County, New York, 1850–1920.* Albany, NY: SUNY Press.

Stone, Lawrence. 1981. "Family History in the 1980s: Past Achievements and Modern Trends." *Journal of Interdisciplinary History* 12: 51–87.

Sweet, James A. 1977. "Demography and the Family." *Annual Review of Sociology* 3: 363–405.

PART ONE

Family Patterns: The Historical Dimension

2

Race and Multigenerational Family Structure, 1900–1980

Steven Ruggles and Ron Goeken

In the late nineteenth century, family and household composition in the United States was more complex than ever before or since.[1] More than a fifth of Americans resided with their extended kin, and about a quarter resided in households with nonrelatives, usually boarders, lodgers, or servants. Most people lived in extended or augmented households at some point during the course of their lives. Fewer than one in twenty households consisted of only one person (Ruggles 1987, 1988).

The 1980s represent the opposite extreme: Households are now simpler than they have ever been. Only 6 percent of households now include extended kin, and the proportion of families with unrelated individuals is even lower. This change does not reflect a new dominance of nuclear households consisting of a husband, a wife, and their children. The frequency of such households has declined by about a third, and by 1983 they accounted for only 29 percent of all households. The change has come through an increase in fragmentary households: married couples without children, unmarried couples, single-parent households, and persons living alone (Ruggles 1988; Sweet and Bumpass 1987; U.S. Bureau of the Census 1983, 1987).

This chapter represents the preliminary stage of a larger project concerning one facet of the simplification of household structure: the decline of multigenerational living arrangements, with a special focus on differentials between blacks and whites. Figure 2.1 shows the percentages of elderly whites and blacks residing with adult children or extended kin in each available census year. There are no data currently available on such living arrangements for the 1920 and 1930 census years, so there may have been fluctuations in the interval between 1910 and 1940 that are not reflected in the graph. At the turn of the century, about 65 percent of whites aged

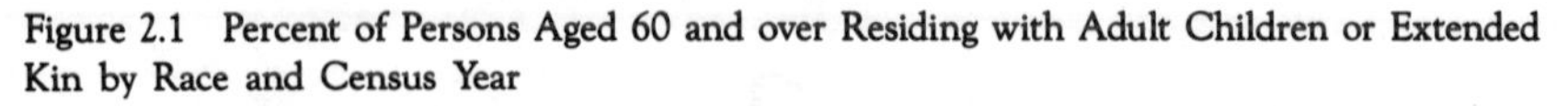

Figure 2.1 Percent of Persons Aged 60 and over Residing with Adult Children or Extended Kin by Race and Census Year

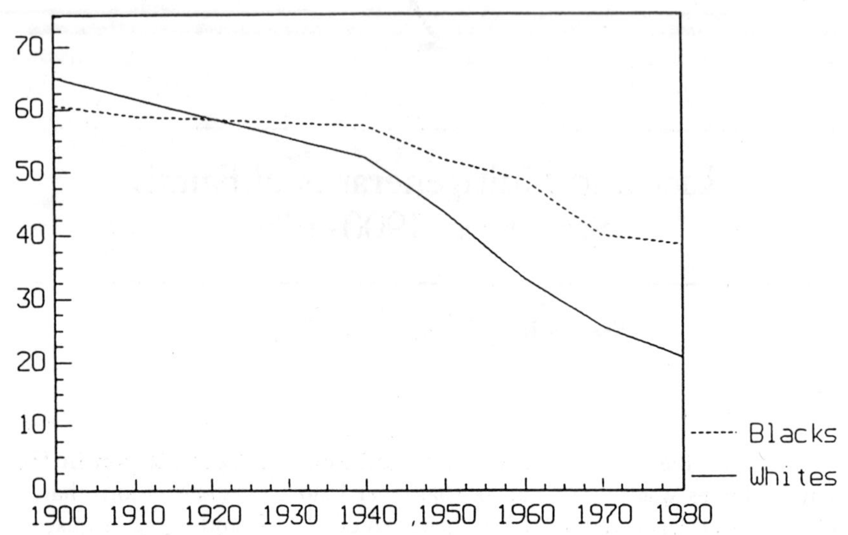

sixty or older resided with their adult children or extended kin. The proportion of elderly blacks with such living arrangements was slightly lower. By 1980, the situation had changed dramatically: Only a quarter of the elderly resided with adult children or kin. Moreover, by the later census year a substantial differential had emerged between elderly blacks and whites; blacks resided with adult children or other kin almost twice as frequently as did whites.

Our research focuses on these dramatic shifts in living arrangements. We are concerned with two basic questions: (1) Why did the frequency of multigenerational and extended families decline during the course of the twentieth century? (2) What is the source of the reversal of the race differential in the family structure of the aged?

Theoretical Considerations

A generation ago there would have been near consensus among historians and sociologists about the causes of the simplification of household structure during the past century. Most scholars regarded the breakdown of complex household structures as an inevitable consequence of economic and social development. Structural-functionalists argued that a shift from family to factory production undermined extended and augmented households (Parsons 1959; Parsons and Bales 1955; Smelser 1959). Modernization theorists pointed to economic and social mobility, the rise of individualism, urbanization, literacy and education, the loss of traditional values, and the decline of community, all of which supposedly reduced the utility of the extended family and contributed to the ideal of the isolated nuclear family (Fletcher 1963; Goode 1963; Nimkoff 1962; Tonnies 1957). Virtually all theorists envisioned a general shift from extended family to nuclear family structure sometime between the seventeenth and the twentieth centuries.

We now know that these models contradict the historical record for Western Europe and the United States. Few people lived in extended families before the nineteenth century. The evidence indicates that the frequency of extended families actually increased during the industrial revolution, as did the incidence of boarding and lodging (Anderson 1971; Laslett 1972; Ruggles 1987; Wall 1983).

Clearly, then, there is no straightforward relationship between economic development or modernization and the decline of complex family structures. In the wake of these findings, the theorists are in disarray. Some historians and sociologists have turned to new kinds of functional economic explanation. They argue that the harsh economic conditions of early industrial capitalism strengthened the interdependence of family members and led to a high frequency of extended families (Chudacoff and Hareven 1979; Hareven 1978; Katz 1975; Modell 1978). According to exchange theorists, multigenerational families served a variety of economic needs for their members (Anderson 1971, 1976). The elderly often lacked sufficient resources to meet their living expenses, but they could provide assistance to their children, especially in the area of childcare for families with working mothers. Many historians agree that extended living arrangements often served as a defense against poverty. By "sharing and huddling," a family could make the most efficient use of limited resources (Foster 1974; Levine 1977; Medick 1976). In the twentieth century, according to this thesis, real wages rose and living conditions improved, and so the functional need for extended families diminished. Thus, the result of the relaxation of economic stress was a general simplification of family structure; people started living independently because they could afford it (Beresford and Rivlin 1966; Michael, Fuchs, and Scott 1980; also, see Angel and Tienda 1982).

Other theorists point to institutional changes in the twentieth century. The institutionalization of fixed retirement ages and the simultaneous introduction of private pensions and Social Security are said to have contributed to the fragmentation of extended families because they provided the means for the elderly to maintain separate residences. The restrictions imposed on welfare recipients under Aid to Families with Dependent Children are also seen as contributing to the fragmentation of households (Anderson 1977; Chevan and Korson 1972; King 1988; Troll 1971).

The black extended family has its own theoretical literature. In the first half of this century, several sociologists argued that conditions of slavery had resulted in disorganization and instability in black families (DuBois 1909; Frazier 1939). The thesis that the black family was pathological became the dominant interpretation of the 1940s and 1950s (Elkins 1959; Myrdal 1944). This school of research culminated with Moynihan's (1965) report, which concluded that the "pathological" nature of black communities could be traced to the deterioration of black family life. In response to Moynihan's study, which emphasized the high frequency of black female-headed households, many sociologists have stressed the strength of extended kin ties among blacks (e.g., Aschenbrenner 1973; Hays and Mindel 1973; Hill 1971; Martin and Martin 1978; McAdoo 1983; Riessman 1966; Staples 1975). Most argue that the black extended family is a defense against poverty or a means of coping with single parenthood (Allen 1979; Billingsley 1968; Farley 1971; Fischer et al. 1968; Hofferth 1984; Stack 1974). Others point to cultural differences between blacks and whites that encourage stronger multigenerational kin ties among blacks (Nobles 1978; Scanzoni 1971; Shimkin, Shimkin, and Frate 1978). Historical research, by contrast, has challenged Moynihan's thesis from the opposite direction by pointing out that most blacks in the nineteenth century resided in male-headed nuclear families (Furstenberg et al. 1975; Gutman 1975, 1976; Lammermeir 1973; Pleck 1972; Riley 1975; Shifflet 1975; Smith et al. 1979).

Social scientists frequently view household structure as a strategic and rational response to prevailing demographic or economic conditions. This functional approach is partly a consequence of static analysis. If we study household structure at a single moment in time, the range of potential explanations is effectively limited to concurrent structural factors. We believe that analyses of household structure should focus on processes of change. This is especially important because a large body of sociological theory rests on untested assumptions about the evolution of the family. Our ability to construct meaningful social theory and to design effective public policy is handicapped if we are limited to static explanation. To understand current residential behavior we should study behavior in the past.

Data Sources

This research is made possible by the recent release of large microdata sets of historical census data. We have used samples drawn from the United States federal censuses for the census years 1900, 1910, 1940, 1950, 1960, 1970, and 1980, and we plan to add data from the 1880 census when it becomes available (Graham 1979; Ruggles and Menard 1990; Strong et al. 1989; U.S. Bureau of the Census 1972, 1973, 1982, 1984a, 1984b). Since 1960, the Census Bureau has made public-use samples of the census available to researchers within a few years of the decennial enumeration. During the past decade, projects carried out at the University of Washington, the

University of Pennsylvania, and the University of Wisconsin in conjunction with the Census Bureau have converted large national samples of the 1900, 1910, 1940, and 1950 census manuscripts into machine-readable form, and a similar project for the 1880 census is currently underway at the Minnesota Social History Research Laboratory.

All these census files provide individual-level information on age, sex, race, family relationships, marital status, occupation, and birthplace. For the most part, these basic variables can be made closely compatible across census years. Although there were significant changes in census definitions and variations in the sampling procedures, it is possible to construct consistent versions of the census files with only a moderate loss of information. For a full discussion of the problems of comparing data from the series of public-use samples and the methods we have used to overcome them, see Ruggles (1991).

Changes in Family Structure and Demography

The dramatic changes in population composition during the course of the twentieth century complicate the study of changing family structure. Life expectancy at the turn of the century was about 47 years, compared with 74 in 1980, and total fertility was twice as high as it is today. These changes had important consequences for extended family structure, because they altered the pool of kin available for coresidence. In addition, massive urbanization during the twentieth century has transformed the social context of family life.

We have only begun to sort out the effects of these changes. An initial attempt to account for the long-term effects of compositional change is given in Figure 2.2. Like Figure 2.1, this graph shows the percentage of elderly blacks and whites residing with adult children or extended kin, but this time we have simultaneously controlled for race and period differentials in age, sex, marital status/presence of spouse, metropolitan residence, and farm residence. The method we used is multiple standardization, which is closely related to the decomposition of rates approach as developed by Kitagawa (1955) and later refined by Das Gupta (1978). The appendix to this chapter describes the methods and decomposes the race and period differentials into the effects of each factor. For whites, the effects of factors tended to cancel one another out; overall, the changes in population composition can account for only 6.2 percent of the overall decline in the proportion of the elderly residing with adult children or other kin. By contrast, among blacks compositional factors account for more than 40 percent of the change in family structure.

For these reasons, in Figure 2.2 the contrast in the historical experience of blacks and whites is magnified. When population structure is held

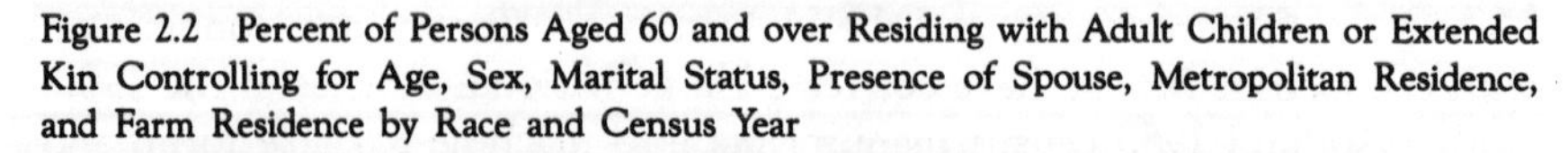

Figure 2.2 Percent of Persons Aged 60 and over Residing with Adult Children or Extended Kin Controlling for Age, Sex, Marital Status, Presence of Spouse, Metropolitan Residence, and Farm Residence by Race and Census Year

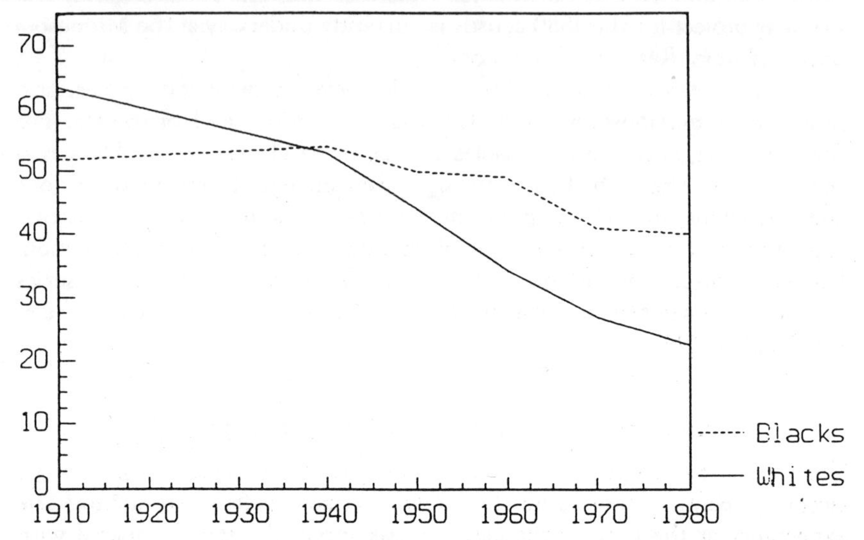

constant, the peak frequency of residence with adult children or kin among blacks occurred in 1940 instead of 1900, and the long-term decline of such families was small. The dramatic simplification of family structure of the elderly in the twentieth century mainly affected whites; among blacks, there has been relatively little change.

The treatment of family structure as a simple dichotomy masks some key differences between blacks and whites. Table 2.1 breaks the living arrangements of the elderly into seven categories. The top section for each race shows the percentages of persons 60 and over residing in simple families, subdivided into those residing without any relatives and those residing with only their spouse or children under 21. Among both blacks and whites, the increase of simple families has been evenly divided between these two categories.

The second section of Table 2.1 shows the percentages of elderly residing in multigenerational families, which we define as residence with children who are older than 21 or ever-married. These are subdivided into residence with never-married adult children, ever-married adult children and no grandchildren, and both children and grandchildren. The final section of the table gives the percentages of elderly residing with other extended kin, broken into residence with grandchildren and no children and residence with other extended kin. This last category of other kin primarily consists of siblings, nephews, and nieces.

TABLE 2.1 Living Arrangements of the Elderly by Year and Race Controlling for Age, Sex, and Marital Status

	1900	*1910*	*1940*	*1950*	*1960*	*1970*	*1980*
Whites, residing in							
Simple families	**34.9**	**38.1**	**47.0**	**55.8**	**65.9**	**74.1**	**78.4**
Unrelated individuals	14.4	15.6	19.3	22.7	26.8	31.8	35.2
Spouse and/or child under 21	20.5	22.5	27.7	33.1	39.1	42.3	43.2
Multigenerational families	**53.4**	**50.1**	**42.2**	**32.9**	**22.3**	**16.4**	**14.1**
Never-married adult child	24.2	23.4	18.8	12.4	9.5	7.2	7.1
Ever-married child	7.2	7.5	9.1	8.6	5.1	3.9	3.6
Child and grandchild	22.0	19.2	14.3	11.9	7.7	5.3	3.4
Other extended families	**11.7**	**11.7**	**10.9**	**11.1**	**11.7**	**9.4**	**7.5**
Grandchild, no adult child	3.7	2.9	2.0	1.5	1.3	1.3	0.8
Other kin	8.0	8.8	8.9	9.6	10.4	8.1	6.7
Total	100.0	100.0	100.0	100.0	100.0	100.0	100.0
Number of cases	5791	11402	12368	17160	10882	13282	15601
Blacks, residing in							
Simple families	**37.2**	**40.9**	**42.2**	**48.7**	**51.9**	**60.5**	**62.0**
Unrelated individuals	15.8	18.4	18.4	21.7	22.6	26.8	28.3
Spouse and/or child under 21	21.4	22.5	23.8	27.0	29.3	33.7	33.7
Multigenerational families	**38.4**	**38.9**	**36.3**	**30.8**	**25.4**	**20.5**	**21.9**
Never-married adult child	9.0	8.9	7.4	4.9	4.6	5.9	7.2
Ever-married child	7.8	8.4	11.4	10.8	8.4	5.9	6.0
Child and grandchild	21.6	21.6	17.5	15.1	12.4	8.7	8.7
Other extended families	**24.4**	**20.0**	**21.5**	**20.5**	**22.7**	**19.0**	**16.2**
Grandchild, no adult child	12.5	11.0	9.1	8.1	7.1	6.4	5.3
Other kin	11.9	9.0	12.4	12.4	15.6	12.6	10.9
Total	100.0	100.0	100.0	100.0	100.0	100.0	100.0
Number of cases	535	1562	4659	6248	8601	11671	14100

For elderly whites, the largest category of multigenerational families in 1900 was comprised of persons living with their adult never-married children. The late-Victorian pattern of coresidence of single children—especially daughters—and their elderly parents is a common theme of nineteenth-century literature, and the phenomenon has also been noted by social historians (Anderson 1984; Auerbach 1978, 1982; King and Ruggles 1990; Mintz 1983; Ruggles 1987; Showalter 1977; Watkins 1984). A high proportion—over 10 percent—of white women in this period never married. Contemporaries generally ascribed this to the "selfishness" of bachelors or to the "surplus of women" (Burgess 1965; Cobbe 1862; Cruikshank et al. 1912:330; also, see citations in Kanner 1972:182–185). Given the social and economic constraints of marriage in the late nineteenth century, no doubt many white women chose not to marry in order to maintain their independence. Those who never married typically remained in their parental households because there were few alternatives available to single women in this period. Moreover, the prescriptive literature of the period is clear on the duties of children to care for their parents in old age (See, for example, Butler 1912; Griffin 1886; Hague 1855; Robins 1896). Indeed, it is likely that some women at the turn of the century never married precisely because they felt obligated to remain in their parental households.

During the course of the twentieth century, it became more socially acceptable for unmarried white women to live alone or in group quarters, and the Victorian sense of duty to parents diminished. Moreover, after the Great Depression the proportion of women marrying increased dramatically. Between 1900 and 1980, the proportion of elderly whites residing with never-married adult children declined from 24.2 percent to 7.1 percent, a change that accounts for over 40 percent of their total decline in the frequency of multigenerational families.

Among blacks, residence of the elderly with unmarried children has never been very frequent, and the frequency of such living arrangements has changed only slightly over the century. This is probably related to higher proportions marrying among blacks; almost 97 percent of blacks at the turn of the century eventually got married. In addition, the social constraints against unmarried women living alone—which were most pronounced among the white bourgeoisie—probably had a smaller effect on blacks than on whites.

A second major difference between blacks and whites in family composition has been the proportion residing with grandchildren but without married children. This category appears near the bottom of Table 2.1. From 1900 through 1980, elderly blacks were three to eight times more likely than whites to reside with grandchildren only. A significant source of this difference is higher mortality among blacks, which left a larger proportion of parentless grandchildren. We have not yet developed estimates of the differential frequencies of parentless grandchildren, but although the mortality differentials are large we expect that they are not great enough to account for the entire race difference in residence with grandchildren. Shimkin, Louie, and Frate (1971) have suggested that the high frequency of blacks residing with grandchildren and no children in the South can be ascribed to the reverse migration of grandchildren whose parents had moved north. However, because northward migration was only a minor phenomenon at the outset of our period, this too is only a partial explanation. A third possibility is that the differential is connected to higher rates of illegitimacy among blacks. All three of these explanations can be investigated further, and we intend to pursue them.

The rest of this chapter focuses on the multigenerational category of Table 2.1. Analyses of the trends and race differentials in multigenerational family structure should take the experience of both the older generation and the younger generation into account, because the power to decide whether to form a multigenerational family often rests with the younger generation. Figure 2.3 compares the frequency of multigenerational families from the perspective of the younger generation and the older generation. The top panel, Figure 2.3a, shows the percentages of persons aged 21 to 59 residing with elderly parents, and Figure 2.3b shows the percentage of persons aged 60 and over residing with adult or ever-married children. Like Figure 2.2, both the graphs in Figure 2.3 use multiple standardization to control for compositional change in age, sex, marital status/presence of spouse, metropolitan residence, and farm residence.

The trends and differentials in multigenerational family structure are strikingly different when we measure them from the perspective of the younger generation. When we control for the changing population composition, the peak frequency of multigenerational residence for the younger generation occurred in 1950 among both whites and blacks. There has been a sharp decline in the frequency of multigenerational families for younger-generation whites since 1950, but for blacks the percentage has remained constant. Equally important, when we control for differential population composition, residence with elderly parents was more common among whites than among blacks in every census year except 1980, when the two were virtually identical.

The contrasts between Figures 2.3a and 2.3b are probably largely a result of demographic patterns. Controlling for the effects of changing population composition only partly accounts for the effects of demography on family structure. The decline in mortality between 1900 and 1950 meant that far more adults had living parents with whom they could reside. Furthermore, declining fertility from the late nineteenth century to the depression meant that adults in 1950 had many fewer siblings than their counterparts of 1900. Because the elderly have rarely resided with more than one of their adult children, the decline of fertility meant that the increasing numbers of parents were divided between a declining number of offspring, so the odds of residence with any particular adult child went up. These two demographic factors are doubtless responsible for the increase in the percentages of adults residing with their parents from 1900 to 1950. After 1950, the mortality trend slowed and the fertility trend reversed, and the overall percentage of the younger generation residing in multigenerational families finally began to go down.

Mortality and fertility also affected the differential frequency with which adult blacks and whites resided with their parents (Ruggles 1986, 1987). Black mortality has been markedly higher than that of whites throughout

Figure 2.3a Percent of Persons Aged 21–59 Residing with Parents Aged 60 or over Controlling for Age, Sex, Marital Status, Presence of Spouse, Metropolitan Residence, and Farm Residence by Race and Census Year

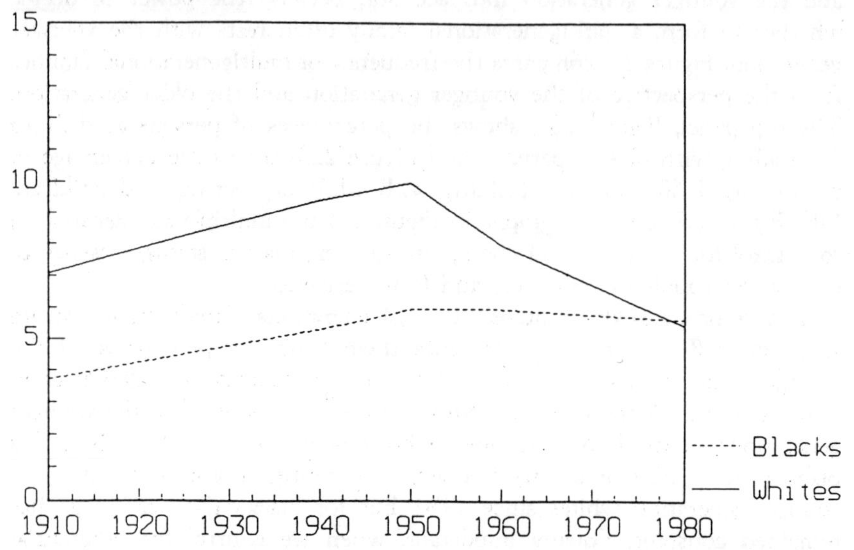

Figure 2.3b Percent of Persons Aged 60 and over Residing with Adult Children Controlling for Age, Sex, Marital Status, Presence of Spouse, Metropolitan Residence, and Farm Residence by Race and Census Year

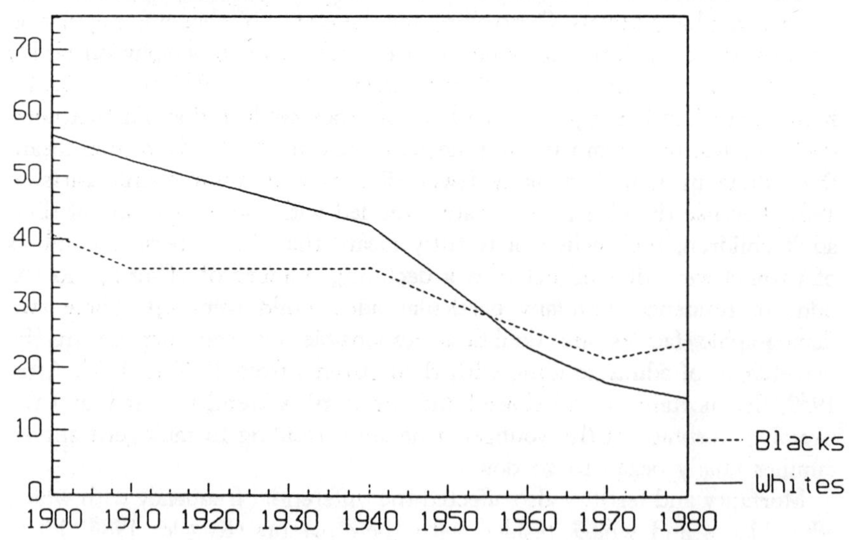

American history, and for most of the twentieth century black fertility has been higher than white fertility. Thus, black adults were less likely to have living parents and had a larger number of siblings competing for the available parents. By comparison, white adults have consistently had greater demographic opportunities to reside with their parents.

The effects of demographic differences on the frequency of multigenerational families are not confined to the younger generation. Clearly, the fertility of the elderly determines their opportunities to reside with children: Those with many children are more likely to have at least one who wants to coreside. Mortality is also a factor, both because it affects the number of surviving children and because the death of a spouse can precipitate the formation of a multigenerational family. The effects of spousal mortality are controlled in Figures 2.2 and 2.3, because they are standardized for marital status and presence of spouse.

Economic Status and Multigenerational Family Structure

The leading explanation for the decline of multigenerational living arrangements among the elderly is that rising incomes allowed increasing numbers of the aged to maintain separate residences. Unfortunately, the census did not provide sufficient information to calculate the total income of the elderly members of each family until 1960. This section will first briefly examine the effects of rising incomes on the family structure of the elderly in 1960 and 1980 and will then turn to alternate measures of economic status to investigate the question in the earlier period.

Figure 2.4 shows the relationship between the income of each generation and the frequency of multigenerational families in 1960 and 1980. The two graphs at the top of the page give the percentages of the elderly residing in multigenerational families for blacks and whites, and the two graphs at the bottom show the percentages of persons aged 21 to 59 residing with elderly parents. In all four graphs, income refers to the sum of own income and spouse's income and is expressed in quintiles.

Among the elderly, low income was associated with a high frequency of multigenerational families among both races in both census years. The same was true for the younger generation in 1980, but in 1960 the frequency of multigenerational families was not consistently related to income of the younger generation for either whites or blacks.

To estimate how much of the decline in the frequency of multigenerational families between 1960 and 1980 should be ascribed to increasing income, we turned to decomposition analysis (Das Gupta 1978; Ruggles 1989). Income was expressed in hundreds of 1967 dollars, and we simultaneously controlled for age, sex, and marital status. Among whites, the rise in incomes of the

Figure 2.4 Percent of Persons in Multigenerational Families Controlling for Age, Sex, Marital Status, and Presence of Spouse by Income, Generation, Race, and Census Year

a) Older Generation (Persons 60 and Over)

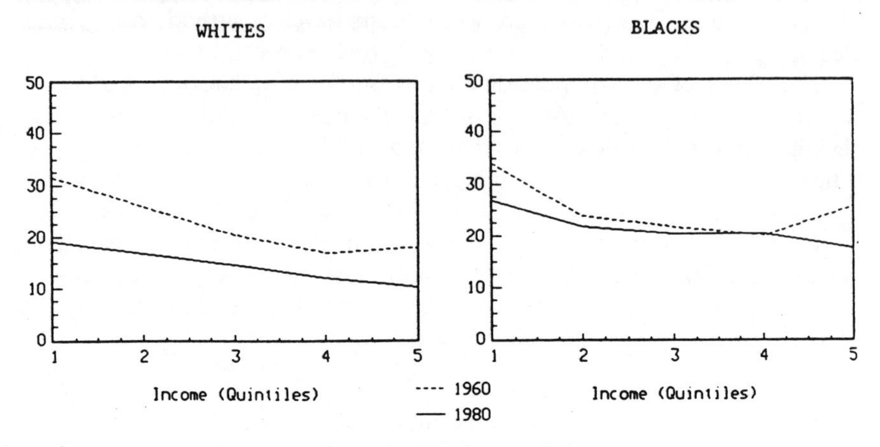

b) Younger Generation (Persons 21-59 Years Old)

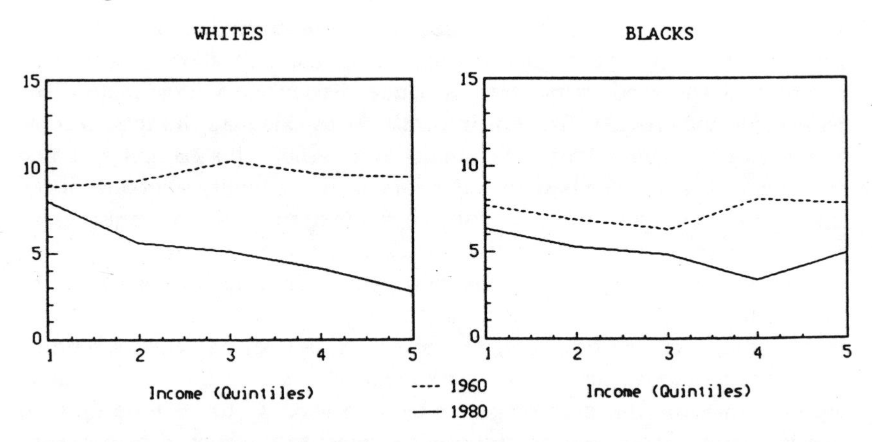

older generation can account for a 3.8 percent drop in the frequency of multigenerational families, or just under half of the change that actually took place. For blacks, the effect of income is a 3.3 percent decline in multigenerationals, which is almost 95 percent of the change that took place. These findings reinforce those studies that have found rising incomes to be a major factor in the simplification of living arrangements of the elderly in the period since 1960 (e.g., Michael, Fuchs, and Scott 1980; compare Pampel 1983). We also carried out decompositions of the effects of the changing income of the younger generation, but we found that this factor could account for only a small percentage of change.

TABLE 2.2 Percentage Residing in Multigenerational Families by Employment Status, Controlling for Age, Sex, and Marital Status

	Whites				*Blacks*			
	1910	*1940*	*1960*	*1980*	*1910*	*1940*	*1960*	*1980*
Older Generation								
In labor force	41.6	30.6	17.8	12.7	33.4	28.7	22.6	21.0
Others	53.6	43.8	24.7	13.8	51.4	40.0	27.9	21.0
Younger Generation								
In labor force	10.5	13.0	10.0	4.9	6.5	8.0	7.4	4.8
Others	11.9	13.9	6.6	6.6	5.6	7.8	4.9	4.7

For the period before 1960, we must turn to alternate measures of economic status. The chief indicator of economic status available in the early period is occupation. This variable, of course, is only available for persons who were in the labor force, and many of the elderly were not. Thus, before turning to the data on occupational status, we examine the effects of labor-force participation on the frequency of multigenerational families.

Table 2.2 shows the percentage of multigenerational families among the elderly and among the younger generation by labor-force status. Persons are considered to be members of the labor force if they or their spouse has an occupation listed (on the limitations of this approach, see Conk 1980). Among both elderly blacks and elderly whites in the first half of the century, those who were not in the labor force were substantially more likely to reside in multigenerational families. The causal mechanism here is ambiguous; on the one hand, elderly persons who did not work may have been forced to reside with their children because they had no income of their own; on the other hand, residence with children may have affected employment because it reduced the need to work. Since 1960, the relationship between employment status and multigenerational family structure has virtually disappeared, perhaps because of the increasing importance of nonwage income among the elderly. For the younger generation, labor-force participation shows no clear relationship to multigenerational living arrangements.

Among whites, there has been little long-run change in the employment status of the elderly; 51.8 percent were classified as labor-force participants in 1910, compared with 49.3 percent in 1980. Thus, for whites labor-force participation has not affected the overall change in multigenerational living arrangements. Among blacks, by contrast, the percentage of elderly in the labor force dropped from 78.3 in 1910 to 46.0 in 1980.

If family structure is considered as a consequence of labor-force status, we can estimate the consequences of declining participation among blacks. Because working blacks were less likely to reside in multigenerational families than those who did not work, the decline in the percentage in the labor force cannot help to explain the decline of the multigenerational family; indeed, all things being equal, we would expect the drop in labor-force participation to contribute to an increase in the frequency of multigenerational families. Decomposition analysis with age, sex, and marital status indicates that the increase resulting from changing labor-force participation would be about 3.5 percent. Thus, if labor-force status were held constant, the total decline in the percentage of multigenerational families would be about 20 percent instead of the actual 16.5 percent.

To assess the role of economic status for persons in the labor force, we have developed a measure we call the economic score. Each specific occupational title that can be identified across census years is assigned a score based on the median income of persons with that occupation in 1950. For occupations held by both men and women in significant numbers, the score is calculated separately for each sex. Of course, this measure is imperfect because it ignores changes in the hierarchy of occupations over time. All conventional occupational classification systems share this problem, however, and the economic score provides a more subtle index of relative economic status than any conventional classification. Moreover, there is considerable evidence that the hierarchy of occupational prestige has changed only modestly since the mid-nineteenth century (Hauser 1982; Hodge, Seigel, and Rossi 1964; Sharlin 1980; Treiman 1976; Tyree and Smith 1978).

Figure 2.5 is analogous to Figure 2.4, except that it is based on economic scores instead of on income and therefore can include figures from the early twentieth century. For the elderly generation in 1960 and 1980, the effect of economic score is similar to the effect of income: low economic status is associated with a high frequency of multigenerational families. But the pattern is quite different for the earlier period. Indeed, at least for elderly whites, there appears to be a positive relationship between economic score and multigenerational family structure in 1910 and 1940. For blacks, the pattern is less clear, but the highest proportion of multigenerational families among the elderly is found in the fourth quintile of economic score. Among the younger generation, there are few consistent effects of economic score on the frequency of multigenerational families.

Because the economic scores only indicate relative economic status within census years, we cannot analyse the impact of changes in economic scores on living arrangements across census years. However, the data in Figure 2.5 strongly suggest that the decline in the frequency of multigenerational families in the first half of the century cannot be ascribed to rising economic

Figure 2.5 Percent of Persons in Multigenerational Families Controlling for Age, Sex, Marital Status, and Presence of Spouse by Economic Score, Generation, Race, and Census Year

a) Older Generation (Persons 60 and Over)

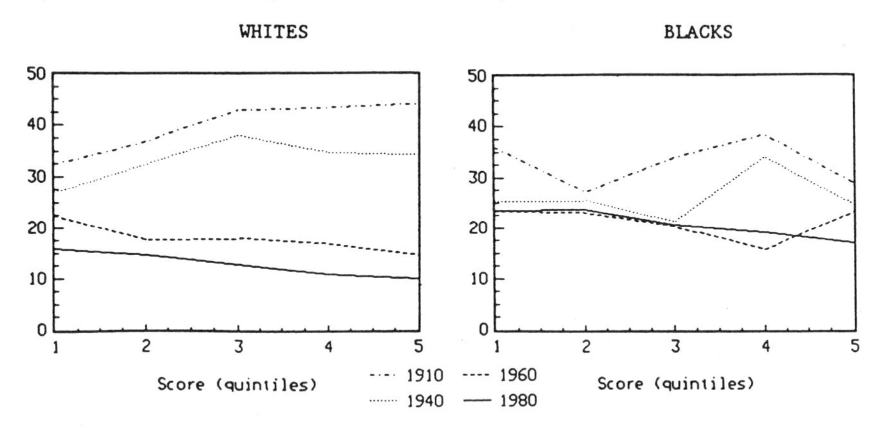

b) Younger Generation (Persons 21-59 Years Old)

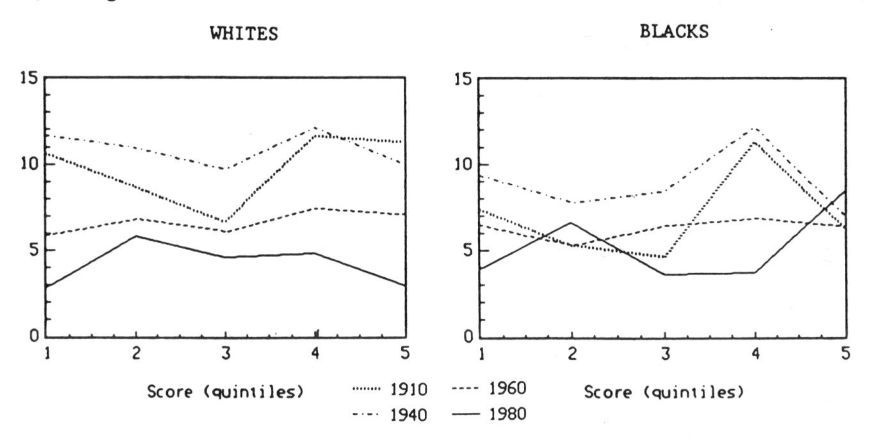

status of the elderly. This does not rule out economic explanations; it simply means that they have to be more subtly constructed.

One approach is to analyze the economic relationships between generations in multigenerational families. Table 2.3 represents an initial step in this direction. The first column in each panel shows the percentage of multigenerational families in which the older generation was the primary income producer or wage earner, accounting for 75 percent or more of the income or economic score. The second column shows the percentage of families in which the presence of the older generation increased the family per-capita income or economic score. In all periods and according to both measures, the economic contribution of the elderly was significantly higher

TABLE 2.3 Measures of the Economic Contribution of the Older Generation in Multigenerational Families, Controlling for Age, Sex, and Marital Status

Income-based measures

	Percent of Families in Which the Older Generation is the Primary Income Producer	*Percent of Families in Which the Older Generation Raises Family Per-capita Income*
Whites		
1960	20.1	32.3
1980	25.6	44.5
Blacks		
1960	31.1	47.5
1980	32.5	51.8

Measures based on economic scores

	Percent of Families in Which the Older Generation is the Primary Wage Earner	*Percent of Families in Which the Older Generation Raises Family Per-capita Economic Score*
Whites		
1910	14.4	31.5
1940	10.7	26.4
1960	15.2	34.1
1980	13.3	34.4
Blacks		
1910	29.0	48.6
1940	22.0	37.7
1960	23.2	42.2
1980	16.3	40.5

for blacks than for whites. In terms of economic score, the contribution of the elderly has diminished over time, but the data on income suggest the possibility that this trend may be counteracted by the increase in nonwage income of the aged.

The evidence on the economic contributions of the elderly in multigenerational families suggests a possible explanation for the greater decline in multigenerational living arrangements among whites. Most elderly whites who did reside in multigenerational families seem to have been economically dependent. The economic incentives for elderly whites to reside with their children are obvious, but the motives of their children are less clear. For many, maintaining their parents was no doubt an economic burden, although it may have been offset by other contributions to family welfare such as homeownership, childcare, and responsibility for domestic duties. But as noted earlier, among whites there were powerful cultural sanctions against those who did not maintain their parents in old age. During the course of the twentieth century, these social norms have shifted dramatically.

Without the force of social obligation, the younger generation has had little incentive to take in their parents.

But the story is somewhat different for blacks. Elderly blacks in multigenerational families have always made a larger economic contribution to the family than elderly whites. From the perspective of the younger generation, the parents have often been an economic asset. Indeed, in many cases it was the younger generation that was dependent. As the century progressed, younger-generation blacks, to a significantly greater extent than younger-generation whites, had a continuing economic incentive to reside with their parents.

Conclusion

Both historians and sociologists have written extensively on family structure. For the most part, however, the historical literature is confined to the nineteenth century and before; the sociological literature has focused on the period since 1960. Moreover, each discipline has adopted different systems of analysis and methods of classification. One of our major aims is to connect the nineteenth-century studies with research on the recent past by analyzing household structure in a consistent way for the entire twentieth century.

One of the difficulties of studying family structure over such a long period is that the magnitude of demographic and economic change in the past century has shifted the social context of family structure. We have attempted to cope with some of the basic structural changes in the population through the use of multiple standardization. A much more intractable problem is posed by the effects of demographic changes on the availability of kin. As we pointed out above, fertility and mortality can have dramatic consequences for the composition of kin groups. Although the census does provide information on the characteristics of kin who reside together, it tells little about relatives beyond the household. The pool of available kin constitutes the context within which residence decisions are made, and that pool is highly sensitive to changing demographic conditions. Therefore, we consider it essential to attempt to control for the effects of changing demography on the population at risk to reside with kin. To that end, we are planning a new demographic microsimulation of kinship that will be specifically tailored to aid analyses of family structure using the public-use samples. We expect that this model will overcome most of the problems that have hampered previous efforts to analyze the demography of kinship (De Vos and Palloni 1989; Ruggles 1990; Ruggles forthcoming).

This chapter represents only a tentative first step; beyond the refinement of the data that will be made possible by the microsimulation, there is a wide range of additional issues and approaches we have yet to explore.

Nevertheless, we owe it to the reader to offer our speculations on the basic questions we posed at the outset: Why did the overall frequency of multigenerational living arrangements among the elderly decline, and why did the differential between blacks and whites reverse?

For whites, much of the decline in multigenerational families came in the category of elderly persons residing with their never-married children. We suggested above that the disappearance of this phenomenon was connected to changing values. First, it became more socially acceptable for unmarried women to live on their own; and second, the social obligations to care for parents in old age diminished. We also suspect that much of the decline in residence with ever-married children results from shifting social norms. Rising economic status of the elderly before mid-century apparently cannot help to explain the decline of the multigenerational family. In the postwar years, however, increasing income does account for much of the change. Finally, we should note that dropping fertility in the late nineteenth century and the first half of the twentieth century markedly reduced the number of options the elderly had to reside in multigenerational families.

Our interpretation depends on a fundamental shift in social norms among the white population, and we are left with the task of explaining the source of change in norms. We could, of course, haul out the usual list of candidates cited by modernization theorists and structural functionalists—urbanization, industrialization, economic and social mobility, loss of traditional values, decline of community. These may indeed have played a role. But we should bear in mind that the anomaly in white family structure is not so much the late twentieth century but rather the late nineteenth century: Nuclear family structure predominated before the industrial revolution, just as it does today. It was the Victorians who were obsessed by the family, not the colonial population. In this light, the interesting question is not so much the source of late twentieth-century norms about living with parents but the source of the late nineteenth-century norms.

For blacks, changes in population composition—age, sex, marital status/presence of spouse, metropolitan residence, and farm residence—explain much of the decrease in multigenerational living arrangements. Moreover, in the period since 1960, income changes alone explain 95 percent of the decline in multigenerational families among blacks. If we measured these variables more precisely and included additional factors such as fertility, geographic mobility and regional variation, compositional changes would very likely account for virtually all of the change among blacks. The question, then, is why the frequency of multigenerational families has been so stable among blacks.

Several studies of the black extended family argue that elderly kin in black families provide assistance to help overcome problems posed by single parenthood or poverty (Anderson and Allen 1984; Goeken 1989; Martin and Martin 1978; Shimkin, Shimkin, and Frate 1978). Some argue that this is a new response, but others stress the cultural continuity of the black extended family.

The evidence on economic relationships within black multigenerational families supports the hypothesis that the elderly have traditionally provided support in black extended families. Multigenerational families among blacks have served the needs of the younger generation as much as the needs of the older, and this may have helped the survival of this family type into the late twentieth century. Because the overall relationship of economic status to multigenerational family structure did not differ markedly between whites and blacks, it does not seem plausible that the differences between black and white multigenerational families were simply a result of greater poverty among blacks. Instead, we suspect that the race differences in family structure during the twentieth century reflect underlying cultural differences between blacks and whites.

Appendix 2.1: Multiple Standardization and Decomposition Analysis

The results presented in this chapter are for the most part the product of multiple standardization or decomposition analysis. They were computed using DECOMP, which is a general-purpose package for multiple standardization and decomposition developed at the Social History Research Laboratory (Ruggles 1989). Multiple standardization is a straightforward extension of the direct standardization technique routinely used by demographers to control for differences in age structure when comparing population rates. In all cases, the standard population was considered to be the sum of all groups being compared. With four simultaneous controls, the standardized rate or percentage for a particular subpopulation—such as blacks in 1910—is calculated as

$$\text{Standardized Rate} = \sum_i \sum_j \sum_k \sum_l R_{ijkl} \cdot P_{ijkl}$$

Where R_{ijkl} is the rate or percentage rates for persons in the subpopulation to be standardized with characteristics i,j,k, and l, and P_{ijkl} is the proportion of the standard population—in this case the sum of all subpopulations—with those characteristics. Thus, the standardized rate simply shows what the rate for the subpopulation would be if the subpopulation shared the population distribution of the standard population.

The closely related technique of demographic decomposition was developed by Kitagawa (1955) to provide a means of partitioning a difference between two rates into components. Later refinements of the method by Das Dupta (1978) increased the power of the technique and simplified the interpretation of results. These methods have proven to be powerful tools for analysis of changing household composition; for examples see Sweet (1984), Kobrin (1976), and Ruggles (1988). Given two populations with differing rates and a set of factors, Das Gupta's approach decomposes the difference between rates into the combined effect of factors, the effect of each factor, and a rate effect. In the four-factor case, the rate effect is considered to be

$$\text{Rate effect} = \sum_i \sum_j \sum_k \sum_l \frac{P_{ijkl} + p_{ijkl}}{2} (R_{ijkl} - r_{ijkl})$$

Where R_{ijkl} and r_{ijkl} are the rates for persons with characteristics i,j,k, and l in the two populations and P_{ijkl} and p_{ijkl} are the proportions of each population with those characteristics. The rate effect is the difference of rates in each cell weighted by the average of population proportions in each cell. This is identical to the standardized difference between the populations, using the average of population proportions as the standard.

The effect of factors is the complement of the rate effect:

$$\text{Combined IJKL effect} = \sum_i \sum_j \sum_k \sum_l \frac{R_{ijkl} + r_{ijkl}}{2} (P_{ijkl} - p_{ijkl})$$

The effect of factors represents the difference in population rates that is entirely accounted for by differences in population distributions. The sum of the rate effect and the effect of factors is equal to the total difference between populations. The effect of factors is then decomposed into the effect of each of the four factors. This procedure is too complicated to explain here, but it involves repeated standardizations by every possible combination of marginal distributions to isolate the independent effects of each factor.

Decomposition is well suited to the problem of analyzing race and period differentials in family structure. The issue here is not one of explaining the variance in family structure, where a form of regression might be more appropriate; rather, we are concerned with assessing the factors associated with a difference of two population rates. Decomposition is especially appropriate where the dependent variable is dichotomous, the factors to be considered are largely categorical or nonlinear, and substantial interactions are suspected. All of these conditions apply in the present instance.

Neither decomposition nor multiple standardization assumes additivity. Because the methods rely on a multiway matrix of rates, they take all interactions among factors into account. This is the greatest advantage of

TABLE 2A.1 Composition of the Aged Population by Race and Period

	Whites				Blacks			
	1910	*1940*	*1960*	*1980*	*1910*	*1940*	*1960*	*1980*
Age								
60–64	36.0	34.3	30.4	28.3	38.1	32.6	32.2	29.8
65–69	27.0	27.1	25.9	23.8	24.5	32.9	28.1	26.5
70–74	18.0	18.4	20.8	19.0	18.0	17.6	19.2	19.8
75–79	11.3	11.5	12.6	14.2	9.2	8.6	11.3	12.4
80–84	5.2	6.0	6.5	8.1	5.7	4.4	5.4	6.6
85–89	2.5	2.7	3.8	6.6	4.5	4.0	3.9	4.9
Marital status								
Mar. w/ spouse	52.8	52.3	55.8	57.8	53.4	45.5	45.2	41.9
Mar. no spouse	3.4	3.7	2.9	2.0	3.7	5.7	7.0	8.0
Widowed	35.9	32.9	30.7	30.3	38.9	41.8	39.9	37.3
Divorced	.8	1.3	2.7	4.2	.5	1.1	2.7	6.4
Never married	7.2	9.8	7.9	5.7	3.5	5.9	5.3	6.3
Metro								
Metropolitan	23.0	53.6	62.1	73.6	12.0	36.6	59.7	82.0
Nonmetropolitan	77.0	46.4	37.9	26.4	88.0	63.4	40.3	18.0
Farm								
Nonfarm	69.3	79.2	92.9	96.1	55.2	65.8	92.1	98.9
Farm	30.7	20.8	7.1	3.9	44.8	34.2	7.9	1.1
Total	100.0	100.0	100.0	100.0	100.0	100.0	100.0	100.0
N	11435	12666	10746	15718	1570	4676	8632	14265

the approach but also its greatest limitation; it is easy to design analyses in which the matrix contains more cells than there are cases in the population. Therefore, decomposition and multiple standardization are most useful when the analyses are relatively simple.

The following tables (2A.1-2A.3) illustrate the decomposition of race and period differentials in the percentage of elderly residing with adult children or other kin. The factors are age/sex, marital status, metropolitan residence, and farm residence. The first two tables give the population marginals and the overall percentages of residence with kin for these variables, respectively, and the decomposition results are given in Table 2A.3.

Notes

1. In this paper, the term family refers to related persons residing in the same household; multigenerational families are those containing two adult generations; and complex households contain either kin or nonkin beyond the nuclear group.

TABLE 2A.2 Percent of the Aged Population with Kin or Adult Children by Race and Period

	Whites				*Blacks*			
	1910	*1940*	*1960*	*1980*	*1910*	*1940*	*1960*	*1980*
Age								
60–64	57.9	50.0	30.3	22.5	57.4	53.1	46.8	40.6
65–69	60.9	50.5	31.7	18.8	58.4	57.3	47.9	37.7
70–74	63.0	52.0	31.1	17.0	59.7	56.0	47.6	37.1
75–79	66.9	56.2	37.6	19.5	59.7	59.8	49.0	33.4
80–84	71.8	59.3	43.4	24.1	60.0	68.4	52.2	39.0
85–89	70.5	69.4	44.7	30.6	65.7	78.8	68.6	45.0
Marital status								
Mar. w/ spouse	56.6	47.0	24.0	15.8	57.3	54.2	43.4	34.8
Mar. no spouse	43.7	42.6	32.7	21.3	46.6	41.6	40.0	37.1
Widowed	74.4	66.0	48.2	27.6	64.5	66.8	58.2	43.2
Divorced	50.6	37.3	36.5	25.2	50.0	37.0	42.4	33.2
Never married	45.4	40.4	37.8	32.6	32.7	32.5	35.8	40.0
Metro								
Metropolitan	65.5	53.4	34.0	20.8	48.4	50.5	46.3	37.8
Nonmetropolitan	60.6	51.0	31.6	20.7	60.2	61.3	52.1	41.0
Farm								
Nonfarm	57.5	50.8	32.3	20.3	51.1	52.4	46.8	38.3
Farm	71.2	57.8	42.7	33.7	68.3	66.9	69.9	47.0
Total	61.7	52.3	33.1	20.8	58.8	57.3	48.6	38.4
N	11435	12666	10746	15718	1570	4676	8632	14265

References

Allen, Walter R., 1979. "Class, Culture and Family Organization: The Effects of Class and Race on Family Structure in Urban America," *Journal of Comparative Family Studies* 10:301–313.

Anderson, Kristine L., and Walter R. Allen, 1984. "Correlates of Extended Household Structure," *Phylon* 45:144–157.

Anderson, Michael, 1971. *Family Structure in Nineteenth Century Lancashire.* Cambridge, U.K.: Cambridge University Press.

______, 1976. "Sociological History and the Working-Class Family: Smelser Revisited," *Social History* 1:317–343.

______, 1977. "The Impact on Family Relationships of the Elderly of Changes Since Victorian Times in Governmental Income Maintenance Provisions," in E. Shanas and M. B. Sussman, eds., *Family, Bureaucracy, and the Elderly.* Durham, N.C.: Duke University Press.

______, 1984. "The Social Position of Spinsters in Mid-Victorian Britain," *Journal of Family History* 9:377–393.

TABLE 2A.3 Decomposition of the Trends and Race Differentials in the Percentage of Complex Families Among the Elderly

	Time Interval			
Change over time	*1910–1940*	*1940–1960*	*1960–1980*	*1910–1980*
Whites:				
Total change in period	9.43	19.16	12.25	40.84
Effects of factors:				
Age/sex	−.14	−.50	−.44	−.99
Marital status	.88	.93	.73	1.84
Metro residence	−1.51	−.19	−.25	−1.92
Farm residence	.71	1.43	.38	3.60
Combined effect of factors	−.06	1.67	.41	2.53
Rate effect	9.49	17.49	11.84	38.30
Blacks:				
Total change in period	1.32	8.70	10.13	19.62
Effects of factors:				
Age/sex	.20	−.98	−.40	−.70
Marital status	.39	.63	.61	.85
Metro residence	1.70	1.11	.70	3.55
Farm residence	.47	4.41	.86	4.26
Combined effect of factors	2.75	5.17	1.76	7.96
Rate effect	−1.43	3.53	8.37	11.67

Differential between blacks and whites

	Year			
	1910	*1940*	*1960*	*1980*
Total difference (whites-blacks)	2.90	−4.96	−15.57	−17.70
Effects of factors:				
Age/sex	−.05	.52	.37	.04
Marital status	−.73	−1.66	−1.90	−1.16
Metro residence	−.05	−.33	−.06	.08
Farm residence	−1.79	−1.49	−.13	.19
Combined effect of factors	−2.62	−2.97	−1.72	−.85
Rate effect	5.52	−1.99	−13.85	−16.85

Angel, R., and M. Tienda, 1982. "Determinants of Extended Family Structure: Cultural Pattern or Economic Need?" *American Journal of Sociology* 87:1360–1383.

Aschenbrenner, Joyce, 1973. "Extended Families Among Black Americans," *Journal of Comparative Family Studies* 4:257–268.

Auerbach, N., 1978. *Communities of Women: An Idea in Fiction.* Cambridge: Harvard University Press.

———, 1982. *The Woman and the Demon: The Life of a Victorian Myth.* Cambridge: Harvard University Press.

Beresford, J. C., and A. M. Rivlin, 1966. "Privacy, Poverty, and Old Age," *Demography* 3:247–258.

Billingsley, Andrew, 1968. *Black Families in White America.* Englewood Cliffs, N.J.: Prentice-Hall.

Burgess, Charles S., ed. 1965. *Health, Growth and Heredity: G. Stanley Hall on National Education.* New York: Teachers College Press.

Butler, Samuel, 1951 (1886). *Note-Books.* London: Cape.

Chevan, A., and J. H. Korson, 1972. "The Widowed Who Live Alone: An Examination of Social and Demographic Factors," *Social Forces* 51:45–53.

Chudacoff, Howard, and Tamara Hareven, 1979. "From the Empty Nest to Family Dissolution: Life-Course Transitions into Old Age," *Journal of Family History* 4:69–83.

Cobbe, F. P., 1862. "What Shall We Do with Our Old Maids?" *Frasers Magazine* 66:694–610.

Conk, Margo A., 1980. *The United States Census and Labor Force Change.* Ann Arbor: UMI Research Press.

Cruikshank, G., et al., 1912. *The Comic Almanack: An Ephemeris in Jest and Earnest, Containing Merry Tales, Humerous Poetry, Quips, and Oddities.* London: Chatto and Windus.

Das Gupta, P., 1978. "A General Method For Decomposing a Difference Between Two Rates into Components," *Demography* 15:99–112.

De Vos, Susan, and Alberto Palloni, 1989. "Formal Models and Methods for the Analysis of Kinship and Household Organization," *Population Index* 55:174–198.

De Vos, Susan, and Steven Ruggles, 1988. "The Demography of Kinship and the Life Course," in P. B. Baltes et al., eds., *Life Span Development and Behavior* 8:259–281.

DuBois, W.E.B., 1908. *The Negro American Family.* Atlanta: Atlanta University Press.

Elkins, S., 1959. *Slavery: A Problem in American Institutional and Intellectual Life.* Chicago: University of Chicago Press.

Farley, Reynolds, 1971. "Family Types and Family Headship: A Comparison of Trends Among Blacks and Whites," *Journal of Human Resources* 6:275–296.

Fischer, Ann, et al., 1968. "The Occurrence of the Extended Family at the Origin of the Family Procreation: A Developmental Approach to Negro Family Structure," *Journal of Marriage and the Family* 30:290–300.

Fletcher, R., 1970. "The Making of the Modern Family," in K. Eliot, ed., *The Family and Its Future.* London: Churchill.

Foster, J. O., 1974. *Class Struggle in the Industrial Revolution: Early Industrial Capitalism in Three English Towns.* London: Arndd.

Frazier, E. F., 1939. *The Negro Family in the United States.* Chicago: University of Chicago Press.

Furstenberg, Frank, T. Hershberg, and J. Modell, 1975. "The Origins of the Female-Headed Black Family: The Impact of the Urban Experience," *Journal of Interdisciplinary History* 6:211–233.

Goeken, R., 1989. "Black Extended Families in the Twentieth Century: A Quantitative Analysis of Research Models." Paper presented at the annual meeting of the Social Science History Association, Washington, D.C.

Goode, W. J., 1963. "Industrialization and Family Change," in B. F. Hoselitz and W. E. Moore, eds., *Industrialization and Society*. Paris: UNESCO.

Graham, Stephen N., 1979. *1900 Public Use Sample: User's Handbook*. Seattle: Center for Demography and Ecology, University of Washington.

Griffin, W. T., 1881. *The Homes of Our Country: Or, The Centers of Moral and Religious Influence; The Crystals of Society; The Nuclei of National Character*. New York: Union Publishing House.

Gutman, Herbert, 1975. "Persistent Myths About the Afro-American Family," *Journal of Interdisciplinary History* 6:181–210.

______, 1976. *The Black Family in Slavery and Freedom*. New York: Pantheon Books.

Hague, W., 1855. *Home Life: Twelve Lectures*. New York: S. S. Dickerson.

Hareven, Tamara, 1978. "The Last Stage: Historical Adulthood and Old Age," *Daedalus* 105:13–28.

Hauser, Robert M., 1982. "Occupational Status in the Nineteenth and Twentieth Centuries," *Historical Methods* 15:111–126.

Hays, W. C. and C. H. Mindel, 1973. "Extended Kin Relations in Black and White Families," *Journal of Marriage and the Family* 35:51–57.

Hill, Robert, 1971. *The Strengths of Black Families*. New York: Emerson Hall.

Hodge, Robert W., Paul M. Siegel, and Peter H. Rossi, 1964. "Occupational Prestige in the United States, 1925–63," *American Journal of Sociology* 70:286–302.

Hofferth, Sandra L., 1984. "Kin Networks, Race, and Family Structure," *Journal of Marriage and the Family* 46:791–806.

Kanner, S. B., 1972. "The Women of England in a Century of Social Change: A Select Bibliography," in M. Vinicus, ed., *Suffer and Be Still: Women in the Victorian Age*. Bloomington: Indiana University Press.

Katz, Michael B., 1975. *The People of Hamilton, Canada West: Family and Class in a Mid-Nineteenth Century City*. Cambridge: Harvard University Press.

King, Miriam, 1988. *Changes in the Living Arrangements of the Elderly: 1960–2030*. (Special study, Congressional Budget Office) Washington, D.C.: GPO.

King, Miriam, and Steven Ruggles, 1990. "Immigration, Fertility, and Race Suicide at the Turn of the Century," *Journal of Interdisciplinary History* 20:347–369.

Kitagawa, E. M., 1955. "Components of a Difference Between Two Rates," *Journal of the American Statistical Association* 50:1168–1194.

Kobrin, Frances, 1976. "The Fall in Household Size and the Rise of the Primary Individual in the United States," *Demography* 13:127–138.

Lammermeir, Paul, 1973. "The Urban Black Family in the Nineteenth Century: A Study of Black Family Structure in the Ohio Valley, 1850–1880," *Journal of Marriage and the Family* 35:440–455.

Laslett, Peter, 1972. "Introduction," in Peter Laslett and Richard Wall, eds., *Household and Family in Past Time*. Cambridge, U.K.: Cambridge University Press.

Levine, David, 1977. *Family Formation in an Age of Nascent Capitalism*. New York: Academic Press.

Martin, Elmer P., and Joanna M. Martin, 1978. *The Black Extended Family*. Chicago: University of Chicago Press.

McAdoo, H. P., 1980. "Black Mothers and the Extended Family Support Network," in L. Rogers-Rose, ed., *The Black Woman*. Beverly Hills: Sage Publications.

———, 1983. *Extended Family Support of Single Black Mothers: Final Report*. Columbia, Md.: N.p.

Medick, H., 1976. "The Proto-Industrial Family Economy: The Structural Function of Household and Family During the Transition from Peasant Society to Industrial Capitalism," *Social History* 1:291–315.

Michael, R. T., V. R. Fuchs, and S. R. Scott, 1980. "Changes in the Propensity to Live Alone, 1950–1976," *Demography* 17:39–53.

Mintz, Steven, 1983. *A Prison of Expectations: The Family in Victorian Culture*. New York: New York University Press.

Modell, John, 1978. "Patterns of Consumption, Acculturation, and Family Income Strategies Late Nineteenth-Century America," in T. K. Hareven and M. Vinovskis, *Family and Population in Nineteenth Century America*. Princeton: Princeton University Press.

Moynihan, D. P., 1965. *The Negro Family: The Case For National Action*. Washington, D.C.: GPO.

Mutran, Elizabeth, 1985. "Intergenerational Family Support Among Blacks and Whites: Response to Culture or Socioeconomic Differences," *Journal of Gerontology* 40:382–389.

Myrdal, G., 1944. *An American Dilemma*. New York: Public Affairs Committee.

Nimkoff, M., 1962. "Changing Family Relationships of Older People in the United States During the Last Fifty Years," in C. Tibbitts and W. Donahue, eds., *Social and Psychological Aspects of Aging*. Ann Arbor: University of Michigan Press.

Nobles, W., 1978. "Toward an Empirical and Theoretical Framework for Defining Black Families," *Journal of Marriage and the Family* 40:679–698.

Pampel, F., 1983. "Changes in the Propensity to Live Alone: Evidence From Cross-Sectional Surveys," *Demography* 20:433–438.

Parsons, Talcott, 1959. "The Social Structure of the Family," in R. Anshen, eds., *The Family: Its Functions and Destiny*. New York: Harper.

Parsons, Talcott, and R. F. Bales, 1955. *Family, Socialization, and the Interaction Process*. Glencoe, Ill.: Free Press.

Pleck, Elizabeth, 1972. "The Two-Parent Household: Black Family Structure in Late-Nineteenth Century Boston," *Journal of Social History* 6:3–31.

Riessman, Frank, 1966. "In Defense of the Negro Family," *Dissent* 13:141–144.

Riley, Peter, 1975. "The Black Family in Transition: Louisiana, 1860–1865," *Journal of Southern History* 41:369–380.

Robins, J. B., 1896. *The Family: A Necessity of Civilization*. Atlanta: N.p.

Ruggles, Steven, 1986. "Availability of Kin and the Demography of Historical Family Structure," *Historical Methods* 19:93–102.

———, 1987. *Prolonged Connections: The Rise of the Extended Family in Nineteenth Century England and America*. Madison: University of Wisconsin Press.

———, 1988. "The Demography of the Unrelated Individual, 1900–1950," *Demography* 25:521–536.

______, 1989. "DECOMP, A Program for Multiple Standardization and Demographic Decomposition: Technical Documentation and User's Guide." Minneapolis: Social History Research Center, University of Minnesota.

______, 1990. "Family Demography and Family History: Problems and Prospects," *Historical Methods* 23:22–30.

______, 1991. "Comparability of the Public-Use Data Files of the U.S. Census of Population," *Social Science History* 15:123–158.

______, forthcoming. "Confessions of a Microsimulator: Problems in Modeling the Demography of Kinship," in Douglas A. Wolf, ed., *Recent Developments in Microsimulation: An International Perspective*. Washington, D.C.: Urban Institute Press.

Ruggles, S., and Menard, R., 1990. "A Public Use Sample for the 1880 Census of Population," *Historical Methods* 23:104–113.

Scanzoni, J., 1971. *The Black Family in Modern Society*. Boston: Allyn and Bacon.

Sharlin, Allen, 1980. "On the Universality of Occupational Prestige," *Journal of Interdisciplinary History* 21:115–125.

Shifflett, Crandall A., 1975. "The Household Composition of Rural Black Families: Louisiana County, Virginia, 1880," *Journal of Interdisciplinary History* 6:235–260.

Shimkin, D., G. Louie, and D. Frate, 1978. "Black Extended Families in Holmes County, Mississippi," in D. Shimkin, E. Shimkin, and D. Frate, *The Extended Family in Black Societies*. The Hague: Mouton.

Shimkin, D., E. Shimkin, and D. Frate, 1978. *The Extended Family in Black Societies*. The Hague: Mouton.

Showalter, E., 1977. *A Literature of Their Own: Women Novelists from Brontë to Lessing*. Princeton, N.J.: Princeton University Press.

Smelser, Neil, 1959. *Social Change in the Industrial Revolution*. Chicago: University of Chicago Press.

Smith, Daniel S., 1978. "A Community-Based Sample of the Older Population from the 1880 and 1900 United States Manuscript Census," *Historical Methods* 11:67–74.

______, 1981. "Historical Change in the Household Structure of the Elderly in Economically Developed Countries," in R. W. Fogel, S. B. Keisler, and E. Shanas, eds., *Aging: Stability and Change in the Family*. New York: Academic Press.

Smith, Daniel S., M. Dahlin, and M. Friedberger, 1979. "The Family Structure of the Older Black Population in the American South in 1880 and 1900," *Social Science Research* 63:544–565.

Stack, Carol, 1974. *All Our Kin: Strategies for Survival in a Black Community*. New York: Harper and Row.

Staples, Robert, 1975. "The Black Family in Evolutionary Perspective," *Black Scholar* 5:2–9.

Strong, Michael, et al., 1989. "User's Guide: Public Use Sample, 1910 Census of Population," Philadelphia: Population Studies Center, University of Pennsylvania.

Sweet, James A., 1972. "The Living Arrangements of Separated, Widowed, and Divorced Mothers," *Demography* 9:143–158.

______, 1984. "Components of Change in the Number of Households, 1970–1980," *Demography* 21:129–140.

Sweet, James A., and Larry Bumpass, 1987. *American Families and Households*. New York: Russell Sage.

Tonnies, F., 1957. *Community and Society*. East Lansing, Mich.: Michigan University Press.

Treiman, Donald J., 1976. "A Standard Occupational Prestige Scale for Use with Historical Data," *Journal of Interdisciplinary History* 7:283–304.

Troll, L. E., 1971. "The Family of Later Life: A Decade Review," *Journal of Marriage and the Family* 33:263–290.

Tyree, Andrea, and Billy G. Smith, 1978. "Occupational Hierarchy in the United States: 1789–1969," *Social Forces* 56:881–899.

U.S. Bureau of the Census, 1972. *Public Use Samples of Basic Records from the 1970 Census: Description and Technical Documentation*. Washington, D.C.: GPO.

______, 1973. *Technical Documentation for the 1960 Public Use Sample*. Washington, D.C.: GPO.

______, 1982. *Public Use Samples of Basic Records From the 1980 Census: Description and Technical Documentation*. Washington, D.C.: GPO.

______, 1983. 1980 Census of Population: Subject Reports. *Persons by Family Characteristics*. Washington, D.C.: GPO.

______, 1984a. *Census of Population, 1940: Public Use Sample Technical Documentation*. Washington, D.C.: GPO.

______, 1984b. *Census of Population, 1950: Public Use Sample Technical Documentation*. Washington, D.C.: GPO.

______, 1987. *Marital Status and Living Arrangements: March 1986*. Current Population Reports, Ser. P-20, No. 410. Washington, D.C.: GPO.

Wall, Richard, 1983. "The Household: Demographic and Economic Change in England, 1650–1970," in R. Wall, ed., *Family Forms in Historic Europe*. Cambridge, U.K.: Cambridge University Press.

Watkins, S. C., 1984. "Spinsters," *Journal of Family History* 9:310–325.

Wolf, Douglas A., 1986. "Kinship and Family Support in Aging Societies." Laxenburg, Austria: International Institute for Applied Systems Analysis, WP-86-81.

3

Group Differences in Economic Opportunity and the Timing of Marriage: Blacks and Whites in the Rural South, 1910

Nancy S. Landale and Stewart E. Tolnay

Economic opportunity plays a prominent role in explanations of nuptiality. Scholars concerned with both historic and contemporary periods have proposed that marriage occurs earlier and is more prevalent where economic opportunity is relatively abundant (e.g., Habakkuk 1971; Hermalin and van de Walle 1977; Malthus [1826] 1986; Wilson and Neckerman 1987; Wrigley and Schofield 1981).[1] Studies linking economic conditions to marriage are generally based on aggregate data and assume that local economic conditions affect all young adults in an area in the same way. However, when society is sharply segmented by class or caste there is reason to doubt the validity of this assumption. In such cases, applying the opportunity thesis of nuptiality requires consideration of group differences in *access* to positions and rewards.

The rural American South during the early twentieth century is an excellent example of a society in which the nature and extent of economic opportunity varied markedly across groups, especially racial groups. At that time, the South was sharply stratified along two distinct dimensions—class and caste. Among rural whites, class position was determined largely by ownership of land. While rural blacks also exhibited class variation, their location in a subordinate caste was more salient (Dollard 1937; Flynn 1983; Mandle 1978). The caste position of southern blacks reduced their access to some forms of economic opportunity and prohibited their access to others. We believe that this stratification system must be considered when

This chapter originally appeared in *American Sociological Review 56* (February 1991). Reprinted by permission.

examining the links between the economy and marriage. In particular, we show that the different economic opportunities open to blacks and whites produced racial variation in the relationships between specific features of the economy and entry into marriage.

We formulate our predictions in terms of the marriage behavior of males. Because of the husband's central economic role in most families during this period, we expect the links between economic opportunity and marriage to be most direct for men. Nonetheless, our analysis also examines the implications of the opportunity structure for the marriage patterns of black and white females. We expect the results to be quite similar to those proposed for males.

Determinants of Nuptial Behavior

Dixon (1971) has suggested a useful conceptual framework for understanding geographic variation in marriage behavior. She delineates three factors that intervene between the social structure and nuptiality: (1) the availability of mates; (2) the feasibility of marriage; and (3) the desirability of marriage. The availability of mates is largely a function of the relative numbers of males and females of marriageable age. The feasibility of marriage depends on a couple's access to economic resources, but also varies according to cultural expectations regarding the financial and residential independence of newlywed couples. Finally, the desirability of marriage reflects the presence or absence of attractive alternatives to marriage. Although not part of Dixon's scheme, we suggest that the desirability of marriage in a given locale may vary by occupation and social position. For example, for those in some occupations, particularly agriculture, marriage (and children) may enhance economic well-being by increasing household production and income.

Consistent with this general framework, we focus first on the *ability* and *motivation* to marry in agricultural societies, like the rural South in the early 1900s. In such settings, access to land is critical to the economic outlook of young adult males. For example, Hajnal (1965) largely attributes the historically late age at marriage in western Europe to land shortages that limited the ability of young adults to establish independent households. Similarly, Levine (1977) credits the shift from household to capitalist production in some rural areas of western Europe with relaxing this constraint by reducing dependence on land acquisition, thereby leading to earlier marriage and childbearing. The American South in the early twentieth century differed in many respects from the western European societies studied by Hajnal and Levine. Southern marriage traditionally occurred much earlier, in large part because land was abundant. However, that began to change during the latter half of the nineteenth century.

Studies of the effects of declining land availability on American family formation in the nineteenth century (e.g., Easterlin 1976; Forster and Tucker 1972; Shapiro 1982; Yasuba 1961) have generally concluded that couples had smaller families where arable land was in short supply. Some scholars have speculated that declining land availability reduced fertility in part by restricting marriage.[2] Where land was readily available, young men could establish themselves as farmers with relative ease; where it was difficult to acquire, they were forced to postpone marriage or to seek nonownership options such as farm tenancy or wage labor.[3] The availability of these alternatives, in turn, depended upon the structure of local economies. Thus, the *feasibility* of marriage was potentially influenced by the availability of agricultural land and alternatives to farm ownership in the local economy.

Less attention has been devoted to understanding the implications of economic conditions for the *motivation* to marry. It is commonly assumed that individuals want to marry, given adequate economic resources (Hermalin and van de Walle 1977; Malthus 1986), but there is reason to believe that the incentives for early marriage also varied with the economic structure. The economic opportunities available in communities determined the employment options faced by young men and women, which entailed distinct conditions and incentives for family formation.

Perhaps most fundamental is the distinction between employment in the wage economy and the family-based farm economy. This distinction has been drawn clearly in a number of studies of economic organization and family formation (e.g., Caldwell 1982; Levine 1977; Tilly and Scott 1978). The farm household, regardless of land tenure, generally functioned as a unit of economic production (Tolnay 1986). All family members, including wives and children, performed valuable economic roles. The labor of wives and children was critical to the success of all but the wealthiest farms—large families could produce higher yields and increase household income. In short, the organization of the farm economy created a clear incentive for early marriage and childbearing.[4]

The situation of wage laborers in the farm and nonfarm sectors differed from that of farmers in several important respects. First, the wage economy was generally organized around the labor inputs of *individuals* rather than families. Because a family was not required for the successful performance of most wage jobs, the organization of the workplace did not encourage early family formation.[5] In fact, it may have *discouraged* youthful marriage by providing an independent source of income for single women. Second, wage labor was generally performed outside the home. Although farm wives could perform productive work while they cared for their offspring, employment outside the home required alternative child-care arrangements. In general, the separation of the workplace from the home reduced the economic contributions of married women. This placed a greater economic burden on husbands, creating a potential disincentive for early marriage. The major exception was married black women, who worked outside the home in significant numbers and contributed substantially to family income.

In sum, the economic structure was linked to marriage in several distinct ways. First, it defined the opportunites for economic self-sufficiency that were critical to household formation. The scarcity or abundance of those opportunities determined the feasibility of marriage. Second, it influenced the employment options available in the local environment. Some options were conducive to marraige while others provided fewer incentives for early family formation. In addition, marriage chances were constrained by the availability of appropriate mates. A relative abundance of potential partners encourages entry into marriage, while a shortage reduces the marriage prospects of the more numerous sex.

Race and Opportunity in the Rural South

During the late nineteenth century the southern caste system shaped all institutions of southern society, from the voting booth to the marketplace. Race was the single most important determinant of economic opportunity. Two by-products of the southern caste system are particularly pertinent to rural marriage patterns. First, by the turn of the century, most rural blacks were locked into a plantation system of agricultural production based on tenancy rather than ownership of land. Second, this agricultural organization was reinforced by the denial of nonagricultural employment opportunities to most black males.

The Southern Tenancy System

The agricultural system of the South was shaped by a complex set of circumstances that arose after Emancipation. Southern planters had to find a substitute for the slave labor they had lost. At the same time, freedmen had to find a niche in the market economy. Solutions to this economic puzzle were constrained by the planters' lack of capital (Jaynes 1986) and the federal government's decision not to require massive land redistribution. After considerable experimentation, an uneasy "compromise" was reached that allowed southern planters to retain ownership of the land, while allowing black farmers more autonomy than the work gang. This compromise was the tenancy system that dominated southern agriculture until the middle of the twentieth century (Ransom and Sutch 1977).

There were different styles of tenancy—some required different resource inputs by tenants, others provided different forms of compensation. Some tenants paid cash rent for access to the land and provided their own tools and work animals. At the other extreme, sharecroppers provided little more than the labor that they and their families could perform and received a share of the cash crop as compensation. Whatever the specific arrangements, however, all forms of tenancy shared the same fundamental characteristic—the tenant family worked land that they did not own.

In some agricultural settings, tenancy is simply a rung on the ladder leading to farm ownership. Through saving, a tenant farmer may gradually accumulate sufficient resources to purchase land and establish economic independence. For blacks in the rural South, however, tenancy was generally a terminal status. A combination of discriminatory treatment, oppressive economic practices, and legal barriers conspired against movement up the agricultural ladder.

The southern caste system guaranteed that blacks would encounter greater resistance to upward mobility than whites. As Flynn noted (1983, p. 24), "The latitude or maneuvering room of blacks within their subordinate position—their ability to demand share privileges, advance to 'independent tenancy', and occasionally even become landowners—was fundamentally offensive to the white sense of social order." As a result, blacks were typically denied credit for investments such as land purchases (Mandle 1978) or driven from their property (Jaynes 1986, p. 256).

Perhaps even more effective in restricting the upward mobility of rural blacks was the system of crop liens and debt peonage that virtually precluded savings by tenant families. For most tenant farmers, the crop in the fields represented their only equity. Especially in lean years, but probably in most years, tenant families could not save enough to meet their expenses from harvest to harvest. Southern merchants were more than willing to extend operating credit at exorbitant rates of interest, using the farmer's maturing crop as collateral (e.g., Ransom and Sutch 1977; Mandle 1978; Schwartz 1976). The merchant's lien assured that the farmer's share of the profits was sliced even thinner. Meager profits and usurious interest rates virtually guaranteed that the farmer's indebtedness extended from one year to the next. Mired in this system of debt peonage, most black tenants found it impossible to accumulate savings. Moreover, this exploitative economic arrangement was buttressed by the southern legal system, which prevented impoverished farmers from escaping the yoke of debt peonage by mechanisms like antienticement and vagrancy laws (Jaynes 1986, p. 310; Myrdal 1975).

Southern whites did not escape the perils of the plantation system of agricultural production. During the last decades of the nineteenth century and the early decades of the twentieth century, more and more rural whites sank into tenancy. Despite the rapid deterioration of rural white fortunes in the South, tenancy remained proportionately far more common among blacks than whites. For example, in 1910 75 percent of all black farm operators were tenants, compared to 39 percent of white farm operators.

Although southern whites were not insulated from the plantation economy, blacks clearly were relegated to the margins of southern agriculture.

Restriction of Nonagricultural Opportunities

Rural black males also faced bleak prospects for employment outside of agriculture due to the relatively retarded development of an industrial economy in the South and the exclusion of blacks from many of those industrial enterprises that did exist (Mandle 1978; Wright 1986). A few industries welcomed black males for the most strenuous and dangerous tasks, e.g., blacks were relatively well-represented in the turpentine and timber industries. The steel mills of Birmingham were another exception to the general exclusion of black males from southern industry (Wright 1986).

More typical was the southern textile industry which effectively excluded black males. Textile manufacturing was the South's most striking success in the development of an industrial base in the late nineteenth and early twentieth centuries. Yet black males were virtually excluded from the textile industry (Jaynes 1986, pp. 272-4). White labor also organized successfully to close other avenues of escape from plantation agriculture. Efforts to exclude blacks from some skilled occupations (e.g., carpentry, brick masonry) were successful, as were efforts to drive black labor from the docks of many southern ports. The result was an occupational structure sharply segmented by race.

In sum, black males who wished to escape the oppressive conditions of the plantation agricultural economy faced disheartening obstacles in the nonagricultural economy. Not only were they virtually excluded from large segments of the southern economy, but within those sectors in which they were allowed to compete they were relegated to the most menial positions. Although not perfectly defined by race, the southern economy reflected the southern caste system. It was a "dual" economy that offered different opportunities and potential for mobility to blacks and whites.

Implications for Marriage Patterns

Racial differences in economic opportunity have important implications for marriage among rural southern males. First, they should generate racial differences in the timing of marriage. Second, and more importantly, they should cause the marital behavior of blacks and whites to respond differently to the prevailing economic structure.

Considering the racial difference in marriage timing, we expect black males to have married earlier than white males. The heavier concentration of rural blacks in tenancy combined with the restricted opportunities for farm ownership likely encouraged early marriage among black males. The tenant household functioned as an autonomous unit and income (for both the tenant family and the landlord) depended on the labor of family members. Male tenant farmers had a strong incentive, then, to marry early (Tolnay 1984). Moreover, there was little reason for black males to postpone marriage while they tried to accumulate sufficient resources to purchase their own land because the road to farm ownership for blacks was littered with obstacles erected by the southern caste system.

We also expect to find significant racial differences in the structural determinants of marriage behavior. The socioeconomic environment varied across regions of the South, e.g., some areas had higher levels of farm tenancy, greater availability of manufacturing employment opportunities, and cheaper land than other areas. These structural characteristics affect marriage patterns by influencing the "desirability" or "feasibility" of marriage. However, we contend that these structural factors had substantially different impacts on marriage for blacks and whites.

We hypothesize that high levels of farm tenancy in an area *encouraged* early marriage for black males and *discouraged* early marriage for white males. For many white males, tenancy was a temporary status and farm ownership was an achievable goal. In areas with high levels of tenancy, however, white males may have had to wait somewhat longer before they were in a financial position to buy land. We also expect the average cost of a farm to have *discouraged* early marriage among white males, for whom higher farm costs likely meant a longer wait to accumulate the resources to purchase land. In contrast, high farm costs would be less relevant to black males because of the social and economic barriers to ownership; they should have no independent effect on their marriage patterns.

Finally, we hypothesize that manufacturing employment opportunities *discouraged* early marriage among whites, but were unrelated to black marriage patterns. Employment in the wage economy had substantially different implications for family formation than farming because it was less dependent on family labor. In addition, some rural white males may have engaged in manufacturing employment temporarily while they saved money to invest in a farm. On the other hand, it is possible (though not expected) that manufacturing employment opportunities encouraged *earlier* marriages for whites by circumventing the need to acquire land before establishing an independent household, as suggested by Levine (1977).[6] Because rural black males were excluded from most segments of the industrial economy, the presence of manufacturing employment opportunities should be largely irrelevant to their marriage behavior.

Data, Measures, and Method

Data from the 1910 Public Use Sample (PUS) of the United States census (Strong, Preston, Lentzner, Seaman, Williams 1989) are employed to test these hypotheses. The 1910 PUS is a nationally representative sample of households drawn from the microfilmed records of the thirteenth census. One in every 250 households originally enumerated was included in the sample, yielding a total sample size of 88,814 households comprising 366,239 individuals. Although the 1910 PUS is a household sample, each sampled household includes information on all individuals residing in the household. We analyze the individual-level data, which include basic demographic and social variables, such as age, sex, race, marital status, birthplace, literacy, and occupation. The household data allow us to locate individuals by county, state, and region of residence.

We restrict our analysis to young men and women living in the rural South in 1910.[7] Individuals are classified as rural if they resided in a place with fewer than 2,500 residents. To provide additional information about the residential environment, we appended county-level data to each of the individual-level census records (Inter-University Consortium for Political and Social Research 1989). The county-level data describe the local economy and population, including the conditions and organization of agriculture and the prevalence of manufacturing activity. Where possible, we include race-specific measures of the local opportunity structure. Where race-specific data are unavailable or inappropriate, our measures refer to the total economy and population of the county. With the exception of two variables described below, the county-level measures are based on data from 1910.

We focus on the young adult population because our interest is in identifying conditions that facilitate or retard *early* marriage. The analysis is restricted to males aged 20-24 and to females aged 18-22.[8] These age groups exhibit substantial variation in marital status in the rural South in 1910. Because females tended to marry at an earlier age than males, we selected a slightly younger age group for the analysis of female marriage behavior. The dependent variable for examining the nuptial behavior of these men and women is a dichotomous measure of marital status in 1910: ever-married vs. never-married. The ever-married (coded 1) includes those who were married, divorced, separated or widowed at the time of the census.[9]

Two types of variables are included as predictors of martial status: individual characteristics of the young men and women and characteristics of the county of residence.

Individual Characterics

The individual characteristics included in the analysis are age, literacy, and occupation.[10] Age is measured in completed years and is included primarily as a control. Literacy is a dichotomous variable that measures the reported ability to read and write in the census year. Occupation for males is a four-category variable that distinguishes farmers (regardless of tenure status), family farm laborers, other farm laborers (primarily wage), and nonfarm workers. This variable reflects the principal options available to males during the period.[11]

No comparable measure of occupation is included for females for several reasons. First, many females reported no occupation in 1910. Second, the occupational activities of women, especially whether or not they were employed, were as much a consequence as a cause of marriage. Women frequently withdrew from the labor force or changed their activities when they married. Thus, a woman's occupation after marriage cannot be used as a predictor of entry into marriage. Because we have no information on occupation *prior* to marriage for the ever-married women, occupation is not a predictor of marital status for females.

County Characteristics

We measure the difficulty of acquiring land with the average value of an acre of farmland in the county of residence. This is a direct measure of the relative cost of purchasing a farm and is highly correlated with other measures of land availability (e.g., population density, proportion of all farmland improved) employed in previous studies (Leet 1977).[12] The prevalence of tenant farming is measured by the ratio of tenant farms (cash or share) to all farms. Because the prevalence of farm tenancy in southern counties varies sharply by race, this ratio is computed separately for farms operated by blacks and whites.

Two indicators of opportunities for nonfarm employment in the county of residence are included: the per capita investment in manufacturing and per capita manufacturing establishments (× 1000). These variables are constructed from 1900 census data because the information is not available in the 1910 census. Although the ten-year lag clearly introduces some error into the measurement of these variables, we believe their inclusion provides important information about alternatives to agricultural employment. Information on employment in manufacturing is not available by race. Thus, these variables describe the role of manufacturing in the *overall* opportunity structure.

To differentiate the effects of manufacturing employment from the more general influence of urbanization, we include as a control a measure of the proportion of each county's population residing in urban areas in 1910. Finally, our indicator of the availability of mates is the race-specific crude sex ratio. Although this is a coarse measure of the marriage market for males and females in young adulthood, county population counts by race and age are not available from the census.

Table 3.1 Means and Standard Deviations for Selected Variables by Sex and Race: Rural Southerners, 1910

Variable	Males Aged 20-24				Females Aged 18-22			
	White		Black		White		Black	
	Mean	Standard Deviation	Mean	Standard Deviation	Mean	Standard Deviation	Mean	Standard Deviation
Individual Characteristics								
Ever-married	.366	.482	.467	.499	.465	.499	.522	.500
Literate	.902	.297	.644	.479	.929	.257	.758	.428
Occupation:								
Farmer (owner or renter)	.276	.447	.260	.439	—	—	—	—
Farm laborer, family	.204	.403	.136	.343	—	—	—	—
Farm laborer, other	.159	.366	.284	.451	—	—	—	—
Nonfarm	.361	.480	.320	.467	—	—	—	—
Age	22.036	1.406	22.003	1.409	19.900	1.413	19.930	1.459
County Characteristics								
Average land cost (per acre)	26.625	20.924	25.122	16.721	26.004	19.720	24.991	17.948
Proportion tenants (race-specific)	.377	.146	.686	.252	.369	.145	.702	.244
Per capita manufacturing establishments (× 1,000)	3.650	1.392	3.207	1.197	3.641	1.338	3.162	1.090
Per capita manufacturing investment	35.222	47.677	35.589	44.427	33.955	46.024	32.061	36.907
Proportion urban	.113	.172	.115	.170	.105	.164	.112	.163
Sex ratio (race-specific)	1.058	.068	1.026	.503	1.053	.055	.998	.086

Findings

Descriptive Racial Comparisons

Table 3.1 presents the means and standard deviations for all variables. Among males aged 20-24, a substantial racial difference in the timing of marriage is evident: 37 percent of white males were ever-married compared to 47 percent of black males. Similarly, white females aged 18-22 were less likely to have entered marriage than their black counterparts, although the difference (47 percent vs. 52 percent) is less than that for males. Clearly, young blacks entered marriage more readily than whites.

A majority of both black and white males were employed in the agricultural sector. White men were slightly more likely to be farmers (owners or renters) than black men (27.6 percent vs. 26.0 percent) and a substantially higher percentage of the young white males worked on family farms (20.4 percent vs. 13.6 percent). A somewhat higher percentage of white men were employed outside of farming though the difference is not striking

(36.1 percent vs. 32.0 percent). The detailed occupational distributions for blacks and whites (not shown) show that young black men in nonfarm employment were more likely to be in unskilled manual occupations than white men.

The ability to read and write was more prevalent among whites than blacks: over 90 percent of the white males and females were literate compared to 64.4 and 75.8 percent of black men and women, respectively. Although literacy was rising among southern blacks during the period, it was by no means universal in rural areas by the early twentieth century.

County characteristics are quite similar across the four race-sex groups with the exception of the race-specific measure of tenancy. The prevalence of tenancy is much higher among black farmers than white farmers. Black males in the sample resided in counties in which, on average, 68.6 percent of black farmers were tenants. In contrast, an average of 37.7 percent of white farmers were tenants in the residential counties of white males. Despite the growth of tenancy in the late nineteenth and early twentieth centuries, farm ownership remained the norm among white farmers in the South.

Zero-order correlations among all variables (available from the authors) reveal the expected relationships between marriage timing and the predictor variables. Moreover, they suggest that collinearity among the independent variables is not a serious problem in our multivariate analysis.

Logistic Regression Results: Males

Table 3.2 presents the multivariate logistic regression results from equations predicting marital status (ever-married vs. never-married). Two equations are presented for each race-sex group, one including only county characteristics (and age), the other adding occupation and literacy. Results from the full equations are used to consider some of the mechanisms through which the opportunity structure influenced nuptiality.

We first examine the influence of agricultural opportunity in the county on the marriage behavior of black and white males. For white males, the predicted effect of land prices on marriage is evident: the higher the average cost of an acre of farmland, the lower the likelihood of marriage (equation 1). This is consistent with our expectation that white males, aspiring to farm ownership, postponed marriage in counties where land was costly. In contrast, the hypothesized effect of tenancy on marriage for white males is not borne out—the effect of tenancy is not significant and its sign is opposite of that predicted.

In contrast to the findings for whites, the timing of marriage was unaffected by land prices for black males (equation 3). The chance that a young black man could acquire the resources to purchase a farm was

Table 3.2 Multivariate Logistic Regression Coefficients for Relationship Between Marital Status and Selected Variables by Sex and Race: Rural Southerners, 1910

	Males Aged 20-24				Females Aged 18-22			
	White		Black		White		Black	
Independent Variable	(1)	(2)	(3)	(4)	(5)	(6)	(7)	(8)
Individual Characteristics								
Literate		-.906*		.219		.529*		-.076
		(-5.389)		(-1.442)		(-3.272)		(-.544)
Occupation:								
Farmer (owner or renter)		—		—				
Farm laborer, family		-3.455*		-3.300*				
		(-16.076)		(-11.214)				
Farm laborer, other		-1.751*		-1.959*				
		(-11.388)		(-9.375)				
Nonfarm		-1.493*		-2.038*				
		(-11.931)		(-9.259)				
Age	.354*	.271*	.456*	.418*	.367*	.365*	.504*	.502*
	(10.715)	(7.235)	(9.533)	(7.784)	(12.372)	(12.280)	(11.855)	(11.774)
County Characteristics								
Average land cost (per acre)	-.006*†	-.003	.002†	.004	-.008*†	-.008*	.001†	.001
	(-2.088)	(-1.123)	(.551)	(.981)	(-3.074)	(-2.978)	(.302)	(.309)
Proportion tenants (race-specific)	.495	-.295	1.134*	.397	1.049*	1.055*	.988*	.980*
	(1.503)	(-.795)	(3.855)	(1.205)	(3.543)	(3.554)	(3.693)	(3.659)
Per capita manufacturing establishments (× 1000)	-.139*†	-.121*	-.027†	-.070	-.081*	-.074*	-.070	-.068
	(-3.519)	(-2.791)	(-.420)	(-.995)	(-2.287)	(-2.069)	(-1.133)	(-1.081)
Per capita manufacturing investment	-.000	.001	-.002	-.001	.002*	.002	.003	.003
	(-.305)	(.798)	(-.899)	(-.297)	(2.000)	(1.891)	(1.362)	(1.332)
Proportion urban	-.264	-.460	.284	.422	-.370	-.372	.360	.370
	(-.750)	(-1.221)	(.557)	(.774)	(-1.165)	(-1.169)	(.757)	(.779)
Sex ratio (race-specific)	-2.331*	-1.946*	-1.882*	-1.996*	2.557*	2.553*	2.980*	3.003*
	(-3.074)	(-2.408)	(-2.514)	(-2.447)	(3.324)	(3.317)	(3.522)	(3.541)
Constant	-5.390*	-1.684	-9.020*	-5.709*	-10.066*	-9.562*	-13.530*	-13.461*
	(-4.913)	(-1.382)	(-6.788)	(-3.835)	(-9.515)	(-8.950)	(-10.370)	(-10.266)
-2 log likelihood	2818.08	2327.53	1364.12	1157.75	3397.67	3386.74	1647.48	1647.19
Number of cases	2,269	2,269	1,085	1,085	2,611	2,611	1,320	1,320

*$p < .05$ †$p < .05$ (one-tailed test) for difference between coefficients for whites and blacks.
Note: t-statistics in parentheses.

sufficiently remote that land prices were largely irrelevant to family formation. Opportunities for tenant farming clearly encouraged early marriage among rural black males. The magnitude of the relationship can be evaluated by comparing the predicted probabilities of marriage at various levels of tenancy. Using equation 3 to predict marital status and setting all covariates (other than tenancy) to their sample means, the predicted probability of marriage is .38 with 40 percent of black farmers engaged in tenant farming, compared to .43 with 60 percent tenant farmers. This indicates a substantial influence of opportunities for tenant farming on marriage among rural black men.

The pattern of results for the manufacturing variables is also consistent with our hypotheses. For white males, per capita manufacturing establishments has a statistically significant negative relationship with the likelihood of marriage (equation 1). This supports our expectation that employment in the wage economy discouraged early entry into marriage. However, per capita manufacturing investments are unrelated to marital status. It is unclear why the two dimensions of manufacturing activity exhibit different relationships with the marriage variable. For black males, neither indicator of local manufacturing activity is related to marriage, reflecting the relative lack of opportunity for blacks in the manufacturing sector.

The sex ratio in the county is an important predictor of marital status for males of both races. A relatively high ratio of males to females indicates a scarcity of potential mates. Accordingly, there is a negative relationship between the sex ratio and marriage for males. The proportion urban in the county population has no effect on marriage patterns among blacks or whites.

We tested the statistical significance of race differences in the effects of the agricultural and manufacturing opportunity variables by pooling the black and white male samples and including multiplicative interaction terms in the logistic regression equations. Only interactions involving the measures of economic opportunity were examined, since our theoretical framework explicitly hypothesizes racial differences in their effects on marriage. We included only county characteristics (and age) in the equation when testing for interactions because our interest is in racial differences in the *overall* effect of the opportunity variables on marriage, i.e., prior to the introduction of controls for the mediating influence of occupation and literacy. The results indicate a significant racial difference in the effect of land prices on marriage, but not tenancy. The effect of per capita manufacturing establishments also differs significantly by race, but there is no difference between blacks and whites in the effect of per capita manufacturing investments.

Equations 2 and 4 add individual measures of occupation and literacy to the predictors in equations 1 and 3. The full equations enable us to assess the mediating role of the socioeconomic attributes of residents. In particular, we are concerned with several issues related to the type of economic activity performed by men. First, we assess whether occupation, broadly defined, affected entry into marriage. Second, we consider whether the effect of occupation on marriage chances was similar for black and white men. And finally, we assess the role of occupation as an intervening variable between the larger economic structure and marriage.[13]

The results for both black and white men show considerable variation in the likelihood of marriage by occupation. Farmers had a much higher likelihood of early marriage than men in other occupations. Farming creates clear incentives for early family formation—whether tenant or owner, the farmer has much to gain from the labor of additional family members. The situation of farmers stands in sharp contrast to that of men employed for a wage. Because the organization of the wage economy was independent of the family unit, these men profited little from early marriage and family formation. Accordingly, they were much less likely than farmers to have married in their early adult years. The magnitude of the difference is illustrated with a comparison of farmers and nonfarm workers. Among whites, farmers were over four times as likely to have married by ages 20-24 than nonfarm men; among blacks, farmers were more than seven times as likely to have married than those employed outside of agriculture.[14]

White males who were unable to read and write were substantially more likely to have married than literate males. In contrast, literacy had a much weaker impact on the likelihood of marriage among black males, perhaps because literacy did not play a major role in determining the career trajectories of young black men.

The effects of the county-level predictors for white men change little from equation 1 to equation 2 with one important exception: the statistically significant negative coefficient for land cost in equation 1 is markedly weakened in equation 2. This is consistent with previous studies of the period (Landale 1989a, 1989b) which show that high land prices impeded entry into farming. Where land was difficult to acquire, young men entered occupations that were less conducive to family formation. Apparently, much of the impact of land cost on marriage was mediated by occupation.

Occupation also appears to intervene between the prevalence of tenancy and marriage for black men. The strong and statistically significant coefficient for black tenancy in equation 1 is no longer significant in the full equation, presumably because blacks residing in areas of widespread tenancy had greater opportunities to become farmers (albeit tenants).

Overall, we find considerable support for our hypotheses. Different features of the opportunity structure were salient to the marriage behavior of black and white males. The marriage behavior of white males responded to land prices and manufacturing activity in the county. Although we expected high levels of tenancy to impede entry into marriage among white men, the results did not support this hypothesis. The single feature of the opportunity structure relevant to marriage among black males was the prevalence of tenant farming in the county. Both land costs and the presence of manufacturing opportunities were much less important for the marriage behavior of black males.

Parallel analyses of black and white males at older ages (results not shown) suggest that it is the timing of marriage, rather than the overall propensity to marry, that is affected by the opportunity structure of the county. The significant effects described above become progressively weaker at older ages. This is demonstrated by the coefficients and t-values associated with different variables across the age groups 20-24, 25-29 and 30-34. While the coefficient for the effect of land prices is −.006 for white males 20-24, it shrinks to −.004 (t = −1.73) and −.001 (t = −0.27) for ages 25-29 and 30-34, respectively. Similarly, the coefficient for the influence of per capita manufacturing establishments among white males falls from −.139 for ages 20-24 to −.065 (t = −1.54) and −.046 (t = −0.93) for ages 25-29 and 30-34, respectively. Finally, marriage among older black males is slightly less sensitive to the prevalence of tenancy in the county—the coefficient declines from 1.134 for ages 20-24 to .945 (t = 2.80) and 1.07 (t = 2.17) for ages 25-29 and 30-34, respectively.[15]

Logistic Regression Results: Females

Table 3.2 also presents results from similar analyses for white and black females aged 18-22. The female equations differ from those for males in omitting occupation from the predictors. Because the results for the females of each race change little after inclusion of individual characteristics, we focus our discussion on the full equations. (Significance tests for racial differences in the effects of the county-level measures of economic opportunity are based on the restricted equation.)

The overall pattern of results for white females is generally similar to that for white males. Literate white females were less likely to have married than those who could not read and write. High land prices reduced the likelihood of early marriage. The number of manufacturing establishments per capita in the county also appears to have discouraged early marriage. The sex ratio among whites has the predicted positive effect on female marriage. Although these relationships are consistent with our hypotheses, the positive and statistically significant coefficient for farm tenancy is clearly contrary to our expectations. It is unclear why a high prevalence of tenancy among white farmers encouraged marriage among young white women in the absence of a similar effect for young white males. We can only speculate that perhaps older tenant farmers were selecting younger women as their brides.[16]

The pattern of results for black women is also consistent with the pattern for black males. Literacy has no effect on the likelihood of marriage. With the exception of the sex ratio among blacks, the only county characteristic that is significantly related to marriage is the prevalence of farm tenancy. Where opportunities for tenant farming were widespread, young black women, like men, were more likely to have married. As with black males, the cost of farmland and the presence of manufacturing opportunities are unrelated to the marriage behavior of black females.

Tests for the statistical significance of race differences in the effects of economic conditions on marriage for females showed that only the price of farmland had a significantly different effect for blacks and whites.

Conclusion and Discussion

A common opportunity thesis underlies explanations of historic patterns of marriage in western societies. The basic argument is summarized by Hermalin and van de Walle (1977): "Our model starts with the proposition that people want to get married. To do so they require a material basis, which includes a place to live and a means of livelihood. It follows logically that they *will* get married, provided dwellings and jobs are available. We assume, on the basis of these premises, that the extent of nuptiality reflects the availability of a material basis of marriage" (pp. 80-1).

We attempted to refine the opportunity thesis of nuptiality, in two ways. First, we argued that the *motivation* as well as the *ability* to marry varies with the economic structure. Some economic activities provide clear incentives for early family formation, while others do not. It is not just the ability to support a family that leads to early marriage; rather, it is some combination of adequate resources and perceived gains. Second, we argued for the importance of systems of stratification for nuptial behavior. Groups in distinct positions in the social hierarchy differ with respect to their *access* to positions and rewards. Thus, the social system mediates the relationship between the economic structure and marriage. When groups are denied access to certain opportunities for social and economic mobility, then conditions in the corresponding sectors of the economy will not figure prominently in their decisions to marry.

We tested these refinements by examining the timing of entry into marriage in the rural South near the turn of the century, when the southern opportunity structure was sharply segmented by race. As anticipated, blacks and whites exhibited different marital timing and responded differently to specific economic opportunities. Although the rural South in the early twentieth century represents an extreme case of social inequality, our findings point to the need to consider differential access to resources in studies of nuptiality.

Acknowledgments

This research was partially supported by a grant from the American Sociological Association's Problems of the Discipline program. The authors thank Mark Hereward and Patty Glynn for their assistance in preparing the 1910 Public Use Sample for analysis, and Avery Guest, Tim Guinnane, S. Philip Morgan, and R.S. Oropesa for comments on an earlier draft of this paper.

Notes

1. Most theoretical statements about the historic relationship between economic opportunity and marriage are drawn from studies of the demographic system in preindustrial northwest Europe. However, the fundamental logic has been applied to societies in which residential and financial independence are prerequisities to marriage.

2. A lack of data on U.S. marriage behavior in the 19th century limits the empirical study of this issue. The U.S. census first collected information on marital status in the census of 1880; marriage data were not included in the published tabulations until 1890.

3. Another alternative was migration to areas of more favorable opportunities. Although migration was important during the period under study, an examination of its effects on marriage is beyond the scope of the present paper. Our cross-sectional census data provide no information on geographic mobility in young adulthood. The relationship between migration and marriage at the turn of the century is examined with longitudinal data in Landale (1989a).

4. The economic contributions of family members are also reflected in the preference of landowners for tenants with wives and children (see e.g., Davis, Gardner, and Gardner 1941, pp. 327-8).

5. Newby's (1989) description of cotton mill production in the New South presents a somewhat different view of the wage labor environment. According to Newby, mill operators sought families with other possible workers—including women and children. In this part of the nonfarm economy, wage labor may not have been incompatible with early family formation. Still, our distinction between employment in the wage economy and the farm economy applies generally.

6. This is not expected because of the differences between the social contexts and marriage patterns of rural western Europe in the eighteenth century and the rural American South in the early twentieth century.

7. Households from the following states are included in our analysis: Alabama, Arkansas, Florida, Georgia, Kentucky, Louisiana, Maryland, Mississippi, North Carolina, South Carolina, Tennessee, Texas, Virginia, West Virginia.

8. Since age-heaping in the 1910 census might disproportionately include poor black males in the 20-24 age group at the lower end (through rounding to age 20), while excluding them at the upper end (through rounding to age 25), we replicated the analysis using ages 22-26 for males. Our substantive conclusions were largely unchanged.

9. Consensual unions were not among the marital status categories included in the 1910 census. However, we believe that most individuals in consensual unions were reported as married by enumerators, though we cannot confirm this. Our conceptual framework need not distinguish between legal and common-law marriage because the two types of unions should respond similarly to local economic opportunity structures.

10. Information for individuals within households was reported by whomever spoke with the census enumerator. Often, though not always, this was the head of the household. This may have some bearing on the accuracy of the individual

characteristics. For example, our measure of literacy is the *reported* ability of household members to read and write rather than a *demonstrated* ability to read and write.

11. It was not possible to differentiate tenant farmers from farm owners. Although the 1910 census includes data on whether a farm was owned or rented, it does not provide information on which household member held the title to owned farms. Preliminary analysis of the ownership data revealed that ownership was confounded with marital status: the majority of men living on owned farms were single men residing in the parental household. Thus, although the farms were owned, the young men were probably not the farm owners. Because a high percentage of the single men continued to live with their families of origin, it was not possible to determine whether the men themselves owned land.

12. Early in our analyses we included a measure of the percentage of all farmland that was improved in 1910. Although it is also considered an indicator of agricultural opportunity, it had no significant independent effect in our equations and was dropped.

13. It may be somewhat problematic to interpret occupation as an intervening variable, since marital status and occupation are measured at the same point in time and "present" occupation may not be the same as occupation at time of marriage. However, because we are considering young men with relatively short marital durations (if married), we believe there is little risk in assuming that occupation at marriage was the same as occupation at the census data.

14. The particularly low marriage chances of family farm laborers undoubtedly reflect, in part, the rules of co-residence. Young men were likely to live and work on their parents' (or other relatives') farms during the years before they married. As a general rule, they were expected to be financially and residentially independent after marriage. Thus, the observed relationship is likely due to the effect of marital status on living arrangements rather than vice versa.

15. Some unexpected findings also emerge from the analyses of older males. For example, among white males, the coefficient for the prevalence of tenancy becomes positive and statistically significant at ages 25-29 and 30-34. We are somewhat reluctant, however, to place as much confidence in the overall pattern of results for older men. For many older men, marriage occurred in the relatively distant past. In the interim, it is possible that they migrated from their county-of-marriage or that the county opportunity structure changed. Although a complete discussion of the equations for older males is beyond the scope of the present paper, results are available from the authors upon request.

16. Tenancy had a significant positive effect on marriage among white males 25-29 and 30-34 years of age.

References

Caldwell, John C. 1982. *Theory of Fertility Decline*. New York: Academic Press.

Davis, Allison, Burleigh B. Gardner, and Mary R. Gardner. 1941. *Deep South: A Social Anthropological Study of Caste and Class*. Chicago: University of Chicago Press.

Dixon, Ruth B. 1971. "Explaining Cross-Cultural Variations in Age at Marriage and Proportions Never Marrying." *Population Studies* 25:215–33.

Dollard, John. 1937. *Caste and Class in a Southern Town*. Garden City: Doubleday.

Easterlin, Richard A. 1976. "Factors in the Decline of Farm Fertility in the United States: Some Preliminary Research Results." *Journal of American History* 63:600–14.

Flynn, Charles L. 1983. *White Land, Black Labor: Caste and Class in Late Nineteenth-Century Georgia*. Baton Rouge: Louisiana State University Press.

Forster, Colin and G.S.L. Tucker. 1972. *Economic Opportunity and White American Fertility Ratios 1800–1860*. New Haven: Yale University Press.

Habakkuk, H. J. 1971. *Population and Economic Development Since 1750*. New York: Humanities Press.

Hajnal, John. 1965. "European Marriage Patterns in Perspective." Pp. 101–43 in *Population in History*, edited by D. V. Glass and D. E. C. Eversley. London: Edward Arnold.

Hermalin, Albert I. and Etienne van de Walle. 1977. "The Civil Code and Nuptiality: Empirical Investigation of a Hypothesis." Pp. 71–111 in *Population Patterns in the Past*, edited by Ronald D. Lee. New York: Academic Press.

Inter-University Consortium for Political and Social Research (ICPSR). 1989. *Guide to Resources and Services 1988–89*. Ann Arbor: University of Michigan, Institute for Social Research.

Jaynes, Gerald D. 1986. *Branches Without Roots: Genesis of the Black Working Class in the American South, 1862–1882*. New York: Oxford University Press.

Landale Nancy S. 1989a. "Opportunity, Movement and Marriage: U.S. Farm Sons at the Turn of the Century." *Journal of Family History* 15:365–86.

______, 1989b. "Agricultural Opportunity and Marriage: The United States at the Turn of the Century." *Demography* 26:203–18.

Leet, Don R. 1977. "Interrelations of Population Density, Urbanization, Literacy and Fertility." *Explorations in Economic History* 14:388–401.

Levine, David. 1977. *Family Formation in an Age of Nascent Capitalism*. New York: Academic Press.

Malthus, Thomas R. [1826] 1986. "An Essay on the Principle of Population, Part II." In *The Works of Thomas Robert Malthus, Volume III*, edited by E.A. Wrigley and David Souden. London: William Pickering.

Mandle, Jay. 1978. *The Roots of Black Poverty: The Southern Plantation Economy After the Civil War*. Durham, NC: Duke University Press.

Myrdal, Gunnar. 1975. *An American Dilemma: The Negro Problem and Modern Democracy*. New York: Pantheon Books.

Newby, I. A. 1989. *Plain Folk in the New South: Social Change and Cultural Persistence, 1880–1915*. Baton Rouge: Louisiana State University Press.

Ransom, Roger L. and Richard Sutch. 1977. *One Kind of Freedom: The Economic Consequences of Emancipation*. New York: Cambridge University Press.

Schwartz, Michael. 1976. *Radical Protest and Social Structure: The Southern Farmers' Alliance and Cotton Tenancy, 1880–1890*. New York: Academic Press.

Shapiro, Morton O. 1982. "Land Availability and Fertility in the United States, 1760–1870." *Journal of Economic History* 42:577–600.

Strong, Michael, Samuel H. Preston, Harold R. Lentzner, Jeffrey R. Seaman, and Henry C. Williams. 1989. *User's Guide: Public Use Sample, 1910 United States Census of Population*. Philadelphia: Population Studies Center, University of Pennsylvania.

Tilly, Louise A. and Joan W. Scott. 1978. *Women, Work, and Family*. New York: Holt, Rinehart, and Winston.

Tolnay, Stewart E. 1984. "Black Family Formation and Tenancy in the Farm South, 1900." *American Journal of Sociology* 9:305–25.

_____. 1986. "Family Economy and the Black American Fertility Transition." *Journal of Family History*. 11:267–83.

Wilson, William Julius and Kathryn Neckerman. 1987. "Poverty and Family Structure: The Widening Gap Between Evidence and Public Policy Issues." Pp. 63–92 in *The Truly Disadvantaged: The Inner City, the Underclass, and Public Policy*, by William Julius Wilson. Chicago: The University of Chicago Press.

Wright, Gavin. 1986. *Old South, New South*. New York: Basic Books, Inc.

Wrigley, E.A. and Roger Schofield, 1981. *The Population History of England, 1541–1871: A Reconstruction*. Cambridge, MA: Harvard University Press.

Yasuba, Yasukichi. 1961. *Birth Rates of the White Population in the United States: An Economic Study* (Studies in Historical and Political Science, Series 79, No. 2). Baltimore: the Johns Hopkins University.

4

The Impact of the Civil War on American Widowhood

Amy E. Holmes and Maris A. Vinovskis

Although much has been written about families and roles of women in the nineteenth century, the experiences of widows have not received much attention (Degler 1980; Mintz and Kellogg 1988). This is disappointing because many women experienced widowhood, and a substantial proportion of children lost one or both of their parents before reaching adulthood (Uhlenberg 1980; Vinovskis 1990). Our neglect of the study of widows becomes even more glaring when we recall that the unusually high casualty rates during the Civil War left many widows in both the North and the South and led to the development of a large federal pension program for disabled Union veterans or their survivors (Holmes 1990; Vinovskis 1989).

This chapter will begin to remedy our neglect of nineteenth-century widows by looking at the impact of the Civil War on spouses of the soldiers and sailors who died as a result of that conflict. First, we examine the extent and nature of nineteenth-century widowhood in general with appropriate comparisons whenever possible to the situation of widows today. Next, we discuss the demographic impact of the Civil War and estimate the number of widows created as well as how local communities tried to assist them during that conflict. Then we trace the establishment and implementation of the federal pension program for widows of Union soldiers and sailors and assess its importance not only to the recipients of that aid but also to the federal budget. Finally, in order to ascertain the actual social and economic impact of the federal pensions upon recipients, we investigate the household arrangements of widows in 1880 in Essex County, Massachusetts, and Kent County, Michigan.

Because almost nothing has been written about Civil War widows, our brief examination does not pretend to provide adequate coverage or to be a sufficiently in-depth analysis to fully assess the impact of that conflict on the life course of nineteenth-century women. Nevertheless, our sketching the broad demographic and social parameters of Civil War widows and providing an exploratory case study of their postwar lives in two counties may stimulate more work on this important but neglected topic. Furthermore, because the federal pension program for Union veterans or their widows may have contributed to the growing interest in state and federal assistance for widows and the elderly in the late nineteenth and early twentieth centuries, there is a need for additional research on these issues.

Widowhood in Nineteenth-Century America

There are important differences in the extent and nature of widowhood in the past and today. The longer life expectancy of women than of men today contributes to the large proportion of them being widows at some point in their lives. White male life expectancy at age twenty was 53.4 years in 1986; that of white females was 59.9 years (U.S. Bureau of the Census 1989:73). But were there similar gender differences in the nineteenth century? The life expectancy at age twenty for males was 44.0 years and for females was 43.0 years in Massachusetts in 1860 (Vinovskis 1972). Similarly, for 1900–1902, the national life expectancy at age twenty was 42.2 years for white males and 43.8 years for white females (U.S. Bureau of the Census 1975:56). Thus, the gender gap in adult mortality appears to have been smaller in the nineteenth century than now and therefore we might expect a more equal proportion of widows and widowers in the past than today.[1]

In the nineteenth century as well as today, widowers were more likely to remarry than widows (Grigg 1984; Lopata and Brehm 1986). Because men married at a later age than women, their chances of surviving their spouse were reduced (Degler 1980). As a result, whereas 4.7 percent of males ages twenty and above were widowers in 1890, 13.2 percent of comparable females were widows. At ages 65 and above this differential increases with 23.4 percent of men widowers in 1890 and 58.7 percent of women widows (calculated from U.S. Bureau of Census 1895:clxxxi).

Another major difference between the nineteenth century and today is that parents were much more likely to die and leave children as orphans in the past. According to Uhlenberg (1980), the probability of one or more parents dying before a child reaches age fifteen decreases from 24 percent in 1900 to only 5 percent in 1976. The proportion of elderly widows among all widows ages twenty and above is much higher today than a hundred years ago (Scadron 1988). Whereas today nearly three-fourths of all widows are aged sixty-five and above, in 1890 that proportion was only one-third (U.S. Bureau of Census 1895:clxxxi; 1989:41). Consequently, widowhood in the nineteenth century left many young women without their spouses and created more problems for the raising of young children than today.[2]

The legal situation of married women and widows improved in the nineteenth century as many states passed legislation before the Civil War allowing married women control over property given to them or inherited by them. Under the common law in most states, a woman whose spouse died intestate received one-third of the estate. By 1890 eight states, mainly in the West, adopted the community property system whereby widows automatically received one-half of all the property acquired by the couple during the marriage. Despite the overall progress, legal advances were usually much slower in the older eastern areas such as Pennsylvania than in the states established after the Civil War (Salmon 1986; Shamas, Salmon, and Dahlin 1987).

If the legal context of widowhood under intestacy improved, what about the actual bequests made through wills? A study of Bucks County, Pennsylvania, in 1685–1756, 1791–1801, and 1891–1893 found that the treatment of spouses by male testators improved by the end of the nineteenth century with a majority of husbands leaving wives a greater share of the estate than the widows would have otherwise acquired intestate (Shamas, Salmon, and Dahlin 1987).

For the few widows whose husbands had accumulated substantial assets, the changes in the provisions and practices of inheritances were beneficial. The estates inherited by these few widows were sufficiently large to allow them to live comfortably and independently. Indeed, Lebsock (1984) has argued that these affluent widows in antebellum Petersburg, Virginia, cherished their independence and demonstrated it by rejecting remarriages, which were forced upon their less fortunate sisters who could not afford to remain single. Lebsock's widely cited explanations for the remarriage pattern of affluent widows are problematic, but she is correct in pointing out that a few wealthy nineteenth-century widows did have considerable control over their own lives and assets.[3]

But most nineteenth-century estates were not sufficient to provide adequate support for widows (Grigg 1984; Trattner 1989). Nor was life insurance, usually just enough to cover the burial expenses, sufficient in coverage or amount to offer much assistance (Kleinberg 1989; Zelizer 1979). As a result, for most women in nineteenth-century America widowhood was associated with poverty—especially if young children were involved.

Driven in part by economic necessity, remarriage often appeared as a necessary and reasonable alternative. Yet widows, especially older ones or those with children, found it difficult to remarry. Throughout the nineteenth century, widowers remarried at significantly higher rates than widows even though the latter would have benefited the most by remarriage (Grigg 1984).

Few married women worked outside the home, but a sizable percentage of widows had to enter the paid labor force to survive (Mason, Vinovskis, and Hareven, 1978). Although society emphasized the importance of the mother being at home with her young children, widows were expected to work outside the home to support their families. The low wages available to widows and other women in the nineteenth century, however, made it difficult, if not impossible, to support and maintain a family (Ryan 1981).

Unable to remarry or to support themselves through their employment, many widows had to turn to others for help. Relatives, neighbors, and sometimes fraternal groups provided some assistance, but the total amount contributed usually was small and sporadic (Clawson 1989; Kleinberg 1989; Motz 1983). Because widows were regarded as part of the "deserving" poor in the nineteenth century, especially if they had lived in that community for some years, private charities and/or public welfare agencies often provided them with assistance—usually in the form of outdoor relief (cash or supplies provided while the recipient lives at home). Yet the limited funds available for private or public assistance to widows meant that the total amount of support would be minimal and often insufficient, even if the widow were working, to support her entire family. As a result, younger children of widows were often sent to an orphanage or, if they were older, apprenticed to someone (Katz 1986; Trattner 1989).

Widows of white, Protestant, and middle-class spouses received the most sympathy and financial assistance in the nineteenth century. Widows of immigrants or of African-Americans not only were poorer to begin with but often faced substantial discrimination both in their jobs and in receiving welfare assistance. Their children were also more likely to be removed from them because those in control of private and public welfare often viewed poor immigrants and African-Americans as inadequate parents (Trattner 1989).

Thus, although the legal situation of widows improved in the nineteenth century and a few of them were able to maintain independent households, most women entering widowhood faced substantial distress and poverty. Remarriage was an option for some, and private and public charities provided assistance for many; but the plight of most widows was difficult—particularly for those who were African-Americans or who had recently immigrated to the country.

Impact of the Civil War

Much has been written about the Civil War, but most of it has been narrowly focused on the military and political aspects of that conflict. The social history of the Civil War remains to be investigated (Vinovskis 1989). Even the few works that do address the Civil War from a social history perspective have little to say about the widows of Union and Confederate soldiers and sailors (Massey 1966; Paludan 1988).

A large number of American males enlisted in the armed forces. Approximately three million men (including 189,000 African Americans) joined the armed forces. Nearly two million whites served in the Union forces and 900,000 whites defended the Confederacy. Although the Union forces were substantially larger than the Confederate ones, the much larger population of the North meant that a smaller proportion of Northerners than Southerners fought in the Civil War. Of the military-age population (aged 13 to 43 in 1860), 35 percent of northern whites served compared to 61 percent of southern whites (Vinovskis 1989).

There is considerable disagreement over the social composition of the Civil War forces. Contemporary critics in both the North and South argued that the Civil War was basically a "poor man's" fight, as middle and upper-class native whites were either exempted from service or able to purchase substitutes (Moore 1924; Murdock 1971). A detailed analysis of Newburyport, Massachusetts, however, suggests that Union soldiers and sailors there were not disproportionately drawn from the lower socioeconomic groups and that the foreign-born were actually less likely to enlist than the native-born population (Vinovskis 1989). Similarly, in Claremont and Newport, New Hampshire, participation in the war was widespread among unskilled and skilled workers. Only farmers or their sons were less likely to enlist (Kemp 1990).[4] Thus, it appears that the Civil War was fought by volunteers and draftees representing a broad spectrum of the population and involved a high proportion of the military-age white population.[5]

Casualties were common, with approximately one out of every five white servicemen dying. Overall, 618,000 Union and Confederate soldiers and sailors died—by far the largest number of dead in any of our wars. The death rate in the Civil War becomes even more glaring when we take into consideration the size of the population. There were 30 American military deaths per 10,000 population in World War II and 3 per 10,000 in the Vietnam conflict; military deaths were 182 per 10,000 inhabitants in the Civil War (Vinovskis 1989).

Northern military deaths (360,000) exceeded southern ones (258,000), but the smaller population size in the South again meant that that region suffered disproportionately. Whereas 6 percent of military-age white males in the North died, 18 percent of their counterparts in the South died. Or approximately one out of six northern servicemen died compared to one out of four southern men in the armed forces (Vinovskis 1989).

Given the large number of participants as well as the high death rate, it is not surprising that the Civil War created many widows. Unfortunately, we do not have any reliable estimates of the total number of married servicemen or of their likelihood of dying during the Civil War.[6]

Because most of those who enlisted or were drafted were young men and some married men undoubtedly were reluctant to leave their families, one might guess that married men were underrepresented. A study of two small New Hampshire communities found that 15 percent of the married men ages 18–45 in Claremont and 19 percent of those in Newport enlisted compared to 18 percent and 29 percent, respectively, of those who were single. Interestingly, there was little difference in enrollment rates between married men with or without children (Kemp 1990).[7]

If married men were somewhat less likely to enlist than single ones, it still does not provide us with an overall estimate of what proportion of Civil War soldiers and sailors were married. The few pieces of information we have give us very different rates. A study of Deerfield, Massachusetts, found that 32 percent of the local servicemen were married (Harris 1984). According to the New York State Census of 1865, however, 44 percent of soldiers were married and 1.5 percent were widowers (New York Secretary of State 1867).[8]

Similarly, we do not have reliable estimates of the likelihood of single or married servicemen dying. Whereas the socioeconomic differences among enlistees in Newburyport were not great, soldiers and sailors from disadvantaged backgrounds were more apt to die; but this still does not address the issue of mortality by marital status (Vinovskis 1989). Using the crude data from New York State in 1865, it appears that single servicemen were slightly more likely to die than those who were married.[9]

In any case, it is clear that a large proportion of Civil War soldiers were married, perhaps in the range of 30–40 percent, and that many of them died of wounds or diseases. As a result, there may have been roughly 150,000 to 250,000 widows of Union and Confederate soldiers and sailors during the Civil War.

Particularly in the North, the families of soldiers were assisted by private and public contributions. With the outbreak of hostilities, individual citizens rushed forth to pledge help for the families of those who volunteered to save the Union. The Massachusetts physicians of Clinton, Worcester, and the Suffolk District Medical Society resolved to provide free medical care for the families of the volunteers, and one real estate owner in Boston even proclaimed he would not charge the families of enlisted men any rent (Reynolds 1970).

Once the fighting started, the casualties mounted and states and local communities had to provide for the growing number of widows. Some widows benefited by receiving whatever remained of the substantial bonuses their husbands obtained for enlisting (Moore 1924; Murdock 1971). Others received preferential treatment in seeking employment (Massey 1966). Most, however, were dependent upon public and private charity to survive. Although private assistance for widows of soldiers was generous in the early months of the Civil War, particularly in the North, it was clear that this would not be enough by itself to help everyone. Therefore states and local communities frequently provided public assistance for the families of soldiers. The Massachusetts legislature, for example, passed an act on May 23, 1861, by which cities and towns were allowed to raise money by taxation to provide aid for the wives, children, or other dependents of soldiers. The town was to be reimbursed by the Commonwealth for these expenditures as long as they did not exceed one dollar a week for the wife and one additional dollar for each child or dependent parent of that soldier; the aggregate payment for the family and parents of each soldier could not exceed twelve dollars a month (Schouler 1868).

The sums of money raised for families of soldiers in the North often were quite substantial. In Massachusetts, towns raised $6,253,455 during the war to help the families of soldiers—in addition to the nearly $43 million the Commonwealth and the local communities paid for bounties and other war-related expenses (calculated from Schouler 1871). The public money raised for aiding the families of Massachusetts soldiers was about a third more than the local communities paid for support of all the public-school teachers during that same period (calculated from Massachusetts Board of Education 1862–1866).

States also tried to help the survivors of deceased soldiers by creating special institutions to care for their children. Championed by the governor, the Pennsylvania legislature in 1865 created orphan schools for the children of Union soldiers and sailors who died as a result of the war. The schools flourished with 1,329 orphans attending at the close of 1865 and their numbers doubling within the next year (Paul 1876).

But there were limits to the generosity of local communities and states as the costs of the war mounted (Holliday 1962). The exorbitant prices for goods due to runaway inflation and the problems of providing for their children made the lives of these women difficult during the war years—particularly for those in the war-devastated areas of the South. Although several states in the Confederacy adopted public assistance programs to assist indigent families of servicemen, the amount of aid they could provide was meager. During the last phases of the war, impoverished women, many of them widows, led bread riots in cities such as Mobile and Richmond (Bremner 1980).

The Federal Pension Program for Union Widows

Military pensions in the United States have a long history. Colonies used pensions as payment for fighting against Indians and for fighting in the American Revolution (Glasson 1918; Resch 1988). The Civil War pension system, however, had much farther-reaching effects than any system preceding it. More money was spent than ever before, a greater proportion of the population received pensions, they received pensions sooner after fighting ended than most previous pensioners, and politicians used pensions to woo voters on a large scale. From the founding of the federal government to the beginning of the Civil War, the U.S. government spent a total of about $90 million on military pensions (Glasson 1918). In the fifteen years after the Civil War, the federal government spent about $5 billion, about 60 times what it had spent before (Glasson 1918). Over 40 percent of the federal budget in 1893 was spent on pension payments to former soldiers and their families (Vinovskis 1989). The Civil War pension also was a source of great debate during the late nineteenth and early twentieth centuries because of its use as political spoils.[10] Ordinary people in the late nineteenth century thus were likely to have contact with the pension system in a variety of ways: by receiving pension payments themselves, by reading about them in newspapers and party platforms, or perhaps by discussing the latest abuses of the system as various pension bureau officials and lawyers were investigated for improprieties.

The Civil War federal military pension had important implications for widows, who made up a substantial proportion of pension recipients. In 1883, one in six on the pension rolls were widows, and over half of them had children under sixteen years of age (Glasson 1900, 1918). Under the pension system enacted in 1862 and modified by subsequent legislation, a widow had to prove that her husband died from service-related wounds or diseases. If the pension was allowed, the widow would receive the same amount that a totally disabled soldier received: from eight to thirty dollars per month. If the widow remarried, pension payments ended. However, she could still receive the sum of payments due to her before she remarried, even if she applied for the pension after her second marriage. Congress, recognizing that widows with minor children had trouble supporting them, provided extra payments to widows with minor children in 1868. Widows who received an eight-dollar pension also received two dollars extra each month for every child under the age of sixteen. Congress raised the amount of pensions in 1886, increasing the amount paid to widows of privates from eight to twelve dollars per month (Glasson 1990). Considering that the average annual earnings for all workers in 1890 was $438 (U.S. Bureau of the Census 1975), a pension of $144 a year represented a significant amount of money. Although widows received the same amount as totally disabled soldiers, these payments represented a larger proportion of wages that widows could earn otherwise. Women could expect to earn approximately three-fifths of the average men's wage in 1885 (Long 1975).

Widows received lump-sum payments in addition to regular pension payments. An act passed soon after the end of the war provided a five-year deadline after which widows could not apply for arrears, but in 1879 Congress allowed payments from the date of death of the husband no matter when the widow applied. Arrears payments could be very substantial. The average first payment to army widows, minor children, and dependent soldiers in 1881 was $1,022, over two times the mean yearly earnings of all workers (Glasson 1918).

Although the pension system passed in 1862 had some impact upon the lives of ordinary people, its impact was limited compared to legislation passed in 1890. This second pension system considerably widened in scope the number of widows eligible for the pension, because it required only that widows prove that their husbands had served ninety days or more. Women no longer had to prove that their husbands died of service-related causes. If she had married the soldier before June 27, 1890, a widow was entitled to a pension of eight dollars each month. This pension was paid not only to women who had been married before or during the war but to women who had married Civil War veterans up to twenty-five years after the war had ended.

The 1890 pension's function as an old-age pension for significant numbers of native-born white Northerners has been noted by several scholars (Haber 1983; Orloff and Skocpol 1984; Vinovskis 1989). Even less work has been done on Confederate pensions. By 1907, every southern state had inaugurated a pension program, although the South was also indirectly paying for Union pensions (Glasson 1907). These state pensions were small. For example, payments to widows in Georgia did not start until 1893, and the average payment to widows in Georgia was about 60 dollars for the whole year in 1906 (Glasson 1907).

States and local communities in the North also helped former Union soldiers and their families (Orloff 1985), so significantly more aid was available for widows there than in the South. Figure 4.1 shows the proportion of widows who were Union widows by state. Union widows made up substantial proportions of widows in northern states, from 6 to 11 percent in most states and as high as 17 percent of widows in one. Pension payments channeled large amounts of federal money to individuals in northern states.

Pensions benefited specific age groups as well. Women whose husbands were of military age during the war received federal pensions. Table 4.1 shows Union and Confederate widows in 1890 as a percentage of all U.S. widows by age cohort. The Census Office in 1890 was ordered to take a special census of Union veterans and widows and began its work using lists of pensioners, so nonpensioners and especially Confederate widows are likely to be underrepresented in this table. Nevertheless, approximately one in six American widows between the ages of 45 and 54 and one in eight ages 35 to 44 were Civil War widows (U.S. Bureau of Census 1890).

Figure 4.1 Union Widows as a Percentage of all Widows by State, 1890

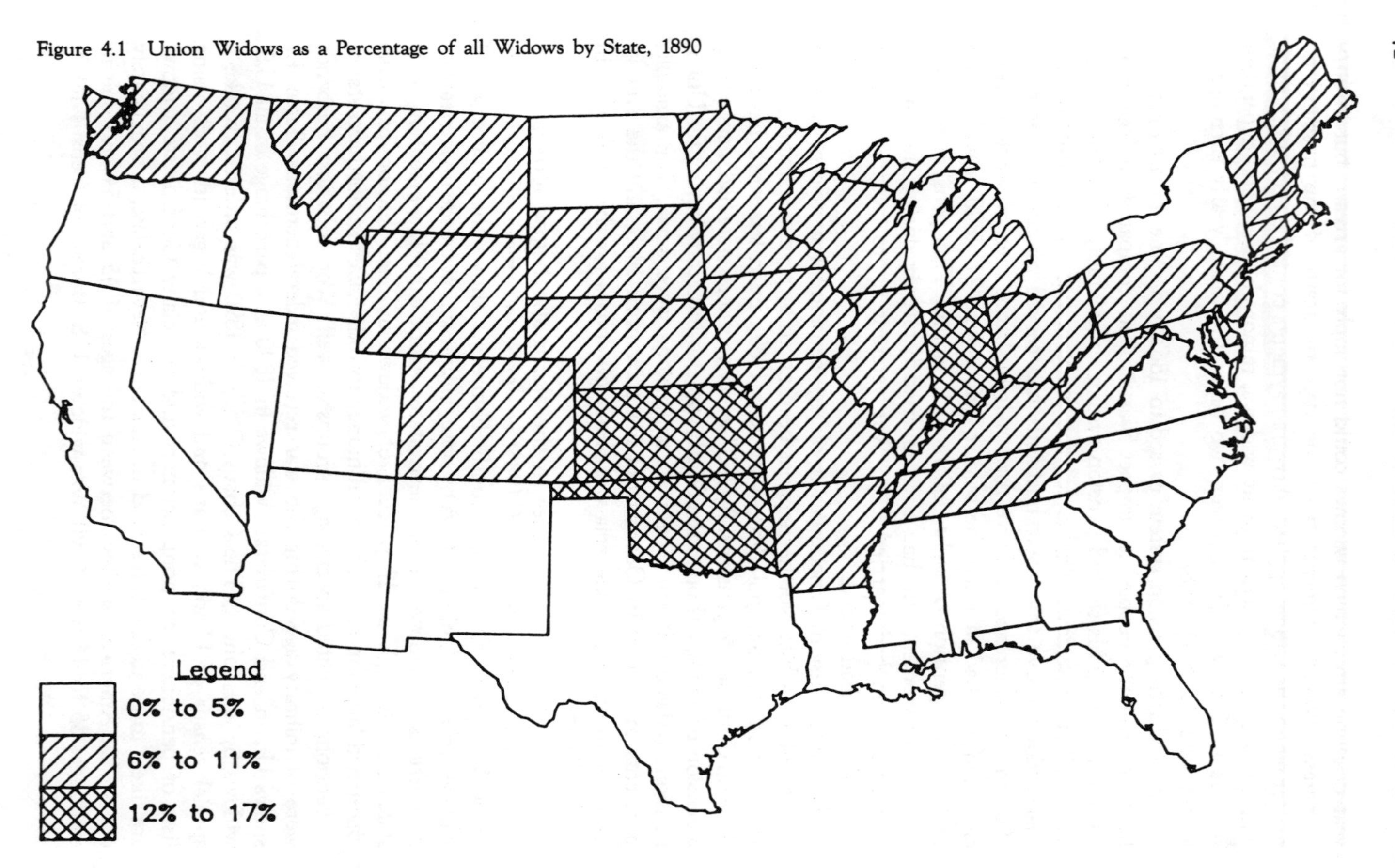

TABLE 4.1 Widows of the Civil War as Percentage of All U.S. Widows in 1890 by Age Cohort

Age Cohort	*Union*	*Confederate*	*Civil War Total*	
Total	7	3	10	(n=205564)
35 to 44	10	3	13	(n=39656)
45 to 54	12	5	17	(n=74812)
55 to 64	8	4	12	(n=56222)
Over 65	3	1	4	(n=29048)

Source: Department of the Interior, Census Office. *Report on the Population of the United States at the Eleventh Census: 1890,* Vol. 1, p. 2, Table 126; Vol. 1, Pt. 1, Table 82.

Widows and Federal Military Pensions in Michigan and Massachusetts Communities

The Civil War pension system is often characterized as a de facto old-age pension system.[11] If the system functioned as an early version of federal social welfare in the United States, what impact did pension payments have on the lives of widows who received them? We can examine the economic and social impact of federal military pensions by looking at the household arrangements of widows in Kent County, Michigan, and Essex County, Massachusetts.[12]

Names of widows from a list of pensioners published in 1883 were matched with the 1880 manuscript census (U.S. Bureau of the Pension 1883). This list includes Union widows from the Civil War and the War of 1812 and dependent mothers of dead Union Civil War soldiers. All received pensions as a result of Civil War pension legislation, so all are included in this discussion.

Unfortunately, only one African-American widow was found in either of these communities, and she did not receive a pension. We know little about the wives and widows of African-American Union troops. African-American troops did not become a common feature of the army corps structure until the last one-and-a-half years of the war (McPherson 1988). Both Michigan and Massachusetts mustered African-American troops, Massachusetts early in the war and Michigan in 1864 (Hargrove 1988:83, 121). Women married to African-American men who joined the army could expect hardships. African-American soldiers were initially paid less than white soldiers. Although recruiting posters in Massachusetts offered $13 per month and state aid to families, African-American soldiers only received $10 per month less $3 for clothing, but white soldiers received $13 per month plus $3.50 for clothing. Massachusetts equalized pay in September of 1863, but African-American soldiers did not receive the pay raise for eighteen months, refusing the raise until it was put into effect nationally (Hargrove 1988:121). Most African-American soldiers were denied commissions as well. The wives and children of African-American soldiers were particularly disadvantaged at home (Berlin, Reidy, and Rowland 1982:656–730). One soldier from Massachusetts described the plight of African-American families: "Our families at home are in suffering condition, and send to their husbands for relief. . . . My wife and three little children at home are, in a manner, freezing and starving to death. She writes to me for aid, but I have nothing to send her" (quoted in McPherson 1965:203–204).

African-American women married to Union soldiers also might expect, in addition to poverty, that they would have to care for men weakened by disease more than would white women and that they would be widowed by disease. African-American Union soldiers were much more likely to die of diseases than their white counterparts (Hargrove 1988:211). Although many widows of African-American Union soldiers did apply for pensions after the Civil War, we do not have any estimates of the extent of their success in receiving them.[13] Unfortunately, much more work needs to be done on both African-American soldiers and their families before we can do anything but speculate about their experiences.

Studying these widows on the community level highlights their uniqueness compared to widows who did not receive pensions. Civil War widows were aged mostly 35 to 64 years in 1883, clearly showing the impact of war deaths on women of marriageable age during the war. As the cohorts of Civil War widows, War of 1812 widows, and Civil War mothers aged, pensions aided groups of women who were increasingly older than other widows. Compared to Civil War widows, nonpensioned widows were more likely to be under age 35 or over 65. In 1890, when the pension expanded considerably, it helped widows in transition from middle to old age.

Age differences between pensioned widows in Michigan and Massachusetts may have implications for those studying social welfare debates in the late nineteenth and early twentieth centuries. Massachusetts was one of the most influential states in debates over old-age pensions in the early twentieth century. Orloff (1984) thought it likely that the Civil War pensions muted demands for old-age pensions in the United States before World War I. An influential report from the Massachusetts Commission on Old Age Pensions in 1910 shows that about 70 percent of the 38,695 aged dependent poor were receiving federal military pensions (calculated from Orloff 1984:74).[14]

The Massachusetts studies may have fostered the perception around the country that the elderly were being taken care of by the military pension. But Civil War widows in Massachusetts were older, mostly aged 45 to 64 years, than those in Michigan. Widows not receiving pensions were older in Massachusetts than in Michigan as well. In fact, the age structure in different states would determine who was being taken care of by military pensions. Consideration of old-age pensions in the United States may have been stalled in part by the particular age structure in one critical state.

We also may speculate that the aging Civil War cohort helped to pave the way for mothers' pensions in the twentieth century because an entire generation of "deserving" widows who had been cared for were aging. Young war widows began with a tiny foothold in receiving federal assistance when Congress authorized pensions during the war. By the time eligibility requirements for federal pensions were loosened with the 1890 legislation, these war widows and others were just beginning to age. Younger non-pensioned widows with children now had fewer resources to help them raise their families than the previous cohort of pensioned Union widows.

Immigration contributed to the relative scarcity of younger widows, especially younger nonnative widows, who received aid. Most widows receiving pensions were born in the United States, especially those living in nonurban areas. In Michigan a far greater proportion of widows receiving pensions were native-born compared to nonpensioned widows.[15] In Massachusetts the two groups did not differ markedly. The "deserving" widows who married soldiers in the Civil War got support that few widows who immigrated afterward were able to receive—a form of outdoor relief in the respectable guise of military pensions.

If the federal government provided early social welfare for these widows, for the most part it did so at the lowest rates. Although it was possible to receive larger pensions, almost all widows on the 1883 pension list in Kent and Essex counties received the eight-dollar-per-month private's pension. Widows in cities received more money than country widows—perhaps because officers were more apt to come from larger communities.

Although most widows received the smallest pension possible, evidence on household arrangements suggests either that younger widows (under 65) receiving pensions were better off financially than older pensioned widows or that pension payments were enough to keep them from seeking other means of support. All younger widows receiving pensions, except those in rural Kent County, were less likely to be employed than widows not receiving pensions. In most communities, more pensioned than nonpensioned widows had no visible means of support.

The support of family members, however, was important for these women; in most areas more than half appear to have been supported by family members. Many widows with minor children also had adult children living in the household who could be sources of emotional and financial support.[16] Pension payments along with the presence of adult children helped Essex County widows to maintain independent households. In Kent County, however, pension payments appear to lessen the need for widows with minor children to retain adult children in the household.[17]

Many of the mothers of Civil War soldiers declaring themselves solely dependent on pensions for support obviously had other sources of support. Overall, older widows who received pensions were more likely to have adult children in their households than widows who did not receive pensions. This lends support to criticisms by contemporaries that some people on pensions were not eligible for payments.

These payments, however, may have given widows more power within the household. Widowhood increasingly meant the end of heading a household for older women in the second half of the nineteenth century (Chudacoff and Hareven 1979).[18] Although age primarily determined whether older widows lived with relatives, it is evident that in some communities pension payments helped widows to head their own households. In Salem, for example, 62 percent of pensioned older widows still headed their own households, even though they were older than nonpensioned widows.

Losing a husband or son in war made little difference in an older widow's resources in terms of whether she had an adult child living with her or other relatives to help support her. Although many older widows were mothers of Civil War soldiers and declared themselves to be solely dependent upon their dead sons' military benefits for support, pension payments eventually contributed to the household incomes of relatives who were in a position to support these widows. Several pensioned widows took in boarders or worked, and even more nonpensioned widows did this, but these means of support were much less important than living with employed relatives. When most widows turned age 65 they were supported by family members or had no visible means of support. About equal proportions of older widows lived with family members regardless of pension status. This finding raises questions about whether financial need primarily determined whether older women lived with relatives or whether other concerns dominated the decision.

Deaths resulting from the Civil War spurred a pension system that was intended to care for widows and children of soldiers and sailors. Pensions clearly did aid widows and widowed mothers of Civil War soldiers and widows of the War of 1812 participants. It is important that this pension came to be considered a right, payment owed to pensioners for their sacrifice, because wartime legislation provided a social welfare foothold for mostly native-born widows in the late nineteenth century. Payments to this cohort of widows, many of whom would be aged by the turn of the century, probably exerted opposing forces upon the discourse about social welfare proposals during this period. A large number of "respectable" native-born white widows and their families received aid through the federal government in an acceptable way—through a pension rather than through institutional or outdoor relief. The pension made it seem more normal for the federal government to help widows, and as they aged, the elderly.

Unfortunately, the pension may have functioned too well as a social welfare system in Massachusetts, where the pensioned population was older than in some other states. Taking their cue from the large numbers of elderly dependents receiving federal pensions in Massachusetts, some states may have rejected systems of their own, in part because they thought that most of the "deserving" aged dependents were already receiving assistance from the federal government.

Conclusion

Compared to single mothers and divorced women, widows have not received as much attention today. In part the relative lack of attention to widows can be explained demographically and economically. Most widows are elderly and supported through the Social Security system, private insurance, and individual savings. Although many widows still experience serious financial and emotional difficulties, compared to single mothers or divorced women with children, they appear to be less disadvantaged.

In the nineteenth century concerns about the well-being and care of widows was much more widespread. In part this was because there were few single mothers or divorced women. But it also reflected the fact that widows were younger and more likely to have young children to support and raise. In addition, the economic situation for widows in the past was very difficult without either a social security program or adequate insurance benefits. Although society looked upon poor widows as among the "deserving" poor, it was unable to provide them with sufficient assistance to lead normal lives. As a result, poor widows were usually forced into the least desirable and low-paying jobs and frequently had their young children removed from them and placed into an institution.

Despite the seemingly obvious importance of widowhood to most nineteenth-century women, most American historians have paid little attention to this phase of the life course. Particularly ignored has been the impact of the Civil War on the lives of women. Perhaps 150,000 to 250,000 women on both sides became widows as a result of that conflict, and many of them had young children. Among certain age-cohorts of the population, a large percentage of all widows came to that status as a result of their spouses dying in the Civil War.

Civil War widows usually were singled out for special treatment during the war, and those in the North greatly benefited from the federal pension program created for Union widows. From a nineteenth-century perspective, the payments to Union widows and their children were generous and readily available. As our in-depth examination of Kent County, Michigan, and Essex County, Massachusetts, reveals, Union widows receiving pensions were more able to live in independent households or stay at home with their children than comparable widows not receiving any such assistance.

The Civil War pension system not only assisted Union widows, it also helped to stimulate demand for national and state programs that would assist widows with young children as well as aid the elderly. Although the United States did not develop a comprehensive national program for widows and the elderly until the 1930s, the Civil War pensions to Union veterans or their widows helped to create a climate of reform opinion in the late nineteenth and early twentieth centuries that was more hospitable to more state and local efforts than before. The Civil War pension program for Union veterans or their dependents also reinforced the nineteenth-century notion that widows are especially deserving of our assistance compared to other needy individuals such as single mothers and divorced women. Not surprisingly, when the Social Security legislation was passed in 1935 and 1939, young widows with children or elderly widows by themselves received much more generous assistance than either single mothers or divorced women.

Notes

1. Information on nineteenth-century mortality remains incomplete and sketchy—especially given the considerable regional and rural-urban differences (Condran and Crimmins-Gardner 1980; Haines 1977, 1979; Haines and Avery 1980; Higgs 1979; Vinovskis 1978). In addition, the 1900–1902 U.S. death registration area life tables appear to significantly overestimate child mortality among African-Americans but to slightly underestimate it for whites. But the aggregate figures may be correct because of the underrepresentation of African-Americans in the death registration area for those years (Preston and Haines 1984, 1991).

2. Differences in the divorce rate as well as in the likelihood of children being born out-of-wedlock, however, have made the probability of a child growing up in a single-parent household more similar between historical periods. The percentage of women ages 35–44, for example, who were either widowed or divorced in 1890 was 14.9 percent in 1987 was 15.8 percent (calculated from U.S. Bureau of Census 1895:clxxxi; 1989:41). On the growth and meaning of divorce in late nineteenth-century America, see Griswold (1982) and May (1980).

3. Lebsock argues that "economic motives for marriage were central" (1984:25) and that wealthy widows who could afford to remain single did so. She bases much of her argument on the rates of remarriage among different economic categories of widows in Petersburg. Unfortunately, her overall sample is modest, and for the periods 1784–1800 and 1801–1820 there is little or no difference in the rates of remarriage between more and less affluent widows. Only in the period 1821–1850 is there a substantial difference, but the sample size is small and she does not control for other factors such as age of the widow or presence of children, which might have affected her results. Furthermore, she acknowledges that "[i]t could be argued that the widows as a group were motivated less by concern with personal

autonomy than by desire to protect the interests of their children. Numbers do not help us distinguish one from the other" (Lebsock:269). Thus, although her book is a major and useful contribution to our understanding of nineteenth-century widowhood, her provocative thesis about the remarriage of affluent widows awaits further conceptual refinement and statistical testing.

4. Kemp (1990) found that in the early phases of the war, the rampant patriotism encouraged high rates of enlistment. As the war continued and casualty rates mounted, both communities increasingly relied upon generous bounties to attract nonresidents to enlist and thereby fulfill each town's state draft quota. A similar pattern was found in Deerfield, Massachusetts (Harris 1984).

5. The proportion of draftees in the Union and Confederate armies was actually quite low. The effect of the draft was mainly to stimulate "volunteers" in local areas as communities strove to avoid conscription (Moore 1924; Murdock 1971). Nevertheless, there was substantial resistance to the draft in both the North and the South (Bernstein 1989; Escott and Crow 1986; Levine 1981).

6. Most of the detailed investigations of Civil War soldiers, including even the most recent ones, do not attempt to estimate the proportion of the troops that were married (Jimerson 1988; Linderman 1987; Mitchell 1988; Robertson 1988; Wiley 1943, 1952).

7. Neither the study of Newburyport, Massachusetts (Vinovskis 1989), nor that of Concord, Massachusetts (Rorabaugh 1986), provided data on the marital status of the enlistees. That information, however, is now being prepared and analyzed for Newburyport.

8. The New York State data refer only to those who were reported by the families to which they belonged as living at the time of the 1865 census. Hence, the data do not include anyone who had died earlier during the war. Also, the report gives soldiers' marital status as of June 1865 rather than at the time of their enlistment and includes a substantial number for whom no marital information is reported. As a result, if many soldiers married near the end or after the war, this figure would overestimate the proportion of those who were married. Therefore, this estimate must be seen as a very crude approximation of the proportion of servicemen married (New York Secretary of State 1867:650).

9. Again, the New York State Census of 1865 provides some useful but very crude information on differential mortality by marital status. We are provided figures on soldiers who are alive in 1865 as well as a separate tabulation of those who have died as a result of the war. Both sets of data are reported by their families in 1865, hence biasing the data against those who were single and left no family to report them. In addition, these data do not include the servicemen who served in New York units but were not residents of the state. The census tabulates 23,294 deaths, but the provost-marshal reports 31,852—a substantial difference. Nevertheless, if we crudely calculate the percentage of single servicemen who died, it would be 17.7 percent compared to 16.1 percent for married ones (New York Secretary of State 1867:650, 683).

10. Morton Keller calls the pension bureau "the most uncompromisingly political branch of the federal government" (Keller 1977:311). Both political parties actively sought votes in close states such as Indiana and Ohio. See also Glasson (1900, 1918), McMurry (1922), Sanders (1980), and Dearing (1952).

11. This literature that mentions the Civil War pension system either points to its function as political patronage (see McMurry, 1922; Sanders, 1980) or to its function as an early version of a federal old-age pension system (see Haber, 1983; Orloff, 1984; Vinovskis, 1989). Although the pension system may have functioned as an early version of social welfare, or even as patronage, it is misleading to think of it solely along functional lines for it may not have been perceived as social welfare at the time. Both of these "functions" need to be better defined and more critically explored.

12. Kent County, Michigan, in the late nineteenth century included a well-populated city, Grand Rapids (pop. 32,106 in 1880) surrounded by rural townships (U.S. Bureau of the Census 1883). Grand Rapids was mainly known for manufacturing furniture. Essex County, Massachusetts, has been well studied; its communities were similar demographically, economically, and socially to many other communities in the Northeast (Modell and Chudacoff 1978). Salem (pop. 27,563 in 1880) had an economy based upon a combination of industry and commerce. People in nonurban areas in this study supported themselves through farming, light manufacturing, transportation, trade, and domestic service (Modell and Chudacoff 1978; Tracy 1878). For details on the specific Kent and Essex County communities included in the sample, see Holmes (1990).

13. Gutman (1976) used the postwar pension records to study the marriage and kinship patterns of African-American families, but he did not investigate either the extent or importance of these pensions for the lives of the widows.

14. Orloff (1985), although conceding that social demand and the large proportions of elderly receiving federal military pensions influenced the "failure" of the United States to adopt widespread social welfare programs in the early twentieth century, argues that the forces that defeated welfare adoption were different. She attributes the failure of the United States to adopt these measures to the different pattern and process of bureaucratization and democratization in Britain and the United States (see also Shefter 1977). She argues that Britain did not develop a corrupt bureaucracy because voting was not widespread and therefore politicians had no need to use the bureaucracy as a system of patronage. Orloff proposes that the political experiences of American reformers led them to believe that political spoils ruined such pension programs in this country. Unfortunately, it is not clear that this was always true or that it influenced many legislators. Further work on the interactions among ideology, demography, and policy decisions about pensions and welfare reforms is needed before we can assess the impact of the Union pensions on social welfare policy in the late nineteenth and early twentieth centuries.

15. Most pensioned widows in Grand Rapids were native-born in a city where about half of widows were foreign-born. This age difference between Kent County pensioned and nonpensioned widows can be attributed in part to high rates of population growth in this county. A large population growth in Kent County brought slightly more foreign-born persons than were already there, but they were newer to the country and had not had the opportunity to fight in previous wars.

16. Minor children here are defined as those below the age of sixteen. This discussion of minor children involves younger widows only—no widows aged sixty-five or older had minor children in this sample.

17. In Grand Rapids, pensioned widows made up the difference by taking in boarders.

18. Nevertheless, almost half of U.S. widows over age fifty-four headed their own households in 1900 (Smith 1979).

References

Berlin, Ira, Joseph P. Reidy, and Leslie S. Rowland (eds.) (1982). *Freedom: A Documentary History of Emancipation, 1861–1867. Series II: The Black Military Experience.* Cambridge: Cambridge University Press.

Bernstein, Iver (1989). *The New York City Draft Riots: Their Significance for American Society and Politics in the Age of the Civil War.* New York: Oxford University Press.

Bremner, Robert H. (1980). *The Public Good: Philanthropy and Welfare in the Civil War Era.* New York: Alfred Knopf.

Chudacoff, Howard P., and Tamara K. Hareven (1979). "From the Empty Nest to Family Dissolution: Life Course Transitions into Old Age." *Journal of Family History,* 4, 69–83.

Clawson, Mary Ann (1989). *Constructing Brotherhood: Class, Gender, and Fraternalism.* Princeton, NJ: Princeton University Press.

Condran, Gretchen, and Eileen Crimmins-Gardner (1980). "Mortality Differentials Between Rural and Urban Areas in the Northeastern United States, 1890–1900." *Journal of Historical Geography,* 6, 179–202.

Dearing, Mary R. 1952). *Veterans in Politics: the Story of the* G.A.R. Baton Rouge: Louisiana State University Press.

Degler, Carl N. (1980). *At Odds: Women and the Family in America from the Revolution to the Present.* New York: Oxford University Press.

Escott, Paul D., and Jeffrey J. Crow (1986). "The Social Order and Violent Disorder: An Analysis of North Carolina in the Revolution and the Civil War." *Journal of Southern History,* 52, 373–402.

Glasson, William H. (1900). *History of Military Pension Legislation in the United States.* New York: Columbia University Press.

______ (1907). "The South's Care for Her Confederate Veterans." *American Monthly Review of Reviews,* 36, 40–47.

______ (1918). *Federal Military Pensions in the United States.* New York: Oxford University Press.

Grigg, Susan (1984). *The Dependent Poor of Newburyport: Studies in Social History, 1800–1830.* Ann Arbor, MI: University Microfilm International Research Press.

Griswold, Robert L. (1982). *Family and Divorce in California, 1850–1890: Victorian Illusions and Everyday Realities.* Albany, NY: State University of New York Press.

Gutman, Herbert F. (1976). *The Black Family in Slavery and Freedom, 1750–1925.* New York: Pantheon.

Haber, Carole (1983). *Beyond Sixty-Five: The Dilemma of Old Age in America's Past.* Cambridge: Cambridge University Press.

Haines, Michael R. (1977). "Mortality in Nineteenth Century America: Estimates from New York and Pennsylvania Census Data, 1865 and 1900." *Demography,* 14, 311–331.

_____ (1979). "The Use of Model Life Tables to Estimate Mortality for the United States in the Late Nineteenth Century." *Journal of Interdisciplinary History*, 11, 73–95.

Haines, Michael R., and Roger C. Avery (1980). "The American Life Table of 1830–1860: An Evaluation." *Journal of Interdisciplinary History*, 11, 73–95.

Hargrove, Hordon B. (1988). *African-American Soldiers in the Civil War*. Chapel Hill, NC: McFarland.

Harris, Emily J. (1984). "Sons and Soldiers: Deerfield, Massachusetts and the Civil War." *Civil War History*, 30, 157–171.

Higgs, Robert (1979). "Cycles and Trends of Mortality in 18 Large American Cities, 1871–1900." *Explorations in Economic History*, 16, 381–408.

History of Kent County, Michigan: Together with Sketches of its Cities, Villages, and Townships . . . Biographies of Representative Citizens (1973). Micropublished as publication No. 143 on Reel 47 of *County Histories of the Old Northwest Series V: Michigan*. Chicago: C. C. Chapman, 1881; New Haven, CT: Research Publications.

Holliday, Joseph R. (1962). "Relief for Soldiers' Families in Ohio During the Civil War." *Ohio History*, 71, 97–112.

Holmes, Amy (1990). "'Such is the Price We Pay': American Widows and the Civil War Pension System." In Maris A. Vinovskis (ed.), *Toward a Social History of the American Civil War: Exploratory Essays* (pp. 171–195). Cambridge: Cambridge University Press.

Jimerson, Randall C. (1988). *The Private Civil War: Popular Thought during the Sectional Conflict*. Baton Rouge: Louisiana State University Press.

Katz, Michael B. (1986). *In the Shadow of the Poorhouse: A Social History of Welfare in America*. New York: Basic Books.

Keller, Morton (1977). *Affairs of State: Public Life in Nineteenth-Century America*. Cambridge: Harvard University Press.

Kemp, Thomas R. (1990). "Community and War: The Civil War Experience of Claremont, New Hampshire, and Newport, New Hampshire." In Maris A. Vinovskis (ed.), *Toward a Social History of the American Civil War: Exploratory Essays* (pp. 31–77). Cambridge: Cambridge University Press.

Kleinberg, S. J. (1989). *The Shadow of the Mill: Working-Class Families in Pittsburgh, 1870–1907*. Pittsburgh: University of Pittsburgh Press.

Lesbsock, Suzanne (1984). *The Free Women of Petersburg: Status and Culture in a Southern Town, 1784–1860*. New York: Norton.

Levine, Peter (1981). "Draft Evasion in the North during the Civil War, 1863–1865." *Journal of American History*, 67, 816–834.

Linderman, Gerald F. (1987). *Embattled Courage: The Experience of Combat in the American Civil War*. New York: Free Press.

Long, Clarence D. (1975). *Wages and Earnings in the United States*. Princeton, NJ: Princeton University Press.

Lopata, Helena Z., and Henry P. Brehm (1986). *Widows and Dependent Wives: From Social Problem to Federal Program*. New York: Praeger.

Mason, Karen Oppenheim, Maris A. Vinovskis, and Tamara K. Hareven (1978). "Women's Work and the Life Course in Essex County, Massachusetts, 1880."

In Tamara K. Hareven (ed.), *Transitions: The Family and the Life Course in Historical Perspective* (pp. 187–216). New York: Academic Press.
Massachusetts Board of Education (1862–1866). *Annual Reports*. Boston.
Massey, Mary Elizabeth (1966). *Bonnet Brigades*. New York: Alfred A. Knopf.
May, Elaine Tyler (1980). *Great Expectations: Marriage and Divorce in Post-Victorian America*. Chicago: University of Chicago Press.
McMurry, Donald L. (1922). "The Political Significance of the Pension Question, 1885–1897." *Mississippi Valley Historical Review*, 9, 19–36.
McPherson, James M. (1965). *The Negro's Civil War: How American Blacks Felt and Acted During the War for the Union*. New York: Pantheon Books.
______ (1988). *The Battle Cry of Freedom: The Civil War Era*. New York: Oxford University Press.
Mintz, Steven, and Susan Kellogg (1988). *Domestic Revolutions: A Social History of American Family Life*. New York: Free Press.
Mitchell, Reid (1988). *Civil War Soldiers: Their Expectations and Their Experiences*. New York: Viking.
Modell, John, and Howard P. Chudacoff (1978). "The Setting: The Essex County Context." In Tamara K. Hareven (ed.), *Transitions: The Family and the Life Course in Historical Perspective* (pp. 99–112). New York: Academic Press.
Moore, Albert Buron (1924). *Conscription and Conflict in the Confederacy*. New York: Nobel Offset Printers.
Motz, Marilyn Ferris (1983). *True Sisterhood: Michigan Women and Their Kin, 1820–1920*. Albany: State University of New York Press.
Murdock, Eugene C. (1971). *One Million Men: The Civil War Draft in the North*. Westport, CT: Greenwood Press.
New York Secretary of State (1867). *Census of the State of New York for 1865*. Albany: Charles Van Benthuysen.
Orloff, Ann S. (1985). "The Politics of Pensions: A Comparative Analysis of the Origins of Pensions and Old Age Insurance in Canada, Great Britain, and the United States." Unpub. Ph.D. diss., Princeton University Press.
Orloff, Ann S., and Theda Skocpol (1984). "Why Not Equal Protection? Explaining the Politics of Public Social Spending in Britain, 1900–1911, and the United States, 1880s–1920s." *American Sociological Review*, 49, 726–750.
Paludan, Philip S. (1988). *"A People's Contest": The Union and Civil War, 1861–1865*. New York: Harper and Row.
Paul, James L. (1876). *Pennsylvania's Soldiers' Orphan Schools*. Philadelphia: Claxton, Remsen, and Haffelfinger.
Preston, Samuel H., and Michael R. Haines (1984). "New Estimates of Child Mortality in the United States at the Turn of the Century." *Journal of the American Statistical Association*, 79, 272–281.
______ (1991). *Fatal Years: Child Mortality in Late Nineteenth-Century America*. Princeton, NJ: Princeton University Press.
Resch, John P. (1988). "Politics and Public Culture: The Revolutionary War Pension Act of 1818." *Journal of the Early Republic*, 8, 139–158.
Reynolds, Robert L. (1970). "Benevolence on the Home Front in Massachusetts During the Civil War." Unpub. Ph.D. diss., Boston University.

Robertson, James I., Jr. (1988). *Soldiers Blue and Gray.* Columbia: University of South Carolina Press.

Rorabaugh, W. J. (1986). "Who Fought for the North in the Civil War? Concord, Massachusetts, Enlistments." *Journal of American History,* 73, 695–701.

Ryan, Mary P. (1981). *Cradle of the Middle Class: The Family in Oneida County, New York, 1790–1865.* Cambridge: Cambridge University Press.

Salmon, Marylynn (1986). *Women and the Law of Property in Early America.* Chapel Hill: University of North Carolina Press.

Sanders, Heywood T. (1980). "Paying for the 'Bloody Shirt': The Politics of Civil War Pensions." In Barry S. Rundquist (ed.), *Political Benefits: Empirical Studies of American Public Programs* (pp. 137–159). Lexington, MA: Lexington Books.

Scadron, Arlene (1988). "Introduction." In Arlene Scadron (ed.), *On Their Own: Widows and Widowhood in the American Southwest, 1848–1939* (pp. 1–21). Urbana: University of Illinois Press.

Schouler, William (1868, 1871). *A History of Massachusetts in the Civil War.* 2 Vols. Boston: William Schouler.

Shamas, Carole, Marylynn Salmon, and Michel Dahlin (1987). *Inheritance in America: From Colonial Times to the Present.* New Brunswick, NJ: Rutgers University Press.

Shefter, Martin (1977). *Patronage and Its Opponents: A Theory and Some European Cases.* Ithaca, NY: Center for International Studies.

Smith, Daniel S. (1979). "Life Course, Norms, and the Family System of Older Americans in 1900." *Journal of Family History,* 4, 285–298.

Tracy, Cyrus M. (1878). *Standard History of Essex County, Massachusetts.* Boston: C. F. Jewett.

Trattner, Walter I. (1989). *From Poor Law to Welfare State: A History of Social Welfare in America.* 4th ed. New York: Free Press.

Uhlenberg, Peter (1980). "Death and the Family." *Journal of Family History,* 5, 313–320.

U.S. Bureau of the Pension (1883). *List of Pensioners of the Roll, January 1, 1883.* Washington, DC: U.S. Government Printing Office.

U.S. Bureau of Census (1895). *Report on the Population of the United States at the Eleventh Census, 1890.* Part 1. Washington, DC: U.S. Government Printing Office.

——— (1975). *Historical Statistics of the United States, Colonial Times to 1970.* Bicentennial edition, Part 1. Washington, DC: U.S. Government Printing Office.

——— (1989). *Statistical Abstract of the United States, 1989.* 109th ed. Washington DC: U.S. Government Printing Office.

Vinovskis, Maris A. (1972). "Mortality Rates and Trends in Massachusetts Before 1860." *Journal of Economic History,* 32, 184–213.

——— (1978). "The Jacobson Life Table of 1850: A Critical Re-Examination From a Massachusetts Perspective." *Journal of Interdisciplinary History,* 8, 703–724.

——— (1989). "Have Social Historians Lost the Civil War? Some Preliminary Demographic Speculations." *Journal of American History,* 76, 34–58.

——— (1990). "Death and Family Life in the Past." *Human Nature,* 1, 109–122.

Wiley, Bell I. (1943). *The Life of Johnny Reb: The Common Soldier of the Confederacy.* Baton Rouge: Louisiana State University Press.

______ (1952). *The Life of Billy Yank: The Common Soldier of the Union.* Baton Rouge: Louisiana State University Press.

Zelizer, Viviana A. R. (1979). *Morals and Markets: The Development of Life Insurance in the United States.* New York: Columbia University Press.

PART TWO

Marriage and Cohabitation: Current Issues

5

American Marriage Patterns in Transition

Neil G. Bennett, David E. Bloom, and Patricia H. Craig

The structure of households in the United States has changed dramatically during the past several decades. In 1960, there were about 3.3 persons per household; 13 percent of households had only one person, 40 percent had four or more persons, and just under 10 percent of family households were headed by females without spouses present. However, by 1990, for example, there were only 2.6 persons per household, with roughly 25 percent of households consisting of a single person, only 26 percent having four or more persons, and 17 percent of family households headed by females without spouses present.

On the surface, it would appear that these changes are closely associated with a long list of social, economic, and other demographic changes that occurred over much the same period. Most noteworthy among these changes are the following: The number of first marriages per 1,000 single females aged fifteen and above declined from 74 to 56 between 1960 and 1987; the crude birth rate declined from 24 to 16 per thousand between 1960 and 1989; the number of divorces per 1,000 married women more than doubled from about 9 to 21 between 1960 and 1987; the proportion of ever-married women aged 20–24 who were childless increased from 24 to 42 percent between 1960 and 1988; the median educational attainment for men and women increased by 16 percent and 24 percent, respectively, between 1960 and 1989; the proportion of adult men and women who had attended college for at least one year more than doubled between 1960 and 1989 to reach levels of 42 percent and 35 percent, respectively; the labor-force participation rate of women increased from 38 percent to 58 percent between 1960 and 1990, with the rates for married women with children below six years of age and for married women with husbands present increasing from 19 and 31 percent, respectively, in 1960 to 58 percent for both groups in 1989; and the proportion of women employed in white collar jobs rose from 55 percent in 1960 to 71 percent in 1990.

All of these trends point to the fact that the United States has been undergoing a significant transformation in the way in which women and men conduct their lives. Today, decisions to pursue a college education or to embark on a professional career are as common among women as they are among men. Years ago, among large numbers of women there was simply no decision to be made. Women would marry and begin their careers of childbearing and childrearing. Men's lives have also been transformed significantly, certainly insofar as they have been faced with a need to adapt to the changing roles of women, both at home and in the workplace (see, e.g., Waite and Goldscheider in this volume).

The major purpose of this chapter is to examine the changing marriage patterns of American women in recent decades and to investigate the causes underlying these changing patterns. In what follows we study a few of the many factors that impinge on the marriage process, including out-of-wedlock childbearing, employment and earnings, and what has come to be known as the marriage squeeze.

Previous Research

Much contemporary research on the family is motivated by recognition of the fact that patterns of marriage and family formation in the United States have changed substantially in recent years. Trends such as the one-third decline in the first marriage rates of women since 1970 (see Figure 5.1), the nearly two-and-a-half-year increase in the median age at first marriage during the same period (see Figure 5.2), and the sharp decrease in the proportion of the population living in husband-wife families over the past twenty-five years have prompted some scholars to agree with popular perceptions: that marriage as a social institution is on the decline (see, e.g., Espenshade 1986). Others emphasize that marriage has remained a cornerstone of American family life (Kitagawa 1981; Rodgers and Thornton 1985). Although single life may now be perceived as more attractive than it was in the past—due to factors like the greater financial independence of women and changing opinions regarding cohabitation—many researchers (see Thornton and Freedman 1983) argue that marriage is unlikely to lose its preeminence as a form of union. Finally, there are those who note that many of these changing marriage patterns have been much more acute among blacks than whites, suggesting that it is important to make the analysis race specific before making sweeping statements about all Americans. Rodgers and Thornton (1985) found that the decline in proportions marrying among whites and blacks that began in the 1950s started earlier and lasted longer for blacks, resulting in markedly lower proportions married for that group. This has led some to speculate that marriage maintains its centrality

Figure 5.1 First-Marriage Rates Among Women Aged 15 and Above, 1970–1987

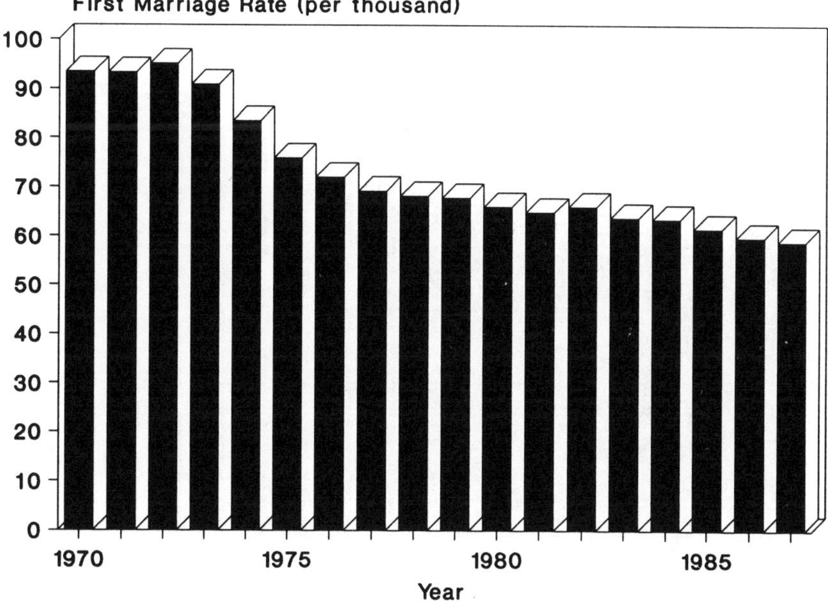

Source: National Center for Health Statistics

for most white Americans but does so to a lesser extent for blacks (Cherlin 1981).

Recent attention to differences in black and white family formation patterns is based largely on concerns about differential resources available to families. Many have found it important to examine economic well-being in conjunction with family composition (Moynihan 1986; Wilson and Neckerman 1986). The decline in the proportion of husband-wife families goes hand-in-hand with the explosive growth of female-headed families: By 1990, 13 percent of white families and 44 percent of black families were headed by women not currently married, representing significant increases from 1960 figures (8 and 21 percent, respectively). Such families tend to be the most impoverished and are increasingly headed by single never-married women (Darity and Myers 1983). Thus, it becomes imperative to include an understanding of declining rates of marriage in the constellation of factors associated with changes in the incidence of poverty.

Interpretation of Cross-Sectional Marriage Trends

Government statistics, as graphed in Figures 5.1 and 5.2, reveal quite clearly that the rate at which individuals are first marrying has fallen steadily over

Figure 5.2 Median Age at First Marriage Among Women, 1970–1987

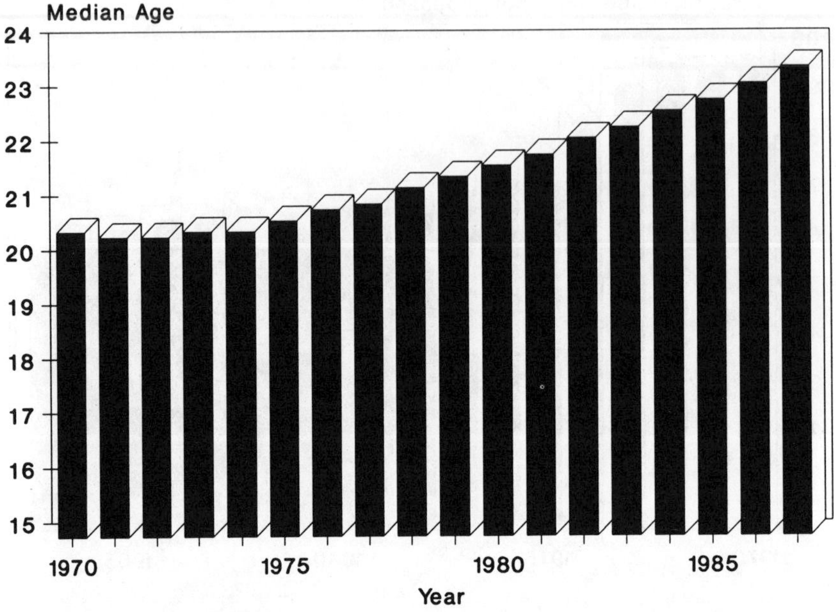

Source: National Center for Health Statistics

a couple of decades and that the median age at first marriage has risen substantially during that same period. This pattern, which has been characteristic of both men and women, has contributed to the increasing proportion of single young adults in the population.

According to some researchers, these facts reflect cohort changes in the timing of marriage and not changes in its ultimate incidence (i.e., not whether but when marriage occurs). For example, Cherlin (1981:11) states, "The higher proportion of single young adults in the 1970s and the early 1980s suggests only that they are marrying later, not foregoing marriage. It is unlikely that their lifetime proportions marrying will fall below the historical minimum of 90 percent."

Another view is presented by researchers such as Becker (1981) and Fuchs (1983), who interpret the data (at least implicitly) not simply as a reflection of delayed marriage but rather as a decline in the proportion of women who will ever marry. The economic opportunities that have opened up for women are unprecedented—not only do they have more options in the labor market but often they are options that imply a permanent rather than temporary state between the end of higher education and marriage or the birth of children. Women with higher economic status or stronger economic prospects may simply have less incentive to marry.

Implicit in both of these views are projections of the future time series of marriage rates. For example, if marriage rates have declined mainly because of an increasing tendency to delay marriage, then the rates should begin to rise as those who are delaying reach their desired ages of first marriage. Alternatively, if the decline is mostly the result of an increasing proportion of women deciding to (or, by default, just happening to) forego marriage, then marriage rates will tend to remain depressed in the future.

Recent Cohort Trends in Marriage

In the present chapter, we consider questions about how and why (1) overall marriage rates have changed, (2) black and white American women differ with respect to patterns of entry into first marriage, and (3) various social, economic, and demographic factors give rise to the racial differences observed. The results that we describe reveal sharp black-white differences.

Many prior analyses are not entirely adequate because they rely on period or cross-sectional measures (i.e., statistics referring to women in a particular calendar year), which do not necessarily provide much insight into the behavioral patterns they are intended to reflect. These measures may fail to describe the marriage process adequately because they are too sensitive to period changes. For example, in a recessionary year in which people put off marrying, cross-sectional statistics would show a decline in marriage rates when in fact only postponement had occurred. A more natural approach to studying marriage patterns might be that based on a life course or cohort perspective. This considers individuals born around the same time (in five-year birth cohorts, for example) and examines their marriage behavior over the course of their lives, which is, in essence, the topic in which we are most directly interested. This is the perspective adopted in this chapter.

The Data

The data set used to estimate the marriage model parameters was obtained from the National Survey of Families and Households (NSFH), the fieldwork of which was conducted between March 1987 and May 1988. The NSFH consists of interviews with 13,017 respondents aged nineteen and older of all marital statuses. Several population groups were double-sampled: minority groups (blacks, Puerto Ricans, and Chicanos), single parents, parents with stepchildren, cohabiting persons, and persons who recently married. The NSFH is extremely useful for this study because it (1) is a nationally representative sample of all women, (2) includes interviews with an exceptionally large number of individuals, and (3) is quite recent.

The Model

Coale (1971) observed that age distributions of first marriages are structurally similar in different populations. These distributions tend to be smooth, unimodal, and skewed to the right, and have a density close to zero below age fifteen and above age fifty. Coale also noted that the differences in age-at-marriage distributions across female populations are largely accounted for by differences in their means, standard deviations, and cumulative values at the older ages, for example, at age fifty. As a basis for the application of these observations, Coale constructed a standard schedule of age at first marriage using data from Sweden, covering the period 1865 through 1869. The model that is applied to marriage data is represented by the following equation (see Rodriguez and Trussell 1980):

$$g(a) = \frac{E}{\sigma} 1.2813 \exp\left\{-1.145\left(\frac{a-\mu}{\sigma}+0.805\right) - \exp\left[-1.896\left(\frac{a-\mu}{\sigma}+0.805\right)\right]\right\}, \qquad (1)$$

where g(a) is the proportion marrying at age a in the observed population and μ, σ, and E are, respectively, the mean and the standard deviation of age at first marriage (for those who ever marry) and the proportion ever marrying.

The parameters of the above equation may be estimated in a variety of ways depending on the nature of the available data. In the present application we work with survey data on age at first marriage for individual women and use a maximum likelihood estimator. Thus, for our sample of all women (i.e., a random sample of ever-married and never-married women in a cohort), we will estimate μ, σ, and E by maximizing the following log likelihood function:

$$\log L_A = \sum_{i\varepsilon M} \log\left[g\ a_i^m \middle| \mu,\sigma,E\right] + \sum_{i\varepsilon \bar{M}} \log\left[1 - G(a_i^s|\mu,\sigma,E)\right], \qquad (2)$$

where $a^m{}_i$ is the age at first marriage for each individual, i, who has married (the set M), a_i^s is the age at the time of the survey for each never-married individual (the set $\bar{M}$), and G(•) is the cumulative distribution function for the density function g(•) expressed in equation (1). The second summation on the right hand side of equation (2) accounts for censoring, which will be present to the extent that not all women who ultimately do marry will have done so by the time of the survey.

The model can be extended to allow for covariate effects by specifying a functional relationship between the parameters of the model distribution and a set of covariates. For example, we may specify these relationships in linear form as follows:

$$\mu_i = X'\alpha$$
$$\sigma_i = Y'\beta\ ,$$
and
$$E_i = Z'_i\gamma\ ,$$

where X_i, Y_i, and Z_i are the vector values of characteristics of an individual that determine, respectively, μ_i, σ_i, and E_i, and α, β, and γ are the associated hyperparameter vectors to be estimated.

Because the model is parametric, it can be applied to data from cohorts that have yet to complete their first marriage experience. In this fashion, the model can be used for purposes of projection (see, e.g., Bloom and Bennett 1990).

Using this model, we derive two sets of statistics: among various birth cohorts, the percentage of women who are expected to ever marry and, for those who eventually marry, their average age at marriage. We are thus able to project the remainder of a cohort's marriage experience even though they might be relatively young (e.g., in their early thirties) at the time of the survey. These results are displayed in Table 5.1.

Examining the figures pertaining to women of all races combined, we find that almost 97 percent of all women born in the late 1930s have already married or can be expected to ever marry, which is certainly consistent with the historical threshold of 90 percent referred to above.

Table 5.1

Percentages of women in various birth cohorts expected to ever marry and the average age of marriage for those who eventually marry, based on data from the National Survey of Families and Households, 1987-1988, and computed using the Coale-McNeil model.

		Period of Birth				
		1935-39	**1940-44**	**1945-49**	**1950-54**	**1955-59**
ALL WOMEN	**Mean Age**	21.0	21.0	21.7	22.0	22.5
	Percentage Ever-marrying	96.8	95.3	95.3	91.3	88.9
WHITE WOMEN	**Mean Age**	20.7	20.9	21.6	22.0	22.4
	Percentage Ever-marrying	97.6	97.0	96.9	93.6	92.9
BLACK WOMEN	**Mean Age**	23.2	21.5	22.2	22.3	24.1
	Percentage Ever-marrying	91.1	81.0	85.4	75.9	72.1

Among women born in the late 1950s, however, the rate had dipped below that figure to 89 percent. Thus, the proportion of all women who forgo marriage has more than tripled between cohorts born twenty years apart.

Young women today who do ultimately marry seem to be postponing that event relative to their counterparts born earlier. Women born in the late 1950s have married at an average age of about twenty-two and one-half years; those born in the late 1930s married, on average, one and one-half years earlier. The remainder of Table 5.1 demonstrates clearly that American patterns of marriage differ substantially depending upon whether one is focusing on blacks or whites. Furthermore, as shown graphically in Figure 5.3, marriage patterns of blacks and whites are diverging as time progresses (see also Schoen and Owens in this volume).

The proportion of white women who never marry has tripled, from just below 2.5 percent among women born in the late 1930s to slightly more than 7 percent among those born in the late 1950s. In addition, for white women who eventually marry, there has been a consistent cross-cohort trend toward postponement. Fewer marry, and those who do marry do so later than was the case one generation ago.

The changing situation among black women is much more dramatic. Just under 9 percent of those born in the late 1930s have never married. That figure has increased to about 28 percent for the cohort born in the late 1950s. The trend in the average age at which black women marry is less certain. However, among blacks who do marry, they do so somewhat later than their white counterparts.

We would be mistaken to believe that all individuals within a particular race behave similarly with respect to their likelihood of entering into marriage or the time at which they do so. Elsewhere (Bennett, Bloom, and Craig 1989), we have found that among both black and white women, those who have more than a high-school education marry several years later, on average, than those who have not graduated high school. In addition, white women who have some higher education are somewhat less likely to ever marry than those who have less education. The opposite relationship holds true among black women. Those with higher education tend to be more likely to marry than those without a high-school degree.

Explanatory Factors Underlying Recent Trends in Marriage

There are various arguments that we might consider in attempting to explain the significant trends in the marriage patterns that we have observed and the pronounced differences in patterns found to exist between the races.

Figure 5.3 Trends in Percentages of Women Never Marrying by Birth Cohort

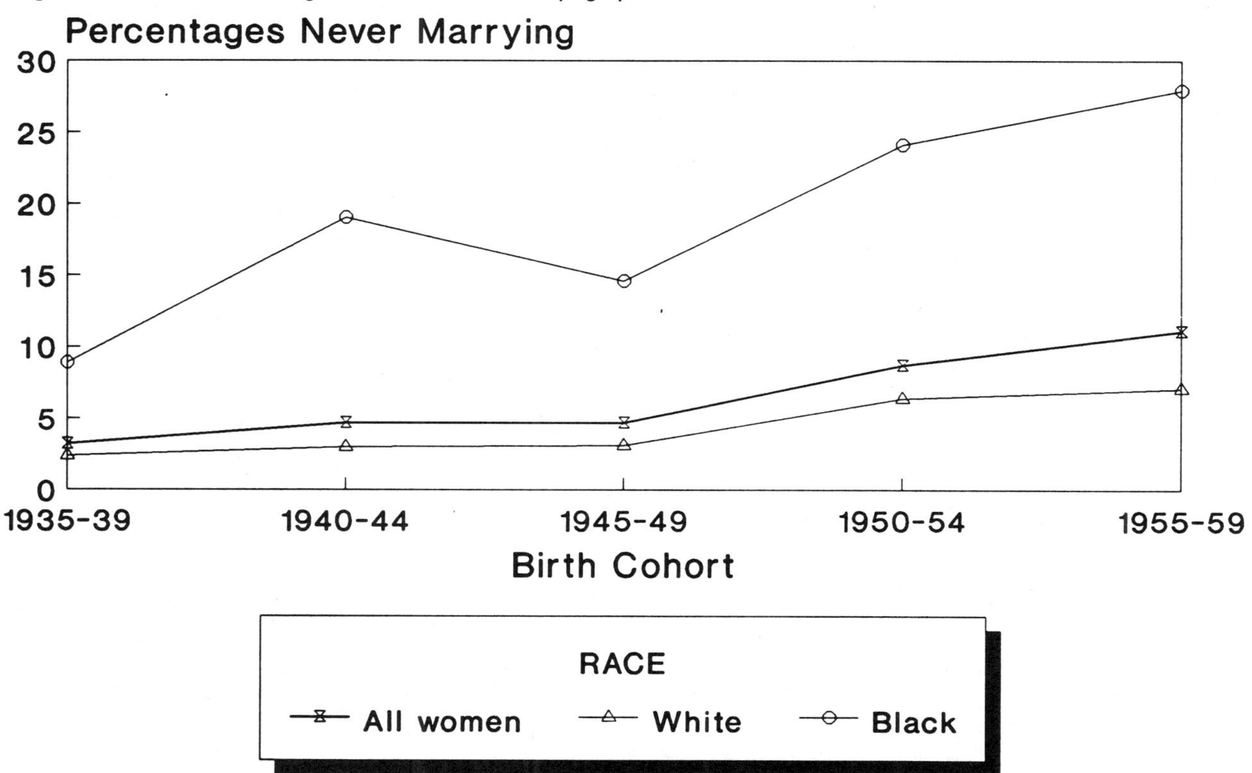

The Marriage Squeeze

First, the issue of imbalances in male-female ratios provides a partial clue to understanding the racial differences in proportions marrying. Declining marriage rates for both white and black women are often seen as a result of what is known as the marriage squeeze. One aspect of the squeeze is that women get caught by demographic factors: At some age women begin to outnumber men in the population, meaning that there are simply fewer men to go around. The sex ratio imbalance occurs several years earlier in life among black women than among white women, in part reflecting factors that are related to the lower socioeconomic status of blacks such as the relatively high rates of death and incarceration among young black men. Further exacerbating the squeeze is the fact that women have traditionally tended to marry slightly older men.

In Figure 5.4 we show the purely demographic effect of the marriage squeeze. For illustrative purposes, suppose that women consider men two years older than themselves to be marriageable. Thus, 20-year-old women would look toward the pool of 22-year-old men for their potential spouses, 30-year-old women would consider 32-year-old men, and so on. Another way of expressing this relationship is to say that women born, for example, in 1957 would match up with men born in 1955. In reality, of course, the majority of women marry men who are anywhere from many years older to several years younger than themselves. Nevertheless, this assumption will highlight for us the effect of the marriage squeeze.

It is useful, then, to examine the size of a birth cohort relative to the cohort arriving two years earlier. In other words, in the example above what is the ratio of the number of male births occurring in 1955 (the future pool of potential husbands) to the number of female births occurring in 1957 (the future pool of potential wives)? Figure 5.4 shows this ratio for the period spanning 1948 through 1972 for the cohorts reflecting (albeit only very roughly) the future wives, and the corresponding birth years reflecting the cohorts of future husbands (i.e., births taking place in 1946 through 1970). We calculate this ratio separately for whites and blacks. We see that in general women born prior to about 1960 face a dearth of men. Furthermore, as anticipated, there is a greater mismatch of sheer numbers of women and men among blacks than among whites for these cohorts. It is interesting to note that in the absence of any marked differences regarding typical age differences between spouses, there generally will be a relative abundance of men in the marriage market for women born in the 1960s and early 1970s.

We should emphasize that the above analysis does not take into account the fact that there is a wide range of differences between the ages of wives and husbands. However, despite the obvious crudity of this exercise, we

Figure 5.4 Ratio of Number of Males Born in a Given Year (t) to Number of Females Born Two Years Later (t+2)

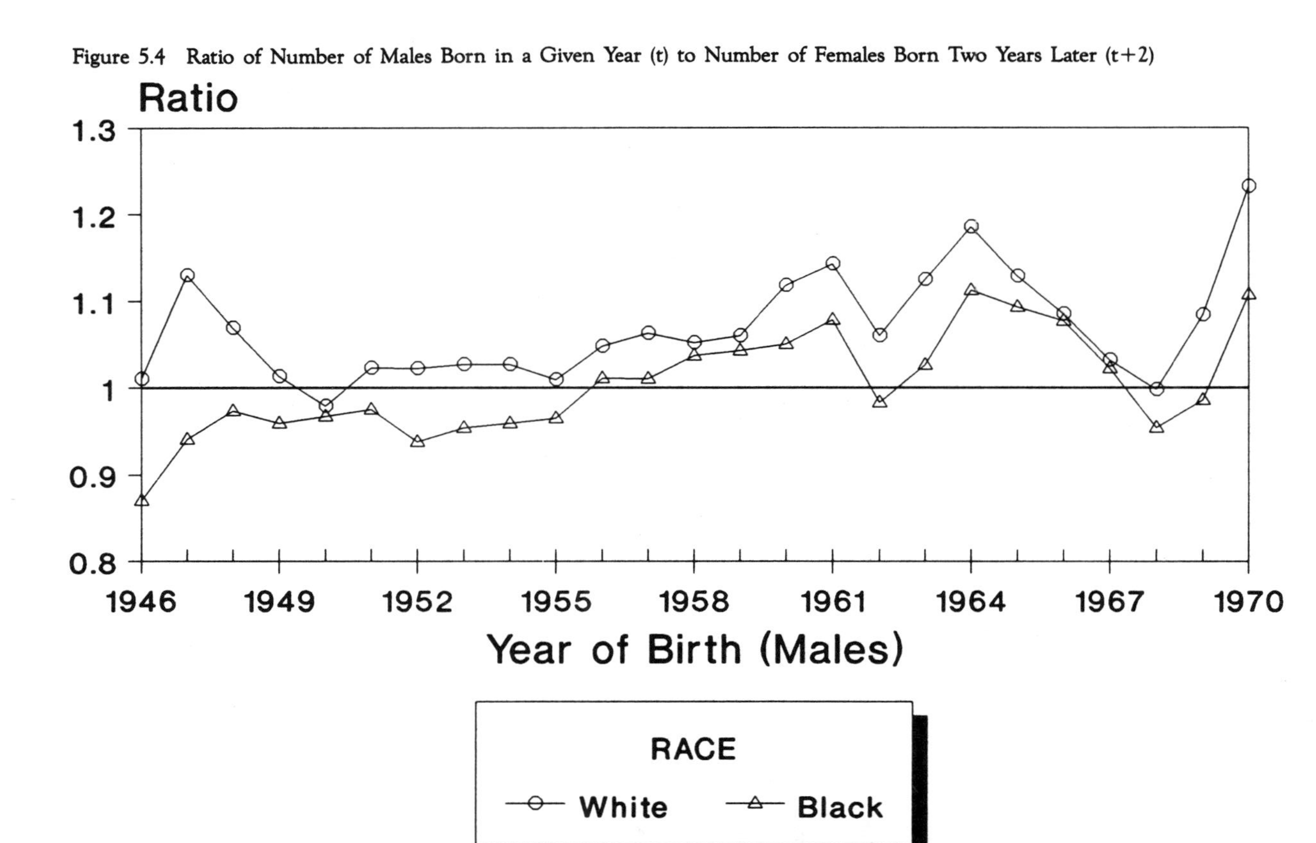

Note: Births are adjusted for underregistration.

may conclude that black women face a shortage of men that is considerably more severe than that experienced by white women.

The results of Table 5.1 are consistent with what we might expect in the presence of a baby-boom-induced marriage squeeze. We would expect, and indeed do find, fewer women marrying in the cohorts who were born after World War II compared with those born just prior to the war when the trend in births was essentially flat. We also find some convergence (not reported in the figure) in the average difference between men and women in their age at first marriage.

The Impact of Economics

The role of economic factors has long been important in explaining marriage patterns. Lower marriage rates are often seen as caused by higher male unemployment (Center for the Study of Social Policy 1984; Edelman 1987; Glick 1981; Moore, Simms, and Betsey 1986; Reid 1982; Stack 1974). We cannot assume, however, that the comparison between patterns of unemployment among blacks and whites is a simple one. We must take into account variations in other factors that might influence unemployment and be correlated with race, such as educational attainment. Thus we have estimated a few simple statistical models in order to determine not only how blacks have fared economically relative to whites in recent years but also whether trends and differentials in race differ by educational attainment (Bennett, Bloom, and Craig 1989).

Our findings indicate that for both sexes during the period 1968 through 1984, unemployment increased substantially among blacks and the less educated relative to whites and those who are better educated. Similarly, for all males actually in the labor force, blacks and the less educated are increasingly losing ground in their average annual earnings relative to other groups. Less-educated women of both races have lower earnings, although no decline over time is apparent. Less-educated black men, throughout this period, exhibit particularly low earnings. In short, less-educated young black men and women find two strikes against them in their race and educational status. We conclude that their relative economic circumstances are generally poor and have deteriorated significantly with the passage of time.

A growing body of literature suggests that these young men and women who are most disadvantaged in terms of education and employment form part of a black "underclass." This group has little hope of the upward mobility that has characterized the American dream. They are an urban population lacking in skills, education, and employment and permanently disaffected from the mainstream labor market (Auletta 1982; Edelman 1987; Hogan and Kitagawa 1985; Wilson and Neckerman 1986). Traditional avenues for improvement are closed to this group, in part because educational credentials are increasingly required for mobility. In addition, though, structural changes in the postwar economy have shut this group out of advancement as the industrial and manufacturing base of the economy has decayed or gone abroad. This has led to declining employment prospects, especially in central cities where blacks are and where these industries were once concentrated. Such a dynamic prevents this group from moving out of poverty (Harrington 1984; Wilson 1978, 1987). An expanding underclass, whose members are unable to gain access to or maintain sufficient resources for marriage, is a factor that must be taken into account in explaining the sharply declining rates of marriage among black women.

Elsewhere, we have established a link between the employment status of an individual and the subsequent likelihood of that individual marrying (Bennett et al. 1989). Analyzing data referring to the 1979 youth cohort of the National Longitudinal Surveys of Labor Market Experience, we have compared the annual probabilities of marriage in a given year among women and men who were employed full time year-round and those who were unemployed (including "discouraged workers") for any time during the previous year. The data indicate that an individual's employment status is positively associated with whether he or she marries, a relationship that is stronger among blacks than among whites.

Out-of-Wedlock Childbearing

The independent effect of out-of-wedlock childbearing on marriage rates must also be considered. We have found that, net of various other socioeconomic factors, a woman who has an out-of-wedlock birth is considerably less likely to ever marry than one who does not (Bennett and Bloom 1991). This ought not surprise us. For many people, marrying is tied to the desire to begin and raise a family; if a woman already has children, then she or her partner may see little or no reason to marry. In addition, potential spouses may think twice before marrying a woman with children because of additional emotional and financial burdens they might bring to a marriage. Although it is also possible that young women have children outside of marriage in response to unsatisfactory marriage prospects, we have found little evidence of this.

Given that having children outside of marriage might make it less likely that women will marry, we want to consider any possible differences in the patterns of childbearing that characterize black and white women because this may add to our explanation about different marriage patterns. Black women have always been more likely to give birth outside of marriage, although recently the gap between the two groups has narrowed (see Figure 5.5). The out-of-wedlock birth rate for white women has risen at every age while for black women it has fallen. However, there is still a substantial

Figure 5.5 Birth Rates Among Unmarried Women Aged 15 Through 44

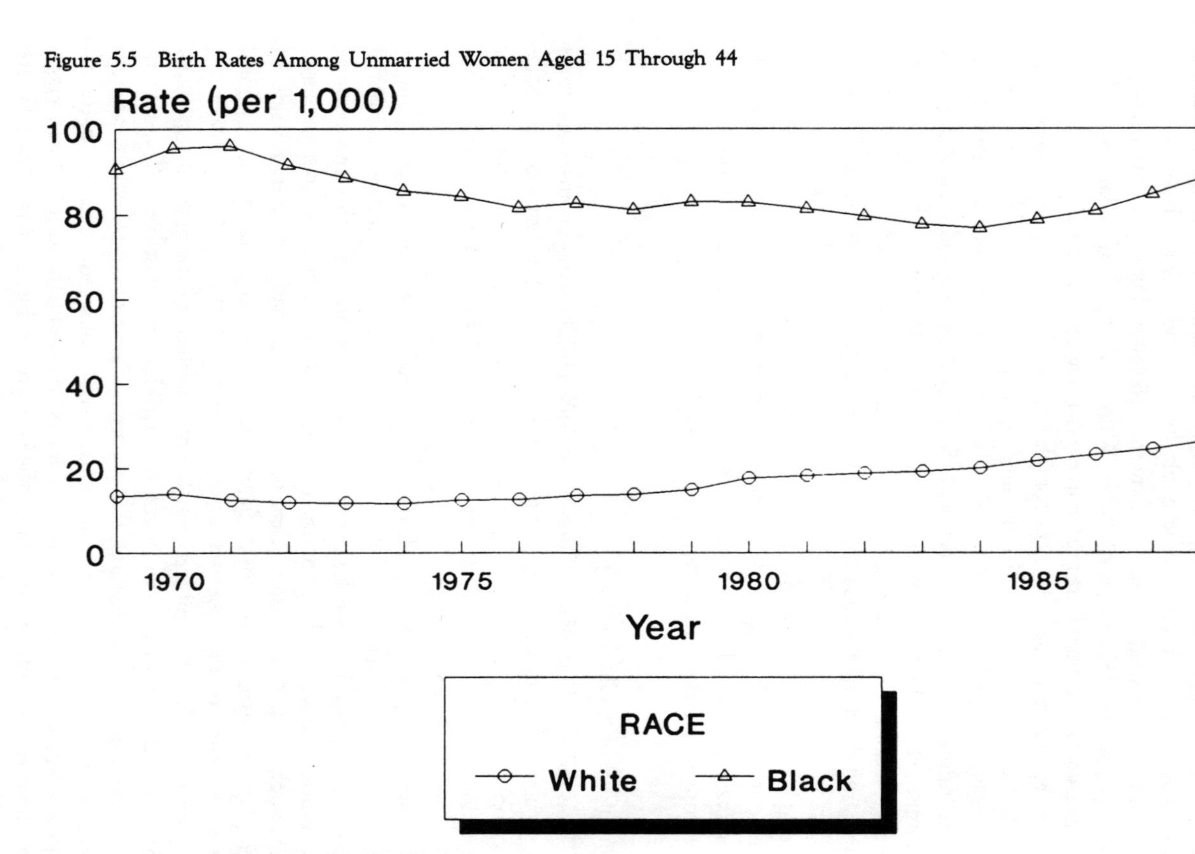

Source: National Center for Health Statistics

Table 5.2

Women in the Labor Force, 1950-1990

Year	Women as a Percentage of Total Labor Force	Labor Force Participation Rates of Women
1950	29.5	33.9
1960	33.4	37.7
1970	38.1	43.3
1980	42.5	51.5
1990	45.4	57.5

gap between the two groups: In 1988 the out-of-wedlock birth rate per thousand women aged 15 to 44 was about 27 among white women and 89 among black women.

As in our previous discussion concerning class differences and their effect on one's ability to enter into marriage, these are again important not simply for their direct effect but also insofar as they affect out-of-wedlock childbearing. We have shown that premarital childbearing disproportionately occurs among women of less-educated parents (Bennett, Bloom, and Craig 1989). For example, about 22 percent of black women aged 15 to 19 whose mothers were not high-school graduates had a premarital first birth versus only 5 percent of the corresponding group of women whose mothers had more than a high-school education. To the extent that a parent's education correlates with social class, the results indicate that having a child out of wedlock is closely related to social class.

Women and Work

Work for pay has become more central to the lives of women, both single and married, than it previously was. Table 5.2 shows the virtual revolution that has occurred in recent decades with respect to the labor-force activity of women. Only one-third of all women were participating in the labor force in 1950; by 1988 that figure had climbed to well over one-half.

The expectations of most young women today have changed with respect to those of earlier generations. They will very probably be working throughout their adult lives. Recognizing this, they may consciously postpone marriage in order to attain the education and resources needed for ad-

Table 5.3

Educational Attainment of American Women, 1950-1989

Year	Median School Years Completed by Women Aged 25 and Over	Percentage of Women who have Completed 4 Years of HS or More
1950	9.6	36.0
1960	10.9	46.0
1970	12.1	55.4
1980	12.4	68.1
1989	12.6	76.6

vancement in the labor market as well as to receive signals from the culture about the appropriate or ideal age at which to marry.

Increasing numbers of women are completing high school and attending college. We see in Table 5.3 that the proportion of women who have obtained a high-school degree more than doubled between 1950 and 1989, from 36 to 77 percent. Women are preparing themselves for, and embarking on, careers in prestigious occupations to an unprecedented extent. Table 5.4 shows the percentage of workers who are female in each of several traditionally "male" occupation. We find, for example, that the proportions of architects, engineers, and lawyers who are female have tripled or quadrupled during the past two decades.

For a number of reasons, postponing marriage may translate into remaining permanently single. Many women who work no longer follow the traditional path of going directly from the home of their parents to the homes they share with their spouses. Rather, because increased earning opportunities permit women to establish more easily lives on their own and because cultural attitudes have not changed about when is the appropriate time for children to leave home, many women set up an independent existence that begins with going away to school or a first job. This may reduce women's orientations to family roles as they begin to enjoy the independence afforded by living on their own (Waite, Goldscheider, and Witsberger 1986). Although the majority of young women indicate a strong desire to marry, those who work for a time may come to see trade-offs between marriage and their careers (Cherlin 1980). Work and education are also strong predictors of nontraditional attitudes toward sex roles and what the division of household labor ought to be (Mason, Czajka, and Arbor 1976; Parelius

Table 5.4

Percentage of Workers in Selected Occupations who are Female		
Occupation	1970	1990
Architects	4.0	18.4
Computer Scientists	13.6	36.5
Dentists	3.5	9.5
Engineers	1.7	8.0
Lawyers	4.9	20.6
Physicians	9.7	19.3
Veterinarians	5.3	23.9

1975; Regan and Roland 1985), although women's attitudes have changed much more quickly and in a more "progressive" direction than men's (Hochschild 1989). Some women may be committed to a more egalitarian concept of marriage than that which pertained under a more traditional model. With respect to issues such as division of household and childrearing labor or career decisions, if women are unable to find spouses with compatible views, they may decide to remain single.

Working relieves many women of the financial need to marry. Researchers have noted the lower rates of marriage among women with many resources (such as education, income, inheritances, etc.), which may indicate that such women use their resources to "buy out" of marriage (Goldscheider and Waite 1986).

Summary and Conclusions

We have demonstrated that American marriage patterns have undergone a profound transformation in recent decades. Fewer young women today can be expected to ever marry and those who do so will postpone relative to previous generations. In modern times, at least 90 percent of individuals in every birth cohort of American women have married at least once, a threshold we now appear to be crossing.

However, we cannot assume that women of all races and levels of educational attainment are similarly likely to marry. Among black women, those who have at least some college marry in greater numbers than those without a high-school degree. Just the reverse is true among white women, though the magnitude of the differential is more modest.

One of the most important facts to note about American marriage patterns concerns the overall racial difference in the likelihood of ever marrying. Blacks are substantially less likely to ever marry than whites. This has long been true; however, the disparity between black and white marriage patterns has increased dramatically over time.

Here we have attempted to show that changing marriage patterns stem from a complex array of circumstances. We have brought to bear arguments that include demographic, social, cultural, and economic factors. It is especially inappropriate today to make broad or sweeping statements about the place of marriage in America. Groups of women differentiated, for example, by race and education have very distinct life courses. The paths by which women have come to remain single have varied enormously. One important task of future research is to assess whether these outcomes have been the result of options exercised by women with increased choices or whether they have been paths involuntarily followed due only to limited life chances.

Acknowledgments

Research for this article was funded by the Russell Sage and Sloan Foundations and by a grant from the Rockefeller Foundation's Gender Roles Program.

References

Auletta, Ken. 1982. *The Underclass*. New York: Random House.

Becker, Gary S. 1981. *A Treatise on the Family*. Cambridge: Harvard University Press.

Bennett, Neil G., and David E. Bloom. 1991. "The Influence of Nonmarital Childbearing on Subsequent Marriage Behavior." Paper presented at the annual meeting of the Population Association of America, Session on Public and Private Influences on Union Formation and Stability, Washington, DC, 21–23 March.

Bennett, Neil G., David E. Bloom, and Patricia H. Craig. 1989. "The Divergence of Black and White Marriage Patterns." *American Journal of Sociology* 95(3): 692–722.

Bloom, David E., and Neil G. Bennett. 1990. "Modeling American Marriage Patterns." *Journal of the American Statistical Association* 85(412): 1009–1017.

Center for the Study of Social Policy. 1984. "The 'Flip-Side' of Black Families Headed by Women: The Economic Status of Black Men." Washington, DC.

Cherlin, Andrew J. 1980. "Postponing Marriage: The Influence of Young Women's Work Expectations." *Journal of Marriage and the Family* 42(2): 355–365.

______. 1981. *Marriage, Divorce, Remarriage*. Cambridge: Harvard University Press.

Coale, Ansley J. 1971. "Age Patterns of Marriage." *Population Studies* 25: 193–214.

Darity, William, Jr., and Samuel Myers, Jr. 1983. "Changes in Black Family Structure Implications for Welfare Dependency." *American Economic Review* 73(2): 59–64.
Edelman, Marian Wright. 1987. *Families in Peril: An Agenda for Social Change.* Cambridge: Harvard University Press.
Espenshade, Thomas. 1986. "The Recent Decline of American Marriage: Blacks and Whites in Comparative Perspective." In Kingsley Davis with A. Grossbard-Schechtman, *Contemporary Marriage: Comparative Perspectives on a Changing Institution.* New York: Russell Sage Foundation.
Fuchs, Victor R. 1983. *How We Live.* Cambridge: Harvard University Press.
Glick, Paul. 1981. "A Demographic Picture of Black Families." In Harriet Pipes McAdoo (ed.), *Black Families.* Beverly Hills: Sage Publications.
Goldscheider, Frances Kobrin, and Linda J. Waite. 1986. "Sex Differences in the Entry into Marriage." *American Journal of Sociology* 92(1): 91–109.
Harrington, Michael. 1984. *The New American Poverty.* New York: Holt, Rinehart and Winston.
Hochschild, Arlie. 1989. *The Second Shift: Working Parents and the Revolution at Home.* New York: Viking.
Hogan, Dennis P., and Evelyn Kitagawa. 1985. "The Impact of Social Status, Family Structure, and Neighborhood on the Fertility of Black Adolescents." *American Journal of Sociology* 90(4): 825–855.
Kitagawa, Evelyn. 1981. "New Life-styles: Marriage Patterns, Living Arrangements, and Fertility Outside of Marriage." *The Annals of the American Academy of Political and Social Science* 453 (January): 1–15.
Mason, Karen Oppenheim, John L. Czajka, and Sara Arbor. 1976. "Change in U.S. Women's Sex-Role Attitudes, 1964–1974." *American Sociological Review* 41(4): 573–596.
Moore, Kristin, Margaret C. Simms, and Charles L. Betsey. 1986. *Choice and Circumstance: Racial Differences in Adolescent Sexuality and Fertility.* New Brunswick, NJ: Transaction Books.
Moynihan, Daniel Patrick. 1986. *Family and Nation.* New York: Harcourt Brace Jovanovich.
National Center for Health Statistics. 1985. "Advance Report of Final Marriage Statistics, 1982." *Monthly Vital Statistics Report,* Vol. 34, No. 3, Supplement. Hyattsville, MD: Public Health Service.
Parelius, Ann P. 1975. "Emerging Sex-Role Attitudes, Expectations and Strains among College Women." *Journal of Marriage and the Family* 37(1): 146–153.
Regan, Mary C., and Helen E. Roland. 1985. "Rearranging Family and Career Priorities: Professional Women and Men of the Eighties." *Journal of Marriage and the Family* 47(4): 985–992.
Reid, John. 1982. "Black America in the 1980's." *Population Bulletin* 37(4).
Rodgers, Willard C., and Arland Thornton. 1985. "Changing Patterns of First Marriage in the United States." *Demography* 22(2): 265–279.
Rodriguez, German, and James Trussell. 1980. "Maximum Likelihood Estimation of the Parameters of Coale's Model Nuptiality Schedule from Survey Data." Technical Bulletin 7, World Fertility Survey, London.
Stack, Carol B. 1974. *All Our Kin.* New York: Harper and Row.

Thornton, Arland, and Deborah Freedman. 1983. "The Changing American Family." *Population Bulletin* 38.

Waite, Linda J., Frances Kobrin Goldscheider, and Christina Witsberger. 1986. "Nonfamily Living and the Erosion of Traditional Family Orientations Among Young Adults." *American Sociological Review* 51(4): 541–554.

Wilson, William J. 1978. *The Declining Significance of Race.* Chicago: The University of Chicago Press.

———. 1987. *The Truly Disadvantaged.* Chicago: The University of Chicago Press.

Wilson, William J., and Kathryn M. Neckerman. 1986. "Poverty and Family Structure: The Widening Gap between Evidence and Public Policy Issues." In Sheldon H. Danziger and Daniel H. Weinberg (eds.), *Fighting Poverty: What Works and What Doesn't.* Cambridge: Harvard University Press.

6

A Further Look at First Unions and First Marriages

Robert Schoen and Dawn Owens

There is a widespread feeling that a fundamental change in American marriage patterns is taking place. Not only are marriage rates declining sharply but there has been an extraordinary increase in the number of couples who are living together without being married. From 1970 to 1982 the incidence of cohabitation increased sixfold to number some 4 million persons. As Glick and Spanier noted (1980:20), "rarely does social change occur with such rapidity. Indeed, there have been few developments relating to marriage and family life which have been as dramatic as the rapid increase in unmarried cohabitation."

Data for the United States that allow cohabitation to be studied in any detail have only recently become available. The present chapter employs the National Survey of Families and Households (NSFH) and is a further look in that it follows the Bumpass and Sweet (1989) and Bumpass, Sweet, and Cherlin (1989) studies, which also used the NSFH. Here we explore the relationship between early cohabitation and first marriage from a life-course perspective and examine how it has changed over time.

Data

The NSFH interviewed a national sample of 13,017 persons between March 1987 and May 1988. The main sample of 9,643 respondents was supplemented by oversamples of certain groups, including cohabiting couples, blacks, and Mexican-Americans (cf. Sweet, Bumpass, and Call 1988). Although the survey covered a broad range of family issues, particular attention was given to cohabitation and its relationship to marriage. In this chapter we examine only female experience, as marital histories for males were found

Figure 6.1 The Marital/Cohabitation Status Life Table Model

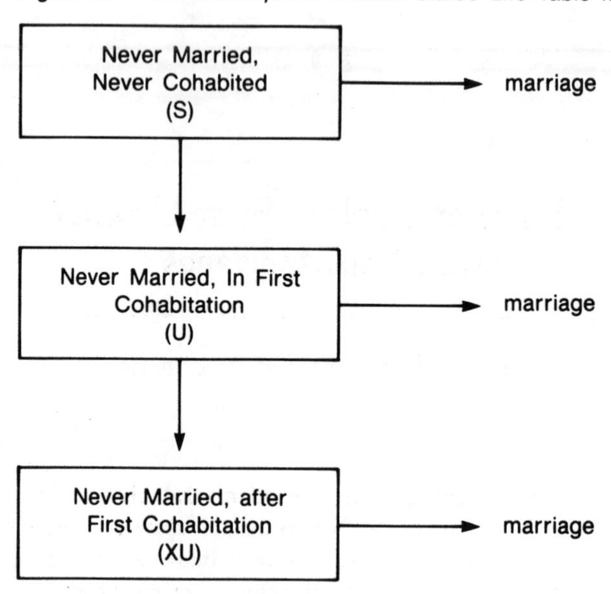

to be of markedly lower quality (or representativeness) (Bumpass, Martin, and Sweet 1989:3).

Methods

The analysis of the NSFH data proceeded in two steps. The first began by specifying a model that has three marital/cohabitation statuses, as shown in Figure 6.1: never married, never cohabited (S); never married, in first cohabitation (U); and never married, after first cohabitation (XU). Persons start in state S and can marry from any of the three unmarried states, but because of the nature of those states, persons cannot return to a previous status. Individual female cohabitation and marriage histories were used to determine the number of person-years lived in each state, by age, and the ages at marriage and at interstate transfer.

In the second step, the study population was restricted to women born between 1928 and 1967, essentially who were between the ages of 20 and 60 at the time of the survey. The study population was divided into eight, five-year birth cohorts, and each cohort was followed through the multistate life table model described previously. In most cases, the reported experience of the cohort provided the necessary life table values immediately. However, in some five-year age groups part of the experience of the cohort was truncated by the survey date. In those cases, the life table values were

TABLE 6.1 Probability of Entering a Cohabitation by Age and Race/Ethnicity, U.S. Females Born 1928–1967

	Cohort Born							
	1928–32	*1933–37*	*1938–42*	*1943–47*	*1948–52*	*1953–57*	*1958–62*	*1963–67*
All females to age								
25	.01	.04	.02	.05	.11	.23	.34	.37
30	.02	.04	.03	.07	.16	.30	.40	—
35	.02	.04	.03	.08	.18	.32	—	—
White females to age								
25	.00	.02	.02	.04	.10	.21	.35	.38
30	.00	.02	.03	.05	.15	.28	.40	—
35	.00	.02	.03	.06	.17	.29	—	—
Black females to age								
25				.12	.17	.31	.40	.34
30				.17	.23	.40	.49	—
35				.19	.24	.42	—	—
Mexican-American females to age								
25				.11	.10	.30	.23	.41
30				.12	.15	.34	.23	—
35				.14	.19	.34	—	—

found using the observed transfer rates and the linear method of multistate life table construction (cf. Schoen 1988, chap. 4). The life table transfer and person-year values were then used to calculate a number of summary measures of cohabitation and marriage experience. In a number of cases, the oversampling makes it feasible to consider the experience of white, black, and Mexican-American women. However, the number of Mexican-American women is small, varying from only 17 in the cohort born 1938–1942 to 59 in the cohort born 1958–1962, and there are fewer than 100 black women in each of the first three birth cohorts.

Results

Patterns of Cohabitation

Table 6.1 shows how the probability of cohabiting increases over time. Only 1 percent of women born in the years 1928–1932 cohabit before attaining age 25, but that figure rises to 37 percent for women born 1963–1967. There are only small increases in the proportion cohabiting between ages 30 and 35, as most women who cohabit before age 35 do so before age 30. Differences by race and ethnicity are present but are not terribly large, with the likelihood of cohabitation generally highest among blacks

TABLE 6.2 Average Duration of a First Cohabitation by Age and Race/Ethnicity, U.S. Females Born 1928–1967

	Cohort Born							
	1928–32	*1933–37*	*1938–42*	*1943–47*	*1948–52*	*1953–57*	*1958–62*	*1963–67*
All females to age								
25	2.7	1.5	1.0	1.6	1.6	1.6	1.5	1.0
30	2.9	2.8	1.2	2.1	1.9	1.8	1.5	—
35	3.3	3.9	1.8	2.4	2.0	1.8	—	—
White females to age								
25			1.0	1.4	1.4	1.4	1.4	0.9
30			1.5	1.8	1.6	1.5	1.3	—
35			2.2	2.0	1.6	1.5	—	—
Black females to age								
25				2.0	2.5	1.8	2.1	1.3
30				2.0	2.9	2.3	2.1	—
35				2.4	3.5	2.4	—	—
Mexican-American females to age								
25				1.6	1.0	2.0	2.0	1.3
30				3.7	2.6	2.6	2.1	—
35				3.6	2.8	2.9	—	—

and lowest among whites. Cohabitation has clearly played a significant role in the experience of U.S. women born after 1950.

Table 6.2 shows that the average duration of a first cohabitation is quite short, typically less than two years. In fact, as cohabitation has become more common, the average length of a first cohabitation has tended to decrease. Again, there are some fairly modest differences by race and ethnicity, with blacks tending to have longer cohabitations than whites.

A cohabitation ends when the partners either marry or separate. Table 6.3 shows that the probability a woman marries her first cohabitation partner is quite high, though it has been declining in the most recent cohorts. Women born in 1943–1947 have a 58 percent chance of marrying their first cohabitation partner before attaining age 25; women born in 1963–1967 have only a 44 percent chance of doing so. The decline characterizes both black and white experience, although black women have always had a lower probability of marrying their first cohabitation partner.

Table 6.4 shows the other side of the coin, the increasing probability that a first cohabitation ends without marriage. For women born since 1953, that probability appears to be greater than one-third. Relatively few women continue to cohabit after age 35. Table 6.2 shows that the average duration of a first cohabitation is quite short, and the average age at first cohabitation (before age 35) is in the early 20s.

TABLE 6.3 Probability of Marrying a First Cohabitation Partner by Age and Race/Ethnicity, U.S. Females Born 1928–1967

	Cohort Born							
	1928–32	*1933–37*	*1938–42*	*1943–47*	*1948–52*	*1953–57*	*1958–62*	*1963–67*
All females to age								
25	.36	.54	.61	.58	.55	.55	.52	.44
30	.52	.63	.69	.65	.67	.62	.63	—
35	.44	.63	.66	.65	.74	.63	—	—
White females to age								
25			.63	.69	.60	.60	.57	.49
30			.76	.76	.73	.68	.69	—
35			.72	.74	.78	.69	-	—
Black females to age								
25				.56	.43	.35	.32	.30
30				.63	.52	.40	.39	—
35				.63	.52	.45	—	—
Mexican-American females to age								
25				.26	.22	.59	.64	.48
30				.46	.27	.59	.64	—
35				.54	.64	.67	—	—

TABLE 6.4 Probability a First Cohabitation Ends Without Marriage by Age and Race/Ethnicity, U.S. Females Born 1928–1967

	Cohort Born							
	1928–32	*1933–37*	*1938–42*	*1943–47*	*1948–52*	*1953–57*	*1958–62*	*1963–67*
All females to age								
25	.45	.09	.13	.13	.20	.27	.30	.40
30	.34	.10	.16	.20	.23	.31	.34	—
35	.45	.20	.23	.25	.23	.34	—	—
White females to age								
25			.09	.08	.20	.25	.25	.41
30			.12	.12	.22	.27	.28	—
35			.14	.17	.20	.28	—	—
Black females to age								
25				.20	.21	.35	.47	.37
30				.21	.32	.47	.56	—
35				.21	.38	.50	—	—
Mexican-American females to age								
25				.16	.09	.23	.28	.35
30				.45	.06	.25	.28	—
35				.39	.18	.30	—	—

TABLE 6.5 Probability of Marriage by Age and Race/Ethnicity, U.S. Females Born 1928–1967

	Cohort Born							
	1928–32	*1933–37*	*1938–42*	*1943–47*	*1948–52*	*1953–57*	*1958–62*	*1963–67*
All females to age								
25	.87	.84	.85	.81	.76	.68	.67	.51
30	.92	.92	.93	.91	.89	.83	.82	—
35	.94	.93	.95	.94	.94	.88	—	—
White females to age								
25	.89	.88	.89	.86	.79	.71	.70	.56
30	.93	.95	.95	.94	.92	.87	.85	—
35	.96	.96	.97	.96	.96	.91	—	—
Black females to age								
25	.81	.65	.62	.68	.65	.50	.39	.24
30	.87	.78	.75	.81	.75	.62	.53	—
35	.90	.80	.84	.84	.79	.71	—	—
Mexican-American females to age								
25	.81	.73	.79	.71	.81	.76	.93	.62
30	.92	.80	.88	.87	.86	.89	.93	—
35	.92	.82	.88	.90	.94	.95	—	—

A number of the noted features of cohabitation in the United States, including the increased incidence of cohabitation and the short duration of such unions, have been reported previously (cf. Bumpass and Sweet 1989; Bumpass, Sweet, and Cherlin 1989). However, we are not aware of any published analysis of the NSFH (or of any other large-scale U.S. data set) that has reported a decreasing trend in either the stability of first cohabitations or the probability that a first cohabitation will lead to marriage.

Patterns of First Marriage

Cohort probabilities of entering a first marriage are shown in Table 6.5. For the first four cohorts, where comparisons are possible, the probabilities are quite consistent with figures calculated from vital statistics data and reported in Schoen et al. (1985). Trends indicating lower proportions ever marrying and later ages at marriage are quite clear. Among blacks, the decline in the proportion marrying before age 30 is particularly pronounced.

Table 6.6 presents marriage probabilities for persons who have ever cohabited. Those figures show little evidence of a decline in the likelihood of marriage. What is most striking about them is that the figure in Table 6.6 is almost always *lower* than the comparable one in Table 6.5 (except for the youngest cohort). Thus the probability of marriage is less for women who cohabit than for women in general. Table 6.7 shows that marriage

TABLE 6.6 Probability of Marriage For Ever Cohabiting Persons by Age and Race/Ethnicity, U.S. Females Born 1928–1967

	Cohort Born							
	1928–32	*1933–37*	*1938–42*	*1943–47*	*1948–52*	*1953–57*	*1958–62*	*1963–67*
All females to age								
25	.44	.54	.74	.60	.60	.65	.59	.54
30	.64	.63	.81	.73	.75	.75	.77	—
35	.54	.63	.83	.75	.85	.79	—	—
White females to age								
25			.65	.72	.64	.73	.64	.60
30			.77	.83	.81	.85	.83	—
35			.73	.80	.90	.87	—	—
Black females to age								
25				.56	.43	.36	.32	.30
30				.77	.48	.43	.43	—
35				.76	.59	.52	—	—
Mexican-American females to age								
25				.26	.39	.70	.71	.64
30				.61	.38	.69	.71	—
35				.80	.73	.86	—	—

chances are even lower for women whose first cohabitation ends without marriage. About half of all females who enter state XU, and roughly a third of white females who do, never marry before age 35.

Discussion

Although many if not most first cohabitations lead to marriage, Tables 6.5 and 6.6 show that women who cohabit are less likely to marry than women who do not cohabit. That finding casts serious doubt on the argument

TABLE 6.7 Probability of Marriage For Persons Whose First Cohabitation Ended Without Marriage by Age and Race/Ethnicity, U.S. Females Born 1943–1967

	Cohort Born				
	1943–47	*1948–52*	*1953–57*	*1958–62*	*1963–67*
All females to age					
25	.15	.20	.37	.22	.25
30	.42	.32	.44	.40	—
35	.39	.46	.47	—	—
White females to age					
25	.45	.23	.52	.31	.29
30	.53	.36	.62	.53	—
35	.31	.61	.66	—	—

that cohabitation is a prelude to marriage. Because marriage has declined more than cohabitation has increased, there is little reason to think that the rise in cohabitation has caused the decline in marriage. What is much more likely is that the same set of factors are responsible for both the rise in cohabitation and the fall in marriage.

What are those factors? One might say that they are related to the larger processes of industrialization, urbanization, and modernization. Those processes have been with us for a long time, however; the dramatic changes in cohabitation and marriage have largely taken place over the past twenty years. It is possible that the new marriage patterns are a result of a serious imbalance in the number of persons available for marriage, but that is not the case in the United States (Schoen and Kluegel 1988), nor is there any evidence that males in general are less suitable as marriage partners now than they were twenty years ago.

Although speculative, our explanation begins with one of the most significant social changes in the United States over the past twenty years, the increased participation of women in the labor force. That greater economic activity of women, and the corresponding decrease in their economic dependence on men, has surely had a strong impact on marriage behavior. A number of writers have examined the "independence" effect, and it is certainly plausible that women who have an economically viable alternative would choose to leave, or not to enter, an unsatisfactory marriage. Moreover, cohabitation seems to fit the lifestyles of dual career couples better than marriage does.

There is more to the story, however. As research has shown (e.g., Bumpass and Sweet 1989), the fall in marriage and the rise in cohabitation have characterized lower socioeconomic status groups more than higher socioeconomic status groups. It is not likely that women with less than twelve years of education are more apt to assert their economic independence than are women with four years of college. Yet the apparent inability of *female* attitudes to explain changes in marriage and cohabitation does not mean that those changes cannot be explained by the changing role of women. *Male* attitudes must also be considered.

If marriage has become less important to economically independent women, it has also become less important to men. The "sexual revolution," a myriad of household conveniences, and the fall, if not the devaluation, of fertility have all diminished the need for marriage. Still, there are many advantages to having a companion. From a male perspective, those advantages may be greater in a cohabitation than in a marriage. Cohabitations minimize long-term obligations. There is less expectation that partners in a cohabitation will share equally, an important consideration as working men earn more overall than working women by a ratio of about 3 to 2. The typically larger economic resources of the male can be translated into greater power more effectively within a cohabitation than within a marriage. That ability accrues to lower- as well as to higher-socioeconomic-status men. Indeed, to the extent that traditional male-female power relationships are more important to lower-socioeconomic-status men, as Scanzoni and Scanzoni (1981:450–451) argue that they are, then cohabitation would be even more appealing to them.

In sum, cohabitation fits this era of individualism by emphasizing autonomy and downplaying commitment. It offers advantages to economically self-reliant women while continuing to offer its traditional benefits to the economically stronger partner.

Acknowledgments

This is a revised version of the paper presented at the April 1990 Conference "Demographic Perspectives on the American Family: Patterns and Prospects," sponsored by the Department of Sociology, State University of New York at Albany. The research was supported by Grant R01 19261 from the Center for Population Research (NICHD) and an award from the Research Board of the University of Illinois at Urbana-Champaign. The assistance of Delores C. Schoen is gratefully acknowledged, as are comments from Nan M. Astone, Andrew J. Cherlin, Jay Teachman, and Robin Weinick.

References

Bumpass, L. L., and J. A. Sweet. 1989. "National estimates of cohabitation." *Demography* 26:615–625.

Bumpass, L. L., T. C. Martin, and J. A. Sweet. 1989. "Background and early marital factors in marital disruption." NSFH Working Paper No. 14, Center for Demography and Ecology, Univ. of Wisconsin, Madison.

Bumpass, L. L., J. A. Sweet, and A. Cherlin. 1989. "The role of cohabitation in declining rates of marriage." NSFH Working Paper No. 5, Center for Demography and Ecology, Univ. of Wisconsin, Madison.

Glick, P. C., and G. B. Spanier. 1980. "Married and unmarried cohabitation in the United States." *Journal of Marriage and the Family* 42:19–30.

Scanzoni, L. D., and J. Scanzoni. 1981. *Men, Women, and Change* (2d Ed.) New York: McGraw-Hill.

Schoen, R. 1988. *Modeling Multigroup Populations*. New York: Plenum.

Schoen, R., and J. R. Kluegel. 1988. "The widening gap in black and white marriage rates: the impact of population composition and differential marriage propensities." *American Sociological Review* 53:895–907.

Schoen, R., W. Urton, K. Woodrow, and J. Baj. 1985. "Marriage and divorce in twentieth century American cohorts." *Demography* 22:101–114.

Sweet, J. A., L. L. Bumpass, and V.R.A. Call. 1988. "The design and content of the National Survey of Families and Households." NSFH Working Paper No. 1, Center for Demography and Ecology, Univ. of Wisconsin, Madison.

7

Cohabitation: A Precursor to Marriage or an Alternative to Being Single?

Ronald R. Rindfuss and Audrey VandenHeuvel

In many societies, the roots of contemporary cohabitation patterns can be traced to the nineteenth century or earlier. Puerto Rican scholars note that consensual unions were present in the period immediately after Spanish colonization in the sixteenth century (Siman de Betancourt 1988). In medieval England, what eventually came to be known as common-law marriage was permitted because in many remote rural areas no justice or cleric was available to preside over an official marriage (Arnold 1951; Houlbrooke 1984). In Sweden, cohabitation was a firmly rooted living arrangement by the early twentieth century (J. Hoem and Rennermalm 1985; Trost 1979).

Apart from the histories that various immigrant groups brought with them to the United States, the American "tradition" of cohabitation is quite recent. It emerged as a popular living arrangement during the 1960s and 1970s (U.S. Department of Commerce 1988; Macklin 1983). Even as late as 1968, a single case of a cohabiting college student was a significant news story (Rindfuss and Stephen 1990), and Margaret Mead discussed the feasibility of cohabitation serving as a functional and appropriate arrangement (Mead 1968).

Despite the recency of cohabitation's popularity in the United States, it is rapidly becoming a life cycle experience of the majority of the younger generation. According to estimates from the recently completed National Survey of Families and Households, almost half of those in their late 20s and early 30s have experienced cohabitation (Bumpass and Sweet 1989). While cohabitation is more common among blacks and those with less education, these differentials are modest. Rather, it appears that fundamental

This chapter originally appeared in *Population and Development Review 16*, no. 4 (December 1990). Reprinted by permission.

changes have occurred in male-female relationships: cohabitation is found among virtually all segments of American society.

Where does cohabitation fit relative to existing institutionalized "marital" arrangements? So far, the sociological and demographic literature has tended to compare the experience of cohabitation with that of marriage. For reasons outlined below, we contend that understanding of this new form of relationship will be better served by also considering the similarities between cohabitation and singlehood. We argue that the evolution of cohabiting relationships is the result of historical changes in the dating and sexual relationships among unmarried individuals (e.g., McLaughlin et al. 1988; Modell 1989), which in turn are grounded in the rise of the individual in Western ideology (e.g., Lesthaeghe and Surkyn 1988).

We realize that the nature of cohabiting relationships is diverse. We suggest, however, that cohabitors and singles have many similarities that are not recognized in the literature. Thus, in this article we explicitly compare the behavior and expectations of cohabitors with those of both single and married persons, in the hope of achieving a better theoretical understanding of cohabitation.

Since cohabitation is now a common experience, its theoretical conceptualization influences the expectations that social demographers, family sociologists, and policymakers have about the effects of rising cohabitation levels. For instance, consider the laws pertaining to cohabitation. If cohabitation is viewed as a form of marriage, attention must be paid to such issues as partner support, inheritance rights, and social security benefits. Alternatively, if it is viewed as a form of being single, such concerns are irrelevant. Early court decisions refused to recognize any rights for cohabiting partners (Gottlieb 1983). Over time, an increasing number of court decisions have afforded nonmarital partners certain rights. For example, a 1976 landmark case in California (*Marvin v. Marvin*) recognized property rights in a cohabiting relationship (Rosen 1984). However, this case, like many others since then, was decided on contract, not family, law. Legal scholars have called on courts to become more responsive to the rights of unmarried couples (e.g., Albano and Schiller 1986; Gottlieb 1983; Rosen 1984).

For theoretical clarity we limit our attention in this article to persons who have never married or are in their first marriage. Our data set is restricted to a cohort that was aged 31–32 years at the most recent follow-up. We expect, however, that many of our arguments would apply to older ages as well.

The evolving definition of cohabitation probably differs from country to country. For example, in Sweden cohabiting relationships tend to be more permanent than in the United States, and childbearing within such unions is common (B. Hoem 1988). Cohabitation in Sweden thus bears a closer resemblance to marriage than it does in the United States. While our empirical evidence relates only to the United States, the question asked in this article is of broad, international significance. A comparison of the nature of cohabitation in different countries could lead to a better understanding of this form of relationship.

We now turn to a discussion of the prevailing views of cohabitation and present an alternative to these views. We then examine a variety of empirical markers that contrast cohabitors with the single and the married. There is no conclusive test indicating how cohabitation can best be conceptualized. Throughout, we will look for the "weight of the evidence."

Conceptualizations of Cohabitation

Cohabitation is generally viewed in one of two ways in the literature: as an alternative form of marriage without the usual legal sanctions; or as the last stage in the courtship process, a type of alternative "engagement." Both views emphasize similarities with marriage and, indirectly, differences from singlehood.[1]

The literature is replete with references to cohabitation as an alternative to or a replacement for formal, legal marriage. For example, Riche (1988), examining the ways in which cohabitors and married couples differ, explicitly recognizes cohabitation as an alternative to marriage. Schoen (1989), reviewing a monograph by Sweet and Bumpass (1987), is concerned with whether the rise in age at marriage in the 1970s is simply an artifact of one form of marriage (legal marriage) being replaced by another form (cohabitation). Willis and Michael (1988) argue for this substitution effect in their analysis of the same data set used here.

A number of authors note that the arrival of a child or the desire to have a child marks the crucial difference between cohabiting couples and married couples (Bachrach 1987; Carlson 1985). Underlying their discussions of the role of childbearing is an assumption, usually implicit, that marriage and cohabitation are similar relationships, and that a couple legally formalizes the relationship to legitimate a child.

The second and more common view of cohabitation is that it has become the final stage in a process leading to marriage (e.g., Gwartney-Gibbs 1986; White 1987). It is thus considered to be a form of "engagement" or the last stage of "courtship." For example, Spanier, who did much of the early census and Current Population Survey work on cohabitation, notes that "cohabitation has become a contemporary extension of courtship" (1982:18).

The use of the term "courtship" is telling. In terms of usage and etymology, it is both old-fashioned and somewhat sexist. For example, the American Heritage dictionary defines "courtship" as "the act or period of wooing a woman." Thus the term stands in sharp contrast to the results of attitudinal studies which suggest that cohabitors tend to have less traditional sex-role attitudes than noncohabitors (Macklin 1978).

These two views of cohabitation take marriage as their vantage point and implicitly assume that cohabiting couples are seeking an alternative to marriage or the traditional step before marriage. This perspective is reasonable, given that some of the components of marriage (such as a shared dwelling unit, shared meals, and sexual intimacy) are present in cohabitation. Yet an alternative perspective, one not often mentioned in the literature, is that cohabitation ought to be compared with single life. Some of the components of the dating experience of the single person are present in cohabitation. A couple who are dating one another often spend a substantial amount of time together—indeed, in some cases they may spend more time together than married couples who are employed and raising children, and they often share meals, particularly the evening meal.

What about sexual intercourse and the nature of the couple's relationship? Traditionally, the institution of marriage governed who had sexual intercourse with whom. Granted that exceptions existed, the expectation was that married individuals had intercourse with their partners and unmarried individuals did not engage in intercourse. However, the twentieth century has witnessed substantial change in the extent to which unmarried individuals have sexual relations. McLaughlin and his coauthors (1988) argue that since the turn of the century there has been a gradual increase in premarital sexual experience, with an acceleration in the rate of increase during the 1960s and 1970s. They state that Kinsey's data suggest that only 8 percent of white women born before the twentieth century reported having had premarital intercourse before age 20. In contrast, using data from Cycle III of the National Survey of Family Growth, Hofferth, Kahn, and Baldwin (1987) report that 65 percent of white women born 1959–61 had had premarital intercourse prior to age 20. Some of Modell's (1989) historical evidence also suggests that changes in the incidence of premarital intercourse were well under way prior to World War II.

McLaughlin and coauthors (1988), as well as others, argue that the United States has witnessed a fundamental change in its normative stance toward premarital sexual behavior. Behavioral evidence clearly supports this position. Given such a change, given the time-consuming nature of many dating patterns, given that many dating couples often share meals, and given that a common euphemism for sexual intercourse among unmarried partners is "sleeping together," it is not surprising that increasing numbers of single people are deciding to live together. Indeed, casual conversations with cohabiting couples suggest that a common reason for deciding to cohabit is that in view of the amount of time they already spend together it would simplify their lives to share a dwelling unit. Further, again based on anecdotal evidence, it seems to be common early in the cohabitation period for couples to live in one partner's dwelling unit, while the other partner maintains his or her own separate unit. In short, the moving-in process is gradual.

When likened to being single rather than to being married, cohabitation does not assume a commitment to permanency at the beginning of the relationship. The necessity of a long-term commitment does not exist, although there may be an understanding that this is a distinct possibility. Indeed, the recent National Survey of Families and Households found that when both members of a currently cohabiting couple were asked about their marriage plans, disagreement between the partners was quite frequent (Bumpass, Sweet, and Cherlin 1989:14).

The possibility that cohabitation should be viewed in contrast to being single has been mentioned in passing by a variety of authors (Bachrach 1987; Davis 1985; Kain 1984; Macklin 1978; Tanfer 1987). None of these authors, however, has systematically compared cohabitors to both single individuals and married individuals. That is the task to which we now turn.

Data

The data used in this article are from the National Longitudinal Study of the High School Class of 1972 (NLS72). The initial interviews took place in the spring of 1972, when the respondents were in their last year of high school. Follow-up interviews were conducted in the fall of 1973, 1974, 1976, and 1979 (Riccobono et al. 1981) and the spring/summer of 1986 (Tourangeau et al. 1987). The number of respondents in the fifth follow-up is 12,841. The NLS72 is an excellent data set for our purposes because of its large sample size, richness of data, and inclusion of both sexes.

The data span the time when cohabitation was increasing in popularity in the United States. Indeed, in the early rounds of the study, the question on marital status did not allow "cohabiting" as a response—reflecting the conventional question design of the time. In the 1986 follow-up, respondents were asked to provide information on their first three marriages or cohabitations. Since less than one percent reported that they had had more than three relationships, this amounts to a virtually complete marriage and cohabitation history. The operational definition for cohabitation is probably best conveyed by examining the preamble to the set of questions for the first marriage or cohabitation: "Please start with the first time that you got married or lived in an intimate relationship with an unrelated adult of the opposite sex. Do not count any living arrangements which lasted LESS THAN ONE MONTH." We have performed a number of consistency checks comparing responses to this 1986 marriage history with the marital status reports in earlier rounds. Bearing in mind that cohabitation was not a permitted response on the earlier rounds, the level of consistency is quite high. The only systematic problem we identified is that approximately 3 percent of first marriages reported in an earlier wave were not reported in 1986. These marriages occurred at relatively young ages. Males and blacks were somewhat more likely to fail to report such marriages.

Perhaps the principal liability of the data set is that the sample frame is restricted to those who were still in school in the spring of their senior year in high school, and thus high school dropouts are not represented. This restriction results in an exclusion of about 9 percent of this cohort (Bogue 1985:396–397). Since high school dropouts have the highest rates of cohabitation (Jacobsen and Pampel 1989; Bumpass, Sweet, and Cherlin 1989), the data set underrepresents the amount of cohabitation for this birth cohort. However, our aim in this article is not to discuss the frequency of cohabitation. Furthermore, we are unaware of any reason why the basic arguments presented here would not apply to high school dropouts; thus the NLS72 data set is adequate for our purposes.

In creating the 1986 follow-up sampling frame, particular groups from the previous rounds were retained with certainty.[2] Such groups are Hispanics, teachers and potential teachers, college graduates, and persons who had already experienced a divorce, widowhood, separation, or an out-of-wedlock birth. The results presented here are weighted to take into account the complex sampling strategy; reports on the number of cases are unweighted. Finally, even though the NLS72 contains information on whites and blacks, the sample size for blacks is relatively small; also there is an expectation that the meaning of cohabitation as well as of marriage differs for whites and blacks (e.g., Espenshade 1985). Thus we restrict our attention to whites.

Childbearing and Marriage Plans

One of the primary roles and normative functions of marriage is childbearing. Ryder (1973:61) discusses how norms have affected trends in American fertility: "These norms specify that all people are expected to marry and have two children as soon as, and providing that, their economic circumstances permit."

The sequential order of marriage and childbearing is important. Even though we have witnessed a substantial increase in out-of-wedlock childbearing (Jones et al. 1985), the prevailing expectation in the United States is still that childbearing is the province of married couples. Further, married couples have historically been expected to have children as reasonably soon after marriage as circumstances allow (e.g., Modell 1989). Thus, when fertility-timing expectations are asked, we would anticipate that among those who are not yet parents, the singles[3] would not expect a child in

Table 7.1 Percent of Respondents Intending to Have a Child Within Two Years Among Those Not Yet Parents, by Marital Status, Sex, and Year

	Marital status			Unweighted N		
Sex and year	Never married	Cohabiting	Married[a]	Never married	Cohabiting	Married[a]
Males						
1976	3	9	43	2650	152	984
1979	5	13	47	1595	159	1149
Females						
1976	4	11	40	2045	176	1397
1979	8	15	52	1118	177	1284

[a] Includes only those who are currently married and still in their first marriage.

the near future but the married would. The question, then, is where do cohabitors fit in?

In both 1976 and 1979 respondents were asked: "When do you expect to have your first (next) child?" The responses ranged from "no children intended" to "within a year." Rindfuss, Morgan, and Swicegood (1988) report that among those who respond "within a year" or "1–2 years" a relatively high proportion become parents in that time period; all the other responses lead to low proportions actually having a child in the short run. Thus, there seems to be a natural break at expecting a child within two years.

Table 7.1 shows the percent intending to have a child within two years for the three marital-status groups of never married, cohabiting, and currently married. Because the first experience of parenthood is quite different from later parity transitions (Rindfuss, Bumpass, and St. John 1980), Table 7.1 is limited to those who were not yet parents in 1976 and 1979. The results are consistent in both years and for both sexes. A substantial fraction (between two-fifths and one-half) of those who are married intend to have a child within the next two years, and fewer than 10 percent of the never married intend to have a child within two years. These results are consistent with our understanding of broad societal expectations governing marriage and childbearing in the United States.

For all four comparisons, the percentage of cohabitors intending to have a child within two years is between the percentages of those married and the never married. However, the cohabitors are clearly more similar to the singles than to the married. Given that these three marital-status groups vary with respect to many background variables, we also examined whether the differences shown in Table 7.1 remain in a multivariate analysis when background variables are controlled. The background variables controlled here and in later multivariate analyses are: family-of-origin socioeconomic status, community size while in high school, educational attainment at

Table 7.2 Among Those Never Married and Never Cohabiting, Percent Distribution of Marital Status 12 Months After Indicated Year, by Marriage Plans[a] and Sex

Marriage plans, sex, and year	Marital status 12 months later				
	Never married	Cohabiting	Married	Total	Unweighted N
Males					
1973 Plans to marry	46	1	53	100	376
No plans	94	1	4	99	3292
1974 Plans to marry	40	2	58	100	371
No plans	94	2	4	100	3154
1976 Plans to marry	48	2	50	100	364
No plans	94	3	3	100	2368
1979 Plans to marry	48	3	49	100	230
No plans	90	5	5	100	1439
Females					
1973 Plans to marry	34	2	63	99	464
No plans	93	3	5	101	2940
1974 Plans to marry	45	2	53	100	408
No plans	92	3	5	100	2610
1976 Plans to marry	38	3	59	100	330
No plans	90	4	6	100	1759
1979 Plans to marry	43	7	50	100	192
No plans	91	4	5	100	1010

[a] Plans to marry within 12 months

follow-up year, grades in the last year of high school, region of residence while in high school, religion, and sex. The results (not shown here) are essentially unchanged. In short, with respect to fertility expectations, cohabitors more closely resemble single respondents.

We now ask whether questions on marriage plans are interpreted to include cohabitation plans. As a component of the question on marital status in each of the first four follow-ups, unmarried respondents were asked whether they had plans to marry in the next 12 months.

For those who were never married and had never cohabited at any of the first four follow-ups, Table 7.2 shows the percent distribution of marital status 12 months later by whether or not respondents had had plans to marry in the next 12 months. Clearly the question on marriage plans is predictive of legal marriage but not of cohabitation. Approximately half or more of those who plan to marry in the next 12 months do so; meanwhile only 4 to 6 percent of those who do not plan to marry actually do so. On the other hand, this question seems to have no predictive power with respect to cohabitation. The probability of cohabitation in the next 12 months appears completely unrelated to short-term marriage plans.

Table 7.3 Percent of Never-Married Respondents Planning to Marry in Next 12 Months, by Whether Cohabiting, Sex, and Year

	Percent planning to marry in next 12 months		Unweighted N	
Sex and year	**Not cohabiting**	**Cohabiting**	**Not cohabiting**	**Cohabiting**
Males				
1973	12	26	3723	53
1974	12	36	3602	97
1976	13	28	2825	170
1979	13	33	1745	191
Females				
1973	15	35	3472	103
1974	16	39	3087	149
1976	16	44	2168	197
1979	16	33	1244	203

While the results in Table 7.2 are consistent with the argument that cohabitation is similar to singlehood, it could also be consistent with the opposite argument. For example, the word "marry" in the question itself may be interpreted in terms of the legal rather than the social institution. Or, it may be that couples view cohabitation as a substitute for marriage and that they plan never to marry. Further, it may be that young adults do not anticipate cohabitation but do anticipate marriage. Nevertheless, we suggest that the results in Table 7.2 are more consistent with an interpretation of cohabitation as similar to singlehood.

A related question is whether cohabitors are more likely to anticipate a marriage in the next 12 months than those who are never married and not cohabiting. Table 7.3 shows the marriage plans for cohabitors and never-married noncohabitors for each of the first four follow-ups. Clearly, the cohabitors are more likely to anticipate a marriage in the next 12 months than the noncohabitors, suggesting that cohabitation may be a stage of the courtship process. Note, however, that the majority of both groups do not plan to marry in the next 12 months. Typically about two-thirds of the cohabitors do not have immediate marriage plans, arguing against the interpretation that cohabitation is equivalent to "being engaged." Rather, such a large number without marriage plans suggests that cohabitation for most is a convenient living arrangement for single individuals not ready to make long-term commitments. Even though they may eventually marry the person with whom they are cohabiting, the purpose of the cohabitation appears not to be marriage.

Table 7.3 also affords insight into male–female differences in the meaning of cohabitation. Prior research (Arafat and Yorburg 1973; Lyness, Lipetz, and Davis 1972) suggests that female as compared with male cohabitors are more likely to view their relationship as leading to marriage. Limited support for this argument is found here. In two of the four years, female cohabitors were significantly more likely than the males to plan marriage within the year, but little difference was observed in the other years. Thus it seems that for females as well as males, cohabitation is generally not viewed as a final courtship stage preceding marriage.

Employment and Educational Activities

Decisions about relationships with members of the opposite sex take place in a context in which the participants are also making decisions about educational and employment opportunities. Due to the complex causal interplay of employment/school decisions with relationship/marriage decisions, we know that employment/school status will be related to marital status. We now consider employment and educational activities by marital status to see where cohabitation fits relative to marriage and being single—without attempting to unravel the causal relationships. For example, compared with those currently married, never-married individuals are more likely to be in school, especially at the ages where higher education is common. The causality here is probably operating in both directions. That is, those who are in school are unlikely to feel that they have the financial resources to get married; those who are married are likely to face constraints that make it difficult to be a student.

We examine the employment/school activities of cohabitors in October of each year from 1973 to 1985, and ask whether the activities of cohabitors are more similar to those who are never married or to the currently married. We focus on October because it is the only month for which employment/school activities are available for each of the 13 years. Since we have data for only one month, it is an advantage that the month is October. It is long enough after the summer months so that the temporary instability often associated with summer is over, and yet long enough past spring that those who have completed their education and desire employment would have had sufficient time to obtain a job.

Two activities are examined: schooling and "other," i.e., being neither in school nor employed.[4] The latter activity is a heterogeneous set of activity states, including homemaker, unemployment, and drifting. The percentages in school and in the residual category are shown in Tables 7.4 and 7.5 respectively. (The proportion employed can be obtained by adding the comparable percents from Tables 7.4 and 7.5, and subtracting the result from 100).

As expected, the proportion attending school is substantially higher among the never married than among the currently married. The differences

Table 7.4 Percent Enrolled in School, by Marital Status, Sex, and Year

	Marital status			Unweighted N		
Sex and year	Never married	Cohabiting	Married	Never married	Cohabiting	Married
Males						
1973	51	45	14	4123	57	441
1974	46	28	17	3762	101	805
1975	49	45	17	3312	132	1182
1976	35	29	16	2842	171	1543
1977	25	25	13	2463	190	1865
1978	21	19	13	2075	201	2166
1979	18	17	12	1747	191	2426
1980	16	17	9	1393	173	2556
1981	14	13	9	1202	177	2757
1982	14	23	9	1049	158	2963
1983	12	20	8	927	143	3121
1984	10	10	7	816	127	3241
1985	9	7	7	740	105	3327
Females						
1973	56	20	9	3765	110	1093
1974	53	26	10	3181	159	1566
1975	54	35	11	2698	182	1936
1976	31	28	10	2178	201	2326
1977	22	20	7	1763	214	2653
1978	21	20	7	1466	216	2835
1979	20	18	7	1245	204	2981
1980	20	14	6	989	165	3083
1981	16	21	6	855	163	3245
1982	13	9	7	761	137	3382
1983	14	9	7	675	130	3472
1984	15	11	6	614	107	3563
1985	15	11	6	567	93	3614

are somewhat higher among females than males, and are substantially larger in the first few years after high school compared to when the cohort members are in their 30s. Almost without exception, the cohabitors are intermediate between the singles and the married. Yet the cohabitors are substantially more similar to the never married than to the married.

For the respondents in Table 7.4, the meaning of schooling varies, ranging from taking a simple course for credit to full-time enrollment in a degree-granting program. Nevertheless, being a student generally consumes financial and other resources and makes it more difficult to work full-time so as to maximize income. Thus, students are less likely to be able to make the long-term commitment typically implied by marriage. Yet, cohabitors show only moderate reluctance to combine cohabitation with the student role, suggesting that the level of commitment involved in cohabitation is of a lower order of magnitude than that involved in marriage. Put differently,

Table 7.5 Percent Neither Employed nor in School, by Marital Status, Sex, and Year

	Marital status			Unweighted N		
Sex and year	**Never married**	**Cohabiting**	**Married**	**Never married**	**Cohabiting**	**Married**
Males						
1973	4	2	2	4123	57	441
1974	6	6	3	3762	101	805
1975	4	4	3	3312	132	1182
1976	8	9	3	2842	171	1543
1977	5	9	2	2463	190	1865
1978	5	3	2	2075	201	2166
1979	5	6	2	1747	191	2426
1980	10	7	6	1393	173	2556
1981	11	9	5	1202	177	2757
1982	10	6	6	1049	158	2963
1983	8	5	5	927	143	3121
1984	8	5	5	816	127	3241
1985	6	6	4	740	105	3327
Females						
1973	7	11	38	3765	110	1093
1974	6	21	40	3181	159	1566
1975	6	9	36	2698	182	1936
1976	8	9	35	2178	201	2326
1977	8	11	35	1763	214	2653
1978	7	7	35	1466	216	2835
1979	6	5	36	1245	204	2981
1980	11	22	37	989	165	3083
1981	11	17	37	855	163	3245
1982	10	11	36	761	137	3382
1983	8	14	35	675	130	3472
1984	9	7	33	614	107	3563
1985	8	8	33	567	93	3614

it appears that the cohabiting role and the student role are much more compatible than the married role and the student role.

Table 7.5 shows the percent who are neither employed nor in school. Due to traditional and continuing gender-role differences in the United States, the composition of this residual group differs by sex. Homemaking is included in this residual group.[5] Since this is overwhelmingly a female role, it is likely that a large proportion of the women in the residual category are homemakers. Alternatively, males in this category are most likely to be unemployed or simply drifting. Since the nature of the activities of those in the residual category differs markedly by sex, the results for males and females are discussed separately.

Given the traditional male role of breadwinner, one would expect that fewer married than cohabiting or single men would be in the residual category of neither employed nor attending school. This is supported by the data. While there are some fluctuations due to the small numbers of cohabitors, the married compared with the cohabitors are less likely (or in four cases, as likely) to be in the residual category. The percentage of cohabitors in the residual category is more similar to the percentage of singles in this category. Again, these results suggest that cohabitors are more similar to singles than to the married.

Married women are more likely than single women to hold the role of homemaker and child-care provider. This is evidenced by the data: single females are substantially less likely than married females to be in the residual category of not employed/not in school. Again, the cohabitors more closely resemble single than married individuals.

Financial Activities and Independence

Delaying both marriage and childbearing has long been an American tradition, one that developed out of the Western European heritage (e.g., Levine 1977; Rindfuss, Morgan, and Swicegood 1988). A major component of this delay is the normative prescription that individuals should neither marry nor have children until they can afford to do so. This affordability clause is clearly supported by Ryder's work quoted earlier, and it is a prescription that is often cited to explain temporal shifts in marriage behavior. Traditionally, financial independence was the male's responsibility. Given the shift in women's work patterns over the twentieth century, the responsibility for financial independence of married couples is likely becoming more mutual. Nevertheless, the prescription regarding financial independence prior to marriage has not waned.

The criteria for when marriage can be "afforded" have changed as the United States has become more affluent and as new "necessities" have been invented (e.g., color televisions, microwaves). Further, the definition of affording marriage is quite heterogeneous, differing by race, class, religion, and ethnicity. This heterogeneity, as well as other determinants of the marriage process, means that there will not be a perfect correlation between financial resources and marital status. Nevertheless, the general expectation is that married individuals will have greater financial resources and independence from parents than those who are single.

One measure of available financial resources is home ownership. Since World War II, home ownership has been a goal of most married couples in the United States, and an attainable one for many. We expect married individuals to be more likely to own their own house or condominium than single individuals, but how do the cohabitors compare? In the fourth and fifth follow-ups, respondents were asked about home ownership. The percent owning a house or condominium is shown in Table 7.6. In both years and for both males and females, those who are married are substantially

Table 7.6 Percent Owning a House or Condominium, by Marital Status, Sex, and Year

Sex and marital status	Year 1979	Year 1985[a]	Unweighted N 1979	Unweighted N 1985
Males				
Never married	14	33	1677	757
Cohabiting	17	33	182	105
Married	56	80	2307	3376
Females				
Never married	7	34	1203	573
Cohabiting	9	27	196	91
Married	63	81	2878	3668

[a] Home ownership in this question refers to February 1986 while marital status refers to October 1985.

more likely to own their dwelling unit than those who are single. The cohabitors in all cases are more similar to the singles than to the married. Indeed, the cohabitors are virtually indistinguishable from never-married noncohabitors. These results are unchanged when we control for possibly confounding variables in a multivariate logit analysis. The cohabitors are not significantly different from the unmarried, and both are significantly less likely to own a home than the married.[6]

For most young men and women, a major component in securing financial independence is ceasing to be dependent on parents for support. For some this might be a sharp break, while for others there may be a gradual reduction. Unfortunately the data set did not systematically explore the issue of financial dependence on parents. However, there are suggestive data. In fall 1976, when the respondents would have been out of high school for somewhat more than four years, and in fall 1979, when the respondents would be about age 25, they were asked whether they were dependent on their parents for more than half of their financial support. The proportion who were is shown in Table 7.7.

In interpreting Table 7.7 it is important to note that for singles only one set of parents is involved, whereas cohabitors and married couples have two sets of parents. The NSL72 inquired about support only from the respondent's parents. Conceptually, if the partner's parents are providing financial support this is equivalent to substituting one type of dependence for another. While we wish that information were available for both sets of parents, we doubt that such information would have a major effect on our findings.

As expected, the proportion of singles financially dependent on their parents is substantially greater than among the married. Also, as the cohort ages, the percent of singles who are financially dependent on their parents

Table 7.7 Percent of Respondents Dependent on Parents for More Than Half of Their Financial Support, by Marital Status, Sex, and Year

	Year		**Unweighted N**	
Sex and marital status	**1976**	**1979**	**1976**	**1979**
Males				
Never married	26	8	2806	1669
Cohabiting	11	5	168	182
Married	2	1	1492	2308
Females				
Never married	31	9	2147	1201
Cohabiting	13	5	188	195
Married	2	1	1870	2879

diminishes, thus reducing the single-to-married differential. Note that among the married, the percentage financially dependent on their parents is truly trivial. The cohabitors fall in between the singles and the married. Particularly in 1976, the percentage difference between the cohabitors and the singles is larger than the difference between the cohabitors and the married. Yet, for cohabitors, the percent financially dependent on parents is not trivial, and thus there is a sharp difference between them and the married.

Examining the financial differences in a logistic regression model (not shown here), we find that the difference between the cohabitors and married respondents remains statistically significant. In 1976, the cohabitors are also significantly different from the singles, but the difference in the coefficients is substantially smaller than the difference involving the married. In 1979, the cohabitors are not statistically different from the never married.

A final way we explore the issue of financial dependence is by examining the financing of schooling. Because the NLS72 was funded primarily by the U.S. Department of Education, detailed data were collected on the financing of education, particularly in the first three follow-ups. Respondents were asked about the components of their school and living expenses and about the sources of income used to cover those expenses. Thus it is possible to determine the fraction of expenses paid by parents. In examining this issue we are constrained by the relatively small number of cases available for analysis because we are examining the intersection of two divergent trends. In other words, as the number of years since high school increases, the number of students decreases. But as the number of years since high school increases, so does the number of cohabitors. It is only for the school years 1974–75 and 1975–76 that sufficiently large numbers of student cohabitors are available for analysis.

Table 7.8 Percent of Students Dependent on Parents for More Than Half of Their Expenses, by Marital Status, Sex, and Year

Sex and marital status	School year 1974–75	School year 1975–76	Unweighted N 1974–75	Unweighted N 1975–76
Males				
Never married	32	30	2284	2026
Cohabiting	14	20	46	68
Married	5	5	201	321
Females				
Never married	42	39	1936	1681
Cohabiting	38	20	59	82
Married	10	9	234	327

Table 7.8 shows the percent of students dependent on their parents for more than half of their expenses. As expected, married students are far less likely than single students to be financially dependent. Consistent with prevailing gender-role expectations, female students are more likely to be financially dependent on their parents than male students. The percent of dependent cohabitors always falls in between that of the singles and the married. They are in some, but not all cases, more similar to the singles than to the married. Thus the evidence from the question on dependence on parents is somewhat mixed, although generally the cohabitors tend to be more similar to the singles.

The small size of the cohabiting-student group and the possibility of confounding variables affecting the relationship require cautious interpretation of Table 7.8. We further explored the issue with a set of logistic regression analyses (not shown here). In all cases, the married were significantly less likely to be financially dependent on their parents than the cohabitors. In three of the four cases, there was no significant difference between the never married and the cohabitors. For females in the 1975–76 school year, the singles were significantly more likely to be financially dependent on their parents than the cohabitors, who in turn were significantly different from the married. These findings tend to support the general conclusion that the cohabitors resemble the singles more closely than the married.

Cohabitors' Self-Identification

The final question we ask is how cohabitors identify themselves when the marital-status question does not allow "cohabiting" as a response. In each of the first four follow-ups (1973, 1974, 1976, and 1979) respondents were

Table 7.9 Among Cohabitors, Percent Reporting Various Marital-Status Categories in Indicated Year, by Sex

	Marital status				
Sex and year	**Never married**	**Currently married**	**Separated, widowed, or divorced**	**Total**	**Unweighted N**
Males					
1973	97	3	0	100	53
1974	96	4	0	100	97
1976	94	6	1	101	170
1979	93	5	2	100	191
Females					
1973	91	9	1	101	103
1974	91	8	1	100	149
1976	96	3	1	100	197
1979	93	3	4	100	203

[a] As identified in the 1986 follow-up. For each year, only those who were cohabiting in that year are included. Further, the table is restricted to never-married cohabitors.

asked about their marital status as of 1 October. The response categories included only conventional marital-status options: never married, currently married; and separated, widowed, or divorced. Those who were cohabiting had to decide which of these best identified their status. The marriage and cohabitation history contained in the fifth follow-up allows us to identify those who were cohabiting as of 1 October in each of the earlier follow-up years. The two sets of information were then compared.

Before examining the results, a note of caution is necessary. Data for each of the follow-ups were obtained by means of a mail-out, mail-back, self-administered questionnaire. Thus respondents could not discuss their particular circumstances with an interviewer. With regard to the first four follow-ups, it is unclear then how cohabitors may have interpreted the term "currently married." They may have done so in the social or the legal sense. If the latter, then it is quite possible that cohabitors view themselves as being in a behavioral situation that is the equivalent of or an alternative to marriage but that is not the same as being legally married.

Despite this very serious ambiguity, the results are striking. For all who were cohabiting in each of the four years, Table 7.9 shows the distribution of the responses to the marital-status question. Those young men and women who were cohabiting overwhelmingly described themselves as never married, and there is little difference by sex.

Although we cannot resolve the inherent ambiguity in the term "marriage," this issue can be further explored by examining the cohabitors' reported living arrangements in each of the first four follow-ups. The basic question is: do cohabitors mention the person with whom they are cohabiting and if so, how do they describe this person? In each follow-up they were asked

Table 7.10 Among Cohabitors,[a] Percent Reporting Various Living Arrangements in Indicated Year, by Sex

	Living arrangement					
Sex and year	**Alone**	**Parents or other relatives**	**Spouse**	**Unrelated individuals**	**Total**	**Unweighted N**
Males						
1973	34	47	1	18	100	54
1974	6	33	4	57	100	97
1976	22	22	8	48	100	163
1979	17	12	8	63	100	180
Females						
1973	17	33	9	41	100	105
1974	11	14	10	66	101	147
1976	13	10	4	72	99	197
1979	15	7	5	73	100	194

[a] As identified in the 1986 follow-up. For each year, only those who were cohabiting in that year are included. Further, the table is restricted to never-married cohabitors.

a closed-ended question about whom they were living with. The allowable responses were: by myself, with my parents, with my husband or wife, with parents and husband or wife, with other relatives, and with persons not related to me. Relatively few were living with other relatives, so this category was combined with the parents-only category. The two categories that include spouse were combined. The resulting distributions for each of the four follow-ups are shown in Table 7.10.

While the small number of respondents causes some instability of the percentages in the early years, the general pattern is clear. As the cohort ages and as cohabitation becomes more socially acceptable during the 1970s, increasing numbers of cohabitors of both sexes report living with unrelated individuals. In no year do more than 10 percent of cohabitors report living with a spouse.

Perhaps most surprising is the relatively high number of cohabitors who report living alone or living with parents or other relatives. This does not necessarily contradict the report of cohabitation given in the 1986 follow-up. Rather, it is probably a reflection of the process whereby individuals become cohabitors. No ceremony, as in the case of marriage, and no biological event, as in the case of parenthood, mark the beginning of cohabitation. For many, the beginning of the cohabiting relationship is likely to be gradual, and a second residence is likely to be maintained for a time. Thus both reports, one of cohabitation and the other of living alone or with relatives, may be accurate.

Further, it is important to remember the age of these respondents. In 1973, when the largest fraction of cohabitors report living alone or with their parents, they would have been out of high school for a year and a half, and be about 19 or 20 years old. Many of the respondents would also have been in their second year of college. At this time of life they are going through the gradual process of leaving the parental household (Goldscheider and DaVanzo 1985), and living arrangements are perhaps most ambiguous. At this time, also, cohabitation is often not full-time; some individuals may have two or more residences. In short, despite the apparent contradiction, it is quite possible to cohabit and to live alone or with one's parents.

Summary and Conclusion

In the last 25 years the United States has witnessed the emergence of cohabitation as a major nontraditional form of male-female relationship. It has many of the characteristics of marriage: shared dwelling unit, shared meals (presumably), and sexual intimacy. Perhaps for this reason, the burgeoning sociological and demographic literature on cohabitation has treated it as an alternative to marriage or as the last stage in the courtship process.

The evidence presented in this article suggests that it is also appropriate to consider cohabitation relative to being single. For the comparisons we make, cohabitors are consistently intermediate between those who are single and those who are married. Furthermore, in almost all comparisons the cohabitors are substantially more similar to the singles than to the married. Cohabitors' fertility expectations, nonfamilial activities, and home ownership rates resemble those of the singles.

We have not addressed a number of important dimensions of cohabitation. These include the sharing of financial resources, the number of hours spent together, and the division of domestic tasks. We wish data on these and related issues were available to see how they might modify our basic findings and to see whether they might show greater gender differences than we have observed. Further, we do not know the decisionmaking steps that precede entry into cohabitation. Instead, we infer from the results that cohabiting individuals tend to be similar to never-married, noncohabiting individuals.[7]

What are the implications of viewing cohabitation as an alternative to the conventional form of being single? The rise in cohabitation may be but another step in the long-term rise of individualism relative to the decline of the institutions of marriage and family. By its very definition, cohabitation requires less "commitment" than marriage. Empirically, we know that cohabiting unions are more likely than marriages to be dissolved by discord.[8] Further, cohabitors are less likely than noncohabitors to hold traditional family values (Bumpass 1990).

The ideology of cohabiting unions does not imply permanence. Thus, the rise in cohabitation implies that individuals will have a greater number of lifetime sexual partners. Further, contrary to earlier expectations, the rise in cohabitation implies an increase in union dissolution rates. This is likely to be the case for cohabiting unions themselves as well as for cohabiting unions that become marriages. Quite possibly, then, the rise in cohabitation could have a feedback effect on the institution of marriage, further weakening its central foundation of permanence.

If we assume for the average heterosexual who has an ongoing relationship with a member of the opposite sex that living with that person is a more enjoyable existence than living alone (or with parents or same-sex housemates)—and we have no evidence to suggest the opposite—then the rise of cohabitation should be viewed in the same context as the rise of premarital intercourse, increases in out-of-wedlock childbearing, and declines in parental authority. When possible, individuals in the United States have attempted to integrate into their lifestyles the appealing components of traditional family forms and customs without also including those components that restrict the individual. For instance, in earlier generations there were struggles with regard to dating behavior and living on one's own, that is, outside the parental household (Modell 1989). More recently, while retaining involvement in intimate relationships, individuals have moved away from the commitment and permanence associated with marriage and the family.

How has this change come about? Economic and occupational changes have been facilitating factors. But this movement has also been fueled by broad and powerful changes—normative, cultural, ideational, and ideological—that occurred in many countries in the West, as discussed by a number of population scholars. Lesthaeghe and Surkyn (1988:8) argued that "The two most salient features of Western ideational change have been the processes of secularization and individuation." Using data from the European Values Studies, they find that approval of sexual freedom and partnership outside of marriage are positively associated with individuation. In his recent presidential address to the Population Association of America, Bumpass (1990) presented a strong case for the "force of secular individualism" affecting a wide variety of family realms. Empirically, one of the strongest and most consistent predictors of who will not cohabit is frequent church attendance (e.g., Clayton and Voss 1977). We would argue that in the United States, at least, cohabitation partially sprang out of the ideology of individualism, despite its action of coupling two individuals.

If the ideology of individualism is the spiritual father of the rise in cohabitation, then we should not be surprised that cohabiting unions are of relatively short duration (Willis and Michael 1988), that they are often terminated by separation rather than marriage (Bumpass, Sweet, and Cherlin

1989), and that when they do end in marriage the resulting union is relatively more fragile (Bennett, Blanc, and Bloom 1988; Bumpass and Sweet 1989). Yet this last finding, that cohabitation prior to marriage increases, rather than decreases, the probability of marital dissolution, has provoked surprise among social scientists and journalists alike. The reason, we would argue, is that they were conceptualizing cohabitation as an alternative to marriage. Viewing cohabitation as an alternative to being single helps explain the various empirical regularities that have emerged regarding the behavior of American cohabitors.

We close with several caveats. The arguments and evidence presented here pertain to the United States, and more specifically to young adults in the United States. In the case of Sweden, cohabitation may be more properly conceptualized as an alternative to marriage. Sweden has had a long history of cohabiting unions, has more cohabiting unions of long duration, and has a higher proportion of cohabiting unions that include childbearing and rearing (B. Hoem 1988; J. Hoem 1985; J. Hoem and Rennermalm 1985; Trost 1979).

Similarly, we should repeat that substantial diversity exists among cohabiting unions in the United States. While most are short lived and do not involve childbearing, some are of long duration and some involve childbearing. If the data set had had enough cohabiting unions of long duration, we would have split the cohabiting group by duration. While we acknowledge the substantial heterogeneity among American cohabitors, we maintain that, taken as a whole and in this time frame, cohabitation in the American context is primarily an alternative to being single.

Acknowledgments

The research on which this article is based has been partially supported by a grant from the U.S. National Institute of Child Health and Human Development, HD-24325; it has also benefited from a Centers grant awarded to the Carolina Population Center by NICHD. Erika Stone provided expert programming assistance. The authors thank the following for helpful comments on earlier drafts: Christine Bachrach, Elizabeth Cooksey, Glen Elder, Barbara Entwisle, John Modell, Elizabeth Stephen, Rebecca Sutterlin, Gray Swicegood, Jay Teachman, J. Richard Udry, participants in the Asian Family Workshop at the East-West Population Institute, participants in the population workshop at the Urban Institute, and participants in the demography workshop at the University of Chicago.

Notes

1. Some authors straddle these two conceptualizations. For example, Bumpass and Sweet (1989) argue: "There is no single answer to whether cohabitation is a late stage of courtship or an early stage of marriage."

2. The number of respondents in the fifth follow-up was intentionally reduced because of budget constraints. Only respondents who took part in the fifth follow-up are considered eligible for inclusion in the current study.

3. Here and throughout the remainder of the article, when we refer to singles or the never married, these are individuals who have also never cohabited.

4. In the case of jointly held activities, we give priority to schooling and then to work. Those in the military are grouped with the employed.

5. Unfortunately, the fifth follow-up did not include a set of questions that allows identification of the homemaker role. The first four follow-ups did; only one male in one of these follow-ups identified himself as a homemaker.

6. One might argue that for married couples home ownership is likely to be joint, and that for cohabiting couples only one of the spouses is likely to own the residence. While we have no evidence for such a pattern, if it did exist it would tend to make the cohabitors more similar to the never married, and thus the results in Table 7.6 might be somewhat exaggerated. Nevertheless, the differences in Table 7.6 are sufficiently striking that the general point about cohabitors being similar to the never married probably remains.

7. We do note, however, that panel data regarding drug and alcohol use following high school provide results congruent with those reported in this article (Bachman, O'Malley, and Johnston, 1984). Drug and alcohol use declines for those who marry, but it increases for those who cohabit and those who neither marry nor cohabit.

8. We hasten to add that we do not suggest it is emotionally or psychologically easy to end a cohabiting relationship. Indeed, the emotional costs may be quite similar to the costs of ending a marital relationship.

References

Albano, Michael S. J., and Donald C. Schiller. 1986. "Cohabitation without formal marriage in the USA," *Family Law* 16 (February): 43–47.

Arafat, I., and B. Yorburg. 1973. "On living together without marriage," *Journal of Sex Research* 9, no. 2:97–106.

Arnold, J. C. 1951. *The Marriage Law of England*. London: Staples Press.

Bachman, Jerald G., Patrick O'Malley, and Lloyd Johnston. 1984. "Drug use among adults: The impacts of role status and social environment," *Journal of Personality and Social Psychology* 47, no. 3:629–645.

Bachrach, Christine A. 1987. "Cohabitation and reproductive behavior in the U.S.," *Demography* 24, no. 4:623–637.

Bennett, Neil, Ann Blanc, and David Bloom. 1988. "Commitment and the modern union: Assessing the link between premarital cohabitation and subsequent marital stability," *American Sociological Review* 53, no. 1:127–138.

Bogue, Donald J. 1985. *The Population of the United States*. New York: Free Press.

Bumpass, Larry L. 1990. "What's happening to the family?: Interactions between demographic and institutional change," *Demography* 27, no. 4:483–498.

______, and James Sweet. 1989. "National estimates of cohabitation: Cohort levels and union stability," *Demography* 26, no. 4:615–625.

———, and Andrew Cherlin. 1989. "The role of cohabitation in declining rates of marriage," Madison: National Survey of Families and Households Working Paper No. 5.

Carlson, Elwood D. 1986. "Couples without children: Premarital cohabitation in France," in Kingsley Davis (ed.), *Contemporary Marriage: Comparative Perspectives on a Changing Institution*. New York: Russell Sage Foundation, pp. 113–130.

Clayton, Richard R., and Harwin L. Voss. 1977. "Shacking up: Cohabitation in the 1970s," *Journal of Marriage and the Family*, 37, no. 2:273–283.

Espenshade, Thomas J. 1985. "Marriage trends in America: Estimates, implications, and underlying causes," *Population and Development Review* 11, no. 2:193–245.

Goldscheider, Frances Kobrin, and Julie DaVanzo. 1985. "Living arrangements and the transition to adulthood," *Demography* 22, no. 4:545–563.

Gottlieb, Arthur H. 1983. "Living together: The need for a uniform nonmarital cohabitation act," *Adelphia Law Journal* 2:79–99.

Gwartney-Gibbs, Patricia A. 1986. "The institutionalization of premarital cohabitation: Estimates from marriage license applications, 1970 and 1980," *Journal of Marriage and the Family* 48, no. 2:423–434.

Hoem, Britta. 1988. "Early phases of family formation in contemporary Sweden," *Stockholm Research Reports in Demography*, No. 47, University of Stockholm.

Hoem, Jan M. 1985. "The impact of education on modern family initiation," *European Journal of Population* 2, no. 2:113–133.

———, and Bo Rennermalm. 1985. "Modern family initiation in Sweden: Experience of women born between 1936 and 1960." *European Journal of Population* 1, no. 1:81–112.

Hofferth, Sandra L., Joan R. Kahn, and Wendy H. Baldwin. 1987. "Premarital sexual activity among U.S. teenage women over the past three decades," *Family Planning Perspectives* 19, no. 2:46–53.

Houlbrooke, Ralph A. 1984. *The English Family 1450–1700*. London: Longman.

Jacobsen, Linda A., and Fred C. Pampel. 1989. "Cohabitation versus other non-family living arrangements: Changing determinants from 1960 to 1980," paper presented at the Annual Meeting of the Population Association of America, 30 March–1 April, Baltimore.

Jones, Jo Ann, et al. 1985. "Nonmarital childbearing: Diverging legal and social concerns," *Population and Development Review* 11, no. 4:677–693.

Kain, Edward L. 1984. "Surprising singles," *American Demographics* 6, no. 8:16–19, 39.

Lesthaeghe, Ron, and Johan Surkyn. 1988. "Cultural dynamics and economic theories of fertility change," *Population and Development Review* 14, no. 1:1–45.

Levine, David. 1977. *Family Formation in an Age of Nascent Capitalism*. New York: Academic Press.

Lyness, J. F., M. E. Lipetz, and K. E. Davis. 1972. "Living together: An alternative to marriage," *Journal of Marriage and the Family* 34, no. 2:305–311.

Macklin, Eleanor D. 1978. "Nonmarital heterosexual cohabitation," *Marriage and Family Review* 1, no. 2:1–12.

______. 1983. "Nonmarital heterosexual cohabitation: An overview," in Eleanor D. Macklin and Roger H. Rubin (eds.), *Contemporary Families and Alternative Life Styles*. Beverly Hills: Sage, pp. 49–72.

McLaughlin, Steven D., et al. 1988. *The Changing Lives of American Women*. Chapel Hill: University of North Carolina Press.

Mead, Margaret. 1968. "A continuing dialog on marriage: Why just 'living together' won't work," *Redbook* 130, no. 6:44–52, 119.

Modell, John. 1989. *Into One's Own*. Berkeley: University of California Press.

Riccobono, John, et al. 1981. "National longitudinal study: Base year (1972) through fourth follow-up (1979) data file users' manual," *National Longitudinal Study Sponsored Report Series*. RTI/0884/73-18S. 3 vols. Research Triangle Park, N.C.: Research Triangle Institute.

Riche, Martha Farnsworth. 1988. "The postmarital society," *American Demographics* 10, no. 11:22–26.

Rindfuss, Ronald R., Larry L. Bumpass, and Craig St. John. 1980. "Education and fertility: Implications for the roles women occupy," *American Sociological Review* 45, no. 3:431–447.

Rindfuss, Ronald R., S. Philip Morgan, and C. Gray Swicegood. 1988. *First Births in America: Changes in the Timing of Parenthood*. Berkeley: University of California Press.

Rindfuss, Ronald R., and Elizabeth Hervey Stephen. 1990. Marital noncohabitation: Separation does not make the heart grow fonder," *Journal of Marriage and the Family* 52, no. 1:259–270.

Rosen, Jeffrey S. 1984. "Taylor v. Polackwich: Property rights of unmarried cohabitants: From Marvin to equity," *Golden Gate University Law Review* 14, no. 3:745–767.

Ryder, Norman B. 1973. "Recent trends and group differences in fertility," in *Toward the End of Growth: Population in America*, ed. Charles F. Westoff. Englewood Cliffs, N.J.: Prentice-Hall, pp. 57–68.

Schoen, Robert. 1989. "Whither the family?" *Contemporary Sociology* 18, no. 4:618–620.

Siman de Betancourt, Aida Veronica. 1988. *Consensual Unions in Puerto Rico: Its Determinants and Fertility Consequences*, Ph.D. dissertation, University of North Carolina at Chapel Hill.

Spanier, Graham B. 1982. "Living together in the eighties," *American Demographics* 4, no. 10:17–19.

Sweet, James A., and Larry L. Bumpass. 1987. *American Families and Households*. New York: Russell Sage Foundation.

Tanfer, Koray. 1987. "Patterns of premarital cohabitation among never-married women in the United States," *Journal of Marriage and the Family* 49, no. 3:493–497.

Tourangeau, Roger, et al. 1987. *The National Longitudinal Study of the High School Class of 1972, Fifth Follow-up, Data File Users' Manual*. Washington, D.C.: Center for Education Statistics, U.S. Department of Education.

Trost, Jan. 1979. *Unmarried Cohabitation*. Vasteras, Sweden: International Library.

U.S. Department of Commerce. 1988. "Households, families, marital status and living arrangements: March, 1988," *Current Population Reports*, P-20, no. 432. Washington, D.C.: U.S. Bureau of the Census.

White, James M. 1987. "Premarital cohabitation and marital stability in Canada," *Journal of Marriage and the Family* 49, no. 3:641–647.

Willis, Robert J., and Robert T. Michael. 1988. "Innovation in family formation: Evidence on cohabitation in the U.S.," paper presented at the IUSSP Seminar on the Family, the Market, and the State in Aging Societies, Sendai City, Japan, September.

8

Young Adults' Views of Marriage, Cohabitation, and Family

James A. Sweet and Larry L. Bumpass

During the past quarter-century it has become very common for unmarried couples to live together. In earlier publications (Bumpass and Sweet 1989; Bumpass, Sweet, and Cherlin 1989) we have documented levels, trends, and differentials in nonmarital cohabitation and have discussed the relationship between increasing cohabitation and decreasing marriage rates. Nearly half of persons entering first marriages in the late 1980s have cohabited prior to marriage, most of them with the person they married. Well over half of persons who remarry live with a partner between their marriages. Nearly a quarter of all American adults have cohabited at some point in their lives. It is clear that what has been normatively proscribed in the recent past has now become the modal behavioral pattern.

The meaning of this trend toward increased cohabitation is not very clear. One issue that has been dealt with in the literature is the extent to which cohabitation is a new stage in the dating and courtship process—an advanced stage of going steady—and the extent to which it is an alternative form of marriage (Caldwell et al. 1988; Henslin 1979; Khoo 1986; Leridon and Villeneuve-Gokalp 1989; Wiersma 1983). We know that the majority of cohabiting persons expect to marry their partners (Bumpass, Sweet, and Cherlin 1989) and that about three-fifths of all first cohabiting relationships are ended by marriage rather than by premarital separation (Bumpass and Sweet 1989).

In designing the National Survey of Families and Households (Sweet, Bumpass, and Call 1988) we focused particular attention on cohabitation:

1. Nearly complete cohabitation histories were collected in conjunction with marriage histories.

2. Cohabitors were asked exactly the same questions concerning their relationship as married respondents.

TABLE 8.1 Distribution of Respondents Aged 19 to 35 by Marital Status and Cohabitation Experience (N = 5650)

	N	%
Never Married		
Previously cohabited	457	8.1
Currently cohabiting	326	5.8
Never cohabited	1158	20.5
Formerly Married		
Previously cohabited	452	8.0
Currently cohabiting	171	3.0
Never cohabited	323	5.7
Currently Married		
Ever cohabited		
married once	831	14.7
married > once	305	5.4
Never cohabited		
married once	1503	26.6
married > once	124	2.2
Total	5650	100.0

3. Unmarried respondents were asked about their marriage and cohabitation aspirations and expectations as well as their perceptions of marriage and nonmarital cohabitation.

4. All respondents were asked about their attitudes toward cohabitation as well as a variety of other family issues.

In this paper we report analyses of some of the subjective measures. Specifically, we will discuss (1) marriage plans and expectations of young adults; (2) their attitudes toward cohabitation; (3) their cohabitation plans and expectations; and (4) differentials in family attitudes among persons by marital and cohabitation status and experience.

We will focus attention on respondents who were aged 35 and younger when they were interviewed. These are the persons who entered adulthood after 1970 when the rate of cohabitation began to rapidly increase. They account for the great majority of all cohabitation experience reported by respondents in the NSFH. We will pay particular attention to differentials in attitudes and expectations by sex, race and ethnicity, parental status, and education (see Table 8.1).

Marriage Aspirations and Expectations

The great majority of young adults expect to marry. All but 5 percent of persons aged 35 and younger report that they have been married or expect to marry in the future.

Despite this, there appears to be a high level of acceptance of nonmarriage. One-quarter of young unmarried persons expressed disagreement with the statement "It is better for a person to get married than to go through life being single." One-third agreed and 40 percent neither agreed nor disagreed. Men are much more likely than women to agree that it is better to be married, but there is no difference between blacks and whites or between the never- and the formerly married.

This acceptance of nonmarriage might be taken as an expression of reservations of a significant minority about marriage as an institution. More likely it represents both the agreement with the idea that some people may be better off not marrying and an acceptance of individual choice in the matter. In the remainder of this section we will look at the marriage aspirations and expectations of unmarried persons aged 35 and younger. We will look separately at persons who are currently cohabiting and at those who are not.

Marriage Plans and Expectations of Current Cohabitors

Half of the cohabiting men and women report that they have "definite plans to marry," and an additional 28 percent think that they will eventually marry their partner. Thus about eight out of ten cohabitors expect to marry their partner. Of the minority who do not, about two-thirds do not expect to marry anyone and one-third expect to eventually marry someone other than their current partner (see Table 8.2).

There are differentials in the proportion expecting to marry. In a multiple classification analysis (data not shown) we find that persons who did not complete high school are considerably more likely to report that they have plans to marry their partner than those with more education. There is little difference among the higher-education groups. Blacks are more likely to plan to marry than whites. These two differentials are consistent with the idea that some people who might like to marry are temporarily cohabiting until their economic condition improves and they can afford to marry.

Cohabiting persons who have previously been married are about 22 points less likely to marry than those who have never been married, after controlling for other characteristics. Persons who have been living with their partner for three years or more are less likely to have definite plans to marry than those who have cohabited for a shorter period of time. There is very little difference between men and women and between persons who have had children (not necessarily in this relationship) and those who have not.

The partners of the respondent were also asked whether they expected to marry their partner. There was a fairly high level of consensus (see Table 8.3). Seventy percent of those who report definite plans to marry

Table 8.2 Distribution of Cohabitors by Marriage Plans

	Male	Female
Definite plans to marry	51.5	48.7
No definite plans, but think will eventually marry partner	28.1	28.3
Don't know if will marry partner	1.1	0.6
Don't think will ever marry partner but will marry someone eventually	6.7	7.3
Don't think will ever marry anyone	12.6	15.0
Total	100.0	100.0

their partner live with partners who report definite plans to marry them. An additional 14 percent have partners who think that they will marry them. Only about 6 percent have partners who do not expect to marry them or who do not know whether they will marry.

We asked persons who reported "definite plans to marry their partner" when they planned to get married. About one-third gave a month and a year and a few others gave a year. But nearly 60 percent reported that they simply did not know when they would get married. "Definite plans to marry" are often not very definite or precise, even when both partners agree that they exist.

We have included a "not ascertained" category in this table for cases where the partner completed the questionnaire but did not answer the marriage expectation question. To the extent that these respondents did not answer these questions because of uncertainty, they should be regarded as not agreeing with their partner. To the extent that their nonresponse was random, they should not be included in the table. Eight percent of the respondents who report definite plans to marry their partner have partners who did not answer the question regarding marriage expectations.

Table 8.3 Respondent's Plans and Expectations Regarding Marrying Partner by Partner's Plans and Expectations

	Marriage Plans of Primary Respondent			
Marriage Plans of Secondary Respondent	Definite Plan to Marry Partner	Thinks Will Marry Partner	Will Marry Someone Else	Will Never Marry Anyone
Definite Plans to Marry Partner	70.3	20.3	4.9	2.2
Thinks Will Marry Partner	14.5	44.9	47.9	17.1
Will Marry but Not Partner	2.7	10.4	15.8	6.2
Will Never Marry	2.8	16.0	11.6	60.3
Don't Know if Will Ever Marry	.0	.6	3.6	2.2
NA	8.3	7.7	16.2	12.0
Total	100.0	100.0	100.0	100.0
N (unweighted)	(230)	(134)	(22)	(79)

Of those reporting that they expect to marry their partners (but do not have definite plans to do so), two-thirds have partners who expect to marry them. Twenty percent have partners who report "definite plans" to marry.

Most of those who do not expect to marry their partner do not expect to marry anyone. Three-fifths of them have partners who similarly do not expect to marry anyone. These individuals who do not expect to marry their partner and do not expect to ever marry anyone else might be regarded as cohabitors who completely reject marriage, at least for themselves. They constitute only 14 percent of all cohabitors. Undoubtedly there are other

Table 8.4 Distribution of Responses to "I would like to get married someday." Nonmarried, Noncohabiting Respondents Age 35 and Younger, by Sex

	Females	Males
Strongly agree	50.8	47.1
Agree	30.7	37.8
Neither agree nor disagree	8.8	5.5
Disagree	4.1	4.7
Strongly disagree	5.6	5.0
Total	100.0	100.0

persons who reject marriage and are open to the possibility of cohabiting but are not currently doing so.

A final caveat concerning the marriage intentions of current cohabitors is in order. These numbers we report are based on currently extant cohabiting unions. This is not a representative sample of all unions that occur. Short-lived unions are underrepresented, and long-duration unions are overrepresented in such a sample. Over 80 percent of respondents who have lived with their partner for less than a year and about half of those who have lived with their partner for four or more years expect to marry them. Those who intend to marry tend to exit the population of cohabiting unions rather quickly (by marrying), leaving in the cross-section a disproportionate number of those who do not. The issue is further confused, however, by changes in orientations toward marriage that may occur over time within a cohabiting union.

Marriage Plans and Expectations of Noncohabiting Persons

Next we turn to the sample of nonmarried, noncohabiting respondents aged 35 and younger. Two different questions were asked pertaining to the respondent's marriage preferences and expectations. The first item asked for agreement or disagreement with the statement "I would like to get married someday." It was answered on a five-point scale from *strongly agree* to *strongly disagree.* The distributions of responses of men and women are shown in Table 8.4.

The other question was asked in the context of finding out about dating behavior and marriage plans and expectations. Those who were "going steady" were asked if they had definite marriage plans. If not, they were asked if they expected to marry their steady boy/girlfriend; if not, they were then asked if they ever expected to marry anyone. Those who were not "going steady" were simply asked if they ever expected to marry. If the respondents answered the questions literally, we have separate measures of marriage preferences and marriage expectations.

A multiple classification analysis of the percent agreeing or strongly agreeing with the statement "I would like to get married someday" and the percent expecting to marry is summarized in Table 8.5. The variation is reported in terms of deviations from the overall sample mean. Gross deviation is the crude or unadjusted deviation of the category mean from the sample mean. Net deviation is the category deviation from the mean after adjusting for the confounding effects of other characteristics included in the model. Note that the means of the two dependent variables are almost identical.

Generally the patterns of differentials are very similar for the two measures. We will summarize the patterns for the preference measure and note the places where the expectation measure gives different results.

Persons under the age of 25 are more likely to want to get married than those who are older. Beyond age 25 the proportion drops rapidly. When other characteristics (particularly prior marital and cohabitation status) are controlled, the differential persists but is attenuated somewhat. It would, of course, not be correct to interpret this age pattern as change that occurs as an unmarried individual ages, because there is attrition to marriage and movement into the unmarried population by separation and divorce (and the termination of cohabitation relationships).

Net of other characteristics there is no difference between men and women in the desire to marry. Men, however, are slightly less likely than women to expect to marry. Whites are about 6 points more likely than blacks to want to get married. This differential is not changed when other characteristics are controlled. The black-white differential in expectations is very similar. There is a sense in which these differentials between majority whites and blacks are quite large. However, considering the enormous difference in marriage behavior, it is surprising that there is not a larger difference in aspirations and expectations.

Never-married persons are much more likely to wish to marry than those who have previously been married. After controlling for other characteristics, the differentials in both expectations and desires are about 10 points. There is not much of a difference by whether the person has previously cohabited.

There is a positive relationship between education level and desire for and expectation of marriage. Persons who are currently enrolled in school are the most likely to want to and expect to marry. This makes sense, because they are currently in, and in most cases have for some time been

Table 8.5 Differentials in Marriage Desires and Expectations of Nonmarried, Noncohabiting Persons Age 35 and Younger

	I would like to get married someday (% agreeing or strongly agreeing)		Percent Expecting to get Married	
	Deviation		Deviation	
	Gross	Net	Gross	Net
19-20	6.4	4.7	5.1	3.5
21-22	4.5	2.2	9.0	6.1
23-24	3.8	3.4	4.7	3.6
25-29	-3.8	-3.0	-2.5	-1.7
30-35	-12.7	-8.5	-16.2	-11.4
Sex				
male	1.4	.1	1.0	-1.1
female	-1.7	-.1	-1.2	1.3
Race/ethnicity				
black	-5.0	-4.2	-8.7	-4.6
non-hispanic white	1.0	0.7	2.2	.9
other	1.0	1.6	-.1	1.7
Marital/cohabitation status				
Never married				
never cohabited	3.9	2.2	4.9	1.6
ever cohabited	-.7	1.8	-1.4	2.2
Formerly married				
never cohabited	-18.8	-13.4	-24.5	-13.0
ever cohabited	-15.9	-10.7	-17.4	-6.9
Education				
<12	-4.4	-3.7	-11.3	-8.1
12	-2.7	-3.0	-1.7	-2.5
enrolled in college	6.4	2.1	9.5	5.5
13-15 (not enrolled)	-.2	2.0	-2.6	-.7
enrolled post-college	2.7	6.2	9.1	11.5
16+ (not enrolled)	-1.6	-.1	4.3	3.3
Children ever borne/fathered				
No	2.8	-.1	4.8	1.6
Yes				
none living w/R	-12.4	-2.1	-21.4	-8.8
some living w/R	-10.7	1.3	-16.7	-5.0
Employment				
part-time	.6	-.2	-.7	-1.6
full-time	-0.9	-.0	1.2	1.9
other	1.6	0.2	-2.3	-3.2
Mean	83.4		81.1	

in, a status that is typically completed before marriage. Ceteris paribus, persons who are not enrolled, especially those with less than a college education, have probably spent more time "in the marriage market," and those that remain unmarried are more likely to have personal characteristics that are impediments to marriage.

Similarly, persons who have never borne or fathered a child are much more likely to want to and expect to marry than those who have. The differential in desire to marry is, however, associated with prior marital status and age and virtually disappears when these other characteristics are controlled. However, after we control for the other characteristics, those persons who have had children are considerably less likely to expect to marry.

We include a measure of current employment status in the analysis as a crude indicator of the attachment to the work force and the economic viability of a potential marriage. As it turns out, persons who work full time are no more likely to want to marry but slightly more likely to expect to marry than those who do not. Obviously, this is a very crude measure of the economic viability of marriage. We would like to expand this analysis to assess the effects of additional dimensions of current economic status as well as economic prospects on marriage desires and expectations. Analyses would have to be done separately for men and women. Unfortunately, apart from education level and race and ethnicity, no good measures of the future economic prospects of young adults exist.

Ninety-two percent of persons who indicated that they "would like to get married someday" reported that they expected to get married. Four subgroups had lower-than-average proportions expecting to marry—older persons (aged 30–35), formerly married persons, persons who did not complete high school, and blacks. For each of these groups, 80–85 percent of those who wanted to marry expected to marry. For other groups the percentage is 93–96 percent (data not shown).

Approval or Disapproval of Cohabitation

We asked NSFH respondents a number of attitudinal items relating to cohabitation and marriage in an effort to better understand the current high level of cohabitation and the recent decline in marriage rates. Respondents were asked to indicate their approval or disapproval of the following situations on a five-point scale ranging from *strongly agree* to *strongly disagree:*

> "It is all right for an unmarried couple to live together as long as they have plans to marry."

Table 8.6 Distribution of Responses to Questions Regarding Approval of Cohabitation in Two Situations

	Couple Has No Interest in Marrying	Couple Has Plans to Marry
Strongly Agree	8.2	5.7
Agree	28.0	24.3
Neither Agree nor Disagree	31.3	41.7
Disagree	18.1	16.4
Strongly Disagree	14.4	11.9
Total	100.0	100.0
	(5055)	(5055)

"It is all right for an unmarried couple to live together even if they have no interest in considering marriage."

These two separate items were included because we thought that respondents might differentiate their approval of cohabitation depending on the circumstances. We expected that cohabitation would be considerably more acceptable as a step in the process of getting married than it would in the absence of an interest in marrying. The data do not support this. See Table 8.6 for the distribution of responses to each of these questions.

Thirty-six percent of respondents agreed that it was all right for an unmarried couple to cohabit even if they have no interest in considering marriage, but only 30 percent approved of cohabitation by a couple with plans to marry. Note that there is also more *dis*approval of cohabitation when the couple has no interest in marriage: 32 versus 28 percent. The neutral category is, therefore, larger for the situation where there are plans to marry. (A discussion and analysis of patterns of response to these items is presented in Sweet 1989.) We have created a composite measure of acceptance of cohabitation from the two items, in which a person is regarded as approving of cohabitation if he or she agrees with either or both of the two items.

Table 8.7 shows the results of a multiple classification analysis predicting the percent of the subgroup that expressed approval. This analysis shows that:

1. Age differences are small. There is no difference by age in approval of cohabitation when there is no interest in marriage. The highest level of approval when there are plans for marriage is found for 19–20-year-olds, and the lowest level for those aged 30–35. (In an analysis of variation in approval of cohabitation in the entire population, the level of approval drops with age after about age 35.)

2. Men are about 6 points more likely to approve than women, under both conditions.

3. There is no difference between blacks and whites in approval of cohabitation when there are plans to marry; however, blacks are about 9 points less likely to approve when there is no interest in marriage.

4. Not surprisingly, prior cohabitation experience is associated with a higher level of approval of cohabitation; the differential is larger when the couple has no interest in marriage than when there are plans to marry. Similarly, currently married persons are more likely to approve of cohabitation if they have previously cohabited than if they have not; there is no difference between those in first- and higher-order marriages. Given cohabitation status, formerly married persons are less likely to approve of cohabitation when there are plans to marry, but there is little difference if there is no interest in marriage.

5. High-school dropouts are most likely to approve when there are plans for marriage; those with college education and students are most likely to approve when there is no interest in marrying.

6. There is no difference in approval of cohabitation under either condition by parental status.

The preceding analysis concerns the acceptability of cohabitation in general. Young unmarried respondents were also asked questions about acceptability of cohabitation for themselves.

> "It would be all right for me to live with someone without being married . . .
>
> - even if we had no interest in considering marriage."
> - to find out if we were compatible for marriage."
> - if we were planning to get married."

The distributions of responses to these items are shown in Table 8.8.

Thirty-one percent think that cohabitation would be acceptable for themselves if they had no interest in marriage; 52 percent to see if they were compatible for marriage; and 58 percent if they were planning marriage. Unlike the previous question series, the acceptability of cohabitation for

Table 8.7 Differentials in Approval of Cohabitation

	Composite Measure			No Interest in Marriage	Plans to Marry
	N	Gross	Net	Net	Net
Age					
19-20	740	5.6	5.7	1.9	7.2
21-22	532	-1.3	-2.7	-3.2	-1.0
23-24	600	4.9	3.1	-.1	1.9
25-29	1389	-2.0	-1.9	-1.5	-.1
30-35	1739	-2.1	-1.2	1.4	-3.3
Sex					
Male	2452	3.5	2.8	3.0	2.3
Female	2548	-3.3	-2.7	-2.9	-2.2
Race/ethnicity					
Black	617	-4.5	-6.5	-7.8	-.4
Non-hispanic White	3813	-.1	.2	1.4	-1.4
Mexican American	276	7.7	8.1	-4.0	10.0
Other	292	2.4	3.2	-.2	9.6
Marital Status/Cohab Experience					
Never Married					
Prev Cohab	341	19.9	20.0	15.2	11.4
Current Cohab	250	25.9	25.6	23.6	16.5
Never Cohab	1577	-1.6	-4.3	-3.6	-2.8
Currently Married					
Married Once					
Prev Cohab	680	17.7	18.6	12.8	11.3
Never Cohab	1372	-19.6	-18.2	-14.9	-9.3
Married >1					
Prev Cohab	221	11.7	13.4	12.9	5.0
Never Cohab	90	-21.3	-18.2	-15.6	-10.4
Formerly Married					
Prev Cohab	210	14.9	17.6	15.2	6.8
Current Cohab	110	23.4	25.3	28.1	9.0
Never Cohab	148	-15.1	-13.2	-8.8	-7.6
Education					
<12	627	8.1	3.2	-.7	7.0
12	1873	-3.2	-2.4	-1.6	-2.0
13-15	991	-1.4	-1.0	-.8	-1.1
16	498	-1.7	2.8	3.2	1.1
17+	299	-.2	.0	1.5	-3.0
Currently Enrolled	712	4.6	3.0	3.2	1.1
Ever Borne/Fathered Child					
No	2566	3.4	.5	-.4	.6
Yes	2433	-3.6	-.5	.4	-.6
Mean		51.3		36.2	29.2

Table 8.8 Distributions of Approval of Cohabitation Under Various Conditions for Nonmarried, Noncohabiting Persons Age 35 and Younger

	No Interest in Marriage	See if Compatible	Planning Marriage
Strongly agree	8.5	15.1	20.6
Agree	22.2	36.0	37.1
Neither agree nor disagree	18.9	18.8	16.8
Disagree	23.7	13.9	10.8
Strongly disagree	26.6	16.1	14.7
Total	100.0	100.0	100.0

oneself exhibits the expected pattern of a higher level of acceptability when there are plans to marry than when there are not. Clearly, the "testing compatibility" condition is much more similar to the planning marriage condition than to situations where there is no interest in marriage.

The differentials are similar to those reported earlier for the items relating to approval of cohabitation in general, with young people, men, majority whites, persons with cohabitation experience, college-educated persons, and parents more favorable to cohabitation. The age, race, and parental status differentials are larger for the "if plans to marry" and "test compatibility" items than for the "no interest in marriage" item.

One additional item gives a slightly different perspective on the issue. Young, unmarried adults were asked a series of questions, with the lead-in "Here are some reasons why a person might NOT want to live with someone of the opposite sex without being married. Please circle how important each reason is to you."

One of the items was "it is morally wrong." Note that this question was not Do you think cohabitation is morally wrong? Instead the question was, in effect, How important is this as a reason to not cohabit? However, it would appear that if a person says "morally wrong" is a very important reason for not cohabiting, they must think that cohabitation is morally wrong. However, a person might feel that cohabitation is morally wrong but that this is not important to them. It does, however, seem to be a reasonably good indicator of the respondent's moral assessment of cohabitation.

The distributions of responses of unmarried noncohabiting men and women to this item were

	Males	Females
1-Not at all important	31.9	27.8
2	11.8	10.6
3	9.8	8.4
4	14.6	14.5
5	8.7	8.0
6	6.4	8.3
7-Very important	16.9	22.4
Total	100.0	100.0

The modal response was "not at all important," which was given by about three respondents in ten. About one in five said it was very important. About half of the respondents gave an answer of "4" or higher. This seems to mean that as many as half of young unmarried noncohabiting adults think that cohabitation is in some sense morally problematic. Women were more likely than men and blacks were more likely than majority whites to feel this way. Three-fifths of persons who disagreed that they "would like to live with someone before getting married" said that the fact that it is morally wrong is an important reason for not cohabiting. (Current cohabitors were also asked this question. One-quarter of them appeared to regard cohabitation as morally problematic.)

Cohabitation Aspirations and Expectations

Respondents were asked two questions regarding their cohabitation desires and expectations. The first question asked whether they agreed or disagreed with the statement "I would like to live with someone before getting married." It was coded on a five-point scale from *strongly agree* to *strongly disagree*. The question was not specific about living with the person to be married or living with any partner. A quarter of the women and 40 percent of the men said that they would like to cohabit. The second question asked about the likelihood that the respondent would live with someone to whom they were not married, on a four-point scale: *very likely*, *likely*, *unlikely*, and *very unlikely*. One-quarter of young unmarried adults reported that they expected to live at some time with a partner to whom they were not married.

Table 8.9 reports the results of a multiple classification analysis of these measures of cohabitation desires and expectations. Young people tend to be more likely to wish to cohabit than older persons, although the differences are rather small and the relationship is not monotonic. The relationship is stronger for the expectations measure than for the preferences measure.

Table 8.9 Differentials in Cohabitation Desires and Expectations of Nonmarried, Noncohabiting Persons Age 35 and Younger

	I would like to live with someone before getting married (% agreeing or strongly agreeing)		% who think it is likely or very likely that they will cohabit	
	Gross	Net	Gross	Net
Age				
19-20	-1.8	2.8	-2.7	1.5
20-22	-2.6	.0	3.8	6.4
23-24	-2.2	-1.4	1.1	2.0
25-29	4.8	1.2	-.3	-3.2
30-35	1.4	-4.4	.0	-5.8
Sex				
male	5.7	6.6	3.5	2.9
female	-6.9	-8.0	-4.1	-3.4
Race/ethnicity				
black	-5.9	-6.8	-2.2	-.7
non-hispanic white	2.1	2.4	-1.0	-1.4
other	-3.8	-4.0	8.6	8.7
Marital/cohabitation status				
never married				
never cohabited	-5.9	-6.4	-4.9	-6.8
ever cohabited	20.9	20.3	17.8	19.0
formerly married				
never cohabited	-7.3	-4.0	-9.4	-2.8
ever cohabited	15.4	18.1	14.6	22.1
Education				
<12	5.7	2.5	5.6	2.5
12	-1.9	-1.5	-.6	-.2
enrolled in college	-3.6	-2.3	-1.5	-.1
13-15 (not enrolled)	3.5	3.0	.6	-.3
enrolled post college	2.7	1.1	3.2	3.3
16+ (not enrolled)	-6.4	-3.5	-6.6	-3.6
Children ever borne or fathered				
none	-1.2	-.6	-.7	.8
some	4.7	2.5	2.4	-3.2
Employment				
part-time	-2.3	-1.4	-.4	.8
full-time	-.1	-1.4	.3	-.4
Not in labor force	2.3	4.6	-.4	.2
Mean	35.1		44.1	

Men are 14 points more likely to wish to cohabit and 8 points more likely to expect to cohabit than women. Majority whites are about 10 points more likely than blacks to wish to or expect to cohabit.

Persons who have cohabited in the past are most likely to wish to and to expect to cohabit in the future. Given prior cohabitation experience, there is little difference between never- and previously married persons. The differential by whether or not the person has had a child is quite small. Those who have had a child are 2 points more likely to wish to but 3 points less likely to expect to cohabit.

The pattern by education is not very clear and consistent. High-school dropouts (and college dropouts) are most likely to wish to cohabit; college students and college graduates are least likely.

Persons who are not working are more likely to want to cohabit than those who are working. If this measure taps the labor-market position of young adults, this differential, net of other characteristics, may be a reflection of the realization of those who are not working that they may not be in a position to marry. However, there is no difference in cohabitation expectations by work status.

Differentials in Family Attitudes by Cohabitation Status and Experience

One issue that has received attention in the literature is the degree to which the behavior of persons who are currently cohabiting or who have cohabited in the past is different from that of persons who have not cohabited. It is easy to document differences, but it is impossible with a single cross-section survey to distinguish between the effects of selectivity on cohabitation and the effects of the experience of cohabitation.

For example, what is the effect of having cohabited on subsequent marital stability? One might think that couples who are unsuitable for each other may find that out while cohabiting and never get married. This might suggest that, other things equal, couples who cohabit before they get married would have a lower rate of marital disruption than those that did not. The data suggest that this is not the case. Persons who cohabited prior to first marriage have a much higher rate of marital disruption than those who did not. If they lived only with their spouse, the rate is 49 percent higher than for those who did not cohabit; if they lived with someone other than their first spouse, the rate is 84 percent higher. These differentials are net of many other characteristics known to be associated with marital disruption (Balakrishnan et al. 1987; Bennett, Blanc, and Bloom 1988; Booth and Johnson 1988; Bumpass and Sweet 1989; Colella and Thomson 1990; Hall 1990). There are at least two alternative explanations for this result. First, there may be something about living together prior to marriage that affects the survival chances of the marriage. Perhaps expectations about the relationship or behavior patterns develop during the cohabitation period that are not conducive to the long-term survival of the relationship. (These would have to be behavior patterns or expectations that would not develop if the couple were married.) We know of no empirical study that gives an indication of what these expectations or behavior patterns might be. Note that they would have to be something that is statistically independent of the structural characteristics that are controlled in the analysis—age, race and ethnicity, education, religious preference, activities early in marriage, and a variety of other characteristics.

The second possibility is that couples who choose to cohabit before getting married are selected on unmeasured characteristics that are not conducive to the long-term survival of marriage. That is to say that these couples would have a higher risk of marital instability even in the absence of cohabitation. They may have a value system that does not place a high priority on relationship stability, or personality characteristics that are not conducive to cultivating and maintaining strong, enduring relationships. Again, we know of no study that has clearly identified such characteristics by showing that when they are present, the effect of cohabitation prior to marriage on marital instability is attenuated. Again such characteristics would have to be independent of the measured characteristics that are already included in the model. There is some interesting evidence that bears on this relationship. In a study of Canadian marriages, Hall (1990) claims that "secular individualism" accounts for the higher disruption rates of persons with cohabitation experience. However, the secular individualism indicators are measured after the experiences of both premarital cohabitation and marital disruption.

In the NSFH we have many measures of family attitudes and opinions. We can compare these attitudes and opinions between persons who have cohabited and those who have not. If, however, we find that persons who have cohabitation experience have a higher level of approval of divorce or more egalitarian sex-role attitudes, we cannot say unambiguously that this would have been true if we had been able to compare the attitudes before they cohabited. It may be that the experience of cohabitation has produced the differential. Nonetheless, it may be suggestive to compare differentials in views of marriage, divorce, sex roles, and other family attitudes by cohabitation experience.

We have run regressions predicting each of a wide range of family-attitude measures by demographic and other structural characteristics of young adults. Two different sets of regressions have been run, each classifying cohabitation status and experience in two different ways.

1. Whether the person has ever cohabited is included in the analysis additively with marital status classified in the conventional way: married, separated, divorced, and never married.

2. A six-category cross-classification of whether the person has ever cohabited is included according to a three-category marital status variable: currently married, formerly married, and never married. This permits the identification of interactions between current marital status and cohabitation experience.

The effects of both of these classifications of marriage-cohabitation status and experience on a variety of family-attitude items are summarized in Table 8.10.

Divorce. Persons with cohabitation experience are 5 points more likely to disagree that marriage is for a lifetime than those without. They are 9 points more likely to approve of divorce for an unhappily married couple with a preschool-age child. These differentials by cohabitation experience are found for never-married and currently married persons but not for the formerly married.

Sexuality. Persons who have ever cohabited are 6 points more likely to agree that a married person ought to overlook occasional sexual unfaithfulness of their spouse. However, even among those with cohabitation experience, only 16 percent agree compared to 10 percent for those who have never cohabited. The differential by cohabitation experience is largest (11 points) for the never married and smallest (3 points) for the currently married.

Similarly, persons who have cohabitation experience are 16 points more likely to approve of premarital sex for 18-year-olds. This differential is found for all marital status groups but is smallest for the never married.

Division of Household Labor and Sex Roles. There is virtually no difference by marital or cohabitation status or experience in agreement with the statement that when both spouses work full time, they should share household tasks equally. Approximately 90 percent of all groups agree with this statement. (This is not to say that they behave this way.)

Persons with cohabitation experience are 8 points less likely to agree that it is better if the man earns the living and the woman cares for the home and family. This differential is largest (11 points) for the currently married and smallest (2 points) for the formerly married. It is interesting that formerly married persons are more likely than currently or never-married persons to agree with this statement.

Having Children. There is no difference by cohabitation experience in agreement with the statement that it is better to have children than to go through life childless. However, persons with cohabitation experience are 10 points more likely to approve of an unmarried woman having a child. This differential is about the same for all marital statuses.

Table 8.10 Net Effects of Current Marital Status and Ever Having Cohabited on Marriage and Family Attitudes—Percent Agreeing or Approving

		Model 1 Ever Cohabited		Model 2					
				Curr Marr		Form Marr		Never Marr	
	Mean	No	Yes	Never Cohab	Ever Cohab	Never Cohab	Ever Cohab	Never Cohab	Ever Cohab
Divorce Items:									
Marriage is a lifetime relationship and should never be ended except under extreme circumstances	71.8	2.0	-3.4	7.2	0.7	-16.9	-19.2	0.2	-4.6
A couple with an unhappy marriage getting a divorce if their youngest child is under age 5	36.2	-3.3	5.7	-8.3	4.1	13.9	15.2	-1.1	5.3
Marriage Items:									
It is better for a person to get married than to go through life being single	36.2	0.7	-1.2	6.2	0.9	-3.7	-6.0	-3.6	-2.9
In a successful marriage, the partners must have freedom to do what they want individually	68.0	-2.9	5.2	-5.4	3.3	-9.1	5.0	0.6	6.2
Parenthood Items:									
It's better for a person to have a child than to go through life childless	32.6	0.1	0.1	2.2	0.8	-5.7	-2.6	-1.8	0.2
Women who have a child without getting married	21.8	-3.9	6.8	-10.0	1.1	-0.6	8.3	2.2	12.7

Table 8.10 *(Continued)*

		Model 1 Ever Cohabited		Model 2 Curr Marr		Form Marr		Never Marr	
	Mean	No	Yes	Never Cohab	Ever Cohab	Never Cohab	Ever Cohab	Never Cohab	Ever Cohab
Sexuality Items:									
Married couples ought to overlook isolated occasions of sexual unfaithfulness	11.9	-2.3	3.8	-0.8	2.5	-6.3	-0.8	-1.0	11.2
It is all right for unmarried 18-year-olds to have sexual relations if they have strong affection for each other	34.1	-5.4	9.6	-9.4	6.9	-7.4	11.5	-1.0	11.2
Sex Role Items:									
It is much better for everyone if the man earns the main living and the woman takes care of the home and family	33.8	3.1	-5.4	6.6	-4.8	-6.2	-7.8	0.9	-5.5
Parents should encourage just as much independence in their daughters as in their sons	83.3	-1.6	2.8	-1.8	4.2	-4.5	3.2	-1.1	0.3
If a husband and a wife both work full-time, they should share household tasks equally	88.5	0.6	-1.0	-0.2	-1.0	2.2	0.7	1.0	-1.7
Maternal Employment Items:									
Preschool children are likely to suffer if their mother is employed	35.8	2.2	-3.8	3.7	-2.9	-6.0	-6.0	1.8	-4.8

	Mean	Model 1 Ever Cohabited		Model 2 Curr Marr		Form Marr		Never Marr	
		No	Yes	Never Cohab	Ever Cohab	Never Cohab	Ever Cohab	Never Cohab	Ever Cohab
Children under 3 being cared for all day in a daycare center	21.3	1.3	2.3	-3.4	2.8	3.9	5.3	-0.2	0.5
Mothers who work full-time when their youngest child is under age 5	30.0	-2.1	3.6	-2.0	5.0	1.7	4.0	-2.8	2.0

Model 1 also includes age, sex, education, race/ethnicity, employment status, and current marital status.

Model 2 also includes age, sex, education, race/ethnicity, and employment status.

Working Mothers. Persons with cohabitation experience are more likely to approve of mothers of preschoolers working full time (6 points), more likely to approve of a child under three being cared for all day in a day-care center (4 points), and less likely to feel that preschool children suffer if their mother is employed (6 points). These differentials are smaller for formerly married persons than for the currently or never married.

Marriage. Persons with cohabitation experience are slightly less likely to agree that it is better to be married than to go through life being single. This differential is found primarily among the currently married.

They are also 8 points more likely to agree with the statement that in a successful marriage the partners should have the freedom to do what they want individually. Although formerly married persons are least likely to agree with this statement, the differential between those with cohabitation experience and those without is greatest for the formerly married (14 points).

Differentials by Cohabitation Desires and Expectations

Additional evidence on selectivity of persons who cohabit with respect to orientations toward marriage, sex roles, and other family issues is presented in Table 8.11. Here we select never-married persons under the age of 36 and predict the same set of family variables as in the previous analysis. Included among the predictor variables in the left panel of the table is whether the person "wants to cohabit" with a partner in the future and in the right panel whether the person expects to do so. Those who want or expect to cohabit are much more likely to accept divorce, less likely to believe that "it is better to be married than to go through life being single," much more likely to approve of an unmarried woman having a child and of premarital sexual relations for 18-year-olds, and more likely to have egalitarian sex-role attitudes and to approve of maternal employment. Thus if the desire and expectation of premarital cohabitation is reflective of actual experience of cohabitation, there is considerable selectivity.

Conclusions

In this chapter we have examined a number of the more subjective aspects of cohabitation in the contemporary United States. What can we conclude from these analyses?

1. The high level of cohabitation in the United States does not appear to be associated with a rejection of marriage.

a. Only a small minority of young adults have never married and do not expect to marry at some point in their lives.

Table 8.11 Net Effects of Cohabitation Plans and Expectations on Marriage and Family Attitudes: Never Married Respondents Under Age 36—Percent Agreeing or Approving (model also includes age, sex, education, race and ethnicity, and prior cohabitation experience)

	Want to Cohabit			Expect to Cohabit		
	No	Yes	NA	No	Yes	NA
Divorce Items:						
Marriage is a lifetime relationship and should never be ended except under extreme circumstances.	11.1	-6.8	.6	4.8	-6.0	-3.3
A couple with an unhappy marriage getting a divorce if their youngest child is under age 5.	-5.2	2.6	1.7	-2.2	5.4	-4.9
Marriage Items:						
It is better for a person to get married than to go through life being single.	4.0	-1.8	-1.8	-.6	-.9	4.4
In a successful marriage, the partners must have freedom to do what they want individually.	-.1	-.9	2.8	-2.2	2.8	1.3
Parenthood Items:						
It's better for a person to have a child than to go through life childless.	-2.1	-.4	4.8	0.2	-.7	1.6
Women who have a child without getting married.	-6.7	4.2	-.5	-4.4	7.0	-0.7
Sexuality Items:						
Married couples ought to overlook isolated occasions of sexual unfaithfulness.	-3.0	1.0	2.1	-1.0	0.1	3.1
It is all right for unmarried 18-year olds to have sexual relations if they have strong affection for each other.	-17.6	10.4	.0	-9.7	14.2	1.6

Table 8.11 *(Continued)*

	Want to Cohabit			Expect to Cohabit		
	No	Yes	NA	No	Yes	NA
Sex Role Items:						
It is much better for everyone if the man earns the main living and the woman takes care of the home and family.	6.7	-6.0	6.1	2.9	-2.6	-4.7
Parents should encourage just as much independence in their daughters as in their sons.	-1.6	-.5	4.4	-.5	5.6	-11.5
If a husband and a wife both work full-time, they should share household tasks equally.	-1.0	-.8	4.2	-.2	.8	-1.0
Maternal Employment Items:						
Preschool children are likely to suffer if their mother is employed.	5.8	-6.6	9.4	5.9	-4.1	-12.1
Children under 3 being cared for all day in a daycare center	-3.5	2.8	-2.2	-2.3	2.1	3.4
Mothers who work full-time when their youngest child is under age 5	-4.6	2.9	-.3	.5	1.4	-5.1

b. Eighty percent of currently cohabiting persons expect to marry their current partner, and there is a high degree of consensus between partners. The majority of those who do not expect to marry their partners do not expect to marry anyone.

c. Among those who are neither currently married nor cohabiting, half strongly agree and an additional third agree that they "would like to get married someday." Only about 10 percent disagree with this statement. There is a similarly high level of expectation of marrying—about 80 percent.

d. There are some differentials in marriage aspirations and expectations. Older persons (those in their 30s), formerly married persons, blacks, persons who have had children, and persons with a high-school education or less are less likely than average to desire to marry.

e. There is some indication that some people (particularly blacks, high-school dropouts, formerly married persons, and those in their 30s) who wish to marry do not feel that they will actually do so. These people who expect to have their marriage aspirations frustrated are, however, only a small minority of each of the subgroups. There is no difference between men and women.

2. There is fairly widespread approval of nonmarital cohabitation among young people. These attitudes, however, seem to be quite complex.

a. In response to general questions concerning cohabitation, half of young adults expressed approval of cohabitation either for a couple planning marriage or for a couple with no interest in marriage.

b. There is not a higher level of approval of cohabitation "if the couple has definite plans to marry" than if they have "no interest in marrying." In fact, the opposite is true. In an earlier publication, we interpreted this as perhaps resulting from some persons feeling that when marriage is planned and feasible, it is best to get married (or, perhaps, it is foolish not to get married). However, for persons who are not currently in the marriage market, cohabitation is acceptable. We also suggested the possibility that some respondents may have misinterpreted the question as approval of cohabitation *only* when there are definite plans to marry.

c. Among young adults, differentials in approval of cohabitation are relatively small, especially when cohabitation experience is taken into account. Men, majority whites, and (when there are plans to marry) persons who did not complete high school have higher-than-average levels of approval.

d. Having said that there is fairly widespread acceptance, there is also a considerable amount of ambivalence about cohabitation. About one-quarter of unmarried young adults seem to see cohabitation as morally wrong, and an additional quarter seem to have some moral qualms about it.

e. Unmarried persons were asked to respond to an additional series of items about the acceptability of cohabitation *for themselves*. Cohabitation is much more personally acceptable if it is in the context of considering marriage than when there is no interest in marriage. In fact, there is nearly as high a degree of acceptability as a means of testing the couple's compatibility for marriage as there is if the couple has marriage plans.

3. There is some evidence that cohabitation serves as an alternative to marriage when marriage is not perceived as feasible. This evidence is, however, quite weak.

a. Among cohabiting couples who report having "definite plans" to marry, the majority cannot specify a month and year. Most simply say that they do not know when they will marry. This suggests that there may be some fairly specific impediment to marriage; our hunch is that the impediment is often primarily economic uncertainty.

b. There is an interesting pattern of differences in approval of cohabitation in general and for the person himself/herself. Groups that are likely to be facing the greatest economic uncertainty (blacks and those with 12 years of education or less) are most likely to approve of cohabitation when there are plans to marry and least likely to approve when there are not. This is consistent with the view that marriage is the preferred state, but when it is not feasible, cohabitation is acceptable (even though it may not be acceptable in the absence of marriage plans).

c. There is an additional legal aspect to this that we have not previously considered. One cohabiting person in eight reports his/her current marital status as "separated." These individuals are legally prohibited from marrying. We have no way of knowing the extent to which they are proceeding to become divorced so that they can marry their partner.

4. There are substantial differences in attitudes and opinions regarding family matters by whether or not a person has had cohabitation experience. Those who have cohabited have less traditional family attitudes than those who have not. They are more likely to approve of divorce, approve of premarital sex, be forgiving of sexual unfaithfulness, approve of unmarried women having children, and believe that married persons need individual freedom. In addition, they are more likely to approve of mothers of preschool-age children working full time and less likely to disapprove of young children being cared for in day-care centers. They also seem to have more egalitarian sex-role attitudes. There is no difference, however, in agreement with the statements that it is better to be married and that it is better to have children. Some of these attitudes may be affected by the experience of having cohabited. However, we believe that it is more likely that those persons with less traditional views of marriage and family are more likely to cohabit. In particular, it does not seem plausible to believe that the attitudes toward maternal employment would have been affected by the experience of having cohabited.

Perhaps the strongest evidence of selectivity is the finding that never-married persons who desire to and expect to cohabit in the future are much more accepting of divorce, less likely to think that it is "better to be married," and more likely to have egalitarian sex-role attitudes than those who do not. Note, however, that the degree of selectivity is probably changing over time. It is likely that there is now less selectivity about cohabitation by persons with nontraditional family views than there was a decade or two ago when premarital cohabitation was much less common and much less accepted. However, if recent trends continue and the proportion with cohabitation experience before first marriage increases to three-quarters or more as in northern Europe, then selectivity may again become important as only those with the most traditional orientations do not experience cohabitation.

The data collected in the NSFH provide considerable perspective on current orientations toward cohabitation and marriage. The planned five-year follow-up interview will allow us to go beyond these cross-sectional relationships. For example, we will be able to observe differential cohabitation rates by prior attitudes and expectations, differential marriage rates by marriage plans of cohabiting partners (and by family orientations more generally), and the extent to which differing value orientations of cohabitors and noncohabitors account for the higher marital disruption rates of the former. The high prevalence of cohabitation makes it essential that we clarify the linkages between cohabitation and marriage and the implications of these for how we conduct demographic research on marriage and for our conceptual understanding of union formation and dissolution.

Acknowledgments

The National Survey of Families and Households was funded by grant HD 21009 from the Center for Population Research of the National Institute of Child Health and Human Development, and the analysis was supported under HD 22433, using facilities provided under HD 05876.

References

Balakrishnan, T. R., K. Vaninadha Rao, Evelyne Lapierre-Adamcyk, and Karol J. Krotki. 1987. "A Hazard Model Analysis of the Covariates of Marriage Dissolution in Canada." Demography 24(3):395–406.

Bennett, Neil G., Ann Klimas Blanc, and David E. Bloom. 1988. "Commitment and the Modern Union: Assessing the Link between Premarital Cohabitation and Subsequent Marital Stability." American Sociological Review 53(1):127–138.

Booth, Alan, and David Johnson. 1988. "Premarital Cohabitation and Marital Success." Journal of Family Issues 9(2):255–272.

Bumpass, Larry, and James Sweet. 1989. "National Estimates of Cohabitation: Cohort Levels and Union Stability." Demography 26(4):615–625. Also NSFH Working Paper No. 2, National Survey of Families and Households, University of Wisconsin, Madison.

Bumpass, Larry, James Sweet, and Andrew Cherlin. 1989. "The Role of Cohabitation in Declining Rates of Marriage." NSFH Working Paper No. 5, National Survey of Families and Households, University of Wisconsin, Madison.

Burch, T. K. 1989. "Common-Law Unions in Canada: A Portrait from the 1984 Family History Survey." In J. Legare, T. R. Balakrishnan and Roderic Beaujot (eds.), *The Family in Crisis: A Population Crisis?* Ottawa: Lowe-Martin Company.

Caldwell, J. C., Pat Caldwell, M. D. Bracher, and Gigi Santow. 1988. "The Contemporary Marriage and Fertility Revolutions in the West." Australian Family Project Working Paper No. 3, Research School of Social Sciences, The Australian National University, Canberra.

Carlson, E. 1985. "Couples Without Children: Premarital Cohabitation in France." In Kingsley Davis and A. Grossbard-Shechtman (eds.), *Contemporary Marriage: Comparative Perspectives on a Changing Institution*. New York: Russell Sage Foundation.

Colella, Ugo, and Elizabeth Thomson. 1990. "Cohabitation and Marital Stability: Quality or Commitment?" NSFH Working Paper No. 23, National Survey of Families and Households, University of Wisconsin, Madison. Paper presented at the annual meeting of the Population Association of America, Toronto, Canada, May 3–5.

Hall, David R. 1990. "Secular Individualism and Divorce: The Link Between Premarital Cohabitation and Marital Dissolution in Canada." Unpublished paper, Department of Sociology, University of Western Ontario.

Henslin, James M. 1979. *Marriage and Family in a Changing Society*. New York: Free Press.

Khoo, S. 1986. "Living Together: Young Couples in De Facto Relationships." Australian Institute of Family Studies Working Paper No. 10, Development Studies Centre, Australian National University, Canberra.

Leridon, H., and C. Villeneuve-Gokalp. 1989. "The New Couples: Number, Characteristics, and Attitudes." *Population* 44:203–235.

Spanier, G. 1983. "Married and Unmarried Cohabitation in the United States: 1980." Journal of Marriage and the Family 34:277–288.

Sweet, James A. 1989. "Differentials in the Approval of Cohabitation." NSFH Working Paper No. 8, National Survey of Families and Households, University of Wisconsin, Madison.

Sweet, James, Larry Bumpass, and Vaughn Call. 1988. "The Design and Content of the National Survey of Families and Households." NSFH Working Paper No. 1, National Survey of Families and Households, University of Wisconsin, Madison.

Thornton, Arland. 1988. "Cohabitation and Marriage in the 1980s." Demography 25(4):497–508.

Wiersma, G. E. 1983. *Cohabitation, an Alternative to Marriage? A Cross-National Study*. Publication of the Netherlands Interuniversity Demographic Institute and the Population and Family Study Centre, Vol. 9. Boston: Martinus Nijhoff Publishers.

Willis, Robert J. and Robert T. Michael. 1988. "Innovation in Family Formation: Evidence on Cohabitation in the U.S." Paper presented at IUSSP seminar "The Family, the Market and the State in Aging Societies," Sendai City, Japan.

9

For Love or Money? Sociodemographic Determinants of the Expected Benefits from Marriage

Scott J. South

Virtually all recent theories of marriage and marital timing call attention to the perceived costs and benefits of marriage versus remaining single. This comparison is made explicit in Becker's (1981) theory of comparative advantage and is at least implicit in Easterlin's (1987) relative income hypothesis; Oppenheimer's (1988) theory of marital search; theories that emphasize the attractiveness of alternatives to marriage (Goldscheider and Waite 1986; Waite and Spitze 1981); and theories that stress the quality and availability of potential spouses (Guttentag and Secord 1983; Wilson 1987). It is surprising, therefore, that the perceived benefits of marriage have received little scrutiny. Most empirical studies of marriage analyze only the actual transition to marriage, with little or no concern for individuals' perceptions of the costs and benefits of making that transition.

An analysis of the expected benefits from marriage may prove particularly useful for explaining group differences in marriage rates. Both marital timing and the probability of ultimately marrying differ significantly by sex (Goldscheider and Waite 1986), by race and ethnicity (Bennett, Bloom, and Craig 1989; Schoen and Owens 1990; Teachman, Polonko, and Leigh 1987), and by age (Rodgers and Thornton 1985). For the most part, these sociodemographic differentials in marital behavior cannot be explained by group differences in other social and demographic attributes (Marini 1978; Michael and Tuma 1985; Testa, Astone, Krogh, and Neckerman 1989).

This chapter uses data from over 2,000 unmarried respondents in the National Survey of Families and Households to examine sociodemographic differences in the anticipated benefits from marriage. Theories of marital entry, especially those emphasizing the structural characteristics of marriage markets, are reviewed to derive hypotheses relating age, race and ethnicity, sex, and other sociodemographic variables to the perceived benefits from marriage. The hypotheses link sociodemographic background to the expected improvement in overall happiness from marriage as well as to specific areas of benefit such as improvement in standard of living, emotional security, sex life, and relationships with friends.

Theoretical Framework

Much like theories of marital formation (Espenshade 1985), explanations for group differences in the expected benefits from marriage can be subsumed under two complementary rubrics: (1) factors related to the attractiveness of alternatives to marriage, especially as reflected by women's economic independence; and (2) the quantity and quality of potential spouses available to an individual. As noted by Lichter, LeClere, and McLaughlin (1991), both categories of explanations derive from the "New Home Economics" school of household production.

Because the utility of marriage is thought to stem from the specialization of the husband in market activities and of the wife in nonmarket roles (Becker 1981), the economic independence of women would be expected to detract from the expected benefit of marriage. According to Becker (1981), there is little advantage to marrying unless each partner brings into the household unique goods and skills. Women with high incomes (and perhaps the men who are likely to marry them), therefore, might anticipate fewer gains or higher costs to marriage. Among women, high wages tend to delay marriage, although education and full-time employment tend to expedite it (Goldscheider and Waite 1986; Teachman et al. 1987). Moreover, women in labor markets characterized by favorable economic opportunities have lower marriage rates (Lichter et al. 1991; Preston and Richards 1975; White 1981). Because men face fewer opportunity costs from marriage, their economic resources are expected to encourage marriage (Teachman et al. 1987; Tucker and Taylor 1989). Their employment and, to a lesser extent, wages are positively related to early marriage (Goldscheider and Waite 1986; Teachman et al. 1987). For both men and women, enrollment in school delays marriage (Hogan 1978; Goldscheider and Waite 1986). Thus, the expected benefits from marriage are likely to increase along with the adoption of traditional sex roles and the absence of conflicting concurrent activities such as school attendance.

A growing explanation for subgroup differences in marital behavior—one with clear implications for the study of the expected benefits from marriage—emphasizes group variation in marriage opportunities. Some observers focus on how sex ratio imbalances influence the sheer availability of potential spouses (Goldman, Westoff, and Hammerslough 1984; Guttentag and Secord 1983; South and Trent 1988; Spanier and Glick 1980; Tucker

1987). Cohort fluctuations in fertility combined with the normative age differential between spouses creates "marriage squeezes" favoring either men or women (Heer and Grossbard-Shechtman 1981; Schoen 1983). The sex differential in mortality and the frequent tendency for older grooms to marry much younger brides reduce considerably the supply of potential mates for older women and for younger men (Goldman et al. 1984). Imbalances in sex ratios among blacks are further exacerbated by very high male mortality and greater rates of incarceration and military service (Farley and Bianchi 1987; Kiecolt and Fossett 1989; Schoen and Kluegel 1988). In 1988, among persons aged 18 to 34, there were approximately 93 unmarried black males per 100 unmarried black females. The corresponding sex ratios among whites and Hispanics were 124 and 138, respectively (U.S. Bureau of the Census 1989). The availability of prospective spouses also varies significantly across local marriage markets (Lichter et al. 1991).

Another slant on the marriage squeeze stresses the quality rather than the quantity of potential spouses (Wilson 1987). From this perspective, a deficit of men with desirable economic characteristics is thought to lie behind women's growing disinclination to marry. Oppenheimer (1988) criticizes conventional marriage models for ignoring the economic attributes of potential husbands and suggests that the retreat from early marriage is as much a function of the declining financial circumstances of men as the rising economic independence of women. The high rates of unemployment, low wages, and low educational attainments of black men place especially severe constraints on the marital opportunities for black women, particularly high-status black women (Spanier and Glick 1980; Tucker and Taylor 1989; Wilson and Neckerman 1986). Wilson (1987) and Lichter et al. (1991) demonstrate that the availability of employed black males increases the probability of marriage among black women.

These two explanations for marital formation—the attractiveness of alternatives to marriage and spouse availability—can be used to generate hypotheses linking the key variables of age, race, sex, and socioeconomic status to the expected benefits from marriage. First, marriage-market theories suggest that age will increase the expected benefits from marriage for men but reduce them for women. Because men tend to marry women younger than themselves, the supply of available spouses increases with age for men but decreases for women (Oppenheimer 1988). Given the greater likelihood that men will find an attractive mate, it seems probable that among men the anticipated happiness from marriage will increase with age; among women, it will decline.

One possible variation in this hypothesized interaction of sex and age involves the expected benefit of marriage to a woman's standard of living. The economic gains to marriage for older women are likely to be greater than those for younger women because the former are more likely to marry older men, whose earnings are higher than younger men's. But this effect should vary further by race because the sex differential in income for never-married persons increases with age for whites but decreases for blacks (Espenshade 1985). Although the sex differential in earnings is generally lower among blacks than whites (Goldscheider and Waite 1986), it is especially low among older unmarried blacks. Hence the expected improvement in economic circumstances should decline with age among black women but increase with age among white women. In statistical terms, this hypothesis predicts a three-way interaction of age, race, and sex in their effects on the expected improvement in standard of living from marriage.

At all ages and for all races, it is reasonable to suggest that women will expect more economic benefit from marriage than will men, although, as noted previously, the sex difference may vary by age and race. Traditionally, women have relied more than men on marriage as a source of economic mobility (Elder 1969; Glenn, Ross, and Tully 1974; Schoen and Wooldredge 1989). It is also reasonable to expect sex differences in the anticipated improvement in emotional security upon marriage, although the direction of difference here is not so clear. On the one hand, although romantic love is the chief motive for marriage among both men and women, women value more highly the affective aspects of marriage such as emotional comfort and support; men, in contrast, are more likely to view marriage as a useful arrangement for dealing with everyday tasks and routines and for regular sexual intercourse (Murstein 1980). On the other hand, men tend to be higher in romantic love than women in premarital relationships (Murstein 1980), they are more likely to rely on their spouse as a confidante, and they benefit more from marriage in mental and physical health (Gove 1972; Gove and Hughes 1979).

Race and ethnic differences in the expected benefits to marriage are also apt to exist. Blacks' marriage rates are considerably lower than whites' (Bennett et al. 1989; Teachman et al. 1987), with the rates for Mexican-Americans generally resembling those of non-Hispanic whites (Schoen and Owens 1990). To the extent that actual marriage rates reflect group differences in the perceived benefits from marriage, significant racial and ethnic differences in expected marital payoffs are likely to exist. It is also known that blacks tend to emphasize the instrumental aspects of marriage more so than whites, who stress its expressive qualities (Heiss 1988; Murstein 1980). The perceptions of Hispanics have been studied less extensively, but the oft-noted emphasis of Hispanic cultures on familial values (Alvirez and Bean 1976; Mindel 1980) suggests that they have higher expectations regarding marriage than do non-Hispanics.

Young black males might be particularly less likely than others to anticipate improvements in personal friendships (other than with one's spouse) upon marriage. Because of their comparatively low marriage rates, relatively few young black males will have friends who are also married. To the extent that personal friendships are homogamous by marital status, marriage can be expected to deteriorate friendships and retard friendship formation more among young black males than among other groups. Also, because black men are significantly more likely than black women to be involved in a nonmarital romantic relationship (Tucker and Taylor 1989), it is conceivable that they would expect less improvement in their sex life from marriage, assuming that the romantic involvement includes sexual relations.

As noted earlier, socioeconomic status is also likely to affect the expected benefits from marriage. Resources such as high income and education, steady employment, and home ownership make marriage less likely to improve one's standard of living. Social and economic resources can also be used to acquire many other advantages outside of marriage, although the relationship between income and perceived benefits from marriage might be tempered by the ability of single persons with high earnings to attract high-quality spouses (Berk and Berk 1983). School attendance is likely to conflict with marital roles, rendering marriage a less attractive alternative.

Finally, the formerly married may view marriage differently than do the never married. Although some divorced persons may have soured on the institution, high remarriage rates suggest that the formerly married see as much benefit and likely more benefits to marriage than do the never married.

Data and Methods

The data source for this analysis is the National Survey of Families and Households (NSFH), a national probability sample of 13,017 adults interviewed between March 1987 and May 1988 (Sweet, Bumpass, and Call 1988). The key questions used here are part of the self-administered questionnaire completed by 2,214 unmarried, noncohabiting persons between the ages of 19 and 35. (Missing data on some items leaves 2,095 respondents available for this analysis.) The NSFH oversamples minority groups, thus facilitating comparisons among blacks, Hispanics, and non-Hispanic whites. Sample weights are used to achieve the proper representation of respondents in the U.S. population.

The dependent variables capture a variety of possible perceived benefits from marriage. Respondents were directed, "For each of the following areas, please circle how you think your life might be different if you were married now." The nine areas of benefit were "overall happiness"; "standard of living"; "economic security"; "economic independence"; "freedom to do what you want"; "emotional security"; "sex life"; "friendships with others"; and "relations with parents." The five possible responses to each item were "much worse"; "somewhat worse"; "same"; "somewhat better"; and "much better." A principal components analysis and an analysis of the correlates of these items indicated that three of them—"standard of living," "economic security," and "economic independence"—tapped a very similar domain; they were combined by taking a simple average, the resulting index hereafter referred to as standard of living.

The items used to measure the expected benefits from marriage have several favorable features. First, the questions require that respondents *compare* their current situation with their perception of their lives upon marriage.[1] As noted earlier, such a comparison is central to several popular theories of marital behavior. Also, the use of several items allows respondents to weigh the pros and cons of marriage for different domains of life, some of which are expected to relate differently to sociodemographic background. Of course, respondents are limited to the benefits listed in the questionnaire. However, most of the life circumstances that could benefit from marriage are included in the survey. Moreover, because the primary focus is on subgroup differences rather than estimates for the total population, the failure to include all possible perceived benefits from marriage is not a serious flaw.

Perhaps the most serious disadvantage of these items is that they were understandably not asked of the married population. If married persons differ from the unmarried (or if the former were different before they married) in their expected benefits from marriage, then the possibility of sample selection bias exists (Berk 1983). In particular, it seems likely that, all else equal, married persons see more benefits to marriage than the unmarried. Although techniques to correct for this bias have been proposed (Heckman 1979), their utility for many sociological problems is questionable. Stolzenberg and Relles (1990) warn that the most common corrections for sample selection bias often do more harm than good. Nevertheless, in supplementary analyses a logistic regression equation predicting exclusion from the subsample of unmarried respondents was estimated using conventional predictors of marital status such as age, race, sex, socioeconomic background, school attendance, and region (Teachman et al. 1987). For each respondent, the predicted probability of exclusion from the sample (i.e., the hazard rate) was then calculated and included as an independent variable in the substantive equations described further on. This correction for possible selection bias had uniformly little effect on the coefficients for variables already in the model. Thus, although the possibility cannot be completely discounted, it does not appear that sample selection bias will severely vitiate the results.

The key independent variables are age, race and ethnicity, and sex. Age is treated as a continuous variable. The (weighted) mean age of the respondents is 24.3 years with a standard deviation of 4.8. Three race and ethnic groups are contrasted in the analysis: whites, blacks, and Hispanics. (Because they are so few in number, members of other racial and ethnic groups are excluded from the analysis). This dummy variable is derived from a single close-ended questionnaire item; hence, it is not known how many black Hispanics self-identified as black and how many self-identified as Hispanic. The possible responses included four different Hispanic categories (Mexican-American, Puerto Rican, Cuban, and other Hispanic), but the relatively small sizes of most of them argued for a single Hispanic grouping. Approximately 72 percent of the sample self-identified as white, 18 percent as black, and 10 percent as Hispanic.[2] In the regression analyses to follow, whites are the reference category. Sex is represented by a dummy variable scored 0 for males and 1 for females. Fifty-four percent of the respondents are male; 46 percent are female.

The other eight independent variables tap respondents' socioeconomic resources, concurrent roles, and geographic context. Earnings include all earnings from wages and salaries in 1986 ($\bar{x}$ = \$9813, s = \$10,432). Because of considerable missing data on this variable, missing values were substituted with the mean.[3] Education is measured by years of school completed ($\bar{x}$ = 13.04, s = 2.26). Weeks unemployed is measured conventionally and refers to the year 1986 ($\bar{x}$ = 4.57, s = 11.80). Home ownership is a dummy variable scored 0 for those who do not own their home and 1 for those who do. Eight percent of respondents own their home. The variable called currently enrolled is scored 0 for the 77 percent of respondents not attending school and 1 for the 23 percent who are. On the variable called formerly married, never-married respondents are scored 0; the widowed and divorced are scored 1. About 11 percent of the respondents are formerly married, almost all of them divorced.

The final two independent variables are characteristics of the county in which the respondent lives: the percentage of the county population that is urban ($\bar{x}$ = 75.7, s = 27.1) and the percentage that is poor ($\bar{x}$ = 12.0, s = 5.8). Urban counties are likely to contain a greater number of alternatives to marriage (Keeley 1977), and thus urbanization might reduce the perceived benefits from marriage. Poor counties are less likely to contain potential spouses with desirable economic characteristics, and hence the perceived benefits from marriage for individuals who reside in them are expected to be lower than elsewhere.

The primary methodological strategy is to analyze the dependent variables as a system of "seemingly unrelated regressions" (Pindyck and Rubinfeld 1981; Zellner 1962). The benefits to marriage are viewed as jointly determined by the exogenous variables, with unmeasured individual-specific factors leading to correlated error terms across equations. The error terms are likely to be correlated because some individuals will see a wide range of benefits to marriage and others will see uniformly few. These correlations can be used, via generalized least squares, to obtain parameter estimates more efficient than those obtained by OLS. The program used (PROC SYSLIN) is part of the SAS software package.

Because the theoretical framework suggests that age, race, and sex interact in their effects on the expected benefits from marriage, appropriate product terms were constructed and included in the equations. Initially, an equation with the three-way interaction of age, race, and sex, along with the lower-order two-way interactions (age by race, age by sex, race by sex) and all other variables in their original metric, was estimated. If the three-way interactions were not statistically significant, the equation was reestimated with only the two-way interactions. If none of the two-way interactions was significant, then the additive model containing no interaction terms was estimated.

Results

Table 9.1 presents some descriptive statistics on the expected benefits from marriage. With the exception of freedom to do what they want, on average the respondents expect marriage to improve their lives. The overall means are above 3, indicating that the mythical average respondent anticipates that most life domains would be somewhat better or much better upon marriage. Although having means above 3, fewer than half of the respondents expect improvement in friendships with others or relations with parents.[4] Most respondents expect no change in these areas upon marriage. If means are used as the yardstick, the respondents expect their sex lives to benefit most from marriage, followed by their overall happiness and emotional security.

The expected benefits to marriage are moderately related to sex and race/ethnicity. Only for relations with parents is the association between these variables not statistically significant by conventional standards, and even here it is of borderline significance. The strongest relationships are between sex/race and expected improvement in standard of living (eta = .25) and freedom (eta = .19). Both variables are characterized by strong sex differences, with females anticipating greater improvement (or less deterioration) than males. Although more modest, race differences are apparent as well. Compared to their white counterparts, blacks and Hispanics are more likely to perceive improvements in both areas. Sociodemographic differentials in the expected improvement in overall happiness are not large but indicate that black females anticipate the greatest benefit, black and Hispanic males the least. Of course, these patterns are useful for descriptive purposes but not for analytical ones because they obtain without controlling for other factors. Moreover, interactions among age, race, and sex cannot be easily discerned from Table 9.1.

Table 9.1 Descriptive Statistics for the Expected Benefits from Marriage by Race/Ethnicity and Sex

Expected Benefit	*White Males*	*White Females*	*Black Males*	*Black Females*	*Hispanic Males*	*Hispanic Females*	*Total*	*P (ETA)*
Overall happiness								
Mean	3.78	3.84	3.55	3.94	3.56	3.97	3.79	.00
Standard deviation	1.03	1.01	1.05	1.03	1.20	1.02	1.04	(.11)
% expecting improvement	64.70	69.00	53.10	70.10	61.50	75.30	66.00	
Standard of living								
Mean	3.01	3.40	3.20	3.75	3.12	3.46	3.25	.00
Standard deviation	.98	.93	.95	.83	1.07	.94	.98	(.25)
% expecting improvement	48.40	65.50	54.40	81.50	53.10	65.60	58.50	
Freedom								
Mean	2.47	2.78	2.60	3.04	2.64	3.06	2.67	.00
Standard deviation	1.05	1.02	1.14	1.18	1.07	1.23	1.09	(.19)
% expecting improvement	11.60	18.20	18.80	28.60	18.00	29.10	16.90	
Emotional security								
Mean	3.57	3.74	3.32	3.77	3.48	3.62	3.62	.00
Standard deviation	.95	.98	1.04	1.00	1.02	1.10	.99	(.13)
% expecting improvement	52.60	62.20	38.60	58.70	49.70	50.90	55.00	
Sex life								
Mean	4.19	4.23	3.79	4.04	4.10	4.08	4.15	.00
Standard deviation	.94	.92	.98	1.02	.83	1.05	.95	(.13)
% expecting improvement	76.30	77.10	61.30	67.80	80.60	74.40	74.80	
Friendships with others								
Mean	3.22	3.09	3.05	3.27	3.22	3.11	3.17	.00
Standard deviation	.83	.74	.83	.86	.76	1.00	.81	(.09)
% expecting improvement	28.70	17.90	20.10	25.90	26.90	27.80	24.20	
Relations with parents								
Mean	3.24	3.20	3.32	3.37	3.33	3.34	3.26	.06
Standard deviation	.80	.76	.81	.81	.89	.98	.80	(.07)
% expecting improvement	25.80	23.00	31.70	27.30	34.10	32.30	26.20	
N (weighted)	871	655	161	208	111	89	2095	

TABLE 9.2 Seemingly Unrelated Regression (GLS) Analysis of the Expected Benefits from Marriage (N=2095; metric coefficient with standardized coefficient in parentheses)

	Dependent Variables						
Independent Vaiables	*Overall Happiness*	*Standard of Living*	*Freedom*	*Emotional Security*	*Sex Life*	*Friendships with Others*	*Relations with Parents*
Age	.013	.034**	.014	.014	.008	.028**	.026**
	(.060)	(.165)	(.061)	(.070)	(.042)	(.166)	(.152)
Sex	.789**	.282	.838**	.690**	.065	.133	.394*
(0=male; 1=female)	(.377)	(.143)	(.383)	(.347)	(.034)	(.081)	(.243)
Race/ethnicity:[a]							
Black	.104	−.098	−.409	−.192	−.271**	−.307	.325
	(.038)	(−.038)	(−.143)	(−.074)	(−.109)	(−.144)	(.153)
Hispanic	−.371	−.129	.280	−.276	−.084	.666	.099
	(−.105)	(−.039)	(.076)	(−.082)	(−.026)	(.240)	(.036)
Education	−.024*	−.000	−.013	.006	−.006	−.023**	−.015
	(−.053)	(−.001)	(−.028)	(.015)	(−.014)	(−.064)	(−.042)
Currently enrolled	−.205**	−.354**	−.054	−.185**	.082	−.129**	−.163**
(0=no; 1=yes)	(−.084)	(−.153)	(−.021)	(−.079)	(.036)	(−.067)	(−.086)
Earnings	−.000	−.001	−.010**	−.002	−.005*	−.005*	−.006**
(in thousands)	(−.004)	(−.013)	(−.100)	(−.023)	(−.052)	(−.060)	(−.085)
Weeks unemployed	−.000	.003	.003	.002	−.000	.001	.003
	(−.003)	(.033)	(.032)	(.018)	(−.004)	(.019)	(.041)
Own home	−.067	−.091	.007	−.047	−.120	−.061	−.082
(0=no; 1=yes)	(−.017)	(−.025)	(.002)	(−.013)	(−.034)	(−.020)	(−.027)
Formerly married	−.018	.158*	.207*	.054	−.138	−.021	−.059
(0=no; 1=yes)	(−.005)	(.051)	(.060)	(.017)	(−.046)	(−.008)	(−.023)

County percent urban	.000 (.011)	.001 (.033)	.001 (.028)	.001 (.020)	−.002* (−.054)	−.001 (−.021)	.002* (.060)
County poverty rate	−.001 (−.004)	.009* (.052)	.002 (.013)	.004 (.025)	−.007 (−.041)	.000 (.002)	.002 (.018)
Age × Sex	−.029** (−.360)	.003 (.044)	−.023* (−.274)	−.021* (−.271)	NI	−.011 (−.178)	−.018* (−.290)
Age × Black	−.014 (−.129)	.009 (.091)	.020 (.177)	−.002 (−.023)	NI	.004 (.054)	−.013 (−.160)
Age × Hispanic	.004 (.024)	.008 (.059)	−.008 (−.051)	.007 (.050)	NI	−.030 (−.266)	−.004 (−.036)
Sex × Black	.284** (.082)	1.611** (.490)	1.357* (.372)	.191 (.058)	NI	1.037** (.380)	.054 (.020)
Sex × Hispanic	.360* (.070)	.194 (.040)	.702 (.130)	−.063 (−.013)	NI	−1.100* (−.273)	.010 (.002)
Age × Sex × Black	NI	−.061** (−.480)	−.051* (−.361)	NI	NI	−.030 (−.285)	NI
Age × Sex × Hispanic	NI	−.013 (−.066)	−.026 (−.119)	NI	NI	.046* (.287)	NI
Constant	3.829	2.109	2.315	3.094	4.324	2.985	2.786

Notes: System weighted $R^2 = .053$.
NI indicates variable not included in equation.

[a] Reference category is whites.

* $p < .05$ (two-tailed test).
** $p < .01$ (two-tailed test).

Table 9.2 shows the results of the regression analyses of the seven possible benefits from marriage.[5] With the sole exception of the expected improvements to one's sex life, some statistically significant interaction between age, race, and sex is apparent. For three of the dependent variables (standard of living, freedom, and friendships with others), one of the three-way interactions of age by race by sex is statistically significant. For three others (overall happiness, emotional security, and relations with parents), at least one of the two-way interaction terms is significant. The nature of these effects is described more fully later; for now it should be emphasized that, by themselves, the component variables involved in these interactions have no clear interpretation.

Two of the variables measuring socioeconomic resources, education and earnings, as well as school enrollment, have fairly consistent negative effects on the expected benefits from marriage. At least one of these characteristics is significantly and inversely related to each of the endogenous variables. Presumably, the availability of desirable alternatives to marriage that accompany these attributes reduces the perceived attractiveness of marriage. By contrast, two other indicators of resources—weeks unemployed (a reverse indicator) and home ownership—have weak and nonsignificant effects on the expected benefits from marriage.

The formerly married differ significantly from the never married on the expected improvements upon marriage in standard of living and freedom. In both cases, the formerly married view marriage in a more favorable light. Having been previously married does not appear to shape substantially, either positively or negatively, marital expectations in other domains. The two contextual variables, the percent of the county population that is urban and the percent in poverty, have inconsistent and relatively weak associations with the perceived benefits from marriage. Respondents in more urban counties tend to anticipate less improvement in their sex lives but better relations with their parents. The former association is perhaps due to higher rates of premarital sexual relations in more urban areas; marriage might lead to a smaller increase in the frequency of intercourse than in less urban areas. The positive association between county percent urban and expected improvements in parental relations is more difficult to explain; it is conceivable that respondents in urban counties anticipate a more marked shift upon marriage toward a family-oriented social network. Contrary to expectations, the county poverty rate is positively related to the expected improvement in standard of living. Perhaps the surrounding poverty makes individuals in poor counties view objectively smaller financial gains as having greater impact on their personal standard of living. Alternatively, perhaps the poverty rate for the total population is an inadequate indicator of the economic circumstances of potential spouses.

Figure 9.1 Effects of Age, Race, and Sex on the Expected Improvement in Overall Happiness from Marriage

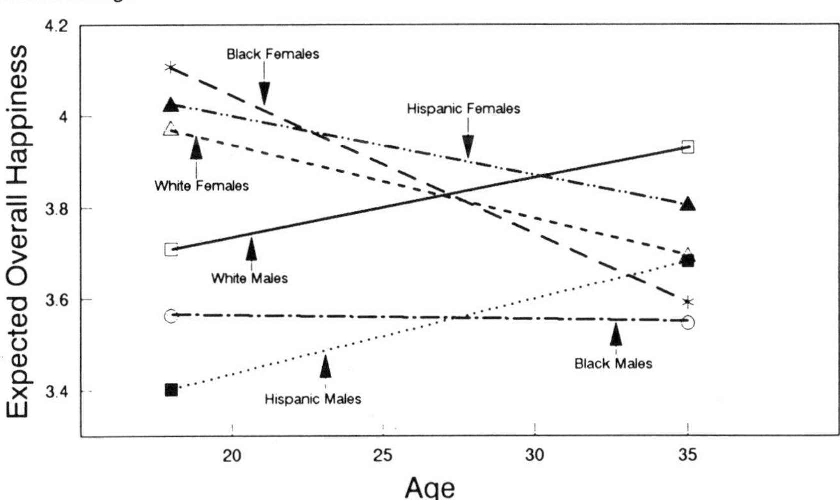

Because age, sex, and race and ethnicity are involved in a complex pattern of interactions, their effects on the dependent variables are shown graphically in Figures 9.1 through 9.6. Each of the figures was constructed by fixing the values of all other variables at their means. Figure 9.1 depicts the relationship between age and the expected improvement in overall happiness separately for the six race/sex groups. As shown in Table 9.2, the effect of age varies significantly by sex, and the sex difference among blacks and Hispanics is significantly different than the sex difference among whites. Figure 9.1 shows that at young ages all three groups of females anticipate greater improvements in happiness than do males. At these ages, the sex difference among whites is smaller than the sex difference among either blacks or Hispanics. Importantly, the slopes for the females groups are all negative, the slopes for white and Hispanic males are positive, and the slope for black males is essentially nil. The difference in the effects of age between white men and women is particularly striking. At ages younger than 27, women anticipate greater improvements in happiness from marriage; after age 27, men anticipate a greater benefit from marriage. In general, the happiness expected from marriage decreases with age for females but increases with age for males, supporting the idea that marriage markets operate differently for men and women. At all ages, black and Hispanic males anticipate less overall happiness from marriage than do black and Hispanic females.

That black males anticipate less improvement in happiness from marriage than do black females suggests that the low marriage rate among black

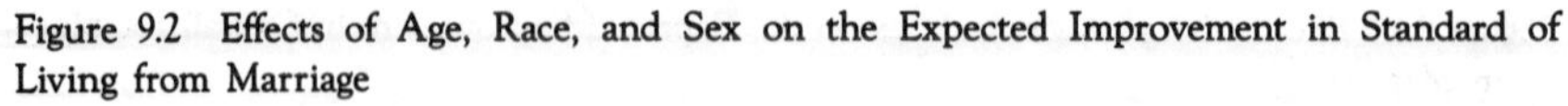

Figure 9.2 Effects of Age, Race, and Sex on the Expected Improvement in Standard of Living from Marriage

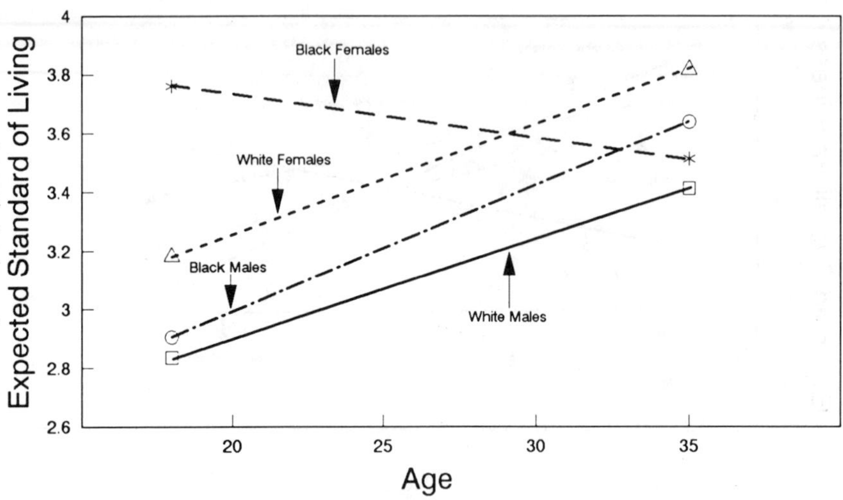

women is not entirely attributable to their disinclination to marry men of relatively low socioeconomic status (Wilson 1987). Rather the marital perceptions of black men appear to play an equally strong role in keeping black marriage rates low. Guttentag and Secord (1983) suggest that the low sex ratios among African-Americans discourage black men from forming stable unions; the oversupply of women provides no incentive for men to commit to one woman.

Figure 9.2 shows the relationship between age and the expected improvement from marriage in standard of living separately for black and white men and women.[6] As Table 9.2 shows, the way in which age and sex interact in affecting the perceived change in standard of living differs for whites and blacks. At young ages, black females expect considerably greater improvement in their standard of living than do others. With age, however, this expectation declines, but it increases for black males and for whites. This three-way interaction of age, race, and sex was predicted by the theoretical framework. Several other hypotheses also find support in Figure 9.2. At all ages, females expect greater improvement in their standard of living than do men of the same race. Also, black men anticipate greater improvement than do white men, although the difference here is not large.

Figure 9.3, which depicts the relationships among age, race, sex, and expected change in personal freedom upon marriage, tells a somewhat similar story. Young black females are the only group to anticipate actual *improvements* in personal freedom with marriage (i.e., the conditional mean is above 3). Again, however, this expectation decreases sharply with age,

Figure 9.3 Effects of Age, Race, and Sex on the Expected Improvement in Personal Freedom from Marriage

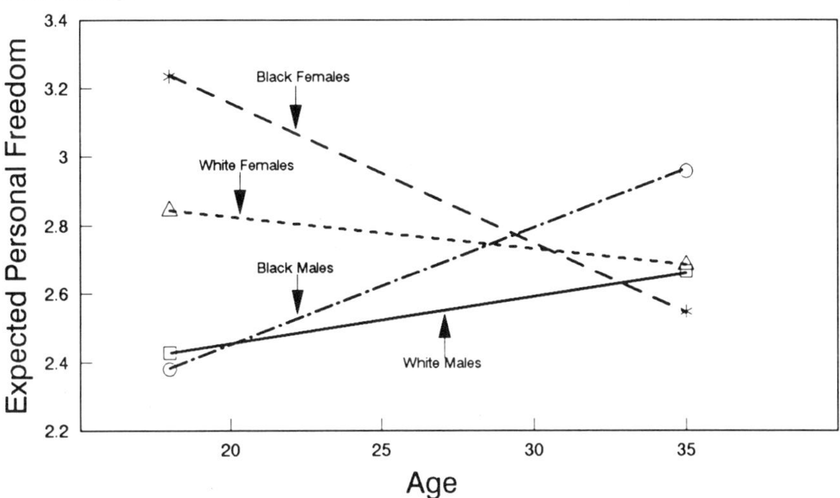

so that by age 35 black females anticipate the greatest *reduction* in freedom. Conversely, among all groups young black males expect the sharpest diminution of freedom; older black males expect the least. At young ages, white men expect greater restrictions on freedom than white women, but with age this difference disappears. Perhaps the sex differences at the young ages reflect young women's anticipation of moving out of the parental household upon marriage and thus either acquiring greater freedom or sacrificing relatively little. Young men, in contrast, are more likely to expect to move from independent living to marriage (Goldscheider and Goldscheider 1987) and thus might perceive a greater loss of freedom.

The effects of age, race, and sex on the expected changes in emotional security from marriage are graphed in Figure 9.4. At most ages, females perceive greater improvement than males of the same race in this domain. The sole exception is among whites older than 33. Moreover, whites tend to anticipate greater emotional benefit from marriage than blacks of the same sex.[7] These results support the idea that whites and women value the expressive aspects of marriage more than do blacks and men (Murstein 1980). Once again, however, it appears that age affects differently men's and women's perceptions, with men's expectations improving with age and women's declining, albeit slightly.

The only benefit from marriage for which no interaction term is significant is the expected improvement in one's sex life. The additive model, shown in Table 9.2, indicates that blacks have lower expectations than whites in this area but that differences by age and sex are not significant. The

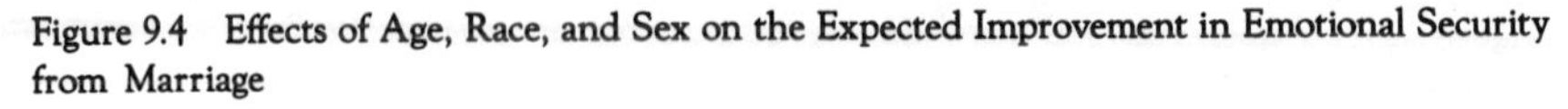
Figure 9.4 Effects of Age, Race, and Sex on the Expected Improvement in Emotional Security from Marriage

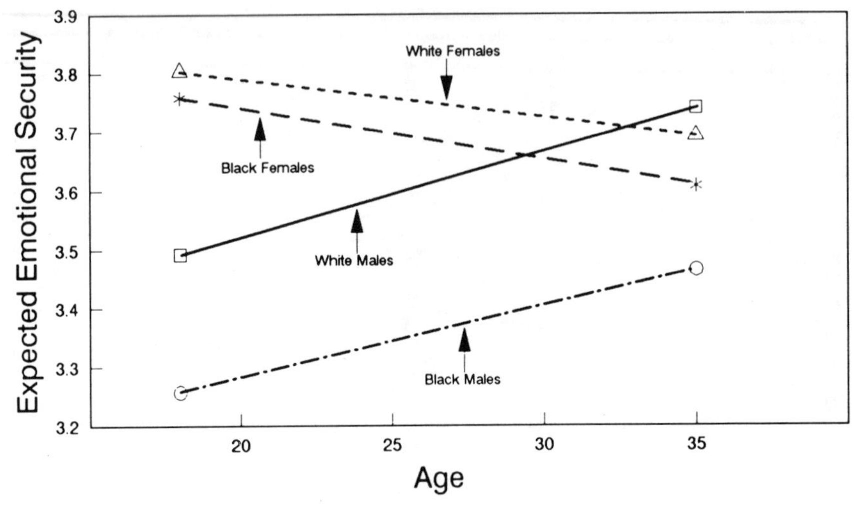

hypothesis stating that compared to whites, black males would anticipate less improvement in their sex lives from marriage than black females because of their more frequent involvement in nonmarital relationships is almost supported; the interaction of sex and race is in the predicted direction but barely fails to attain statistical significance ($p = .07$).

As shown in Figure 9.5, the relationships between age, sex, race/ethnicity, and expected improvement in friendships with others from marriage are complex. As predicted, young black males have the lowest expectations in this area. However, they differ very little from Hispanic females, and their expectations increase sharply with age, as do those of white men and women. One pattern found for several of the other marital benefits is echoed here: Single black females begin their prime marriage-formation years with high expectations, but in contrast to most other groups, these expectations appear to decrease as they grow older. At the youngest ages, black women and men have, respectively, the highest and lowest means on the expected improvement in friendships. Curiously, Hispanic men and women show the opposite pattern, with the conditional male mean higher than the female mean, although the order is reversed at older ages.

The pattern for black men and women is at least partially consistent with the hypothesis that the expected improvement in friendships will covary with the proportion of one's age, race, or sex group that is married. This hypothesis was developed on the assumption that friendships are largely homogamous by marital status (as well as by age, race, and sex), so that if many of one's actual or potential friends are married, the volume

Figure 9.5 Effects of Age, Race, and Sex on the Expected Improvement in Friendships from Marriage

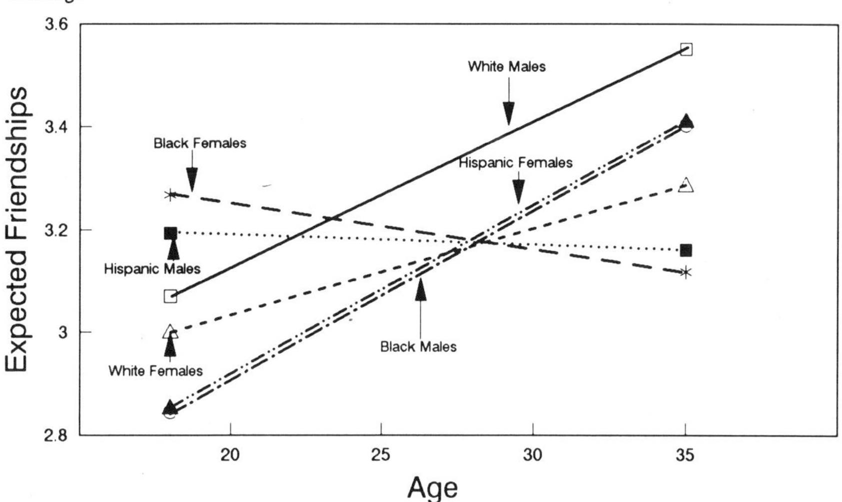

and quality of friendships would improve upon marriage; conversely, if most of one's friends are single, friendships would be expected to deteriorate or improve less markedly. Among blacks aged 20 to 24, a larger percentage of females than males are married with spouse present (18.2% vs. 11.4%); at ages 30 to 34, more males than females have that marital status (40.3% to 38.3%) (U.S. Bureau of the Census 1989). However, the hypothesis is not strongly supported among whites or Hispanics, because throughout the age range considered here the percent of males that are married is consistently lower than that of females, and all white males and young Hispanic males expect greater improvements in friendships than their female counterparts. Moreover, although the percent married for all six groups increases over this age range (U.S. Bureau of the Census 1989), the perceived improvements in friendships for black females and Hispanic males actually decline with age.

Finally, Figure 9.6 displays the effects of age, race, and sex on the expected change from marriage in relations with parents. As Table 9.2 shows, the effects of age vary significantly between men and women. Although for this variable differences between races are not significant, the effects of age are shown separately for blacks and whites to facilitate comparisons with the other benefits from marriage. As they do with several other benefits, young black women see a comparatively large improvement from marriage in their relations with parents, and older black women see relatively little benefit. Among black men, white women, and white men, the expectation of improvement in parental relations tends to increase with

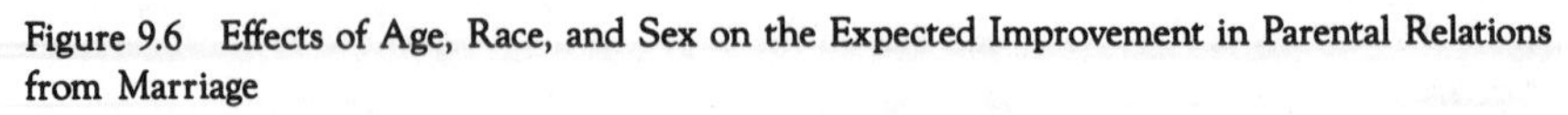
Figure 9.6 Effects of Age, Race, and Sex on the Expected Improvement in Parental Relations from Marriage

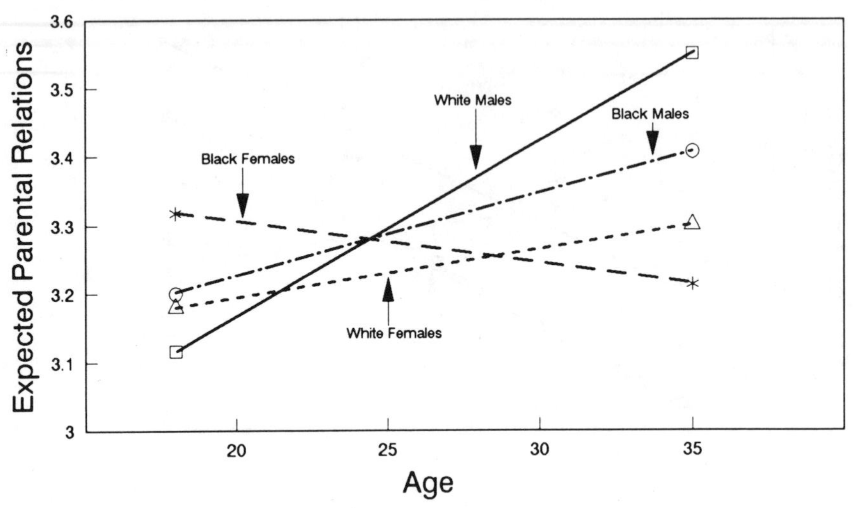

age. By about age 25, men expect a greater improvement from marriage than do women in relations with their parents.

Discussion and Conclusion

By and large, the findings are consistent with the hypotheses drawn from the theoretical framework. Individuals with greater personal resources tend to see fewer benefits to marriage than persons from less advantaged backgrounds. Presumably, individuals with greater resources have available more attractive alternatives to marriage, especially in the labor market. The perceived benefits to marriage increase with age for males; among females they either decrease or increase more slowly. These differences are consistent with an improvement in the quantity and quality of potential wives as men age and with a deterioration of the pool of eligible husbands for women as they grow older. Given the deficit of employed young black males, young black women appear to perceive greater benefits in marriage than their position in the marriage market warrants. However, the often precipitous decline with age in their expectations does accord with the hypotheses.

One striking result is that young black men and women have quite different visions of how marriage will affect their lives. Although these differences tend to converge and sometimes reverse themselves at older ages, at the youngest ages black men see much less benefit in marriage than black women. The low rates of marriage among black women appear to be as much a function of black males' reticence to marry as of black females' inability to find attractive mates (cf. Wilson 1987). These sex differences at the younger ages are also apparent among whites but in more muted form. It seems unlikely that market differentials can completely explain these sex and race differences, because black women are usually considered the most disadvantaged group in the marriage market. One possible explanation for young black women perceiving more benefits from marriage than others could be differential selection out of the unmarried population. If, because of a more severe marriage squeeze among black women than black men or whites, fewer black women who wish to marry are able to do so, then the remaining pool of unmarried black women might contain a relatively larger number who see substantial benefit to marriage. However, this explanation does not appear readily capable of explaining the different effect of age among black women than among others.

The larger sex difference among blacks than whites in the expected benefits from marriage might also be partly attributable to the experience of growing up in fatherless families. The higher proportion of female-headed families among blacks, coupled with the severe financial hardships endured by female-headed families (McLanahan 1985), might lead young black women to value marriage very highly. This might be especially true for unmarried mothers. Relatedly, the deficit of black fathers to serve as role models for young black men may make it difficult for the latter to see the benefits of marriage. Again, however, it is not certain that this explanation can account for group differences in the effect of age on the expected benefits from marriage. Just as no single explanation can account for black-white differences in marital formation (Cherlin 1981), there is no simple interpretation of these patterns. Theories of the marriage market appear capable of explaining some of the sociodemographic determinants of the expected benefits from marriage, but the complexity of the differentials demands supplementary explanations.

Although racial differences in the expected benefits to marriage are fairly regular, differences between Anglos and Hispanics are weaker and less consistent. No support is found for the hypothesis that Hispanic men and women see greater benefits to marriage than do non-Hispanics or blacks.

These results also suggest that increased attention be paid to the role of age in the marital formation process. The age differences observed here in the cross-section could conceivably result from one of two processes. Individuals could change their minds about the expected benefits from marriage as they grow older (i.e., an aging effect), or older individuals could hold different attitudes than younger ones throughout their lives (i.e., a cohort effect).[8] It is impossible with these data to choose unequivocally between these alternatives, but both aging and cohort explanations can be accommodated by a theoretical framework emphasizing disequilibria in marriage markets. For example, imbalances in the number of marriageable men and women can be created by cohort fluctuations in fertility combined with the traditional age difference between spouses; by increasing sex differentials in mortality throughout the prime marriage years; and by changes in the volume of "competition" from other ages for spouses, as when older men court young brides, a situation that both increases competition among younger men and leaves older women facing a dwindling supply of older grooms. Clearly, the secular rise in age at marriage and the increase in remarriages warrant further analysis of marital attitudes and behavior at the older ages.

Finally, further analyses of the expected benefits from marriage seem justified. Not only are the anticipated costs and gains of marriage critical for evaluating theories of marital timing, but social changes that might alter the ledger of costs and benefits (and allegedly undermine the fundamental basis of marriage) are apt to continue in the future. Women's growing economic independence is the most cited change, but the deterioration of male earnings (Oppenheimer 1988), a weakened normative commitment to marry (Thornton 1989), and changes in the marriage squeeze may also affect perceptions of marital costs and benefits. The consequences of these perceptions might also be worth exploring insofar as unmet expectations can influence marital quality and stability.

Acknowledgments

This research was partially based on work supported by a grant from the National Science Foundation (Grant No. SES8820743). I am grateful to Glenna Spitze and Katherine Trent for helpful comments.

Notes

1. As with similar attitudinal variables, establishing the validity of these items is not a simple task. The questions appear straightforward enough to acquire face validity. Construct validity was assessed by correlating these items with a question asking respondents how much they agree or disagree (on a 5-point Likert-type scale) to the statement, I would like to get married someday. Presumably, individuals who see more benefits to marriage would express greater desire to marry, although clearly these variables are not intended to measure the same theoretical construct. The correlations between the desire to marry and the seven perceived benefits to marriage are all positive and statistically significant. Perhaps because of relatively little variance in the former variable (almost 80% of respondents agreed or strongly agreed) and random measurement error, the correlations are not overly strong, ranging from .09 (for relations with parents) to .30 (for overall happiness). That the strongest correlation is for overall happiness rather than the specific life domains, however,

argues further for the validity of the dependent variables. It is perhaps worth stressing that the expected benefits from marriage are not intended to measure the desire to marry or the ultimate probability of marrying.

Of course, when some individuals answer these questions, they have a specific potential spouse in mind; others are considering a hypothetical partner. The theories under consideration do not appear to deem this an important distinction, nor is there reason to expect important differences between these two groups of respondents. Nonetheless, additional analyses controlled for whether respondents reported having a steady boyfriend or girlfriend, with no appreciable changes in the results.

2. For stylistic reasons, the term *racial* will frequently be used as shorthand for *racial and ethnic.*

3. Including a dummy variable for individuals whose earnings are imputed has no appreciable impact on the findings.

4. For the composite variable, standard of living, the percentage expecting improvement is the percentage of respondents whose average on the three items is greater than 3. For all other variables, this is the percentage of respondents expecting this area of their lives to be "somewhat better" or "much better" upon marriage.

5. As expected, correlations between the error terms across equations are all positive. They range from a low of .22 for the regressions of expected change in freedom and sex life to a high of .64 for the equations predicting the expected change in overall happiness and emotional security.

6. Because interactions involving Hispanics are only significant for the expected changes in overall happiness and friendships with others, the slopes for Hispanics are not shown in the graphs for the other dependent variables.

7. The slopes are shown separately for whites and blacks because the interaction of sex and race just barely fails to reach statistical significance ($p = .07$).

8. In theory, the observed age differentials could also be caused by a selection effect if individuals are selected out of the unmarried population on the basis of their expectations about the benefits from marriage. However, the correction for sample selection bias left the effects of age unchanged, suggesting that other interpretations are required. It is also worth noting that if selection effects are operating, they must be very complex, because they would have to operate differently for the various race/sex groups.

References

Alvirez, David, and Frank D. Bean. 1976. "The Mexican-American Family." Pp. 271–292 in Charles H. Mindel and Robert W. Habenstein (eds.), *Ethnic Families in America.* New York: Elsevier.

Becker, Gary S. 1981. *A Treatise on the Family.* Cambridge, MA: Harvard University Press.

Bennett, Neil G., David E. Bloom, and Patricia H. Craig. 1989. "The Divergence of Black and White Marriage Patterns." *American Journal of Sociology* 95:692–722.

Berk, Richard A. 1983. "An Introduction to Sample Selection Bias in Sociological Data." *American Sociological Review* 48:386–398.

Berk, Richard A., and Sarah Fenstermaker Berk. 1983. "Supply-side Sociology of the Family: The Challenge of the New Home Economics." *Annual Review of Sociology* 9:375–395.

Cherlin, Andrew J. 1981. *Marriage, Divorce, Remarriage*. Cambridge, MA: Harvard University Press.

Easterlin, Richard A. 1987. *Birth and Fortune: The Impact of Numbers on Personal Welfare*. Second edition. Chicago: University of Chicago Press.

Elder, Glen H., Jr. 1969. "Appearance and Education in Marriage Mobility." *American Sociological Review* 43:510–533.

Espenshade, Thomas J. 1985. "Marriage Trends in America: Estimates, Implications, and Causes." *Population and Development Review* 11:193–245.

Farley, Reynolds, and Suzanne M. Bianchi. 1987. "The Growing Racial Difference in Marriage and Family Patterns." Research Report No. 87-107. Ann Arbor, MI: Population Studies Center, University of Michigan.

Glenn, Norval D., Adreain A. Ross, and Judy Corder Tully. 1974. "Patterns of Intergenerational Mobility of Females through Marriage." *American Sociological Review* 39:683–699.

Goldman, Noreen, Charles F. Westoff, and Charles Hammerslough. 1984. "Demography of the Marriage Market in the United States." *Population Index* 50:5–25.

Goldscheider, Calvin, and Frances K. Goldscheider. 1987. "Moving Out and Marriage: What Do Young Adults Expect?" *American Sociological Review* 52:278–285.

Goldscheider, Frances Kobrin, and Linda J. Waite. 1986. "Sex Differences in the Entry into Marriage." *American Journal of Sociology* 92:91–109.

Gove, Walter R. 1972. "Sex Roles, Marital Roles and Mental Illness." *Social Forces* 51:34–44.

Gove, Walter R., and Michael Hughes. 1979. "Possible Causes of the Apparent Sex Differences in Physical Health: An Empirical Investigation." *American Sociological Review* 44:126–146.

Guttentag, Marcia, and Paul F. Secord. 1983. *Too Many Women?* Beverly Hills, CA: Sage.

Heckman, James J. 1979. "Sample Selection Bias as a Specification Error." *Econometrica* 45:153–161.

Heer, David M., and Amyra Grossbard-Shechtman. 1981. "The Impact of the Female Marriage Squeeze and the Contraceptive Revolution on Sex Roles and the Women's Liberation Movement in the United States, 1960–1975." *Journal of Marriage and the Family* 43:49–65.

Heiss, Jerold. 1988. "Women's Values Regarding Marriage and the Family." Pp. 201–214 in Harriette Pipes McAdoo (ed.). *Black Families*. Second Edition. Newbury Park, CA: Sage.

Hogan, Dennis P. 1978. "The Effects of Demographic Factors, Family Background, and Early Job Achievement on Age at Marriage." *Demography* 15:161–176.

Keeley, Michael. 1977. "The Economics of Family Formation." *Economic Inquiry* 15:238–250.

Kiecolt, K. Jill, and Mark A. Fossett. 1989. "Mate Availability, Economic Opportunity, and Marital Quality among Black Americans." Paper presented at the annual meeting of the American Sociological Association, San Francisco.

Lichter, Daniel T., Felicia B. LeClere, and Diane K. McLaughlin. 1991. "Local Marriage Market Conditions and the Marital Behavior of Black and White Women." *American Journal of Sociology* 96:843–867.

Marini, Margaret Mooney. 1978. "The Transition to Adulthood: Sex Differences in Educational Attainment and Age of Marriage." *American Sociological Review* 43:483–507.

McLanahan, Sara. 1985. "Family Structure and the Reproduction of Poverty." *American Journal of Sociology* 90:873–901.

Michael, Robert T., and Nancy Brandon Tuma. 1985. "Entry into Marriage and Parenthood by Young Men and Women: The Influence of Family Background." *Demography* 22:515–544.

Mindel, Charles H. 1980. "Extended Familism Among Urban Mexican-Americans, Anglos, and Blacks." *Hispanic Journal of Behavioral Sciences* 2:21–34.

Murstein, Bernard I. 1980. "Mate Selection in the 1970s." *Journal of Marriage and the Family* 42:777–792.

Oppenheimer, Valerie Kincade. 1988. "A Theory of Marriage Timing." *American Journal of Sociology* 94:563–591.

Pindyck, Robert, and Daniel Rubinfeld. 1981. *Econometric Models and Economic Forecasts.* New York: McGraw-Hill.

Preston, Samuel H., and Alan Thomas Richards. 1975. "The Influence of Women's Work Opportunities on Marriage Rates." *Demography* 12:209–222.

Rodgers, Willard L., and Arland Thornton. 1985. "Changing Patterns of First Marriage in the United States." *Demography* 22:265–279.

Schoen, Robert. 1983. "Measuring the Tightness of a Marriage Squeeze." *Demography* 20:61–78.

Schoen, Robert, and James R. Kluegel. 1988. "The Widening Gap in Black and White Marriage Rates: The Impact of Population Composition and Differential Marriage Propensities." *American Sociological Review* 53:895–907.

Schoen, Robert, and Dawn Owens. 1990. "A Further Look at First Unions and First Marriages." Paper presented at the Conference on Demographic Perspectives on the American Family: Patterns and Prospects, April 6–7, Albany, NY.

Schoen, Robert, and John Wooldredge. 1989. "Marriage Choices in North Carolina and Virginia, 1969–71 and 1979–81." *Journal of Marriage and the Family* 51:465–481.

South, Scott J., and Katherine Trent. 1988. "Sex Ratios and Women's Roles: A Cross-National Analysis." *American Journal of Sociology* 93:1096–1115.

Spanier, Graham B., and Paul C. Glick. 1980. "Mate Selection Differentials Between Whites and Blacks in the United States." *Social Forces* 58:707–725.

Stolzenberg, Ross M., and Daniel A. Relles. 1990. "Theory Testing in a World of Constrained Research Design: The Significance of Heckman's Censored Sampling Bias Correction for Nonexperimental Research." *Sociological Methods and Research* 18:395–415.

Sweet, James, Larry Bumpass, and Vaughn Call. 1988. "The Design and Content of the National Survey of Families and Households." Working Paper NSFH-1, Center for Demography and Ecology, University of Wisconsin–Madison.

Teachman, Jay D., Karen A. Polonko, and Geoffrey K. Leigh. 1987. "Marital Timing: Race and Sex Comparisons." *Social Forces* 66:239–268.

Testa, Mark, Nan Marie Astone, Marilyn Krogh, and Kathryn M. Neckerman. 1989. "Employment and Marriage among Inner-City Fathers." *Annals of the American Academy of Political and Social Sciences* 501:79–91.

Thornton, Arland. 1989. "Changing Attitudes Toward Family Issues in the United States." *Journal of Marriage and the Family* 51:873–893.

Tucker, M. Belinda. 1987. "The Black Male Shortage in Los Angeles." *Sociology and Social Research* 71:221–227.

Tucker, M. Belinda, and Robert Joseph Taylor. 1989. "Demographic Correlates of Relationship Status among Black Americans." *Journal of Marriage and the Family* 51:655–665.

U.S. Bureau of the Census. 1989. "Marital Status and Living Arrangements: March 1988." *Current Population Reports,* Series P-20, No. 433. Washington, DC: U.S. Government Printing Office.

Waite, Linda J., and Glenna D. Spitze. 1981. "Young Women's Transition to Marriage." *Demography* 18:681–694.

White, Lynn K. 1981. "A Note on Racial Differences in the Effect of Female Opportunity on Marriage Rates." *Demography* 18:349–354.

Wilson, William Julius. 1987. *The Truly Disadvantaged.* Chicago: University of Chicago Press.

Wilson, William Julius, and Kathryn M. Neckerman. 1986. "Poverty and Family Structure: The Widening Gap between Evidence and Public Policy Issues." Pp. 232–259 in S. H. Danziger and D. H. Weinberg (eds.), *Fighting Poverty.* Cambridge, MA: Harvard University Press.

Zellner, Arnold. 1962. "An Efficient Method of Estimating Seemingly Unrelated Regressions and Tests for Aggregation Bias." *Journal of the American Statistical Association* 57:348–368.

PART THREE

Families, Parents, and Children

10

The Disappearing American Father? Divorce and the Waning Significance of Biological Parenthood

Frank F. Furstenberg, Jr., and Kathleen Mullan Harris

The place of fathers in the family has long been viewed by social scientists as potentially precarious. From the time of Malinowski's writings, family theorists have recognized the comparatively weak link between biological fathers and their children—at least in contrast to the more obvious maternal bond created by pregnancy and childbearing (Malinowski 1930; Davis 1939, 1949; Goode 1960). Malinowski was among the first to observe that marriage is a cultural invention that establishes men's parental rights and responsibilities. The near universality of marriage and its effectiveness in licensing parenthood have been taken as evidence that culture could regulate behavior no less successfully than biology.

Recent changes in marriage practices throughout the Western world have challenged this assumption. The sudden and sweeping transformation in the family during the second half of the twentieth century has caused social theorists to reconsider both the institution of marriage and men's role in the family. (Cherlin 1981, 1988; Davis 1985; Levitan, Belous, and Gallo 1988; Popenoe 1988; Spanier 1989). This chapter will neither consider the sources of this transformation—a subject that has been much addressed in previous writings—nor review in detail the abundant demographic and sociological evidence showing the declining significance of marriage (Cherlin 1988; Davis 1985; Popenoe 1988; Thornton 1989). Our main objective is to examine the impact of family changes on patterns of fathering in families where men and their children live apart.[1]

The data presented here are principally drawn from the National Survey of Children, an eleven-year longitudinal study of children first interviewed in middle childhood (Furstenberg et al. 1983; Moore, Nord, and Peterson 1989). Our results take on added meaning when they are placed in the context of other research. A number of recent studies seem to indicate that a substantial and growing fraction of nonresidential fathers spend little time with their biological offspring or offer them much in the way of material or emotional assistance. The picture that emerges is not an optimistic one. It raises serious questions about what can and should be done to strengthen the position of fathers in the family or make up for their absence. We address though do not resolve these questions in the concluding section of the chapter.

The Transformation of the American Family

The reconsideration of the role of fathers has been forced by a remarkable confluence of family changes during the past quarter-century. By now, it is well known that beginning in the mid-1960s, marriage patterns began to digress sharply from what has now become known as traditional practices. In fact, the very early age at marriage and the relatively low rates of divorce characteristic of the postwar period were discontinuous with preexisting as well as subsequent patterns of marriage behavior. The era of domestic mass production during the baby boom was in fact as anomalous as it was short-lived (Cherlin 1981; Thornton and Freedman 1983).

The declining centrality of marriage can be described as the uncoupling of a sequence of closely timed events in the process of family formation. First, the link between marriage and the onset of sexual behavior was severed; then, the link between marriage and parenthood was attenuated (Cherlin 1988; Furstenberg 1982). Then, couples began to live together outside of marriage, further postponing marriage. The incidence of non-marital childbearing soared as fewer couples felt compelled to marry merely because of pregnancy. At the same time the stability of marital unions plummeted. Marriage became a less secure arrangement for childbearing and for guaranteeing the continued presence of the biological father in the home (McLanahan and Booth 1989).

The simultaneous growth of out-of-wedlock childbearing and marital instability resulted in a sharp rise in female-headed families. Male-headed families have risen as well over the past two decades at an even slightly faster rate. Still, 87 percent of all single-parent families were headed by a mother in 1988. The proportion of children in mother-headed families stood at 21.4 percent in 1988, nearly twice the proportion in 1970 (Select Committee on Children, Youth, and Families 1989).[2]

From the vantage point of children, the probability of growing up with both parents sharply declined during the latter third of the twentieth century. At mid-century, children probably had a higher chance of being raised by both biological parents than at any time in previous history. Rates of nonmarital childbearing were low; death rates had declined from their still steep levels in the early part of the century; and divorce rates, except for a brief period after World War II, were fairly stable. Roughly three out of four children born in the period from 1930 to 1960 would spend their entire childhood with both of their parents (Bumpass and Sweet 1989; Furstenberg and Cherlin 1991; Uhlenberg 1974).

Compare that figure with the status of children born today. Just about a quarter of all children are now born out of wedlock (Select Committee on Children, Youth, and Families 1989). A few of these nonmarital births actually occur in stable unions, but the great majority are to single parents or temporary unions. Add to that the substantial fraction of children born into marriages that will not survive. Bumpass and Sweet (1989) estimate that 44 percent of the children—36 percent of whites, 60 percent of African-Americans, and 43 percent of Mexican-Americans—born between 1970 and 1984 will spend some time in a single-parent family by age 16. Divorce rates have leveled off, perhaps even declined, since the mid-1970s. But nonmarital childbearing has continued to rise, more than offsetting any increase in marital stability (Furstenberg 1990). What do these high rates of marital instability imply for patterns of childbearing, and especially for fathers' involvement with their children?

Parenting Apart: A Research Review

How parents living apart coordinate childcare is a new topic in sociology of the family. The management of parenthood across households has received some attention in the growing literature on unmarried parenthood (Elster and Lamb 1986; Parke and Neville 1987; Robinson 1988; Schultz 1969). It has also come up in studies of the process of separation and divorce (Fox 1985; Lamb 1987; Wallerstein and Kelly 1980). A review of these separate two bodies of research can lead to the impression that fathers often remain involved in their children's lives and continue to play an important role in their upbringing (Children's Defense Fund 1988; Schultz 1969; Thompson 1983). However, recent evidence from several large surveys suggests a more cautious and less optimistic interpretation of the existing data on the role played by outside fathers, the actual amount of co-parenting, or even the unqualified benefits of paternal involvement for the well-being of children (Furstenberg 1989).

Data on child support provide the first piece of evidence that does not square with the impression that most unmarried and formerly married fathers continue to play an active role in the family. From the mid-1970s onward, the Census Bureau has been collecting information on child support payments to single mothers. The earliest of these surveys demonstrated that a relatively small proportion—little more than a third—of nonresidential fathers provided payments, and the level of payments was quite meager.

Never-married mothers were far less likely to receive payments. But even among formerly married mothers, the proportion receiving payments is a distinct minority (Select Committee on Children, Youth, and Families 1989).

Survey Data on Relations Between Nonresidential Fathers and Their Children

The child-support data may conceal informal patterns of paternal support or they may fail to reveal recent trends of increasing support among younger cohorts of fathers. During the past decade several national surveys have provided a cross-sectional picture of the extent of paternal participation in childrearing among nonresidential fathers. The second wave of The National Survey of Children conducted in 1981 provided the first systematic data on patterns of parenting among parents living apart. Three other national surveys conducted since the 1981 survey have also provided information on the relationships between nonresidential fathers and their children (Mott 1989; Seltzer 1989, Seltzer and Bianchi 1988). We shall make no attempt to summarize the results of these studies in detail, but a few general results give the flavor of the overall findings.

All of the surveys reveal a high level of disengagement among fathers not residing with their children. In the NSC, close to half of all children living apart from their fathers had not seen them in the previous year. Most children who had had some contact with fathers saw or heard from them only sporadically. Just a sixth of the children had seen their fathers once a week or more in the past year on average. In a typical month, two-thirds of the children had no contact at all. Phoning and letter writing were also infrequent. Less than half had ever been in their father's home and only a fifth said that they had slept over at their father's house in a typical month.

More recent surveys reveal a high level of paternal disengagement, although not as steep and immediate a decline as was discovered in the NSC. Possibly, recent cohorts of fathers are more likely to retain contact with their children. Or differences in design may explain the lower level of attenuation found in recent surveys.[3] Nonetheless, all studies show a sharp decline in contact over time. Many fathers who appear to initially retain contact with their children ultimately diminish their involvement in the relationship. The dynamics of this changing relationship are not well understood, but it seems that geographical mobility, remarriage, and a declining commitment to child support all figure into the attenuation of bonds between fathers and their children. The inability of many formerly married couples to negotiate a stable and viable childrearing arrangement also appears to undermine the father's continued involvement (Furstenberg and Cherlin 1991).

Given the infrequent interaction between children and their fathers, residential mothers also report rather little communication between them and their former partners. Two-thirds report that they rarely or never discuss matters concerning the child with the father and three-fourths say he takes little responsibility for childrearing decisions (Furstenberg and Nord 1985). The low level of collaboration is primarily due to the father's infrequent contact. But even when he is on the scene, cooperative parenting is not the characteristic style of interaction between parents living apart. Most develop a style that might be termed "parallel parenting": They carry on their childrearing with a minimum of consultation. This style of parenting among couples who do not live together reduces the possibilities of conflict even if it occasionally places burdens on children who must live a highly segregated existence in the two separate households.

Finally, a comment about the couples who shared joint physical custody of their children. Actually, so few turned up in the second wave of the NSC that it is impossible to develop a reliable profile of their behavior. Such families may have become more prevalent in the past decade, but in the early 1980s, at least, they remained a rare breed. As for the handful of couples who did share parenting responsibilities, it appears that many experience a moderate to high amount of conflict in their dealings. As mentioned above, cooperative parenting after divorce is an elusive ideal.

It is interesting to observe the situation for the small number of children living apart from their mothers. Nonresidential mothers were more involved than fathers who lived outside the home. Still, a third of the children not living with their mothers had not seen them in the past month and 40 percent had not spent even a single night at their house. According to the custodial parent (fathers or grandparents), mothers living apart from their children were generally uninvolved with childrearing decisions and had little or no influence in day-to-day matters concerning the child. Apparently, living outside the home erodes parental participation—even when the absent parent is the mother.

Although the research to date has identified some striking trends, an incomplete picture of relations between fathers and their children in disrupted families remains. Because they have been observed at only one point in time, it is difficult to uncover much about when and why fathers disengage from their children or to discern the consequences of different patterns of paternal involvement for children.

This chapter uses both cross-sectional and longitudinal data from three successive waves of the National Survey of Children to examine the dynamics of paternal involvement over time. After a brief description of the data, we examine the changing patterns of contact between children and fathers at three points in time. We then analyze shifts in the affective bond between children and their nonresidential fathers at two points in time as they move from early adolescence to early adulthood.

The Data

Our data are from the National Survey of Children (NSC), a panel study of a nationally representative sample of children interviewed in 1976, 1981, and 1987. The sample was developed from a household enumeration that screened families with children in the designated age range of 7 to 11 years in 1976. The survey was originally designed to be a broad assessment of the social, physical, and psychological characteristics of U.S. children and of family and neighborhood circumstances in which they grow up. In 1976, in-person interviews were obtained for 2,301 children from 1,747 households, with a completion rate of 80 percent.

In 1981, a second wave of interviews that focused on the effects on children of marital conflict and family disruption was carried out among a subsample of the children interviewed in 1976. All children who had experienced the disruption of their families or who had been living in high-conflict families at the time of the 1976 survey were reinterviewed, as was a subsample of children who had been living in stable families at that time. Eighty-two percent of those selected for follow-up were interviewed yielding a sample of 1,423 children between the ages of 11 and 16.

The focus of the third wave of interviews in 1987 was on the social, psychological and economic well-being of sample members as they became young adults. Telephone interviews were conducted with 1,147 youth or 82.4 percent of those interviewed in previous waves. Adjustments were made in the weighting of the data to correct for differential sample attrition by age, sex, race of child, and residential location so that the sample resembles the distribution of children born between September 1964 and December 1969 and living in the United States in 1976. For further details on sample selection and data collection, see Furstenberg and Nord (1985), Furstenberg, Nord, Peterson, and Zill (1983), and Moore and Peterson (1989).

Marital Disruption and Contact with Fathers

We first examine the prevailing levels of contact between children and their nonresidential biological fathers at three points in time for the sample as a whole.[4] Figure 10.1 presents the cross-sectional data on children's contact with their nonresidential fathers by the length of time since the marriage was disrupted at the three interview points—in 1976 when children were between the ages of 7 and 11, in 1981, and in 1987 when the children were 18 to 23. The two panels of the figure show the proportion of children who have *any* contact and those with *regular* contact—at least once a week

Figure 10.1 Contact with Biological Fathers, by Length of Time Since Separation, NSC 1976, 1981, 1987

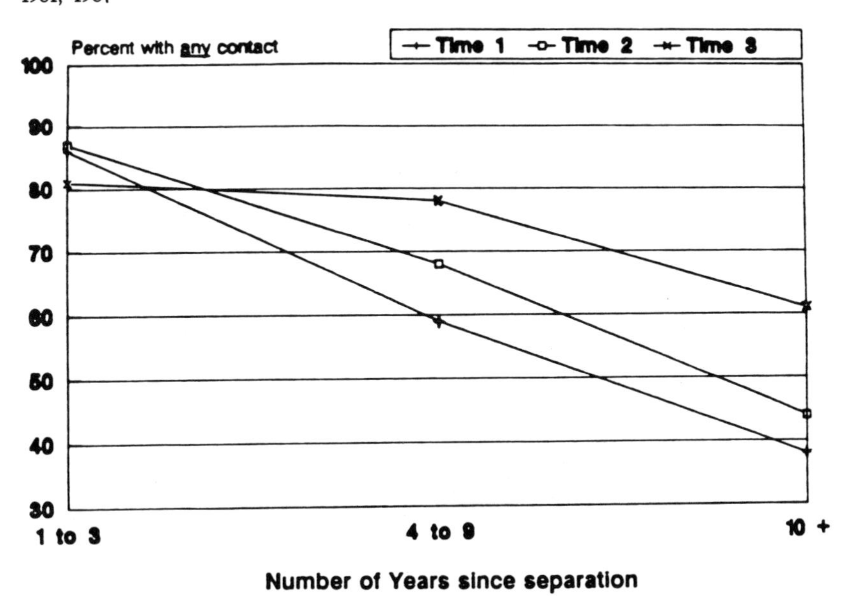

Percent with regular contact

time 1 time 2 time 3

60
50
40
30
20
10
0

1 to 3
4 to 9
10 +

Number of Years since separation

or more on average—in the 12 months preceding the survey. Obviously, one might expect to find differing levels of contact at each survey wave both because the children are getting older and because the interval since separation is lengthening on average. Because disruptions of marriages continue throughout the study, we are able to contrast patterns of contact with fathers among children whose parents divorced in middle childhood, in early and in late adolescence.

The patterns of contact at all three cross-sections appear to be roughly similar—that is, contact diminishes sharply over time. But the slope of the decline changes. It is steepest at the initial wave when children were quite young at the time of divorce and least marked when the parental separation occurred in middle childhood or later in adolescence. This suggests that a later age at separation may counteract the pattern of attenuation so evident in the initial two waves of the study.

Tables 10.1a and 10.1b explore this possibility by examining age-at-separation and duration-since-separation effects simultaneously. Although some cell sizes are too small to provide reliable estimates, it would appear that age at separation and duration since separation are both influencing the resultant pattern of contact. But age effects are much more important in determining whether children have any contact with their fathers (Table 10.1a). Duration effects are observed only among the children who were separated from their fathers before age five. (This can be seen by comparing the column and the row differences in Table 10.1a). However, when we examine regularity of contact (Table 10.1b), the results are not as clear cut. Here age-of-separation effects may be less important than duration effects. In others words, all children, regardless of when their parents separate, experience a sharp drop-off in the regularity of contact over time. However, the inconsistencies in the table suggest either that the numbers are too small to reveal regularities or that the cross-sectional data may be masking more complex changes in patterns of contact. A longitudinal examination of the data should help us to understand better the dynamics of change hinted at in the cross-sectional information presented above.

A Longitudinal Analysis of Contact

Up to this point we have assumed that contact can only diminish over time. But fathers and children may resume contact or begin to see one another more frequently. The cross-sectional snapshots provide only net effects, concealing the actual declines and increases that occur over the three time points. The next pair of tables takes advantage of the longitudinal data by observing a child's pattern of contact with his or her father from one interview to the next.[5] We compare two sets of transitions—the first

Table 10.1a Percent of Youth Having Contact with Outside Father, by Age at Separation, Number of Years Since Separation, and Year of Interview[1]

	Time 1 (1976)			Time 2 (1981)			Time 3 (1987)		
Years since separation	1-3	4-9	10+	1-3	4-9	10+	1-3	4-9	10+
Age at Separation									
1-4	-	55 (129)	38 (13)	-	62 (21)	42 (117)	-	-	52 (95)
5-9	86 (72)	83 (24)	-	-	66 (95)	67 (12)	-	-	69 (84)
10+	-	-	-	86 (44)	93 (15)	-	81 (37)	77 (48)	73 (11)

Table 10.1b Percent of Youth Having Regular Contact at Least Once a Week on Average with Outside Father, by Age at Separation, Number of Years Since Separation, and Year of Interview[1]

	Time 1 (1976)			Time 2 (1981)			Time 3 (1987)		
Years since separation	1-3	4-9	10+	1-3	4-9	10+	1-3	4-9	10+
Age at separation									
1-4	-	5 (129)	15 (13)	-	19 (21)	9 (117)	-	-	21 (95)
5-9	49 (72)	4 (24)	-	-	25 (95)	-	-	-	21 (84)
10+	-	-	-	43 (44)	0 (15)	-	32 (37)	27 (48)	9 (11)

when children moved from preadolescence to adolescence (time 1 to time 2) and the second from adolescence to early adulthood (time 2 to time 3).

Looking first at the total number of children who had experienced a separation by the 1976 interview and who were reinterviewed in 1981, we observe a familiar pattern of attenuation in paternal contact (see Table 10.2a). Just under one-third of the children in contact with their fathers at time 1 lost contact by time 2; only 1 in 5 moved from no contact to some contact during the same time period. The most common pattern over time was consistency. The odds ratio of children continuing their previous pattern of contact, that is of remaining on the diagonal, was 10.3.[6]

A similar analysis of the changing pattern of contact between times 2 and 3 also reveals a pattern of consistency, though to a lesser extent (see Table 10.2a). An odds ratio of 7.0 indicates greater flux in father-child relations as children move from adolescence into early adulthood. Not only are the patterns of contact less stable in later adolescence but the direction of the change is more toward reinitiation of contact. In fact, among those who change their pattern of visitation from one time to the next, children were about as likely to gain as to lose contact during late adolescence. This has the effect of stemming the rapid decline in contact that occurs in the early years following divorce.

Regular contact exhibits a similar pattern of consistency during the two time periods—that is, stability is more characteristic in the earlier (odds ratio = 11.3) than the later period (odds ratio = 3.9—see Table 10.2b). However, the increasing amount of change reveals a different pattern of asymmetry than the pattern found for any contact. Children are far more likely to experience a sharp decline in *regular* contact during late adolescence and early adulthood than to increase their level of contact. Of course, this pattern may not be peculiar to nonresidential fathers. After all, a growing number of young adults interact less frequently with their residential parents during this time as well (Goldscheider and Lebourdais 1986).

In part, the shifting patterns of contact and regular contact described above could be artifacts of the high rates of attenuation early in children's lives. By late adolescence, so many fathers have lost contact with their children that those who remain in contact are no doubt more committed to an enduring relationship. In other words, the subgroup of fathers and children that remain in touch with one another over time becomes more selective—accounting for the declining level of attrition in contact. Also, youth with sporadic patterns of paternal contact were slightly more likely to exit from the study before time 3, further adding to the selectivity of those who maintain contact.

An additional clue to understanding the changing patterns of contact is provided by analyzing whether these patterns differ by factors such as children's sex, age, age at separation, race, their mother's educational level,

Table 10.2a Change in Patterns of Contact (at least once in previous year) from Time 1 to Time 2 and from Time 2 to Time 3

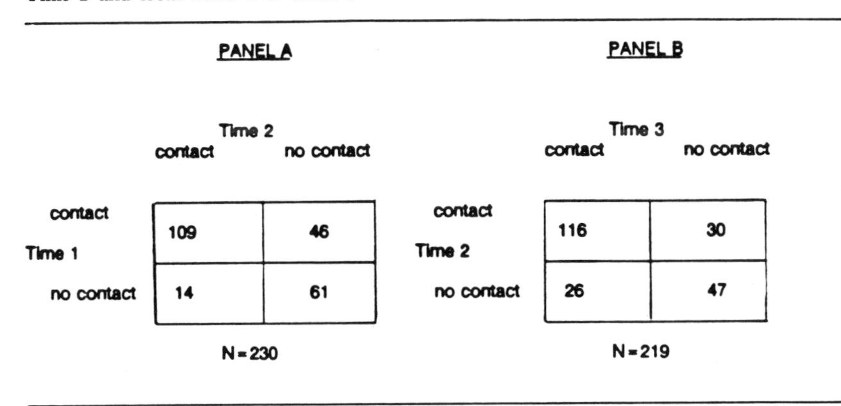

PANEL A

		Time 2: contact	Time 2: no contact
Time 1	contact	109	46
	no contact	14	61

N=230

PANEL B

		Time 3: contact	Time 3: no contact
Time 2	contact	116	30
	no contact	26	47

N=219

Table 10.2b Changes in Patterns of Regular Contact (at least once a week on average) from Time 1 to Time 2 and from Time 2 to Time 3

PANEL A

		Time 2 regular contact: yes	Time 2 regular contact: no
Time 1 regular contact	yes	24	21
	no	17	168

N=230

PANEL B

		Time 3 regular contact: yes	Time 3 regular contact: no
Time 2 regular contact	yes	22	33
	no	24	140

N=219

and whether or not she remarried during the course of the study. The results of these analyses (not shown) reveal an interesting story. In the first transition period, many of these factors showed significant differences in the pattern of continuity and in the direction of the turnover, in particular race and the education level of the mother. Blacks experienced much greater instability in their patterns of contact than whites, and children of better educated mothers (more than high school) experienced greater continuity in contact with outside fathers than children of less educated mothers.

These differences disappear in the period between time 2 and 3. That is, the same pattern observed for the entire sample is replicated within every subgroup; a decline in stability of contact and an increasing proportion of reinitiation of some contact (relative to loss of contact). Although certain groups experience more rapid disengagement of the father following separation than other groups, over time *all groups* experience the same collective pattern in changing contact with outside fathers.

Our analysis of paternal contact has uncovered a growing amount of instability in patterns of interaction during the later stages of the study. A small number of children who had lost contact with their fathers at time 2 begin to see them on an occasional basis, but few with any regularity. Moreover, just a tenth of the children reported regular contact at both times 2 and 3—exactly the same proportion who had regular contact at both times 1 and 2. A central question is whether this modest level of contact is sufficient for many youth to sustain meaningful relationships with their fathers. In the next section of the paper, our attention turns from the quantity to the quality of relationships. The information on the changing level of affective bonds provides a clearer indication of the significance of nonresidential fathers in their children's lives.

Marital Disruption and Paternal Involvement

The quality of the father-child relationship is measured by children's reports about the level of closeness to, warmth toward, and identification with their fathers. Based on three items in the interview, we developed an affect scale that ranges from 0, when the father-child bond is very weak, to 3, when father involvement is very high. Unfortunately, no such measures were collected in the first interview, so we can only examine changing levels of affect between time 2 and 3. (See Appendix 10.1 for a description of these items and construction of the scale.) Table 10.3 provides a cross-sectional picture of relations between children and their parents, contrasting fathers in intact families with mothers and fathers in nonintact families. The top panel shows the percent of adolescents who report high levels of parental involvement for each of the three items, "closeness," "be like," and "gives affection," and the percent distribution on the 3-item affect scale for time 2. The bottom panel presents the distributions for time 3. The first column reveals the quality of the father-child bond in intact families; the remaining columns focus on nonintact families (the biological father lives outside the home). The second column shows the levels of closeness with the biological mother in nonintact families and the third column shows levels of closeness with all outside biological fathers including in the base those who had no contact with the child in the last year. The final column restricts the base of outside fathers to those with whom the adolescent has contact.

Contrasting the quality of the father-child bond in intact families with nonintact families (columns 1 and 3), we see a striking difference in the

Table 10.3 Measures of Affect in the Parent-Child Relationship by Family Structure, at Time 2 (1981) and Time 3 (1987)

	Intact Families	Non-Intact Families		
	Fathers (n=533)	Mothers (n=216)	All Fathers (n=216)	Father with contact (n=116)
Time 2				
closeness	.79	.86	.38	.53
be like	.72	.64	.32	.44
gives affection	.73	.75	.36	.53
Affect scale				
no contact			.32	
0	.07	.04	.19	.30
1	.15	.17	.15	.21
2	.25	.31	.13	.18
3	.54	.49	.21	.31
Time 3				
closeness	.71	.78	.28	.45
be like	.71	.61	.26	.42
gives affection	.71	.67	.26	.42
Affect scale				
no contact			.36	
0	.12	.13	.26	.39
1	.14	.17	.11	.18
2	.23	.23	.10	.18
3	.51	.48	.17	.25

levels of affect. The proportion of adolescents in intact families who report having a strong bond with their fathers is more than twice as high as that of the adolescents in nonintact families. At time 2, for instance, 79 percent of the adolescents in intact families say they are very close to their fathers. By contrast, 38 percent of adolescents in nonintact families report as strong a bond with their outside fathers. The weaker bond between children and their outside fathers is also suggested by the distribution of the affect scale at time 2. Almost 80 percent of the adolescents in intact families fall into the two highest levels of affect on the index compared to 34 percent of those in nonintact families.

Differences in father-child relations between intact and nonintact families are even more dramatic at time 3. Although levels of father involvement drop slightly within intact families, the decline in closeness with outside fathers is still greater. By time 3, when the children are in late adolescence and early adulthood, almost 3 times as many children from intact families as from nonintact families experience a high-quality relationship with their father. Clearly, fathers in intact families are more involved and enjoy a closer relationship with their children than nonresidential fathers and this advantage apparently increases over time.

Focusing only on nonintact families, the child's bond to the residential mother is substantially stronger than it is to the outside biological father. By a ratio of more than 2 to 1, adolescents report stronger affective ties to their mothers than to their nonresidential fathers. Attenuation in closeness to mothers is slight compared to the decline experienced by outside fathers. The proportion of adolescents in nonintact families reporting strong affective bonds with their mothers (the two highest levels on the affect scale) drops from 80 percent to 71 percent from time 2 to 3; whereas the proportion who are close to their fathers drops from one-third to one-quarter. Thus, as adolescents from nonintact families enter early adulthood, practically three times as many report having a strong emotional bond with their mothers than with their fathers.

The affect measures in column 3 of Table 10.3 include all nonresidential fathers, including roughly a third of those at each time who have no contact at all. These fathers are omitted from the base in the fourth column. The levels of paternal affect increase due to the smaller denominator, but the data still indicate that outside fathers have much weaker bonds with their children than intact residential fathers and than nonintact residential mothers. Closeness levels with outside fathers are one-third lower at time 2 and 42 percent lower at time 3 than the levels of affect with fathers in intact families.

Among children in nonintact families who are in contact with their outside fathers, about half experience a warm and close relationship with their fathers when they are in mid-adolescence, and this proportion drops to about 43 percent as they become young adults. Thus, not only does contact decline over time, but among those who have contact, the cross-sectional perspective reveals a modest decline in closeness as well. Although the overall pattern is one of general decline in closeness over time, a sizable minority of 50 adolescents (43%) report a strong attachment with their outside fathers at time 3. Whether high levels of father involvement have a significant impact on the child's life and whether high-quality father-child relations that are sustained over time make a difference in child outcomes is currently under investigation in a separate analysis.

Paternal Involvement Where Contact Was Lost or Regained

It is especially interesting to examine the quality of the paternal relationship when contact between the outside father and adolescent was either lost or reinitiated between time 2 and time 3. Table 10.4 displays the levels of father involvement for those adolescents who lost and who regained contact

Table 10.4 Affective Measures of Paternal Involvement for Adolescents Who Lose Contact with Fathers by Time 3 and for Adolescents Who Reinitiate Contact with Fathers at Time 3

	Lose contact time 2 affect (n=31)	Reinitiate contact time 3 affect (n=22)
Affect items		
closeness	.65	.41
be like	.61	.36
gives affection	.48	.32
Affect scale		
0	.16	.55
1	.26	.14
2	.26	.00
3	.32	.32

from time 2 to time 3. Among adolescents who subsequently lost contact, we anticipated that father involvement at time 2 would be relatively weak. These children, we reasoned, would be more susceptible to losing contact when they already had previously deteriorating relations. Surprisingly, however, adolescents who lost contact over time resemble those who maintained contact in their levels of affect with their fathers. The contrasting group—adolescents who regained contact with their father—conformed more to our prior expectations. The reinitiated bond is relatively weak compared to those who had contact throughout the time period. Evidently, reinitiation of contact in the father-child relation does not lead to a high-quality relationship, at least not initially, and this hints at the possibility that fathers rather than children are responsible for the restoration of contact.

Affective Mobility

We now turn our analysis to tracking the course of father-child relations in nonintact families over time. Given a starting level of paternal involvement, what are the chances of an improvement or a deterioration in relations? In other words, how stable is the affective relationship through adolescence? To investigate the association between the levels of affect at two points in time, we use categorical data analysis to model the extent to which father-child relations change during adolescence (Fienberg 1989). When the affect

Table 10.5 Affective Mobility: Time 2 Affect Scale by Time 3 Affect Scale for Nonresidential Fathers (N = 116)

		Time 2 Affect Scale				
		0	1	2	3	total
Time 3 Affect Scale	0	19	7	10	9	45
	1	3	7	3	8	21
	2	7	4	3	7	21
	3	6	6	5	12	29
	total	35	24	21	36	116

scale at time 2 is cross-classified with the affect scale at time 3, a square contingency table is obtained revealing the turnover or mobility in closeness over time and is shown in Table 10.5.[7] If there were perfect association in the table, then affect responses would tend to cluster along the diagonal. That is, given an initial level of paternal involvement at time 2, it would remain the same at time 3. The extent to which the counts cluster on the diagonal reveals the stability in relations between fathers and children during adolescence.

Table 10.5 shows instead that there is a fair amount of movement in affective relations with outside fathers: 65 percent of the adolescents in time 2 are at a different level of closeness with their fathers at time 3. Furthermore, of those whose paternal relations change over time, 59 percent experience a decline in closeness, and 41 percent experience an improvement in relations. Therefore, for those father-child dyads that do experience changing relations, on balance, the direction of movement or change in affect over time is toward weaker rather than toward closer bonds.

Using log-linear analysis, we estimated a variety of association models to determine whether the affective mobility was due to a general change in the underlying distributions of father-child affect over time, to some systematic association in affect over time, or to random fluctuation (Hout et al. 1987). The fit of various association models to the affective mobility table in Table 10.5 is shown in Appendix 10.2. The most parsimonious description of the changing patterns in father-child affective relations is the model specifying symmetry and independence (model #1).[8]

The symmetry in the model implies that there is no significant difference in the marginal distributions of affect between time 2 and time 3. That is, in the aggregate, affective relations with outside fathers do not change over time. Independence implies the absence of a significant association between the two affect scores over time. In other words, the level of affect in the father-child relation at time 3 is independent of the level of affect at time 2. Thus, although the underlying collective distribution of paternal involvement remains stable over time, relations with outside fathers are just as likely to improve or to deteriorate as they are to stay the same.

To explore the possibility of differences in affective mobility by subgroups of the population of nonintact families, association models were also estimated to test for gender, age, race, and family-structure interactions. The results (not shown) revealed that these factors did not determine differential affective mobility in father-child relations over time. Within each subgroup (males/females; less than 14 years of age/14+ at time 2; whites/blacks; and stepfamilies/mother-only families) the association is symmetric and independent. It should be noted that these factors may determine differences in the *levels* of affect at a point in time, but they do not determine differences in the *pattern of change* in affect over time.

What does this mean for the course of father-child relations through adolescence and into early adulthood? The underlying dimension of closeness with outside fathers does not change significantly over time. But for an individual father-child dyad, the quality of the relationship is highly unstable and unpredictable over time. A strong affective bond at time 2 is not a guarantee that the relationship will remain strong by time 3. Conversely, adolescents who have a poor relationship with their outside father at time 2 are equally likely to improve as they are to stay the same through time. These data imply wide fluctuation in the affective bonds between adolescents and outside fathers over time.

These results contrast distinctly with a similar analysis of affective mobility within intact families (Harris and Furstenberg 1990). Father-child relations in intact families were markedly more stable over time—given a level of affect at time 2, the chances of staying at that level were much greater than moving either up or down on the affect scale. By comparison, relations with outside fathers are much less stable—perhaps because they are subject to the vicissitudes of living arrangements, marriage, and economic security that accompany family life when biological parents divorce. Possibly, too, the instability of the emotional bond could indicate a more superficial relationship between children and their nonresidential fathers that is prone to frequent emotional reassessments.

The Place of Surrogate Fathers

A shortcoming of our analysis is its exclusive focus on relations between biological fathers and their children. We have ignored the obvious fact that in the course of childhood many children acquire stepfathers or other surrogate fathers who may offer the emotional and material assistance not provided by the biological father. In a subsequent analysis we will give more attention to the role of surrogate fathers and their consequences for the well-being of children. However, we can report here that close relations with a surrogate father were about as prevalent as they were with outside biological fathers.[9]

Although adolescents were not as strongly attached to stepfathers living inside the home as they were to biological fathers in the home, levels of affect for stepfathers were very similar to those for outside fathers in early- to mid-adolescence. Within stepfamilies at time 2, about 60 percent reported feeling very close to their stepfather compared to 61 percent who reported a close relationship with their outside biological father. On the affect scale, 62 percent enjoyed a strong bond with their stepfather; 61 percent enjoyed the same degree of attachment with their biological father. As adolescents enter young adulthood, relations with stepfathers decline as do relations with biological fathers. At time 3, 38 percent report a close relationship with their stepfather compared to 43 percent with their biological fathers. Clearly some youths are able to establish strong bonds with a stepparent. The level of affective attachment with stepparents does at least indicate the possibility that many youths do form significant attachments with surrogate fathers. This may be one of many factors that accounts for the high amount of emotional instability in relations with biological fathers described previously.

Summary and Conclusion

When we look at maritally disrupted families over time, the picture that emerges confirms the impression provided by cross-sectional studies. Relationships with outside fathers are neither prevalent nor predictable. Children generally experience a declining amount of contact with their fathers. The drop-off is especially evident among children whose fathers moved out when they were quite young—many of whom lose contact with their fathers for most or all of their childhood.

The pattern of declining contact is not uniform over time. Fathers do not continue to fade out as much when children reach adolescence, and some even become more active as their children reach late adolescence and early adulthood. Patterns of contact were more stable from early childhood to adolescence than from adolescence to early adulthood when losses in contact declined and reinitiation of contact increased. As a result, the balance of gains to losses of contact shifts dramatically, favoring a slightly higher proportion of gains as youth move from early adolescence to early adulthood.

These results suggest that we should give greater recognition to the capacity of children and fathers to resurrect their relationship later in life. Adolescents sometimes migrate from their mothers' to their fathers' households during this time. Even when they don't shift residence, they may be responsive to emotional bids from their fathers or even seek such bids. Mothers may be less able or inclined to play the role of gatekeeper. For their part, fathers may be more willing to establish ties with their children when they do not have to deal with their former spouse. Many men seem to regard childrearing as part of a bundle of marital responsibilities attached to the household where they reside. When they leave the household, they find it difficult to maintain bonds with their children at the same time that they relinquish ties to their former spouse. That mind-set may change when children no longer are so rooted to their mother's household.

Unfortunately it is difficult to establish a convincing case on the basis of our data that the mild resurgence of contact between children and their fathers is very consequential. To the contrary, reinitiation only rarely resulted in strong bonds between fathers and their offspring. And interestingly, the opposite pattern—loss of contact with fathers—is not necessarily the result of weak ties: Fathers who lost contact with their children during adolescence had just as strong ties as those who remained in contact. Such unpredictability in father-child relations when the father lives outside the home was reflected in our analysis of changing affective ties with outside fathers. Even among those children who sustain contact with their fathers, affective relations vary widely over time and paternal involvement fluctuates as children move through adolescence and into early adulthood.

Our analysis of the sources of disengagement by fathers following divorce revealed that although a few factors determined greater rapidity in disengagement, ultimately the trends we have described occur among all subgroups that we observed. That is, over time, all groups of fathers and children collectively experienced the same overall decline in contact and instability in emotional attachment.

Implications: The Effect of Fathers on Children's Welfare

This chapter has not looked at the critical question of whether or how various behavioral outcomes—schooling, early labor-market participation, teenage childbearing, crime and substance abuse, or mental health—are linked to children's relations with their fathers. We are in the midst of that analysis and will present its findings in another publication. However, it is not difficult to anticipate some provisional findings even from the partial evidence assembled in this chapter. First of all, there are few families in which nonresidential fathers maintained frequent contact and a close relationship with their children. After all, just 10 percent of the children had regular contact with their fathers at both of the first two survey points and just 5 percent at all three. And of those who maintained contact from time 2 to time 3, just 10 percent sustained a strong affective bond compared with 34 percent in intact families. True, other fathers who had episodic and weak ties to their children strengthened their bonds during adolescence. But again, the number of such cases is small. Thus, we can anticipate that the overall impact of paternal participation on children's behavior is not likely to be very great. Of course, it is nonetheless important to look at the special subset of involved fathers to see if they provided critical assistance to their children. An earlier cross-sectional analysis using cruder measures failed to turn up evidence that children did better when their nonresidential fathers were highly involved in their upbringing. But a stronger test of this hypothesis is presently in the works.

Implications: The Changing Role of Men in the Family

This paper has emphasized the negative side of what Furstenberg (1988) previously described as the good dads–bad dads complex, a simultaneous trend in American society that gives men latitude to become highly involved caretakers or to play a relatively minor role in family life. We do not discount the abundant evidence suggesting that more residential fathers are assuming a greater level of parental responsibility. Men in the family may be gradually, sometimes willingly and sometimes reluctantly, sharing more childcare. In so doing, they may be expanding their paternal repertoire and forging much closer emotional links with their children.

But this emergent trend is more than offset, we believe, by the enormous growth in the number of nonresidential fathers. If we take seriously the evidence in this paper, active childcare among nonresidential fathers is limited. Parenting apart, whether after marriage or when marriage never occurs, introduces enormous complications in developing an effective alliance between parents, who frequently harbor considerable resentments toward one another (Furstenberg and Cherlin 1991). Is it reasonable to expect these parties to exchange information, provide mutual support, and coordinate their activities on behalf of their children?

Nonresidential parents are likely to fade into a secondary role when faced with the current constraints imposed by parenting apart. Frequently, fathers adopt the alternative strategy of shifting their allegiance to a new household either by starting a new family or acquiring an existing one. This pattern of swapping families may be a rational adaptation to the relative ease of managing children inside as opposed to outside the household. In effect, most men and women find it easier to see marriage (or its equivalent) and childrearing as a package deal than as two discrete and unrelated enterprises.

If we are correct, the role of fathers is being redefined by a changing marriage system. The responsibilities of fathers are carried from one household to the next as they migrate from one marriage to the next. Some men who become stepparents or surrogate parents in a new household often transfer their loyalties to their new family. Relations with their biological children become largely symbolic if they survive at all.[10]

We are arguing then that the fusion of biological and sociological fatherhood that has traditionally been accomplished by marriage may be undergoing a radical transformation as the institution of matrimony is declining. Many men are biological fathers and sociological fathers, but a growing proportion are not both at the same time. This observation has important implications for policymakers who are keen on restoring men's obligations to their biological offspring.

Implications for Public Policy

A succession of child-support enforcement bills were enacted in the 1980s, culminating in the Family Support Act passed in 1988. This latter piece of legislation was designed to require biological fathers to pay a larger share of child support. A major objective of the bill was to reinforce a father's financial obligation to his offspring. Many proponents of this legislation hope that compelling fathers to pay may also strengthen the social and emotional bonds between men and their offspring.

Although we do not disagree with the efforts to enforce child support, we are skeptical that such efforts are likely to result in stronger ties between nonresidential parents and their children. We believe that the possibilities of fostering effective paternal bonds by compelling child support are likely to be modest at best. The limitations of nonresidential fatherhood are quite real. Men are likely to develop competing obligations in other households. Residential mothers, too, sometimes have conflicting interests that may lead them to spurn or even undermine a nonresidential father's emotional claims.

We recognize that some parents manage to cooperate when they no longer reside together. Others peacefully coexist even when they cannot cooperate. Still, we believe that policies that assume a high level of collaboration between parents are doomed to produce disappointing results. The Family Support Act may well increase the level of child-support payments; however, it is not likely to reintegrate fathers back into the family.

What are our options for strengthening ties between men and their offspring? The only obvious alternative that we see is to strengthen our faltering marriage system—a remedy that may be unappealing to some and unthinkable to others. We must admit that we have no obvious prescriptions for rejuvenating marriage. Many advocates of economic reform believe that improved economic prospects, especially among minorities, would encourage couples to enter marriage and remain wed in the face of emotional discontents. But few now argue that economic opportunities should be differentially available to men. Expanded job opportunities for women as well as men may sustain the trend of delayed marriage and high rates of conjugal instability.

Involving men in parenting could have a salutary effect on marital stability, assuming the formation of a union. All other things equal, men who actively participate in raising their children may be more reluctant to leave marriage. Furthermore, men's childrearing efforts may constitute a form of emotional capital in marriages that are badly in need of greater investment. Hence women may be less likely to experience discontents in marriage when their husbands more actively participate in childrearing (Harris and Morgan 1990). And even when marriages do not survive, more active fathers might be more likely to sustain relationships with their children after divorce. The cultural promotion of the "good dad" ideal may be one of our best defenses against the withdrawal of fathers from the family.

It should be clear that we are not very sanguine about the possibilities of reversing the general decline in the institution of marriage in modern society. But we are fairly confident that the ideal of the conjugal family system is not likely to disappear and be replaced by another family form. What we foresee is greater diversity, an expansion of our already pluralistic kinship system. Were it not the case that children experienced greatly different life chances in different family forms, the idea of pluralism might be celebrated. Perhaps, then, we ought to think about ways of ensuring that children's futures are not so tightly linked to their parents' choices of whether or not to live together.

Acknowledgments

The authors are grateful to Julien Teitler for data analysis and editorial assistance and to Herbert Smith for invaluable methodological advice. We also thank Kristin Moore for reviewing an earlier draft. Data collection was funded by NICH ASPE/DHHS, made to Child Trends, Inc., under Grant #HD21537-03. The analysis was funded by ASPE/DHHS under the same grant.

Appendix 10.1: Description of Affect Measures and Scale

The following three items were asked of the child in both the 1981 and 1987 interviews:

1. How close do you feel to your father:
   1) extremely close,
   2) quite close,
   3) fairly close, or
   4) not very close?

2. How much do you want to be like the kind of person he is when you're an adult:
   1) a lot,
   2) quite a bit,
   3) just a little, or
   4) not at all?

3. Does your father give you:
   1) all the affection you want,
   2) slightly less than you want,
   3) much less than you want, or
   4) don't you want affection from him?

We combined the three items above to construct an index of affect or closeness in the father-child relationship for each of the time 2 (1981) and time 3 (1987) interviews. We first standardized each item by dichotomizing the response distribution into a low and high response. On the "closeness" and "be like" items, we dichotomized the distribution as high when the respondent reported feeling extremely or quite close (1 and 2) to the parent and wanting to be like the parent a lot or quite a bit (1 and 2); and low for responses 3 and 4. On the "gives affection" item, high was indicated by the first response—when the adolescent reported that the parent gives all the affection that is wanted—and low for the remaining responses (2 through 4).

We then added the number of high responses to indicate the level of paternal involvement at the two time points. Thus, this affective dimension is measured by a scale that ranges from 0, when the child reports the affect in the relationship as low on all three items, to 3, when the child says he/she is very close to the father, wants to be like the father, and receives all the affection he/she needs from the father. The reliability

(Cronbach's alpha) of this affective scale is .78 at time 2 and .81 at time 3.

The same three items were asked of the child about the mother and an affect index was similarly computed for the mother-child relationship (with a reliability of .71).

Appendix 10.2 Likelihood-Ratio Chi-Squared Statistics for the Fit of Selected Association Models to Affective Mobility Tables for Nonresidential Fathers (N = 116)

Model	L^2	df	L^2 for rejection of model: $\alpha = .05$
1. symmetry + independence	13.43	12	21.03
2. independence	11.22	9	16.92
3. symmetry	3.55	6	12.59
4. quasi-independence	3.20	5	11.07
5. quasi-symmetry	0.53	3	7.81
6. symmetry + uniform	10.19	11	19.68
7. uniform association	7.64	8	15.51

Notes

1. We have chosen not to give equal attention to fathers who remain with their children, which is treated in a separate analysis (Harris and Furstenberg 1990).

2. Children in father-headed households climbed from 1.1 percent to 2.9 percent during the same period.

3. Variations in the age of children, the interval since separation, or the measure of contact might account for some of the differences.

4. Only mother's reports of contact between children and their biological fathers were available in the first wave of the survey. Third-wave contact information was only available from the youth, while in the second wave of the survey we were able to use both mothers' and youths' reports for consistency checks. In only a small number of instances did mothers and children not agree and in all but one of these cases we favored the greater amount of contact based on the assumption that children may have been seeing their fathers without their mother's knowledge and mothers would be recalling instances of paternal contact that the children had

forgotten. One case was omitted altogether because the difference in the amount of contact reported was too great for us to reconcile.

5. The data are confined to children who were already living apart from their fathers at the prior interview.

6. This is interpreted as the chances of maintaining contact at time 2 relative to losing contact at time 2 are more than 10 times greater if there is contact at time 1 as opposed to no contact at time 1. Similarly, the chances of having no contact at time 2 are 10 times greater if there was no contact at time 1 relative to having contact at time 1.

7. This affective mobility table includes only those adolescents who have contact with their fathers at both points in time.

8. When we compare the fit of model 1 with that of the independence model (#2), the difference is an L^2 of 2.21 with 3 degrees of freedom, which is not a significant improvement in fit over the symmetry + independence model. Similarly, the comparison between model 1 and model 6, symmetry + uniform, results in an L^2 of 3.24 with 1 degree of freedom—again not a significant improvement in fit.

9. Because the affect measures regarding the stepfather were not available at all times we were not able to analyze affective mobility with stepfathers.

10. Remarriage is not the only source of reduced commitment to biological offspring. Some men who never remarry may nonetheless shift their allegiance from their biological children as they take on responsibilities for other children. For example, it has been observed, especially among African-Americans, that many men are called upon to care for their mother's or sister's children who may lack a residential father. In this chapter we have not examined the parenting patterns of unmarried fathers, a topic that will be explored in a separate analysis.

References

Bumpass, L. L., and J. A. Sweet. 1989. Children's experience in single-parent families: Implications of cohabitation and marital transitions. *Family Planning Perspectives, 21*(6), 256–260.

Cherlin, A. J. 1981. *Marriage, divorce, remarriage.* Cambridge, MA: Harvard University Press.

Cherlin, A. J. 1988. The weakening link between marriage and the care of children. *Family Planning Perspectives, 20*(6), 302–306.

Children's Defense Fund. 1988. *Adolescent and young fathers: Problems and solutions.* Washington, DC: Adolescent Pregnancy Prevention Clearinghouse.

Davis, K. 1939. Illegitimacy and the social structure. *American Journal of Sociology,* Vol. 45, 215–233.

Davis, K. 1949. *Human society.* New York: The Macmillan Company.

Davis, K. (ed.). 1985. *Contemporary marriage: Comparative perspectives on a changing institution.* New York: Russell Sage Foundation.

Elster, A., and M. E. Lamb. 1986. *Adolescent fatherhood.* Hillsdale, NJ: Lawrence Erlbaum Assoc.

Fienberg, S. 1989. *The analysis of cross-classified categorical data.* Cambridge, MA: The MIT Press.

Fox, G. L. 1985. Noncustodial fathers. In S. Hanson and F. Bozett (eds.), *Dimensions of fatherhood,* pp. 393–415. Beverly Hills, CA: Sage.

Furstenberg, F. F., Jr. 1982. Conjugal succession: Reentering marriage after divorce. In P. B. Baltes and O. G. Brim (eds.), *Life span development and behavior* (Vol. 4), pp. 107–146. New York: Academic Press.

______. 1988. Good dads–bad dads: The two faces of fatherhood. In A. J. Cherlin (ed.), *The changing American family and public policy,* pp. 193–218. Washington, DC: Urban Institute Press.

______. 1989. Supporting fathers: Implications of the Family Support Act for men. Paper presented at the forum on the Family Support Act sponsored by the Foundation for Child Development November 9–10, 1989, at the National Academy of Science in Washington, DC.

______. 1990. Divorce and the American family. *Annual Review of Sociology 16,* 379–403.

Furstenberg, F. F., Jr., and A. J. Cherlin. 1991. Divided families: What happens to children when parents part. Cambridge, MA: Harvard University Press.

Furstenberg, F. F., Jr., and C. W. Nord. 1985. Parenting apart: Patterns of childrearing after divorce. *Journal of Marriage and the Family,* 47(4), 898–904.

Furstenberg, F. F., Jr., C. W. Nord, J. L. Peterson, and N. Zill. 1983. The life course of children and divorce: Marital disruption and parental conflict. *American Sociological Review,* 48(5), 656–668.

Goldscheider, F., and C. Lebourdais. 1986. The falling age at leaving home, 1920–1979. *Sociology and Social Research,* 70, 99–102.

Goode, W. J. 1960. A deviant case: Illegitimacy in the Caribbean. *American Sociological Review,* 25(1), 21–30.

Harris, K. M., and F. F. Furstenberg, Jr. 1990. Affective mobility: The course of parent-child relations in adolescence. Paper presented at the annual meeting of the American Sociological Association, Washington, DC, August 1990.

Harris, K. M., and S. P. Morgan. 1990. Fathers, sons and daughters: Differential paternal involvement in parenting. Paper presented at the annual meeting of the American Sociological Association, Washington, DC, August 1990.

Hout, M., O. D. Duncan, and M. E. Sobel. 1987. Association and heterogeneity: Structural models of similarities and differences. In C. C. Clogg (ed.), *Sociological Methodology,* pp. 145–184. Washington, DC: American Sociological Association.

Lamb, M. E. 1987. *The father's role: Applied perspectives.* New York: John Wiley & Sons.

Levitan, S. A., R. S. Belous, and F. Gallo. 1988. *What's happening to the American family? Tensions, hopes, realities* (revised edition). Baltimore: Johns Hopkins University Press.

Malinowski, B. 1930. Parenthood, the basis of social structure. In R. L. Coser (ed.), *The Family: Its Structures and Functions,* pp. 51–63. New York: St. Martin's Press.

McLanahan, S., and K. Booth. 1989. Mother-only families: Problems, prospects, and politics. *Journal of Marriage and the Family,* 51(3), 557–580.

Moore, K. A., and J. L. Peterson. 1989. The consequences of teenage pregnancy: Final Report. Washington, DC: Child Trends, Inc.

Moore, K. A., C. W. Nord, and J. L. Peterson. 1989. Nonvoluntary sexual activity among adolescents. *Family Planning Perspectives, 21*(3), 110–114.
Mott, F. 1989. When is a father really gone: Patterning of father-child contact in father-absent homes of young children born to adolescent and young adult mothers. Report prepared under Grant Number 1R01 HD23160 with the National Institute of Child Health and Human Development.
Parke, R. D., and B. Neville. 1987. Teenage fatherhood. In S. L. Hofferth and C. D. Hayes (eds.), *Risking the future,* pp. 145–173. Washington, DC: National Academy Press.
Popenoe, D. 1988. *Disturbing the nest.* New York: Aldine De Gruyter.
Robinson, B. 1988. *Teenage fathers.* Lexington, MA: Lexington Books.
Schultz, D. A. 1969. *Coming up black: Patterns of ghetto socialization.* Englewood Cliffs, NJ: Prentice-Hall.
Select Committee on Children, Youth, and Families. 1989. *U.S. children and their families: Current conditions and recent trends, 1989.* Washington, DC: U.S. Government Printing Office.
Seltzer, J. A. 1989. Relationships between fathers and children who live apart. Paper presented at the 1989 annual meeting of the American Association for the Advancement of Science, San Francisco, CA.
Seltzer, J. A., and S. M. Bianchi. 1988. Children's contact with absent parents. *Journal of Marriage and the Family, 50,* 663–677.
Spanier, G. B. 1989. Bequeathing family continuity. *Journal of Marriage and the Family, 51*(1), 3–13.
Thompson, R. A. 1983. The father's case in child custody disputes: The contributions of psychological research. In M. E. Lamb and A. Sagi (eds.), *Fatherhood and family policy,* pp. 53–100. Hillsdale, NJ: Lawrence Erlbaum Assoc.
Thornton, A. 1989. Changing attitudes towards family issues in the United States. *Journal of Marriage and the Family 51* (4), 873–893.
Thornton, A., and D. Freedman. 1983. The changing American family. *Population Bulletin, 38*(4), 2–44.
Uhlenberg, P. 1974. Cohort variations in family life cycle experiences of U.S. females. *Journal of Marriage and the Family, 36*(2), 284–292.
Wallerstein, J. S., and J. B. Kelly. 1980. *Second chances: Men, women, and children a decade after divorce.* New York: Ticknor & Fields.

11

Intergenerational Resource Transfers Across Disrupted Households: Absent Fathers' Contributions to the Well-Being of Their Children

Jay D. Teachman

Over the past quarter of a century divorce rates have risen precipitously. Recent estimates indicate that as many as 50 percent or more of recently contracted marriages will end in divorce (Martin and Bumpass 1989). A substantial majority of these divorces will involve children (Bumpass 1984). Given the centrality of marriage in Western social structure for the sustenance and socialization of children, it is natural to ask what arrangements divorced parents make concerning the welfare of their children. Prior research has focused almost exclusively on child support (in the form of a monetary transfer from the absent parent to the custodial parent) as the primary means by which absent parents provide for their children. In this chapter, I examine the nature and extent of other contributions made by absent parents (fathers) to the well-being of their children following divorce. I also investigate the determinants of variation in the regularity with which these contributions are made and the degree to which such contributions are interrelated.

The results indicate that absent fathers seldom provide other than monetary forms of assistance. Absent fathers are especially unlikely to become involved in activities with their children that require their direct participation and thus an investment of time. An analysis of the determinants of resource transfers indicates that fathers who make child-support payments are more likely than other fathers to provide other forms of assistance. More generally, fathers who provide at least one form of assistance are more likely to provide other contributions.

The Problem and Research Goals

Concern over the consequences of marital disruption has spurred considerable research. Within the current matrix of relationships between gender and economic opportunity, various researchers have documented the negative consequences of marital dissolution for female-headed families (Garfinkel and McLanahan 1986; Hoffman and Duncan 1988) and the long-term negative consequences for children (McLanahan and Bumpass 1988). At least part of the negative impact of divorce on women and children can be traced to the loss of economic support from absent fathers. Traditionally, fathers in intact families have assumed primary responsibility for the economic support of their children (England and Farkas 1986). Although women have increased their rates of labor-force participation in recent decades, their ties to the labor force, and thus economic resources, are still more tenuous than those of men (Masnick and Bane 1980; Moen 1985). In addition, the presence of children continues to have a "traditionalizing" effect on the family, with men increasing their involvement with labor-market activities and women becoming more concerned with home activities (Waite, Haggstrom, and Kanouse 1985). Divorce often disrupts a traditional division of labor in which women and children are economically vulnerable.

Historically, as it has evolved through the political and legal systems (Kahn and Kamerman 1988), the central mechanism by which resources are transferred across households from absent fathers to their children has been court-ordered child-support payments.[1] Yet recent estimates indicate that nearly 20 percent of divorced mothers do not have a child-support award (Office of Child Support Enforcement 1988). Moreover, of women with an award, less than 75 percent receive payment, and the amount of support received is generally below the costs associated with rearing children (Beller and Graham 1985; Seltzer 1990). Because the centrality of child-support payments for the economic well-being of children following divorce and the variability in child-support outcomes is recognized, considerable research has been done to identify the determinants of whether child support is awarded and received, as well as the amounts involved (Beller and Graham 1985, 1986; Hill 1984; O'Neill 1985; Peterson and Nord 1988; Robins and Dickinson 1986; Seltzer and Garfinkel 1990).

However, almost nothing is known about the nature of other forms of social and economic transfers across households from absent fathers to their children. In addition to making child-support payments, absent fathers can make economic contributions by purchasing clothing for their children or by paying for medical expenses and so on. By making child-support payments, fathers may be fulfilling their economic and legal responsibilities to their children—at least as defined by the content of court settlements. However, simply making child-support payments only partially fulfills the more general role of "fathering." By making economic contributions other than child-support payments, fathers can not only increase the material well-being of their children, they can remain more involved in their children's lives, continuing to fulfill the parental roles they performed while married. Such economic contributions imply greater involvement on the part of fathers as they gather information about their children (likely through increased contact) and make decisions about how much to contribute, when to contribute, and in which areas.

Absent fathers can also elect to participate more or less fully in their children's daily activities. For example, absent fathers can take an active interest in the schooling of their children. Such contributions of time, as opposed to economic contributions, are even more likely to indicate the efforts of fathers to continue fulfilling their parental role after divorce. Noneconomic contributions by absent fathers are also potentially important components of the socioeconomic and emotional well-being of children of disrupted marriages. Although the roots of the effects are not entirely clear, children from divorced families are more likely to drop out of high school, experience disciplinary problems in school, and engage in delinquent behavior (Hetherington, Cox, and Cox 1979; Matsueda and Heimer 1987; McLanahan 1985). It has been suggested that these outcomes may be due partly to the lack of participation and supervision on the part of absent fathers.

Given the paucity of empirical evidence and the potential importance of absent fathers' contributions to the well-being of their children, my first goal is to describe the nature and extent of such contributions (including child-support payments but with greater emphasis on other forms of assistance). My second goal is to estimate the effects of selected predictor variables on the transfer of various resources across households from absent fathers to their children. Following research investigating the determinants of the receipt of child support (Beller and Graham 1985; Hill 1984; Peterson and Nord 1988), I assume that variables tapping the motivation of parents concerning the absent father's investment in the well-being of his children are the primary determinants of the receipt of various forms of assistance. Specific expectations about the effects of particular covariates are elaborated in a later section.

My third goal is to ascertain the degree to which fathers who provide one form of assistance are likely to provide other forms of assistance, with particular attention to the association between making child-support payments and providing other contributions. I assume that the provision of most types of contributions are positively correlated, because fathers who are more concerned about the well-being of their children are more likely to provide a variety of types of assistance. Support for this assumption is indicated by research showing that fathers who pay child support are more likely to continue to have contact with their children (Furstenberg et al. 1983; Seltzer, Schaeffer, and Charng 1989). The positive association between paying child support and retaining contact with children, the extent to which it reflects an underlying dimension of concern for children's well-being, is thereby generalizable to other forms of assistance. In addition, fathers who have contact with their children have both the information and opportunity needed to provide a variety of forms of assistance.

There is, however, an argument in the literature that when extrapolated suggests that fathers opt to substitute, not supplement, other forms of assistance for making child-support payments. Weiss and Willis (1985) argue that fathers may hesitate to pay child support because they cannot control how their support payments are divided between the personal consumption of the custodial parent and the children.[2] Their argument is congruent with reports from absent fathers who state that inability to control how their child-support payments are allocated by the custodial mother is a primary reason for not making support payments (Haskins 1988). By examining the relationship between making child-support payments and providing other forms of assistance, I am able to test whether other forms of assistance may be substitutes for making child-support payments.

Data

The data are taken from the fifth round of the National Longitudinal Study of the High School Class of 1972 (NLS). The NLS has followed respondents from their senior year in high school to early 1986, with intervening follow-ups in 1973, 1974, 1976, and 1979. The original sample was a stratified random sample of all high-school seniors enrolled in public, private, and church-affiliated high schools in the United States (Tourangeau et al. 1987). The fifth follow-up is a subsample of about 14,500 cases of the original sample of over 22,000 men and women and contains a supplement with detailed information from ever-married custodial parents about the nature and extent of assistance provided by absent parents. Because very few divorced fathers in the NLS data have custody of their children, I conduct the analyses based on responses provided by mothers.

The NLS misses individuals who were not in school the spring of their senior year in high school. Variation in providing assistance to children according to education is thus truncated, as well as are other variations related to education. However, this restriction is likely to have less impact on ever-divorced mothers, because they are more likely than never-married mothers to have graduated from high school. In general, though, the higher education of the NLS sample compared to the U.S. population means that respondents are more likely to have the resources needed to provide other

TABLE 11.1 Definitions of Variables Used in Analysis of Contributions Fathers Make to the Well-Being of their Children

Variable	*Values*	*Mean*	*sd*
Assistance other than paying child support:			
"Other than child support payments that your first spouse may make, how regularly does your first spouse do the following?"	1=Very regularly 2 3 (2–4 are not labeled) 4 5=Never		
1. Pay for clothes for the children 2. Pay for presents for the children 3. Take the children on vacation 4. Pay for routine dental care 5. Carry medical insurance for the children 6. Pay for uninsured medical expenses 7. Help the children with homework 8. Attend school events			
Predictor variables:			
Voluntary agreement	1 = Child support agreement reached voluntarily 0 = Otherwise	.54	.50
Visitation	1 = Visitation rights not granted at divorce 0 = Otherwise	.07	.26
Child < 6 at divorce	1 = At least one child < 6 at divorce 0 = Otherwise	.78	.42
Number of children	Number of own children at divorce	1.50	.70
Duration of marriage	In months	70.67	37.74
Duration since divorce	In months	78.57	46.19
Log of mother's income	Log of income at divorce in 1985 dollars	6.94	4.10
Mother college	1 = College degree or higher 0 = Otherwise	.08	.27
Mother some college	1 = At least some college 0 = Otherwise	.34	.47

(Continued)

TABLE 11.1 (*Continued*)

Variable	*Values*	*Mean*	*sd*
Log of father's income	Log of income at divorce in 1985 dollars	9.17	2.62
Joint custody	1 = Joint physical custody 0 = Otherwise	.10	.30
Spouse relationship during divorce	1 = Bitter 2 = Many disputes 3 = Some disputes 4 = Friendly	2.64	1.09
Black	1 = Black 0 = Otherwise	.14	.35
Regularity of support	1 = Never 2 = Seldom 3 = Occasionally 4 = Regularly	2.31	1.28
Proximity medium	1 = Same state or different state < 500 miles 0 = Otherwise	.38	.49
Proximity low	1 = Different state > 500 miles or don't know 0 = Otherwise	.28	.45
Mother remarried	1 = Mother has remarried 0 = Otherwise	.48	.50
Father remarried	1 = Father has remarried 0 = Otherwise	.53	.50

Note: The following variables were used in the equation for making child-support payments but not in the equations for the receipt of other forms of support. Mother retained a lawyer at divorce (1 = No; 0 = Otherwise; mean = .11; sd = .31); Divorce occurred in "no fault state" (1 = Yes; 0 = Otherwise; mean = .71; sd = .46); Child support was awarded at divorce (1 = Yes; 0 = Otherwise; mean = .81; sd = .39); Log of amount of child support awarded at divorce (In log of 1985 dollars: mean = 4.33; sd = 2.29).

TABLE 11.2 Regularity with Which Absent Fathers Provide Each Form of Assistance (%)

	Very Regularly to Never				
Form of Assistance	*1*	*2*	*3*	*4*	*5*
Pays for clothes	5.2	2.5	11.6	15.4	65.1
Pays for presents	12.7	8.0	20.1	19.1	40.1
Takes the children on vacation	8.0	4.1	11.4	11.3	65.2
Pays for routine dental care	12.6	3.1	5.2	4.6	74.5
Carries medical insurance	27.8	2.6	4.9	3.6	61.1
Pays for uninsured medical expenses	11.6	2.6	5.9	4.1	75.7
Helps the children with homework	2.3	1.6	4.9	6.2	84.9
Attends school events	3.6	2.9	6.9	11.8	74.8

	Regularly	*Occasionally*	*Seldom*	*Never*
Regularity of child-support payments	43	11	18	28

forms of assistance, most likely leading to an upward bias in the results reported further on.

Respondents in the NLS are followed from approximately age 18 until approximately age 32, a span of ages over which both marriage and divorce are likely to occur. However, disruptions of late marriages (after age 32) and marriages of long duration (more than 14 years) are not observed. This also means that older women at divorce are not included. However, the ages covered in the NLS are those at which parents are likely to have children requiring assistance from absent fathers (e.g., have children under the age of 18). The final sample size is 644 mothers.

The questions used to determine the nature and extent of assistance provided by absent fathers for their children, as reported by custodial mothers, are shown in Table 11.1. In all, the NLS contains information about eight types of assistance (not counting information about child-support payments); clothes, gifts, vacations, dental care, medical insurance, uninsured medical expenses, help with homework, and attending school events.[3] Also included in Table 11.1 is a description of the predictor variables used in the multivariate analysis as well as their means and standard deviations.

Descriptive Results

Responses for the regularity with which each type of assistance, including child support, is provided by absent fathers are shown in Table 11.2. Excluding the payment of child support, the results indicate that noncustodial fathers seldom provide any type of assistance shown. For only one item,

TABLE 11.3 Percent of Absent Fathers Making Different Numbers of Contributions

Number of Different Contributions Made	*Excluding Child-Support Payments (%)*	*Including Child-Support Payments (%)*
None	31	19
One	10	16
Two	12	10
Three	11	11
Four	9	10
Five	6	8
Six	6	6
Seven	5	6
Eight	11	8
Nine	—	6

purchasing gifts for the children, have more than 50 percent of the fathers ever provided the assistance in question. Except for providing medical insurance, which is the one form of assistance other than child-support payments most likely to be included in divorce settlements, fewer than 1 out of 7 fathers provides assistance on a very regular basis. The results indicate that more fathers have at some time paid child support (almost 3 out of 4) than have ever provided any of the other forms of assistance (this item is measured on a different scale).

Fathers are somewhat more likely to provide economic assistance than noneconomic assistance. The proportion of fathers who participate in the schooling of their children is particularly low. Fewer than 1 father out of 27 regularly assists his children with homework or attends school events. Over three-quarters of absent fathers have never participated in the schooling of their children. Slightly more fathers (1 out of 12) take their children on vacation, however, substantiating the observation made by Furstenberg and Nord (1985) that absent fathers are more likely to act like pals to their children than parents. This notion is also consistent with the fact that a majority of absent fathers (3 out of 5) have purchased gifts for their children.

Because it is possible for fathers to provide only a subset of the types of assistance being considered, the data in Table 11.2 likely underestimate the percent of fathers who have ever provided *any* type of assistance. The data in Table 11.3 address this possibility by presenting the percent of fathers who have ever provided different numbers of contributions. The first column of figures excludes making child-support payments; the second column of figures includes these payments. The results indicate that a greater percent of fathers have at some time provided at least one type of assistance than is evident from considering each type of assistance separately. If we exclude child-support payments, about 2 out of 3 fathers have made one or more types of contributions to the well-being of their children. If we include child-support payments, this figure increases to about 4 out of 5 fathers. Note, however, that these figures refer to having *ever* provided assistance—the percent of fathers that provide assistance on a very regular basis would be much smaller. Moreover, the fact that 1 out of 5 fathers has never provided *any* of the types of assistance considered here speaks to the frailty of father-child relationships outside of marriage.

Multivariate Analysis

Expected Relationships

The multivariate analysis is designed to identify the key determinants of the provision of various forms of support and to ascertain whether fathers who provide a given form of assistance are more likely to make other contributions. In the paragraphs below, I outline the expected relationships between several variables contained in the NLS and the provision of other forms of support. Before discussing the results, I also describe the statistical model to be estimated.

I expect that generalized resource transfers across disrupted households are related to the expectations and motivations of both parents concerning the degree to which absent fathers will remain involved in the lives of their children. In turn, the expectations and motivations of parents are based on at least two interrelated factors: (1) the degree of emotional and instrumental interdependencies between the absent father and his children and (2) the quality of the relationship between the parents. Fathers who have developed stronger interdependencies with their children are more likely to be motivated to continue to fulfill the role of parent following divorce; custodial mothers who enjoy a good relationship with the absent father are more likely to expect and solicit his active participation in the rearing of their children. These two factors are interrelated according to the extent that absent fathers are motivated to provide for the well-being of their children by seeking to maintain a good relationship with the custodial mother and according to the degree that a good relationship between parents increases fathers' motivations to transfer resources to their children.

In the multivariate analysis, the strength of interdependencies between absent fathers and their children and the nature of the relationship between parents are measured by the following variables: marital duration, whether the divorce agreement allows the father to visit his children, whether the divorce agreement was reached voluntarily, the mother's report of the quality of the relationship (from bitter to friendly) between the parents during the divorce, and the nature of the custody agreement.[4] Longer marriages, through greater economic and emotional investments, are more likely to develop strong emotional and instrumental interdependencies between parents and between fathers and their children. Visitation rights are more likely to be granted and the divorce settlement voluntarily agreed upon when both parents intend for fathers to remain involved with their children and when fathers are more concerned about their children's future welfare.[5] Similarly, a good relationship with the custodial mother reduces the emotional and logistical frictions involved in transferring resources across households and increases the likelihood that mothers will expect and encourage the contributions of the absent fathers. Thus, I expect that fathers who were married longer, who entered into a voluntary divorce agreement, who have visitation rights, and who enjoy a better relationship with the custodial mother will be more likely to provide various forms of assistance to their children.

The custody arrangement parents made for their children at divorce is also included in the analysis. Although still relatively rare, the incidence of joint physical custody has been increasing (Seltzer 1990)—in the NLS-72 sample about 10 percent of the mothers report that fathers have joint physical custody of their children. I assume that joint physical custody results when the parents enjoy a reasonably good relationship and when they are highly motivated to continue parenting jointly. As such, I anticipate that fathers with joint physical custody will be more likely to make various contributions to the welfare of their children. However, the nature of joint physical custody requires that its effect be evaluated somewhat differently from the effects of other variables. By the very nature of the custody arrangement, resources are provided to children by sharing households as well as by transferring resources across households. Thus, without additional information, the effect of joint physical custody cannot be interpreted as affecting the degree to which absent fathers transfer resources to their children's household.

The multivariate analysis also contains a number of control variables that might mitigate the relationship between the covariates discussed above and the provision of various types of assistance. These controls include the socioeconomic resources of parents (measured at divorce), race, the number and ages of children, elapsed time since the divorce, the physical proximity of the father, and the current marital status of each parent.[6] The socioeconomic resources of the parents are included in order to control for the overall ability of parents to provide for the well-being of their children. The number and ages of children are included to control for differences in the level of household expenses as well as types of expenses that are faced by custodial mothers as a result of variations in household composition. Race is included as a control on the basis of research that indicates that black mothers (at least among women who are ever married) are less likely to receive transfer payments from the absent father (Beller and Graham 1985). The assumption is that black mothers are less likely to receive other forms of assistance.

The length of time since divorce is included to control for the erosion of emotional and instrumental interdependencies between fathers and their children that may occur with increased time spent in separate households. Similarly, the remarriage of either parent is included to control for changes in interdependencies that take place as allegiances are shifted to a new family and new boundaries are erected between the absent father and his children. The physical proximity of the absent father is included to control for the ability of absent fathers to provide particular forms of assistance (e.g., help with homework) and the opportunity to maintain emotional and instrumental interdependencies through frequent contact. I anticipate that a longer time since divorce, the remarriage of either parent, and greater physical distance reduce the likelihood that absent fathers transfer resources to their children.

Statistical Model

The multivariate analysis is conducted using a simultaneous equation procedure in which each type of assistance is made jointly dependent and errors are allowed to be correlated across equations. This is sometimes known as a "seemingly unrelated equations model" (Pindyck and Rubinfeld 1981). The model is appropriate when the dependent variables are conceptually related. I assume that making child-support payments and the provision of other forms of support are interrelated indicators of the absent father's propensity to transfer resources to his children in order to provide for their well-being. Consequently, I anticipate that the error terms across the models for each type of assistance will be correlated. As indicated below, the expected direction of the correlations across error terms will vary according to whether one assumes that fathers use various forms of assistance as either supplements to or substitutes for each other (in particular, whether other forms of assistance are supplements to or substitutes for making child-support payments).

The model estimated takes the following general form:

$$Y_1 = X_1\beta_1 + \varepsilon_1$$

$$\vdots$$

$$Y_n = X_n\beta_n + \varepsilon_n$$

where $Y_1, \ldots, Y_n$ are the forms of assistance provided by absent fathers, including child support, $X_1, \ldots, X_n$ are vectors of predictor variables that may overlap, $\beta_1, \ldots, \beta_n$ are vectors of parameters associated with the predictor variables and $\varepsilon_1, \ldots, \varepsilon_n$ are error terms with $Cov(\varepsilon_i, \varepsilon_j)$ not restricted to equal 0. The model is estimated using a two-step, generalized least-squares procedure (PROC SYSLIN in SAS).

The regularity with which child support and each of the eight other forms of assistance are provided constitute the dependent variables.[7] The relationships between providing the various forms of support are indicated by the correlations between the error terms of the model. Positive correlations indicate that fathers who more regularly provide at least one type of support also more regularly provide other types of assistance. Negative correlations indicate that fathers substitute types of support.

Results

The results from estimating the seemingly unrelated equations for the various types of assistance provided by fathers are presented in Table 11.4.[8] Although there are some minor variations in effects across forms of assistance (some of which would be expected due to chance), the general pattern is clear. Consistent with the expectations outlined above, fathers who enjoyed a friendlier relationship with the mother during the divorce (for all forms of assistance except child support and medical insurance) and who reached an agreement on the divorce settlement voluntarily (for child support, clothes, medical insurance, and vacations) more regularly transfer resources to their children. Also as expected, fathers who share joint physical custody of their children are more likely to provide assistance than fathers not sharing custody (medical insurance and child support being exceptions), although the magnitude of the effects indicate that fathers who share joint custody do not uniformly transfer resources to their children on a very regular basis. That joint physical custody does not affect the payment of child support is not unexpected given the sharing of costs that most likely occurs under this custody arrangement and the resulting latitude that parents have in structuring if and when one spouse will make a monetary compensation to the other spouse (Seltzer 1990).

Most of the control variables shown in Table 11.4 have only modest effects on the father's contributions and mostly in expected directions. Higher-income fathers are more likely to pay child support, carry medical insurance, and pay for uninsured routine medical bills but are not more likely to provide other forms of assistance. Neither the economic and educational resources of the mother nor the age and number of children have a consistent effect on the transfer of resources from the absent father. Elapsed time since divorce is negatively related to the provision of gifts and the payment of medical bills. The effect of propinquity is particularly

TABLE 11.4 GLS Regression (seemingly unrelated equations) of Various Forms of Assistance on Predictor Variables and Additional Controls[a]

Variable	Child Support[b]	Clothes	Gifts	Dentist	Medical Insurance	Medical Bills	Vacations	Homework	School Events
Predictor variables:									
Voluntary agreement	.403*	.260*	.193	.078	.394*	.153	.312*	.095	.108
Marital duration	.004	−.001	.001	.001	.004	−.001	.002	−.001	.001
Spouse relationship	.041	.155*	.144*	.212*	.082	.157*	.149*	.062*	.083*
No visitation	−.265	−.232	−.850*	−.264	−.624*	−.192	−.319	−.085	−.156
Joint custody	−.168	.979*	.734*	.690*	.268	.893*	.580*	.787*	.582*
Control variables:									
Black	−.150	.126	−.454*	−.264	−.146	−.220	.007	.008	−.108
Father's earnings	.058*	.024	.018	.038	.084*	.051*	.042*	−.004	.018
Mother's earnings	.003	−.008	−.002	.000	.004	−.005	.015	.003	.004
Mother some college	.168	.046	.222	.103	.279	.134	.144	−.007	.008
Mother college	.172	.089	.148	.133	.077	.057	.418*	.093	.218
Number of children	−.089	−.056	.012	−.026	−.053	−.075	−.052	.039	.035
Child < 6 at divorce	.135	−.138	−.086	−.399*	−.118	−.291	−.183	−.053	−.080
Divorce duration	−.003	−.003	−.004*	−.002	−.003	−.005*	−.000	.000	−.000
Mother remarried	−.031	−.030	.008	.054	−.047	−.011	.088	−.031	.050
Father remarried	.230*	.061	.139	.024	.038	.022	.106	.042	−.036
Proximity medium	−.072	.010	−.021	−.008	−.178	−.033	.261*	−.128	−.166
Proximity low	−.605*	−.344*	−.510*	−.443*	−.785*	−.519*	−.029	−.323*	−.540*

System weighted R^2 = .102*

[a] Direction of coding for regularity of receipt of other forms of assistance is reversed from that shown in Table 11.1.

[b] Model for receipt of child support also includes controls for whether child support was awarded at divorce, the amount of child support awarded, whether the mother retained a lawyer, and whether the divorce occurred in a state with a "no fault" provision.

* $p < .05$.

strong—fathers who live farthest from their children are the least likely to provide assistance (vacations being the one exception). The marital status of mothers and fathers has little effect on whether fathers provide assistance to their children except that remarried fathers are more likely to make child-support payments.[9]

The cross-model correlations for the seemingly unrelated equations are shown in Table 11.5. The correlations are all positive (and statistically significant with one exception), indicating that fathers who provide at least one form of assistance for their children are more likely to provide other forms of assistance. The positive correlations between the error terms for making child-support payments and the other forms of support are in line with the notion that fathers supplement child support with other contributions. Note, however, that the correlations between paying child support and other forms of assistance are generally smaller than those observed between other pairs of support (the correlations between support received and both assisting with homework and attending school events are very small). On one hand, this suggests that a proportion of fathers restrict the transfer of resources to making child-support payments. On the other hand, these results indicate that if fathers contribute more than just child-support payments, they are likely to provide several types of assistance.

To examine both possibilities in greater detail, the extent to which absent fathers provide more than one form of assistance to their children, conditional on having ever provided a given type of assistance, is shown in Table 11.6. The mean number of other forms of support ever provided is indicated according to whether each type of assistance has ever been provided. As suggested by the correlations in Table 11.5, the results show that if fathers provide one form of support, they are likely to provide other types of support. For most forms of assistance, fathers who have ever provided the assistance in question have provided between five to six types of assistance (including the type of support being considered). Of particular note is the number of other types of support provided by fathers who help their children with homework or attend school events. Although these forms of assistance are relatively rare (see Table 11.2), the fathers that do provide this sort of support make a substantial number of other contributions. One might expect this result to occur due to the selectivity of fathers who participate in their children's school activities (i.e., only the most motivated fathers participated).

It is also instructive to consider the small number of other types of support contributed by fathers conditional on never having provided the type of support being considered. For example, among fathers who have never provided gifts for their children, the mean number of other types of support provided is just .35. This represents the smallest value in Table 11.6, but the results for other forms of support are also small (the largest

TABLE 11.5 Cross-model Correlations for Seemingly Unrelated Equations[a]

Variable	*Support Received*	*Clothes*	*Gifts*	*Dentist*	*Medical Insurance*	*Medical Bills*	*Vacations*	*Homework*	*School Events*
Support received	1.00								
Clothes	.14	1.00							
Gifts	.28	.58	1.00						
Dentist	.20	.49	.42	1.00					
Medical insurance	.33	.35	.43	.56	1.00				
Medical bills	.25	.51	.37	.67	.52	1.00			
Vacations	.24	.52	.52	.41	.35	.38	1.00		
Homework	.03	.52	.36	.36	.28	.41	.39	1.00	
School events	.15	.52	.42	.37	.29	.39	.35	.66	1.00

[a] All correlations except that between support received and homework are significant at $p < .05$.

TABLE 11.6 Mean Number of Other Forms of Assistance Ever Provided by Absent Fathers According to Whether Each Type of Assistance Has Ever Been Provided

Variable	*Mean Number of Other Forms of Assistance*[a]	
	Ever Provided	*Never Provided*
Child support payments	3.31	1.35
Clothes	5.54	1.20
Gifts	4.41	0.35
Dentist	6.30	1.44
Medical insurance	5.23	1.15
Medical bills	6.32	1.50
Vacation	5.41	1.30
Homework	6.87	1.88
School events	6.10	1.54
Mean number of forms of assistance provided:	2.86	

[a] All differences between value for ever provided and never provided are significant at $p < .05$.

being 1.88 for fathers who have not assisted their children with homework). Of some interest is the fact that the most common contribution made by fathers who have not provided other forms of assistance is buying gifts for their children (data not shown). In other words, even if a father has not made the contribution in question, he is likely to have provided a gift at some point, and this is consistent with the notion that many fathers elect to act as pals toward their children.

Next, consider the relatively small number of other forms of assistance provided by fathers who have ever paid child support (3.31). This value is much smaller than comparable figures for other forms of assistance and occurs because a substantial proportion of fathers, about 20 percent (data not shown), make child-support payments but do not provide other types of assistance. That is, the mean number of other forms of assistance provided by fathers who make child-support payments is weighted downward by the proportion of fathers who make child-support payments but provide no other contributions to their children's welfare. These are most likely fathers who define responsibilities to their children as those that are outlined in their divorce settlement.

I conclude the multivariate analysis by considering the predictors of the number of different contributions ever made by absent fathers. The cross-model correlations shown in Table 11.5 and the means shown in Table 11.6 indicate that fathers who provide at least one type of assistance are more likely to provide other contributions; I anticipate that the predictors of the number of contributions ever made will be similar to those for the regularity with which individual types of assistance are provided. As shown in Table 11.7, the pattern of effects for the number of different contributions

TABLE 11.7 OLS Regression of Number of Contributions Made by Absent Fathers on Predictor Variables and Controls[a]

Variable	*Excluding Child-Support Payments*	*Including Child-Support Payments*
Predictor variables:		
Voluntary agreement	.731*	.877*
Marital duration	.006	.006
Spouse relationship	.260*	.273*
No visitation	−.902*	−1.188*
Joint custody	1.133*	.929*
Control variables:		
Black	−.167	−.288
Father's earnings	.089*	.108*
Mother's earnings	−.019	−.018
Mother some college	.224	.297
Number of children	−.256	−.278
Child < 6 at divorce	−.251	−.190
Mother college	.469	.507
Divorce duration	−.004	−.004
Mother remarried	−.223	−.239
Father remarried	.204	.291
Proximity medium	−.498*	−.498*
Proximity low	−1.644*	−1.862*
R^2	.23*	.25*

[a] Direction of coding for regularity of receipt of other forms of assistance is reversed from that shown in Table 11.1.

* $p < .05$.

made by absent fathers is indeed very similar to that observed in Table 11.4. Fathers who voluntarily agreed to the divorce settlement, who enjoyed a friendlier relationship with their spouse during the divorce, who live closer to their children, who earn more, who have visitation rights, and who have joint custody all provide a greater number of contributions. Thus, the factors that lead fathers to make at least one type of contribution more regularly also act to increase the diversity of the types of resources they provide for their children.

Discussion

Using data from a nationally representative sample, I examined the extent to which absent fathers transfer various types of resources, ranging from clothes to help with homework, to their children. Other than paying child support and buying gifts, the majority of fathers have never provided assistance. Absent fathers are particularly unlikely to provide assistance that requires their direct participation (e.g., helping their children with homework or attending school events). These results are consistent with other studies that show that absent fathers have little contact with their children (Furstenberg et al. 1983) and indicate that divorce disrupts the links between a substantial proportion of fathers and their children.

The picture is less dramatic, but still telling, when considering the percent of fathers who have ever provided at least one type of assistance. Other than paying child support, about 1 out of 3 absent fathers have never provided assistance to their children. Considering both child-support payments and other forms of assistance, about 1 out of 5 absent fathers has never provided any form of assistance. These figures show that a majority of fathers have provided at least some form of assistance to their children, but they also indicate that a substantial minority have never contributed to the well-being of their children (at least with respect to the forms of assistance considered in this chapter). Moreover, the figures refer to having ever provided assistance and ignore the regularity with which contributions are made. For example, not one of the absent fathers in the NLS-72 sample has provided each of the types of support on a very regular basis (data not shown). If we include child-support payments, only 50 percent of the fathers have provided at least one type of assistance on a very regular basis (data also not shown).

These results indicate that a substantial proportion of absent fathers either abandon or significantly restrict their fulfillment of the parental role. One consequence of this pattern is that children from disrupted families are more likely to experience some form of deprivation than children from intact families. Subsequent research needs to more clearly document the parameters of this deprivation, its long-term consequences, and the role of various types of contributions from absent fathers in alleviating deprivation. It would also be useful to obtain a better understanding of the socioemotional consequences for children of variations in the nature and extent of contributions made by absent fathers.

Despite the generally negative tone of the findings, the data indicate that there is a subset of fathers who appear to be concerned about the well-being of their children. Both the cross-tabular and multivariate analyses indicate that fathers who regularly make child-support payments supplement those payments with other forms of assistance. More generally, there is a positive correlation between the provision of various types of support. There is no evidence to indicate that various forms of assistance may serve as substitutes for each other.

The multivariate analysis indicates that objective measures of household socioeconomic status (i.e., mother's education and income, fathers income, number and ages of children) are less important in predicting whether assistance is provided than are indicators of the parental relationship. These results suggest that assistance is more likely to be transferred across households when both parents are motivated to have fathers continue to fulfill the parental role following divorce. It should be emphasized, however, that the nature of the NLS-72 data is such that only indirect indicators of parental expectations and motivations can be considered. The development of policy aimed at maximizing the welfare of the children of divorce will require a more direct test of the importance of parental expectations and motivations, as well as their determinants.

The effect of joint physical custody on the provision of assistance is also important to note. It is clear that absent fathers who share physical custody of their children are more likely to transfer resources to their children (with the exception of child-support payments). On one hand, this finding suggests that legislative efforts aimed at increasing the prevalence of joint physical custody may have the desired effect of increasing the participation of absent fathers in raising their children. On the other hand, such a conclusion must be made with a significant caveat—under the current regime of divorce settlements, parents who agree to a joint physical custody arrangement are likely to be an unusually motivated subset of all parents (as noted above, in the NLS-72 data, joint physical custody arrangements characterize only about 10 percent of the divorces). It is likely that attempts to unilaterally increase the prevalence of joint physical custody would result in rapidly diminishing returns in terms of the father's participation in the raising of his children. It remains an open question as to the nature and extent of this selectivity problem—but a question that is crucial for the development of policy initiatives.

Acknowledgments

This research was supported by funds provided by the Institute for Research on Poverty at the University of Wisconsin, NSF grant SES-8812215 and a Semester Research Award from the University of Maryland. Research conducted at the Center on Population, Gender and Social Inequality is facilitated by a grant from the William and Flora Hewlett Foundation.

Notes

1. I understand that both mothers and fathers are absent parents. However, given the fact that the substantial majority of such parents are fathers, and recognizing the limitations of the data used in this paper, I couch the discussion in terms of fathers as the noncustodial parents.

2. In a separate paper, Weiss and Willis (1989) estimate that only one out of four dollars transferred by absent fathers is spent directly on children.

3. I originally considered two measures of receipt of child support, whether support was received in the past month and the regularity with which support was received, because each is subject to different sorts of error. The indicator of whether

support was received in the past month is likely to suffer from recall bias; the indicator of the regularity of receipt of support more accurately captures fluctuations over time in the absent father's propensity to make support payments. There is little substantive difference in results when using the two measures.

4. It is possible to specify a more specific set of causal relationships between many of the variables considered here (e.g., marital duration precedes characteristics of the divorce settlement). I ignore this causal structure for two reasons. First, recognizing the potential for substantial indirect effects to occur, I am concerned only with the direct impact of each variable. Second, and more important, several of the questions used in the NLS-72 to measure particular variables are ambiguous with respect to the time period they reference, making it difficult to sort out causal order (I refer to this problem in note 8 while discussing the possibility that some covariates may be endogenous).

5. Theoretically, a divorce settlement reached voluntarily can encompass virtually any agreement between parents, including one in which fathers are not expected to have anything to do with their children following divorce. In practice, however, the evidence suggests that voluntary agreements are much more common among parents who anticipate that fathers will remain involved with their children after divorce (Teachman 1990).

6. Because the marital status of each parent is determined from responses provided by mothers, whether the mother has remarried is measured with little error. There is likely to be greater error in measuring whether the absent father has remarried. Indeed, about 20 percent of the mothers stated that they did not know the marital status of the absent father. These cases are coded in the zero category (father not remarried). A similar problem occurs for physical proximity of the father—in many cases, the mother does not know the location of the father. In these cases, the father's proximity is coded as low. Preliminary analyses indicated that including separate indicators for whether the mother knew the location and marital status of the father does not lead to a better-fitting model and does not affect the parameter estimates for other variables.

There are two reasons for including the earnings of parents measured at the time of divorce. First, and most important, the NLS does not contain a measure of the absent father's income following divorce. Second, it is likely that variations in earnings potential are reasonably well captured by earnings at divorce, especially given the relatively short period covered by the NLS data. The education of fathers is not included in the model given its colinearity with his income and the education and income of mothers.

7. I recognize that the use of an ordinal scale to measure the regularity with which types of assistance are provided may lead to biased estimates of coefficients when GLS regression is used. However, least-squares regression is generally quite robust to departures from normality. To ascertain some idea of the robustness of the GLS results, I fitted a logistic regression equation to each of the forms of assistance separately using 1 to indicate that the assistance had ever been received and 0 otherwise. The results (not shown) correspond closely to those shown in Table 11.4.

8. Several additional models were also estimated due to the possibility that the ambiguous time reference of several questions used in the NLS-72 introduces

endogeneity (e.g., providing assistance influences the values taken by the covariates). Specifically, it is possible that endogeneity biases the effects of proximity of the absent father and the marital status of the parents. Using a stepwise procedure to enter these variables in various orders does not alter the pattern of results for other covariates. I do not attempt to explicitly model possible endogeneity, because I am less interested in partitioning the direction of causality and more interested in determining whether a relationship holds. I am also concerned with the change in the effects of other variables once the additional variables are included.

9. The positive effect of the father's remarriage on the payment of child support is contrary to the expectation outlined earlier in the chapter but is consistent with other reports (Beller and Graham 1985; Hill 1984). The explanation invoked to explain this finding is that fathers who remarry are more family oriented than are fathers who do not remarry, leading to the positive impact on child-support payments. The failure of remarried fathers to provide other forms of assistance may be attributed to the demands on their time and resources made by their new families.

References

Beller, Andrea, and John Graham. 1985. "Variations in the economic well-being of divorced women and their children." Pp. 471–506 in Martin David and Timothy Smeeding (eds.), *Horizontal Equity, Uncertainty and Economic Well-Being*. Studies in Income and Wealth Series, Vol. 50, National Bureau of Economic Research. Chicago: University of Chicago Press.

______. 1986. "Child support awards: Differentials and trends by race and marital status." *Demography* 23:231–246.

Bumpass, Larry. 1984. "Children and marital disruption: A replication and update." *Demography* 21:71–82.

England, Paula, and George Farkas. 1986. *Households, Employment and Gender: A Social, Economic and Demographic View.* New York: Aldine De Gruyter.

Furstenberg, Frank, S. Philip Morgan, and Paul Allison. 1987. "Paternal participation and children's well-being after marital dissolution." *American Sociological Review* 52:695–701.

Furstenberg, Frank, and Christine Nord. 1985. "Parenting apart: Patterns of child-rearing after marital disruption." *Journal of Marriage and the Family* 47:893–904.

Furstenberg, Frank, Christine Nord, James Peterson, and Nicholas Zill. 1983. "The life course of children of divorce: Marital disruption and parental contact." *American Sociological Review* 48:656–667.

Garfinkel, Irwin, and Sara McLanahan. 1986. *Single Mothers and Their Children.* Washington, DC: Urban Institute.

Haskins, Ronald. 1988. "Child support: The men's view." Pp. 306–317 in Sheila Kamerman and Alfred Kahn (eds.), *Child Support: From Debt Collection to Social Policy.* Newbury Park, CA: Sage.

Hetherington, E. Mavis, Martha Cox, and Roger Cox. 1979. "Play and social interaction in children following divorce." *Journal of Social Issues* 35:26–49.

Hill, Martha. 1984. "PSID analysis of matched pairs of ex-spouses: Relation of economic resources and new family obligations to child support payments." Unpublished manuscript, Institute for Survey Research, University of Michigan, Ann Arbor.

Hoffman, Saul, and Greg Duncan. 1988. "What are the economic consequences of divorce?" *Demography* 25:641–645.

Kahn, Alfred, and Sheila Kamerman. 1988. *Child Support: From Debt Collection to Social Policy*. Newbury Park, CA: Sage.

Martin, Teresa, and Larry Bumpass. 1989. "Recent trends and differentials in marital disruption." *Demography* 26:37–51.

Masnick, George, and Mary Jo Bane. 1980. *The Nation's Families: 1960–1990*. Boston: Auburn House.

Matsueda, Ross, and Karen Heimer. 1988. "Attitudes toward women's familial roles: Change in the United States, 1977–1985." *American Sociological Review* 52:826–840.

McLanahan, Sara. 1985. "Family Structure and the reproduction of poverty." *American Journal of Sociology* 90:873–901.

McLanahan, Sara, and Larry Bumpass. 1988. "Intergenerational consequences of family disruption." *American Journal of Sociology* 94:130–152.

Moen, Phyllis. 1985. "Continuities and discontinuities in women's labor force activity." Pp. 113–155 in Glen Elder (ed.), *Life Course Dynamics: Trajectories and Transitions, 1968–1980*. Ithaca, NY: Cornell University Press.

Office of Child Support Enforcement. 1988. Twelfth Annual Report to Congress for the Period Ending September 30, 1987. Washington, DC: Government Printing Office.

O'Neill, June. 1985. "Determinants of child support." Report prepared for the National Institute of Child Health and Human Development under grant No. RO-1-HD-16840.

Peterson, James, and Christine Nord. 1988. "The regular receipt of child support: A multi-step process." Unpublished manuscript, Child Trends, Washington, DC.

Pindyck, Robert, and Daniel Rubinfeld. 1981. *Econometric Models and Economic Forecasts*. New York: McGraw-Hill.

Robins, P. K., and K. P. Dickinson. 1984. "Receipt of child support by single-parent families." *Social Service Review* 58:622–641.

Seltzer, Judith. 1991. "Legal custody arrangements and children's economic welfare." *American Journal of Sociology* 96:895–929.

Seltzer, Judith, and Irwin Garfinkel. 1990. "Inequality in divorce settlements: An investigation of property settlements and child support awards." *Social Science Research* 19:82–111.

Seltzer, Judith, Nora Cate Schaeffer, and Hong-wen Charng. 1989. "Family ties after divorce: The relationship between visiting and paying child support." *Journal of Marriage and the Family* 51:1013–1031.

Teachman, Jay. 1990. "Socioeconomic resources of parents and the award of child support in the United States: Some exploratory models." *Journal of Marriage and the Family* 52:689–699.

Tourangeau, Roger, Penny Sebring, Barbara Campbell, Martin Glusberg, Bruce Spenner, and Melody Singleton. 1987. *The National Longitudinal Study of the*

High School Class of 1972 (NLS-72) Fifth Follow-up (1972) Data File User's Manual. National Opinion Research Center, University of Chicago.

Waite, Linda, Gus Haggstrom, and David Kanouse. 1985. "Changes in the employment activities of new parents." *American Sociological Review* 50:263–272.

Weiss, Yoram, and Robert Willis. 1985. "Children as collective goods and divorce settlements." *Journal of Labor Economics* 3:268–292.

______. 1989. "An economic analysis of divorce settlements." Discussion Paper No. 89–5, Economic Demography Group, Economics Research Center, NORC/University of Chicago.

12

The Influence of the Parental Family on the Attitudes and Behavior of Children

Arland Thornton

This chapter begins with the observation that although there are many institutions socializing children in today's complex world—including peer groups, schools, the mass media, and work groups—the family continues to be a potentially powerful influence on the lives of children. The family provides children a set of values and norms that may be important in the formation of attitudes and preferences. It provides children role models that they can refer to as they develop their own ways of doing things. It provides children an emotional environment in which their own personalities are nurtured and formed. And, the family provides children a set of resources, including financial ones, that they can call on in making their way through life.

This research was motivated by an interest in the general question of the impact of parents on their growing children. How are the family experiences and attitudes of children influenced by the families that raise them? To what extent are parents successful in passing on their family values to their children? What is it about the parental family that influences the family behavior and attitudes of young people?

Three specific questions are addressed in this chapter. The first concerns the issue of aggregate intergenerational similarity, investigating overall differences between young adults and their parents. In order to address this issue thoroughly we make two different sets of comparisons: one between young adults and their middle-aged parents, with both being observed at the same point in time; and the other between young adults and their parents when their parents were themselves young adults.

The second issue shifts the locus of inquiry from the aggregate level to the microlevel and asks the extent to which individual parents and their children are alike. More specifically, we will be asking to what extent the family attitudes of parents are passed on to their individual children.

Finally, we ask how the family attitudes and decisions of children are influenced by a broad range of parental family characteristics and experiences. One issue concerns parental religious affiliation and commitment to religious institutions and how they influence children's attitudes and behaviors. We also ask questions about the influence on children of the marital histories of the parents. Also of interest is the socioeconomic position of the parents, as is family size and the mother's experience in the work force.

This chapter will cover several dimensions of young people's family attitudes and behaviors. On the attitudinal side, we will investigate ideas about marriage, divorce, cohabitation without marriage, childlessness, premarital sex, and appropriate roles for women and men. And, on the behavioral side, we will focus primarily on premarital sex, cohabitation, and marriage.

Data and Methods

This chapter relies on data from a panel study of mothers and children. The families were selected from a probability sample of first, second, and fourth-born white children drawn from the July 1961 birth records of the Detroit Metropolitan Area. Approximately equal numbers of families were selected from each family-size group. The mothers were first interviewed in the winter of 1962, and subsequent interviews were conducted in fall 1962, 1963, 1966, 1977, 1980, and 1985. The children were interviewed in 1980 when they were eighteen and in 1985 when they were twenty-three.

The original 1962 survey included interviews with 92 percent of the sampled mothers, and the study has maintained the cooperation of a large percentage of the families over the full twenty-three years. In 1985, interviews were obtained with both mothers and children in 867 families, representing 82 percent of the families originally interviewed in 1962.

The seven interviews with the mothers resulted in a wide-ranged collection of information about the mothers and their families. Included is information about the socioeconomic position of the family, the marital history of the mother, her childbearing, her religious affiliation and activity, and a wide array of attitudes toward family issues. In the interviews with the young adult children in 1980 and 1985 we gathered similar attitudinal information as obtained from the mother as well as extensive information about the children's experiences and plans. Of particular importance for this chapter is the battery of behavior information obtained from the children about premarital sex, marriage, and nonmarital cohabitation.

Intergenerational Differences in Family Attitudes

We begin our analysis of the influence of the parents on their young adult children by addressing the aggregate differences between parents and children in family attitudes and values. We do this by comparing the distribution of parental attitudes concerning appropriate roles for men and women, marriage, divorce, childlessness, cohabitation without marriage, and premarital sex with the attitudes of their children on these same family issues. In making these parent-child comparisons I focus primarily on mothers and their daughters because this strategy controls for the effects of gender. However, where appropriate, I point out important contrasts between mothers and their sons and also between sons and daughters. Table 12.1 provides useful information for making these intergenerational comparisons.

It is useful to preface our analysis of intergenerational differences in family attitudes and values with the observation that the children participating in our study have lived their childhood and adolescent years during a period of dramatic social changes in family attitudes. Between these children's births in 1961 and their first interview in 1980, the United States experienced dramatic shifts in family attitudes and values (Cherlin and Walters 1981; Mason et al. 1976; Thornton 1989). As the data in Table 12.1 demonstrate, the mothers of these children clearly participated in this rapid social change. During the lifetimes of these children, their mothers' attitudes toward appropriate roles for men and women, on average, became more egalitarian; mothers became more accepting of divorce and more tolerant of voluntary childlessness. For example, whereas only one-third of the mothers in 1962 disagreed with the statement "most of the important decisions in the life of the family should be made by the man of the house," by 1985 more than three-fourths rejected this statement. Similarly, whereas 51 percent of these mothers disagreed in 1962 with the statement "when there are children in the family, parents should stay together even if they don't get along," by 1985, 82 percent disagreed. And, for attitudes toward childlessness, the percentage of mothers saying "almost all married couples who can ought to have children" declined from 85 percent in 1962 to 43 percent in 1985. Although our study does not contain the relevant information to document changes in attitudes toward such issues as marriage, premarital sex, and extramarital sex, we know from other sources that Americans during this period also became more tolerant toward remaining single and toward sexual relationships outside of marriage (Thornton 1989; Thornton and Freedman 1982; Veroff et al. 1981).

There are clearly important differences between mothers and children in their attitudes toward family issues, although the magnitude of the differences varies across specific issues. In 1980 daughters expressed more egalitarian attitudes than their mothers on six of the eight sex-role-attitude items measured, with four of these differences being statistically significant. The differences between mothers and daughters generally widened between 1980 and 1985, with daughters being more egalitarian than their mothers on all eight sex-role items (and all but one of these differences were

TABLE 12.1 Distributions of Attitudes Toward Family Issues

	Mothers				*Daughters*		*Sons*	
Variable	*1962*	*1977*	*1980*	*1985*	*1980*	*1985*	*1980*	*1985*
A. Percentage with egalitarian sex-role attitudes[a]								
Decisions	32.3	67.6	71.2	77.7	66.1	85.3	44.9	64.9
Women active	44.1	58.5	64.8	71.5	72.2	89.2	72.6	85.1
Men's/women's work	56.9	77.5	66.8	75.0	68.7	79.6	52.0	63.7
Housework	46.9	61.9	69.6	75.6	72.5	86.4	76.1	88.1
Relations/working mother	—	65.4	78.6	75.2	74.1	78.0	66.1	69.8
Men work/women home	—	34.5	38.9	47.9	57.2	64.2	48.0	62.1
Women happier home	—	67.0	72.3	70.6	78.9	81.4	72.6	76.7
Husband/wife career	—	49.0	53.9	62.7	79.4	86.9	76.3	85.8
B. Percentage negative toward marriage[b]								
Married happier	—	—	35.6	31.7	46.8	44.5	37.1	40.0
Few good marriages	—	—	36.6	31.5	36.5	27.1	32.6	26.2
Better married	—	—	67.9	67.2	71.5	72.6	60.0	64.1
Better single	—	—	9.5	10.0	23.5	13.4	35.3	21.4
C. Percentage approving of divorce[c]								
Not stay together	51.0	80.4	82.1	82.3	82.8	89.9	65.2	70.7
Divorce best	—	—	61.8	60.7	33.5	32.8	31.9	33.9
D. Percentage approving premarital sex[d]								
Before marriage	—	—	32.0	37.1	65.1	76.8	77.9	82.8
Planning marriage	—	—	36.5	41.8	66.9	80.2	77.4	81.7
E. Percentage approving cohabitation without marriage[e]								
Live together all right	—	—	23.2	26.9	44.7	56.9	59.2	69.4
Should not live together	—	—	26.2	36.0	57.9	69.0	72.0	79.0
F. Distribution of attitudes toward childlessness[f]								
All couples parents								
Yes	84.8	—	42.8	42.6	35.8	32.6	41.9	40.6
Depends	8.4	—	3.6	5.3	6.2	3.2	5.6	5.1
No	6.8	—	53.6	52.1	58.0	64.2	52.6	54.3
Total	100	—	100	100	100	100	100	100
Number of respondents	867	—	867	867	436	436	431	431

(Continues)

TABLE 12.1 (*Continued*)

[a]The question wording for each item is listed below, with the response codes in parentheses. The underlined codes were treated as egalitarian (nontraditional) in this analysis.

Decisions: Most of the important decisions in the life of the family should be made by the man of the house (strongly agree "SA"; agree "A"; undecided, don't know, depends "DK"; disagree "D"; strongly disagree "SD").

Women active: It's perfectly all right for women to be very active in clubs, politics, and other outside activities before the children are grown up (SA; A; DK; D; SD).

Men's/women's work: There is some work that is men's and some that is women's, and they should not be doing each other's (SA; A; DK; D; SD).

Housework: A wife should not expect her husband to help around the house after he comes home from a hard day's work (SA; A; DK; D; SD).

Relations/working mother: A working mother can establish as warm and secure a relationship with her children as can a mother who does not work (SA; A; DK; D; SD).

Men work/women home: It is much better for everyone if the man earns the main living and the woman takes care of the home and the family (SA; A; DK; D; SD).

Women happier home: Women are much happier if they stay at home and take care of their children (SA; A; DK; D; SD).

Husband/wife career: It is more important for a wife to help her husband's career than to have one herself (SA; A; DK; D; SD).

[b]The question wording for each item is listed below, with the response codes in parentheses. The underlined codes were treated as "negative toward marriage" in this analysis.

Married happier: Married people are usually happier than those who go through life without getting married (strongly agree "SA"; agree "A"; disagree "D"; strongly disagree "SD").

Few good marriages: There are few good or happy marriages these days (SA; A; D; SD).

Better married: It's better for a person to get married than to go through life being single (SA; A; D; SD).

Better single: All in all, there are more advantages to being single than to being married (SA; A; D; SD).

[c]The question wording for each item is listed below with the response codes in parentheses. The underlined codes were treated as approving in this analysis.

Not stay together: When there are children in the family, parents should stay together even if they don't get along (strongly agree "SA"; agree "A"; don't know "DK"; disagree "D"; strongly disagree "SD").

Divorce best: Divorce is usually the best solution when a couple can't seem to work out their marriage problems (SA; A; DK; D; SD).

[d]The question wording for each item is listed below with the response codes in parentheses. The underlined response codes were treated as approving of premarital sex.

Before marriage: Young people should not have sex before marriage (strongly agree "SA"; agree "A"; don't know "DK"; disagree "D"; strongly disagree "SD").

Planning marriage: Premarital sex is all right for a young couple planning to get married (SA; A; DK; D; SD).

[e]The question wording for each item is listed below, with the response codes in parentheses. The underlined codes were considered as approving in this analysis.

Live together all right: It's all right for a couple to live together without planning to get married (strongly agree "SA"; agree "A"; don't know "DK"; disagree "D"; strongly disagree "SD").

Should not live together: A young couple should not live together unless they are married (SA; A; DK; D; SD).

[f]The question wording is listed below with response categories exactly as shown in table.

Do you feel almost all married couples who can *ought* to have children?

statistically significant). Of course, if we compare the attitudes of the daughters in the 1980s with those of the mothers at about the same position in the life course—in 1962 just after the daughters were born—the contrasts between the mothers and daughters are much sharper. This comparison makes it very clear that young women today are approaching adulthood with very different sex-role attitudes than did their mothers. The intergenerational differences noted in these data are also consistent with cross-sectional age differences observed in sex-role-attitude data from the General Social Survey (Mason and Lu 1988; Thornton 1989).

Regarding attitudes toward marriage, Table 12.1 (Panel B) provides evidence of only one consistent intergenerational difference between mothers and daughters. In both 1980 and 1985 daughters were significantly more likely than mothers to disagree with the statement "married people are usually happier than those who go through life without getting married" (Married Happier), with the differences being more than 10 percentage points each year. Apparently the daughters, most of whom had never been married, even by the 1985 interview were less willing to impute more happiness to the married state than their mothers. A second intergenerational difference was evident in 1980 but had largely disappeared by 1985. In 1980, when the daughters were eighteen, more than twice as many of them as their mothers agreed that "there are more advantages to being single than to being married" (Better Single). By 1985 when the daughters had matured to age twenty-three, substantially fewer actively endorsed remaining single, and their distribution of attitudes was much more similar to that of the mothers (with the statistically significant difference of 1980 no longer being statistically significant).

Intergenerational differences on attitudes toward divorce are quite complex (Table 12.1, Panel C). For one of the divorce-attitude questions—"when there are children in the family, parents should stay together even if they don't get along" (Not Stay Together)—the distributions of mother and daughter attitudes are almost identical in both 1980 and 1985. There is, however, a statistically significant difference of 12–17 percentage points between mothers and sons on this question, with mothers being more accepting of divorce than sons. Although this difference between mothers and sons is clearly an intergenerational difference it probably reflects a gender effect rather than an intergenerational effect because the young women are also more accepting of divorce than the young men. This pattern of young women being more accepting of divorce than young men when there are children in the family may be due to the prevailing pattern of child custody arrangements following divorce in the United States, where most children live with their mothers. Thus, divorce is much more likely to cause a disruption of the father-child bond than of the mother-child bond. Also, because there is evidence that fathers develop closer ties with their sons than with their daughters (Morgan et al. 1988), divorce and maternal custody of children would have a greater impact on the paternal relationships of boys than girls. The likely result is that when there are children in the family, men view divorce less approvingly than do women. This interpretation is strengthened by the fact that there is no gender difference in the distribution on the other divorce-attitude measure (Divorce Best), which contains no reference to children. Note, however, that although there was no difference between mothers and daughters in the 1980s, the daughters were entering their young adult years in the 1980s with substantially more approving attitudes toward divorce than their mothers had in the 1960s. This is due to the large increases in acceptance of divorce occurring across the 1960s and 1970s.

When we turn our attention from the "oughtness" of staying together as measured by the Not Stay Together question to whether or not "divorce is usually the best solution when a couple can't seem to work out their marriage problems" (Divorce Best), we find no gender difference but a substantial intergenerational effect. Mothers are nearly twice as likely as their children to endorse the proposition that "divorce is usually the best solution." This generation difference probably reflects the different meanings of divorce in the lives of children and their parents. At the same time that divorce breaks marital relationships that are judged by at least one spouse to be deficient, divorce also disrupts parent-child relationships that may not have any serious problems (Thornton 1985a). The same divorce that is judged to be a positive factor for adult relationships may be a very negative factor in the lives of children. Thus, divorce is probably much more likely to be the best solution to an unhappy marriage for parents than for children, and Wallerstein and Kelly (1980) report that children who experience divorce report substantially more regret about the divorce than do their parents. It may also be difficult for children to understand and appreciate the perspectives of parents. Young people tend to be idealistic about marriage and have not had to deal directly with the adjustments required in marriage. As a result they may overestimate the power of personal adjustment and dedication to avert separation and divorce. At the same time, parents who have a fuller appreciation of the adjustments marriage requires and the difficulties of working out problems may not fully appreciate the difficulties divorce produces for children.

Turning now to issues of premarital sexuality and cohabitation (Table 12.1, Panels D and E), we observe a substantial generation gap between parents and children. Whereas about one-third of the mothers in 1980 expressed approving attitudes toward premarital sex, approximately two-thirds of their daughters had accepting attitudes. And, between 1980 and 1985 as the daughters matured and became even more approving of premarital sex, the intergenerational gap widened even further. Whereas there was about a 33 percentage point difference between mothers and children in 1980, by 1985 the differential had grown to nearly 40 percentage points. Because young men tend to be more approving of premarital sex than young women, the intergenerational difference between mothers and sons is even larger than between mothers and daughters.

The young people also appear to understand the existence of the generation gap in attitudes toward premarital sex. Fifty percent of the daughters perceived that their mothers disapproved strongly, with another 41 percent perceiving that their mothers disapproved somewhat; only 8 percent perceived their mothers as not disapproving. In contrast, fully two-thirds of the daughters perceived their male friends as not disapproving and one-half perceived their female friends as not disapproving (Thornton and Camburn 1987). All of these data suggest that there are probably many families in America today where there are substantial disagreements between parents and children over the issue of premarital sex.

Panel E of Table 12.1 reveals a similar picture for attitudes about cohabitation without marriage, although overall levels of approval appear to be lower than for premarital sex. Whereas approximately one-quarter of the mothers in 1980 expressed approving attitudes toward cohabitation, around one-half of the daughters were approving. This gap also widened between 1980 and 1985. Also, because sons are more accepting of cohabitation than daughters, the intergenerational differences between sons and mothers are even greater than those between daughters and mothers.

The final panel in Table 12.1 documents attitudes toward childlessness and suggests a modest intergenerational effect. Apparently, young women making the transition to adulthood today are more likely to reject the requirement of parenthood than are their mothers. Whereas 52 percent of the mothers in 1985 said that it was not necessary for almost all married couples to have children, 64 percent of the daughters took this position (difference statistically significant). Because of the large increases in acceptance of childlessness during the 1960s and 1970s, the gap between the mothers when they were entering adulthood and their daughters in the 1980s is even greater than the cross-sectional gap observed in the 1980s. Also observe that because sons in the 1980s were more likely than daughters to believe that all couples should have children, their attitudes, on average, were almost identical to those of their mothers at the same point in time.

Intergenerational Differences in Religious Commitment

Table 12.2 provides documentation of the religious commitment of mothers and children in 1980. Just as Table 12.1 demonstrates important intergenerational differences in attitudes toward family issues, Table 12.2 indicates important differences in commitment to religion, with mothers being

TABLE 12.2 Distributions of Religious Attendance and Importance, 1980

Variable	*Mothers*	*Daughters*	*Sons*
Attendance at services[a]			
Never	5.7	5.2	9.2
Less than once a month	30.9	37.7	46.7
Once a month	5.3	7.8	7.6
A few times a month	10.5	14.8	7.9
Once a week	38.9	28.9	24.9
Several times a week	8.7	5.6	3.7
Total	100.0	100.0	100.0
Importance of religion[b]			
Not important	5.5	9.7	19.8
Somewhat important	26.2	48.3	50.6
Very important	68.3	42.0	29.6
Total	100.0	100.0	100.0

Note: The number of mother-child dyads in the analysis sample is 888.

[a]The question was, "How often do you usually attend religious services—would you say several times a week, once a week, a few times a month, once a month, or less than once a month?" Although the category "never" was not suggested to the respondents, a number of them volunteered that they never attended services.

[b]The importance of religion was ascertained by the question "Quite apart from attending religious services, how important would you say religion is to you—very important, somewhat important, or not important?"

significantly more religious than their children. Whereas 48 percent of the mothers reported attending religious services at least once a week in 1980, only 34 percent of the daughters and 29 percent of the sons reported attending that frequently. Similarly, more than two-thirds of the mothers reported religion to be very important to them, and less than one-half of the daughters and less than one-third of the sons reported religion to be that important. This substantial intergenerational difference is also reflected in the fact that 7 percent of the daughters and 12 percent of the sons reported having no specific religious affiliation and only 4 percent of the mothers reported having no religious preference (data not shown in tables). Because there have been declines in the church attendance of the mothers between 1962 and 1980, the differences in church attendance between mothers and their children at approximately the same position in the life course are even greater than the 1980 cross-sectional differences reported in Table 12.2 (Thornton and Camburn 1987).

Intergenerational Transmission of Family Attitudes

We now shift our emphasis from an examination of the similarities and differences of the aggregate distributions of attitudes of mothers and children to consider the similarities of individual mothers and children. By focusing on intergenerational similarities we are able to examine the extent of intergenerational transmission of attitudes at the individual level. That is, we are able to see the extent to which the relative position of a specific mother in the distribution of maternal attitudes is related to the relative position of her own child in the distribution of children's attitudes. The family attitudes investigated for this purpose included attitudes toward divorce, premarital sex, and appropriate roles for men and women.

This question was addressed by examining the extent to which the 1980 attitudes of individual children reflect the 1980 attitudes of their mothers. In order to preclude the possibility that any observed correlations between the attitudes of mothers and children were simply the result of the attitudes of both mothers and children being jointly determined by structural characteristics of the family such as socioeconomic position, the intergenerational effects of mother's attitudes on children's attitudes were estimated using multivariate causal models in which the mother's attitude and a number of characteristics of the parental family were used to predict the child's attitude. The characteristics of the parental family used in the equations included religious identification, attendance at religious services, education, age, work history, marriage history, and number of children.[1]

Measurement error is also an issue that must be dealt with in such analyses, because any error of measurement in the attitudinal variables will downwardly bias the estimated intergenerational effects. This problem was handled by using latent variable procedures to adjust for the effects of measurement unreliability. This approach was possible because the data set has multiple measures of the different substantive variables obtained at multiple time points. The substantive and measurement models were estimated simultaneously using the maximum likelihood procedures outlined by Joreskog and Sorbom (1978 and 1979). In order to evaluate the differential effects of mothers on sons and daughters the equations were estimated separately for families with sons and daughters.[2]

The standardized regression coefficients representing the effects of maternal attitudes on those of their children were generally in the neighborhood of .3. The lowest standardized regression coefficient was .22 and was observed for premarital sex attitudes among sons; the highest coefficient of .36 was observed for sex-role attitudes among daughters. The similarity of coefficients across substantive domains suggests the tentative conclusion that there are no important differences in the extent to which specific family attitudes are passed across generations.

I also began this research with the assumption that the transmission of maternal attitudes would be greater for daughters than for sons. Therefore, the models of intergenerational transmission have been consistently evaluated by gender. The estimated effects of maternal attitudes on children, however, have been about the same for sons as for daughters. For example, for sex-role attitudes the estimated standardized regression coefficient was .36 for daughters as compared to .32 for sons. Similarly for attitudes toward premarital sex, the coefficients were .27 and .22 for females and males, respectively. Thus, although there is a tendency for the effects to be somewhat larger for daughters than sons, the differences are quite small, suggesting that the influences of mothers on their male and female children are very similar.

In order to put the magnitude of this intergenerational transmission of attitudes into perspective, it is useful to compare the size of these intergenerational coefficients with the coefficients estimating the amount of attitudinal stability within the same generation. Using similar procedures, the standardized regression coefficient measuring the effect of the mothers' 1962 sex-role attitudes on their 1977 sex-role attitudes was estimated to be .30; the comparable measure of intragenerational stability in divorce attitudes over the same fifteen years was estimated to be .35. However, the intragenerational stability in maternal attitudes between 1977 and 1980 was estimated to be .80 for sex roles and .86 for divorce. Thus, the extent of intergenerational transmission of attitudes is very similar to the level of intragenerational stability across a fifteen-year period but much smaller than the magnitude of intragenerational stability across just three years.

This same line of research also demonstrates that parental attitudes not only influence the attitudes of their children but also their behavior. The same analysis showing that parental attitudes concerning premarital sex influence children's attitudes also indicates that those same parental attitudes also influence whether the children have ever had sexual intercourse, the number of sexual partners they have had, and the frequency of intercourse during the month immediately preceding the 1980 interview (Thornton and Camburn 1987).

This research has also shown that the influence of parental attitudes toward premarital sex on the attitudes and behavior of young adult children depends upon the quality of the relationship between parents and children. More specifically, the observed impact of maternal attitudes on the premarital sexual attitudes and behaviors of children is stronger in families where children and mothers have a close communicative relationship (Weinstein and Thornton 1989; also see Moore et al. 1986). This finding suggests that parents are better able to communicate their values and influence the ideas and behavior of their children when they have strong and supportive relationships with those children.

One more conceptual and methodological point before leaving the issue of intergenerational transmission of family attitudes. In order to estimate the causal models it was necessary to assume that all intergenerational causation goes in only one direction: from parents to children and not from children to parents. Although this is a reasonable first approximation of reality in that the bulk of the causal influence between parents and children through age eighteen probably goes from parents to children rather than the other way around, there are also good theoretical reasons to expect that children may also influence the attitudes and values of their parents, especially during the years the children are making the transition to adulthood. To the extent that there is any influence of children on parents, the estimates presented above of the influence of parents on children would be biased, but because I expect the bulk of the intergenerational influence to go from parents to children, such bias is likely to be modest.

In work that I currently have underway I am evaluating the impact of children's behavior on their parents attitudes. More specifically, this analysis is investigating the extent to which children's cohabitation experience between 1980 and 1985 impacts on their parents' attitudes toward cohabitation.

The Structure and History of the Parental Family

In the previous section we considered the impact of maternal attitudes concerning family issues on children's family attitudes and behaviors. In this section we broaden the analysis of the determinants of children's behavior and experience to include a wide range of family experiences and characteristics including religion, both religious identification and commitment; socioeconomic position; maternal work experience; number of children; and parental marital history, including age at marriage, whether the mother was pregnant at her own marriage, and divorce and remarriage experience. The dependent variables to be considered include sex role-attitudes, marriage attitudes, divorce attitudes, premarital sex attitudes and behavior, contraceptive behavior among the sexually active, and cohabitation and marriage experience. All of the analyses of the dependent variables have been conducted using multivariate models. Although the exact specification of the explanatory variables has varied across dependent variables, many of the explanatory variables listed have been included in most of the analyses reported. This summary will, of necessity, highlight only the most interesting conclusions. Throughout this discussion the reader will be referred to individual papers for the details of both the analyses and the conclusions. The reader, however, should make no assumptions about the possible relationships not summarized here, because a fair number of the possible effects from the previous list of independent and dependent variables have not yet been analyzed in detail.

Religion

Religious institutions have long been important sources of family values and norms in Western societies. Religious institutions and their leaders have historically taken strong positions concerning such issues as marriage, divorce, childbearing, premarital sex, and appropriate roles for women and men. Although the authority of religion as a source of moral guidelines concerning family and personal behavior may have declined in recent years, there is still reason to believe that commitment to religious institutions continues to influence behavior (D'Antonio and Aldous 1983; Glenn 1987; Lesthaeghe and Surkyn 1988; Thornton 1985b).

In our work we have concentrated on two main dimensions of religion: religious affiliation and religiosity. Religious affiliation is of importance because of the great diversity of religious institutions in their positions concerning family and personal behavior. Our work has focused on the Catholic-Protestant distinction, and because of the heterogeneity within the Protestant group, we have further subdivided that group into Fundamentalists and Baptists and all others. Religiosity is important because it indicates the degree to which people are integrated into and committed to their religious group. Religiosity has been measured by two separate concepts: frequency of attendance at religious services and the importance of religion in the life of the individual.

Our research is consistent with a growing literature indicating the declining uniqueness of Catholic family behavior (Alwin 1984; Blake 1984; Jones and Westoff 1979; Mosher and Hendershot 1983). On several family issues including sex-role attitudes, divorce attitudes, and premarital sexual behavior and attitudes, Catholic young people are very similar to nonfundamentalist Protestants.

Our data also suggest that fundamentalist Protestants have become increasingly distinct. During the past two decades when there have been important changes in attitudes toward family issues, fundamentalist Protestants have also changed, but the amount of change they have experienced has been less than for nonfundamentalist Protestants. Consequently, when the sons and daughters in our sample of fundamentalist families reached adulthood in the early 1980s, they had more negative attitudes toward divorce and premarital sex and reported less premarital sexual intercourse (Thornton 1985a; Thornton and Camburn 1987).

Our research also indicates that the mother's religiosity may have more influence than her religious affiliation on her children's family attitudes and behavior. On average, children whose mothers attended religious services frequently were less accepting of divorce and premarital sex than children whose mothers attended less frequently. They also had less premarital sexual experience.

Because of the differences among religious groups in official positions toward premarital sex and divorce, we originally thought that the impact of maternal religiosity would be greater for Catholics and fundamentalist Protestants than for nonfundamentalist Protestants. Detailed investigations of the interaction effect of religious affiliation and attendance, however, revealed that the effect of religious attendance was similar for all of the major religious groups (Thornton 1985a; Thornton and Camburn 1987).

Our research has also considered the relationship between the children's own religiosity and two dimensions of adolescent reproductive behavior: their premarital sexual experience and, for those who have experienced sexual intercourse, their contraceptive behavior. On the first issue, we have documented a strong correlation between adolescent premarital sexual attitudes and behavior and two measures of religiosity: frequency of attendance at religious services and the importance of religion in one's own life (Thornton and Camburn 1987; also see Chilman 1983; DeLamater and MacCorquodale 1979; Zelnik et al. 1981).

Most previous research has assumed that the correlation between adolescent sexual experience and attitudes and religiosity reflects causal influence from religiosity to sexual experience and attitudes. Our research accepts the plausibility of this path but also argues for the possibility of reciprocal causation—with sexual behavior and attitudes significantly influencing religious involvement. We estimated a reciprocal causation model and found evidence for both theoretical arguments in that there were significant empirical effects in both directions (Thornton and Camburn 1987).

Our research concerning the interrelationships between religiosity and contraceptive behavior among sexually active young people was motivated by the expectation that the psychological and social costs of using medical methods of contraception would be lower for young people less involved in religious institutions. Our findings were consistent with this hypothesis in that sexually active young women who attended religious services infrequently were more likely than others to use medical methods of contraception (Studer and Thornton 1987; also see Tanfer and Horn 1985).

Parental Marital History

The social sciences are rapidly accumulating an extensive body of research documenting the importance of the marital experiences of parents for their children. There are good theoretical reasons to believe that premarital pregnancy, age at marriage, divorce, and remarriage in the parental generation would influence the lives of both parents and children (Hayes 1987; Hetherington 1979; Pearlin and Johnson 1977), and recent empirical evidence has demonstrated such impacts on the behaviors, relationships, and health outcomes of both children and adults (Glenn and Kramer 1985; Hayes

1987; Hogan and Kitagawa 1985; McLanahan 1985; McLanahan and Bumpass 1988; Menaghan and Lieberman 1986; Udry and Billy 1987; and Wallerstein and Kelly 1980). We have studied how parental marital history influences children's divorce attitudes, their attitudes and behavior concerning premarital sex, their attitudes and behavior concerning marriage, and their nonmarital cohabitation experience.

This body of research demonstrates that several dimensions of the parental marital history have strong effects on children's attitudes and behavior. Looking first at the mother's age at marriage, we find children whose mothers married young had more accepting attitudes toward premarital sex, were more likely to have experienced sexual intercourse, and had more sexual partners. Children whose mothers married young also entered into both marital and cohabiting unions faster than others, with the effects on the rates of entrance into cohabiting and marital unions being similar. The more rapid rate of entrance into unions also extends to the decision to marry after entrance into a cohabiting union (Thornton 1991; Thornton and Camburn 1987). These findings clearly indicate an important intergenerational transmission of the rapidity of union formation.

As part of this study we ascertained the premarital pregnancy status of the mother from birth and marriage records and investigated the relationship of her premarital pregnancy experience to the attitudes and behavior of her young adult child. We found consistent and strong evidence suggesting that mothers who were premaritally pregnant had children who were more approving of premarital sex, perceived their mothers as more approving, and were more sexually active themselves (including a higher probability of experiencing sexual intercourse, having had more sexual partners, and having more sexual experience in the month preceding the 1980 interview). Children whose mothers were premaritally pregnant also had higher rates of union formation, including both marriage and cohabitation. Note that these effects are not just the result of a young age at marriage, because maternal age at marriage was included as a control in all of the analyses (Thornton 1991; Thornton and Camburn 1987). It is useful in considering the importance of these findings to remember that the premarital pregnancies in question occurred more than a decade before the children entered the adolescent years, and the existence of effects over that length of time reflects an impressive impact of parental experiences over a long period of the children's lives.

Parental divorce and remarriage also have important and pervasive influences on a broad range of children's behaviors and attitudes. Young people whose parents experienced a divorce were less positively oriented toward marriage themselves, had more positive attitudes toward divorce, and were more positive toward premarital sex (Thornton and Freedman 1982; Thornton and Camburn 1987). They also were more likely to report premarital sexual intercourse, more sexual partners, and more sexual partners in the month before the 1980 interview (Thornton and Camburn 1987). Parental divorce also influences coresidential union formation—increasing the overall rate of leaving singlehood for a coresidential union while at the same time shifting the first union experience away from marriage and toward cohabitation (Thornton 1991). The result is that children who experienced a marital dissolution during the years they were growing up are more likely than others to cohabit before marriage. In all of these comparisons the influence of experiencing a marital dissolution as a child is substantial. For example, the cohabitation rate among the children who had experienced a childhood family disruption was more than twice as high as the cohabitation rate among children with stably married parents (Thornton 1991).

One particularly interesting finding is that a maternal remarriage tends to exacerbate the effects of divorce rather than ameliorate them. Among the children experiencing divorce, those whose mothers had remarried had more positive attitudes toward premarital sex and more sexual experience than those whose mothers had not remarried (Thornton and Camburn 1987). The children whose mothers had divorced and remarried also had higher rates of cohabitation and marriage, although this tendency seems to be limited more to daughters than to sons (Thornton 1991). Elsewhere (Thornton 1991) I discuss several causal mechanisms that could possibly account for the influence of parental divorce and remarriage on children's union-formation experience and suggest that the most likely mechanism is through children's attitudes toward marriage, premarital sex, and cohabitation.

Socioeconomic Position

Our analyses have consistently found important effects of the mother's education on her own attitudes toward sex roles, divorce, and premarital sex, with more educated mothers having more egalitarian sex-role attitudes and less restrictive attitudes toward divorce and premarital sex. At the same time, however, we have not found the influence of parental education on children's attitudes and behavior to be strong or consistent. Perhaps the most important effect we have observed of parental education on children's family behavior is its depressing effect on the children's rate of entrance into marriage (Axinn and Thornton 1989).

There are good theoretical reasons to expect that parental preferences for the timing of their children's marriages would interact with their financial resources in affecting their children's actual rates of entrance into marriage (Waite and Spitze 1981). That is, parents with more financial resources might have more capacity to influence their children in the direction they desire. We tested this hypothesis by constructing an interactive model and using it to predict the rate of marriage of young adult children. The data provided partial support for this interactive hypothesis (Axinn and Thornton 1989).

Maternal Employment

We investigated the possible impact of maternal employment on several dimensions of the behavior and attitudes of young adult children, including sex-role attitudes, divorce attitudes, and premarital sexual behavior and attitudes. Contrary to expectations, we found no substantial or consistent effect of maternal employment on any of these dimensions of adolescent life (Thornton 1985a; Thornton and Camburn 1987; Thornton et al. 1983), casting doubt on the importance of the work histories of mothers on the kinds of childhood outcomes studied here.

Family Size

The number of children born to the mother was included in the analyses of premarital sexual behavior and attitudes and attitudes toward divorce, premarital sex, and appropriate roles for men and women. For the most part the effects of family size were small. The only statistically significant effect suggested that children from larger families had more restrictive attitudes toward premarital sex, but this effect did not extend to sexual behavior (Thornton and Camburn 1987).

Acknowledgments

Many people have contributed to this research. Of particular importance are the mothers and children who participated in the 23-year panel study on which it is based. The interviewers, coders, and computing personnel of the Survey Research Center of the University of Michigan provided expertise and commitment in collecting and processing data. Ronald Freedman, David Goldberg, and Lolagene Coombs directed the early data collections, and Deborah Freedman collaborated with the author in directing later waves of data collection. Donald Camburn provided assistance in collecting the later waves of data, and Linda Young-DeMarco provided assistance in managing the data and in conducting analyses. Judy Baughn prepared the manuscript. Funding for data collection and analysis was provided by the National Institute of Child Health and Human Development. The author is greatly appreciative of these many contributions but retains the usual responsibility for any errors.

Notes

1. Both the divorce and premarital sex attitude analyses also included age at marriage. The premarital pregnancy status of the mother was also included in the analysis of premarital sex attitudes.

2. Full details of the individual analyses reported here can be found in Thornton 1985a; Thornton and Camburn 1987; Thornton et al. 1983.

References

Alwin, Duane F. 1984. Trends in Parental Socialization Values: Detroit, 1958 to 1983. *American Journal of Sociology* 90:359–382.

Alwin, Duane F., and Arland Thornton. 1984. Family Origins and the Schooling Process: Early Versus Late Influence of Parental Characteristics. *American Sociological Review* 49:784–802.

Axinn, William G., and Arland Thornton. 1989. The Influence of Parental Resources on the Timing of the Transition to Marriage. Paper presented at the Annual Meeting of the Population Association of America.

Blake, J. 1984. Catholicism and Fertility: On Attitudes of Young Americans. *Population and Development Review* 10:329–340.

Cherlin, Andrew J., and Pamela B. Walters. 1981. U.S. Men's and Women's Sex-Role Attitudes. *American Sociological Review* 46:453–460.

Chilman, C. S. 1983. Coital Behaviors of Adolescents in the United States: A Summary of Research and Implication for Further Studies. Paper presented at the annual meeting of the American Psychological Association, Anaheim, CA, August 26–30.

D'Antonio, W. V., and J. Aldous. 1983. *Families and Religions: Conflict and Change in Modern Society*. Beverly Hills, CA: Sage Publications.

DeLamater, J., and P. MacCorquodale. 1979. *Premarital Sexuality*. Madison: University of Wisconsin Press.

Glenn, Norval D. 1987. Social Trends in the United States: Evidence from Sample Surveys. *Public Opinion Quarterly* 51:S109–S126.

Glenn, Norval D., and Kathryn B. Kramer. 1985. The Psychological Well-Being of Adult Children of Divorce. *Journal of Marriage and the Family* 47:905–912.

Hayes, Cheryl D. (ed.) 1987. *Risking the Future*. Washington, DC: National Academy Press.

Hetherington, E. Mavis. 1979. Divorce: A Child's Perspective. *American Psychologist* 34:851–858.

Hogan, Dennis P., and E. M. Kitagawa. 1985. The Impact of Social Status, Family Structure and Neighborhood on the Fertility of Black Adolescents. *American Journal of Sociology* 90:825–855.

Jones, E. F., and C. F. Westoff. 1979. The End of "Catholic" Fertility. *Demography* 16:209–217.

Joreskog, K. G., and D. Sorbom. 1978. *LISREL IV—A General Computer Program for Estimation of a Linear Structural Equation System by Maximum Likelihood Methods*. Chicago: National Educational Resources.

———. 1979. *Advances in Factor Analysis and Structural Equation Models.* Cambridge, MA: Abt Books.

Lesthaeghe, Ron J., and Johan Surkyn. 1988. Cultural Dynamics and Economic Theories of Fertility Change. *Population and Development Review* 14:1–45.

Mason, Karen O., and Yu-Hsia Lu. 1988. Attitudes Toward Women's Familial Roles: Changes in the United States, 1977–1985. *Gender & Society* 2:39–57.

Mason, Karen O., John L. Czajka, and Sara Arber. 1976. Change in U.S. Women's Sex-Role Attitudes, 1964–1974. *American Sociological Review* 41:573–596.

McLanahan, Sara. 1985. Family Structure and the Reproduction of Poverty. *American Journal of Sociology* 90:873–901.

McLanahan, Sara, and Larry Bumpass. 1988. Intergenerational Consequences of Family Disruption. *American Journal of Sociology* 94:130–152.

Menaghan, Elizabeth G., and Morton A. Lieberman. 1986. Changes in Depression Following Divorce. *Journal of Marriage and the Family* 48:319–328.

Moore, K. A., J. L. Peterson, and F. F. Furstenberg. 1986. Parental Attitudes and Early Sexual Activity. *Journal of Marriage and the Family* 48:777–782.

Morgan, S. P., D. N. Lye, and G. A. Condran. 1988. Sons, Daughters, and the Risk of Marital Disruption. *American Journal of Sociology* 94:110–129.

Mosher, W. D., and G. E. Hendershot. 1983. Religion and Fertility Reexamined. Paper presented at the annual meeting of the Population Association of America, Pittsburgh, PA, April 14–16.

Pearlin, Leonard I., and Joyce S. Johnson. 1977. Marital Status, Life-Strains and Depression. *American Sociological Review* 42:704–715.

Studer, Marlena, and Arland Thornton. 1987. Adolescent Religiosity and Contraceptive Usage. *Journal of Marriage and the Family* 49:117–128.

Tanfer, Koray, and Marjorie C. Horn. 1985. Contraceptive Use, Pregnancy, and Fertility Patterns Among Single American Women in Their 20s. *Family Planning Perspectives* 17:10–19.

Thornton, Arland. 1985a. Changing Attitudes Toward Separation and Divorce: Causes and Consequences. *American Journal of Sociology* 90:856–872.

———. 1985b. Reciprocal Influences of Family and Religion in a Changing World. *Journal of Marriage and the Family* 47:381–394.

———. 1989. Changing Attitudes Toward Family Issues in the United States. *Journal of Marriage and the Family* 51:873–893.

———. 1991. Influence of the Marital History of Parents on the Union Formation Experience of Children. *American Journal of Sociology* 96:868–894.

Thornton, Arland, and Donald Camburn. 1987. The Influence of the Family on Premarital Sexual Attitudes and Behavior. *Demography* 24:323–340.

Thornton, Arland, and Deborah Freedman. 1982. Changing Attitudes Toward Marriage and Single Life. *Family Planning Perspectives* 14:297–303.

Thornton, Arland, Duane F. Alwin, and Donald Camburn. 1983. Causes and Consequences of Sex-Role Attitudes and Attitude Changes. *American Sociological Review* 48:211–227.

Udry, J. Richard, and John O. G. Billy. 1987. Initiation of Coitus in Early Adolescence. *American Sociological Review* 52:841–855.

Veroff, Joseph, Elizabeth Douvan, and Richard A. Kulka. 1981. *The Inner American.* New York: Basic Books.

Waite, Linda J., Frances K. Goldscheider, and C. Witsberger. 1986. Nonfamily Living and the Erosion of Traditional Family Orientations Among Young Adults. *American Sociological Review* 51:541–554.

Waite, Linda J., and Glenna D. Spitze. 1981. Young Women's Transition to Marriage. *Demography* 18:681–694.

Wallerstein, Judith S., and Joan Berlin Kelly. 1980. *Surviving the Breakup*. New York: Basic Books.

Weinstein, Maxine, and Arland Thornton. 1989. Mother-Child Relations and Adolescent Sexual Attitudes and Behavior. *Demography* 26:563–577.

Zelnik, M., J. F. Kantner, and K. Ford. 1981. *Sex and Pregnancy in Adolescents*. Beverly Hills: Sage.

13

Work in the Home: The Productive Context of Family Relationships

*Linda Waite and Frances K. Goldscheider**

The home is the primary site for interaction between husbands and wives, parents and children, brothers and sisters, residents and guests. Until the nineteenth century, the home was also the context for nearly all productive activities, which were performed by family members either in or near the home. As a result, family relationships, although surely hierarchical and structured, nevertheless took place in a context of joint production, in which men, women, and children were working together for their collective well-being.

But the development of paid employment outside the home increasingly took men from the household during the nineteenth century to earn money for family consumption (Tilly and Scott 1978). This left the tasks associated with the home and garden to women and children, who worked together to keep the household running and to provide a haven for their returning husband and father—the ideal-typical pater familias—and as a consequence domestic productive interaction focused increasingly around the mother-child relationship, intensifying and redefining it in important ways (Lasch 1977; Shorter 1975). Then the expansion of schooling and a new definition of childhood emphasizing school and a future of employment outside the home took boys away as well (Zelizer 1985). This left the home and its chores to women and their daughters, recreating the home as *women's place* where women serve men, and where even very young boys resist participation in what had become exclusively "girls' work" (Chodorow 1978; White and Brinkerhoff 1981a; White 1989). However, the growth of women's education and an increasingly egalitarian approach to women's roles in the workplace

The authorship of this paper is equal and joint. The names are presented in reverse alphabetical order.

have now weakened parents' justification for treating their children differently; girls' curricula and goals in school have come increasingly to resemble boys', with the result that girls' participation in the home has dwindled in many households to boys' levels (Goldscheider and Waite 1991, chap. 9).

Many of the processes of industrialization that affected men's roles in the workplace and children's requirements for education have also reduced the tasks associated with maintaining a home, and a long-term decline in fertility has limited the number of years of direct childcare, leaving even adult women time to take on paid employment. Nevertheless, many tasks remain that are essential if families are to be clothed, fed, and sheltered and if children are to be socialized in privacy, comfort, cleanliness, and security. The movement of most productive activity to sites removed from the family residence has not changed the home's importance for family interaction, but it has limited and shifted the context of this interaction. Thus, not only is work in the household no longer seen as directly productive (because it is "simply" the work that frees family members for wage labor—or preparation for wage labor—outside the home), it has also been degraded to one-way rather than shared service activities. Home-based family interaction now takes place in a setting in which the remaining productive tasks are almost entirely the province of adult women, who have become responsible for making a home *for*, and no longer *with*, their partners and children, whose primary activities take place elsewhere.

Thus, the tasks that remain within the household are an anomaly in a society that has focused its attention only on the value of activities outside the home. These tasks have been devalued further by their linkage to women and made more unattractive to women, who have lost their team of helpers and their satisfaction in training others to do a job well. Women increasingly find themselves using their skills in nearly total isolation, their activities ignored and not appreciated, with only the task not done rising above the surface of family awareness. When men and children have almost no social support for helping out (in fact, quite the reverse), women find themselves seen as coercive in their efforts to get help, efforts that most therefore abandon. As such, the performance of household tasks has become a painful issue in increasing numbers of families (Fuchs 1988; Ross and Mirowsky 1989).

Thus, the growth in female labor-force participation has sharply unbalanced the work effort of married men and women. This effort, which was about equal (and unending) in subsistence households and which was equal as well when only men worked outside the home, is clearly not equal among modern two-earner families (Coverman and Sheley 1986; Sanik 1981; Walker and Woods 1976). Employed women work many more hours—at their job plus at home—than do men or women who are not employed outside the home. An important reason why young women are delaying marriage is likely to be that their expectations for shared household roles are higher than those of the men they meet (Thornton 1989), and children's decreased participation in household tasks may well be contributing to couples' greater unwillingness to bear them. If so, then studying the patterns that underlie the domestic division of labor is the first task in understanding the basic family and demographic trends now characterizing Western society.

This chapter is a step in this direction. We examine the ways in which families allocate the labor of their members to the productive activities that constitute housework. We build on two streams of research, one that has examined the division of household labor between husbands and wives (Ross 1987; Spitze 1986) and another independent line of research that examines the participation of children in "chores" (Duncan and Duncan 1978; White and Brinkerhoff 1981a; Propper 1972). But researchers have almost never looked at the family economy as a whole, considering all those in the household—wives, husbands, and children—as potential workers.[1] This chapter extends and elaborates previous research, explicitly examining trade-offs between the adults in the household and the children, and between the spouses.

Background

Research on the division of labor between husbands and wives suggests that the traditional basis for this division still provides a strong justification for it: Husbands work more hours than wives in the paid labor force, influencing the spouses' respective shares in domestic tasks via their *time availability*. The husband's participation in housework tends to decrease as his hours of work outside the home increase, and increase if the wife is employed (Coverman and Sheley 1986; Gershuny and Robinson 1988; Miller and Garrison 1982).

But there is clearly more to it. Higher wages outside the home evidently confer power over the decision about how to balance leisure and work within the home, so that husbands and wives with higher wages perform fewer household tasks than do their relatively less powerful counterparts (Farkas 1976; Ross 1987; Spitze 1986). Further, social definitions of performance of housework depend on the sex of the worker, so that women ordinarily perform more of the tasks in the domestic "gender factory" in order to reinforce traditional gender identities in household members (Berk 1985).

Not all accept traditional gender roles, however; some husbands think they *should* participate more and some less. Hence, a husband's attitudes about sex roles appear to influence his share of housework (Ross 1987). Those husbands who express support for nontraditional roles for the sexes appear more likely to take nontraditional roles at home themselves. But even when the wife faces severe constraints on her time because of full-time employment, she tends to retain responsibility for the substantial majority of the housework (Ross 1987; Spitze 1986). So husbands' support for equality between the sexes moves the division of labor toward equal participation, but it doesn't move it very far and only from a base of extreme inequality.

The small amount of research literature on children's roles in household tasks reflects some of these concerns but is primarily focused on other issues. The gender-role question has only appeared in the literature on children's roles in terms of trade-offs between boys and girls rather than among children, mothers, and fathers (Duncan and Duncan 1978; White and Brinkerhoff 1981a). There are no studies on change over time in children's share relative to adults', although a historical decline in children's participation is suggested by findings that rural and farm children are responsible for more chores than urban children (Light, Hertsgaard, and Martin 1985; Roy 1961). There is some evidence that children take more responsibility when their mothers are employed (Cogle and Tasker 1982; Timmer, Eccles, and O'Brien 1985). However, because the effects found in most of these studies have been extraordinarily weak and because children of working mothers in two-parent families take on far less responsibility than children in mother-only families, even when their mother works few hours (Goldscheider and Waite 1991; Weiss 1979), it is very likely that the underlying role structure shaping the participation of parents and children in domestic tasks does not depend in any simple way on the mother's time availability.

In fact, parents appear to be quite ambivalent about their children's participation in household chores. When mothers and fathers are asked *why* they expect their children to share some responsibility for household tasks, there is little consistency in their answers beyond a vague concern about developing character and a sense of responsibility (White and Brinkerhoff 1981b). Only a few report that they require the child's labor in running the house, and even fewer indicate that they view "chores" as a way to prepare the child for the performance of household tasks as adults—learning to cook, do laundry, and clean up one's room—although this answer is more often given by families with daughters. Another minority response, most commonly given in large families, is that parents want children to feel they have a responsibility to participate in the work of the household enterprise. However, because more than a third of parents *pay* children for work around the house, they are really reinforcing a view that such work is optional.[2]

Nevertheless, in addition to focusing on what husbands and children each do, it is important to study how they are trading off with each other and with their wives and mothers. Most tasks can be done, at least in part, by children or by either parent. And the amount that needs to be done by any family member depends on how much the others are already doing. The vast majority of studies of husband-wife sharing exclude the role of children and may be seriously incomplete; the few studies on children's roles in the household may also have missed something important by not including the extent of the husband's share.

In this chapter we extend and elaborate previous research by explicitly examining trade-offs between family members. We allow the share done by the father to depend on the share done by the children and the share done by the children to depend on the share done by the father. We develop and test hypotheses about the characteristics of mothers, fathers, and children that influence the ways they share responsibility for housework.

Data

Data for this analysis come from the National Longitudinal Surveys of Young Women and Mature Women. Conducted by the Ohio State University Center for Human Resource Research, these surveys include information over a recent 15-year period on more than 10,000 women. Personal interviews were conducted with national probability samples of young women ages 14 to 24 in 1968 and older women ages 30 to 44 in 1967. Those included responded to lengthy interviews in many of the succeeding years through the early 1980s. Attrition from the sample over the panel period has been relatively low.

The sample for this analysis consists of married women with at least one child in the household who is over the age of 5 and under the age of 19. We restrict the sample to those families eligible to share across the three categories of interest: wife, husband, and children. We reason that children cannot begin to assume responsibility for household chores before about age 6 and that adult children in the household take on a different role—and have different responsibilities outside the household—than younger children. The women in our sample may have older or younger children but must have at least one child old enough to share housework and not yet an adult.

How Women Provided Information on Sharing

The Mature and Young Women data contain identical sets of items on household tasks. Women were asked about household tasks:

> Now I would like to ask you a few questions about work around the home. . . . Would you say that—week in and week out—you have the sole responsibility,

> someone else has the sole responsibility, or that you share responsibility with someone else for—grocery shopping? child care, including helping with children? cooking? cleaning the dishes after meals? cleaning the house? washing the clothes? yard and home maintenance? family paperwork, like paying bills and balancing the checkbook?

In each case, the woman could report that she has sole responsibility, others have responsibility, that she shares responsibility with others, or that the particular task is not applicable, for example if she had no children and thus did not have or share responsibility for childcare.

For each task that was shared or for which others had responsibility, the woman was asked, "Who usually performs this task or shares it with you?" The response categories included husband, children, hired help, and other. These categories allow us to distinguish among categories of others but not, except for husbands, the particular individual with whom the woman shares.[3] If the woman reported that she shared responsibility for a task, she was asked, "Would you say that you are responsible for this task less than half of the time, about half of the time, or more than half of the time?"

This measure provides information on *responsibility* for various commonly done household tasks. It is not without drawbacks; in particular, it does not allow for sharing with more than one other category of others. For example, a woman might share grocery shopping not only with her husband but also with one of her children, but she is allowed to name only one other class of individuals with whom she shares. This feature of the question series introduced a negative correlation between sharing with husbands and sharing with children, although this correlation is modest (about 0.2) in the data used here. But although our measures ignore the *number of hours* spent on the tasks, the hours measure is likely to reflect other issues less central to our concerns such as individual differences in how efficient people are or how much they like spending time on a particular task. We think our sharing measures are conceptually more appropriate for the questions we pose, because they tell us how much each person does *of the work that the family has decided needs to be done.*

The reader will note that the mentioned list of household tasks includes a sizable number usually considered "female" and two—maintenance of yard and home and family paperwork—that are either stereotypically male (like yard and home maintenance) or neutral (like paperwork). Together, these tasks account for about 90 percent of all household time inputs according to a landmark study (Walker and Woods 1976). But the six traditionally female tasks predominate in the time they require in the average household.

Using these data, we created measures that reflect the extent women share with husbands and children, considering each task separately as well as the array of tasks. To measure the amount of responsibility for each separate task, such as cooking, assumed by children, we created a measure of sharing that ranged from zero, if the woman did not share at all with children, to four, if children had sole responsibility for the task (a rare occurrence). The complete coding of this measure is

0 if mother does not share with children[4]
1 if children do less than half
2 if children do about half
3 if children do more than half
4 if children have sole responsibility

We created an identically-coded set of measures for each task for sharing with husbands.

To consider household tasks as a group, we constructed two indices of sharing household tasks, one for the extent of sharing with children and one tapping the extent of sharing with husband. Before combining the individual tasks into a single measure of sharing, we first examined the relationships among the tasks shared, considering sharing with children and sharing with husbands separately. This analysis showed that in each case, there were five chores for which patterns of sharing were closely related. These chores are dishwashing, clothes washing, housecleaning, cooking, and grocery shopping.[5] Our scales sum the scores for each chore for children (KIDSHARE) and husbands (HUBSHARE), coded as described previously. The resulting scales each had a possible range of 0 to 16, but most of the cases were concentrated at the low end with nearly identical means (2.96 for KIDSHARE and 3.01 for HUBSHARE for the families in our sample).

Estimation Techniques

Our analysis of the relative responsibility of husbands, wives, and children for household tasks uses two multivariate techniques, multinominal logistic regression and two-stage least squares (2SLS). For each individual chore, we use multinomial logistic regressions to predict the odds that women shared any responsibility for performing it (1) with husbands or (2) with children, relative to being wholly responsible, herself, for the given chore.[6] The level of sharing with anyone outside the immediate family is very small: The task most likely to be shared outside the family is household cleaning, but only 4 percent of women report sharing any responsibility for cleaning house with paid help. Because the supervision of such others usually is the wife's responsibility, we felt that including those wives sharing only with nonfamily members with those not sharing at all made the most appropriate contrast to sharing with nuclear family members.

We model variation in HUBSHARE and KIDSHARE using 2SLS regression, in which (1) the extent of sharing with husbands is expected to affect the extent of sharing with children and vice versa; (2) a set of factors influences sharing with both; and (3) other factors either influence sharing with husbands only through their effect on sharing with children or influence sharing with children only through their effect on sharing with husbands.

We hypothesized that the number of the husband's hours of paid work should directly affect his ability to take responsibility for household tasks but should not directly influence the children's level of participation (controlling for the earnings his hours yield, of course, which could be spent on hiring nonhousehold members).[7]

Our theorizing with regard to sharing with children was somewhat more complex: We reasoned that families with teenage daughters feel at least some responsibility to train them in domestic tasks, training that few husbands would be able to provide. Hence, the presence of such children will increase a woman's reported sharing with children but affect sharing with husbands only through the effect sharing with children has on sharing with husbands. Table 13.1 presents the means of the independent and dependent variables for this analysis.

Hypotheses

We expect that in addition to the hypotheses already noted—which are necessary to perform 2SLS regression—many factors will affect a woman's sharing household tasks either with her husband or with her children.[8] Further, the literature on sharing with husbands and sharing with children has generally focused on different issues. In our combined analysis we will be able to see the extent to which this separation is justified, because it is likely that factors that have primarily been examined in the context of analyses of the husband-wife division of labor also affect sharing with children and vice versa. We have three general categories of hypotheses drawn from the literature on husband-wife division of labor, which we generalize to the entire household economy: (1) those that affect the spouses' time and energy to do the work; (2) those that indicate differences in resources and power over the decision of how the work is to be shared; and (3) those that could be expected to influence attitudes and values about the "proper" roles of husbands and wives (and perhaps parents and children) in the household. We include as well an additional category of hypotheses

Table 13.1 Definitions, Means, and Standard Deviations of Variables

Variable	Definition	Mean	Standard Deviation
HUSSH2	Husband Sharing on 4 Tasks	3.0100	4.0182
KIDSH2	Kids Sharing on 4 Tasks	2.9489	4.1369
STPFAM1	Lived in Remarried Household as Teen	0.0396	0.1951
FHHFAM1	Lived in Female Headed Household as Teen	0.1177	0.3223
STEPPAR	Step Parent Present Indicator	0.4165	0.4931
KIDSLT4	At Least One Child Less than 4	0.1542	0.3612
KIDS46	At Least One Kid 4, 5 or 6	0.2358	0.4246
GIRL1218	At Least One Girl 12 to 18	0.4085	0.4916
GIRLGE19	At Least One Girl GE 19	0.1108	0.3139
BOYS1218	At Least One Boy 12 to 18	0.4354	0.4959
BOYSGE19	At Least One Boy GE 19	0.1158	0.3200
TOTKIDS	Total Number of Children	2.4439	1.1451
BLACK	If Black then Black=1 Else=0 *1982*	0.2046	0.4035
SOUTH	Region of Residence *1982*	0.3969	0.4894
SIZE	Size Labor Force, R Labor market *1982*	2.8623	2.2122
EDATT	Highest Grade Completed *1977*	12.3023	2.5160
EMPLOYED	Respondent Employed=1	0.6042	0.4891
WCHR	Hrs Worked	17.6792	18.5880
WFDISAB	Woman Has Health Limit	0.0873	0.2823
WINC	Wife Combined Wage and Business Inc.	5807.4146	7420.8209
AGECADJ	Age in a Continuous Form Minus 27	12.1546	7.8343
FAMROLES	Family Role Attitude Factor	–0.0523	0.9275
JOBROLES	Job Role Attitude Factor	–0.0310	0.7277
HUSGRD	Highest Grade Comp Pres/Recent Hus *1982*	11.8735	4.4156
HEARN	Husband Combined Wage and Business Inc.	20655.9611	13175.2799
HUSCWH	Number of Hours Worked, Husband *1982*	40.6765	17.0945
HDISAB	Husband Has Health Limit	0.1365	0.3434

drawn from the literature on children's involvement in household tasks: (4) those relating to the ages and genders of the children.

Constraints on Parental Time and Energy

One of the most critical questions facing modern families is how to get the work of the household done when both husband, whose "job" once included many of these tasks, and the wife, whose "job" they now are, are employed outside the home. We constructed three indicators of contraints on husbands' and wives' time and energy for performing household tasks based on their paid employment. We consider the number of hours on the job for both men and women; and for women, we also wanted to examine the fact of such employment per se. A woman's being employed at all outside the home, even relatively part time, should increase the husband's and children's shares of household tasks, because any employment involves time costs of transportation to and from work and the necessity of purchasing and maintaining appropriate work clothes (Ross 1987; Spitze 1986); and the fact of the wife and mother's employment reduces the justification for her doing all the domestic work.

1. Spouses' Employment and Paid Work Hours: We hypothesize that wives' employment and the number of hours of paid work of husbands and wives should increase the shares of other members of the family.

Resources and Power

Research on the division of labor between husbands and wives has focused to a considerable extent on their relative power in the relationship, assuming that power derives from command over resources and hence, particularly for women, the existence of alternatives to the current marriage.[9] The implicit assumption underlying the linkage of marital power and division of household labor is that housework is undesirable and low status and therefore performed mostly by those who cannot enforce a more equitable division of labor (Spitze 1986). If neither cares particularly, or if the spouses agree on the appropriate division of labor, then who the boss is will never come into the decisionmaking process. Increasingly, however, who does household tasks has become an issue, with men holding very different attitudes than women on the appropriateness of their doing such chores (Berk 1985).

Our data do not include measures of all these issues. However, the critical power issue for most in deciding to break up a relationship is the extent of husbands' and wives' financial resources. The higher a given spouse's earnings, the more he or she has the power to leave a relationship, which can be used to influence decisionmaking; however, the higher the other spouse's earnings, the more costly it is to leave.[10]

It is less clear how such power should influence sharing with children. Children may follow their father's lead in pitching in with housework as their mother's employment brings in greater financial rewards and is taken more seriously, but it is also possible that increased parental earnings could lead to greater purchasing of outside goods and services, reducing further the need for the children to share.

2. Husband's and Wife's Income: We expect that as adults' earnings increase, so does the opportunity cost of their time spent in housework and their power to define how family leisure time is spent, increasing the share of the chores that other family members do.

Attitudes Toward the Division of Household Labor

To analyze the attitudinal dimension of family sharing, we focus on two direct measures of the wives' general sex-role attitudes and on the education level of husbands and wives. Our scales of sex-role attitudes tap two somewhat different dimensions of changing family roles. One seems to reflect less traditionally sex-typed ideas about the importance of women's roles in the workplace, emphasizing the importance of a woman's pay to her family and the satisfactions that she might derive from working, which we call *job roles;* the other, which we call *family roles,* focuses on women's traditional roles in the home. We scaled these questions so that a high value means a less traditional response. (More information about the construction of these scales is presented in Appendix 13.1.)

These measures are only available for women, not for their husbands (or children). This presents a problem, because most studies of couples have shown that *his* attitudes are much more important than hers when they differ. However, their attitudes tend to be closely related; further, we have educational measures for both spouses, and education is closely related to holding more egalitarian sex-role attitudes among males (Goldscheider and Waite 1991).

It was not at all clear to us how sex-role attitudes, which measure attitudes about *men's and women's* roles in the workplace and in the home, would relate to sharing household tasks *with children*. Mothers who place a high value on the importance of home-based roles for women might spend more time at home, have higher standards for home maintenance, and so place high demands on their children (and particularly want to train their daughters "appropriately"). However, what they are saying in their responses to these questions is that they gain tremendous satisfaction from their roles in the home and might thus be less willing to share them.

Higher education is also associated with more modern sex-role attitudes and thus to greater sharing between men and women, but it may lead to less sharing with children. Families with more education are more likely to define childhood as a time of preparation for the world of achievement outside the home and to give priority to homework over housework and perhaps be more concerned about giving children leisure to prevent "burn-out" from their competitive quest for achievement through the educational system. If so, household tasks would become the purview of adults among families with more education.

3. Sex-Role Attitudes: Women with less traditional sex-role attitudes should share household tasks more with husbands and perhaps with children.
4. Educational Attainment: Those with more education, both husbands and wives, would be more modern in their definitions of family responsibilities, involving husbands more and children less in domestic tasks.

Ages and Sexes of Children

Previous research and common sense suggest that the age and sex composition of the children in the household will affect their involvement in household labor. Many families assign tasks to children along lines segregated by traditional notions of gender (Berk 1985; Brody and Steelman 1985; Thrall 1978). Further, children clearly become better able to take on household tasks as they grow, with preteens able to perform fewer tasks than teenagers. So the presence of an "appropriate" child for a given task is likely to lead to greater sharing of that task, because the alternative is to train a less "appropriate" child, pay an outsider, not do the task, or for the parents, usually the mother, to take on the task herself.

5. Families with older children, particularly girls, will involve children more in household tasks.

Results

Table 13.2 presents the results of the 2SLS analyses of the extent to which wives share household responsibilities with their husbands and children. Column 1 shows coefficients for factors influencing sharing with husbands and column 2 shows those for sharing with children. Table 13.3 presents polytomous logit coefficients indicating the likelihood of sharing with husbands (column 1 for each chore) relative to the wife taking complete responsibility for that task and the likelihood of sharing with children (column 2 for each chore), again relative to not sharing with either.

Children Versus Husbands

Do families substitute the household labor of husbands for children? Or do families in which both adults share household tasks also involve their children more as well, thus reducing the wife's share? Given the fact that children's and husbands' shares of housework are relatively low (Goldscheider and Waite 1991), families have much more leeway to reduce the amount of housework done by the wife and mother than they do to reduce the already low amounts done by husbands or children.

Our results show that families appear to treat husbands as substitutes for children but to treat children as substitutes for the wife (Fig. 13.1). Each additional task done by the husband reduces the amount done by children by nearly one task (87 percent); for every eight tasks husbands do, children do seven fewer. Apparently the wife gets very modest relief from her mate's efforts on housework. He reduces the tasks that need to be done, so children are not called on to do them; but the wife still does

Table 13.2 Two-Stage Least-Squares Models of Sharing with Husbands and Children, Total Population

	Children's Share	*Husband's Share*
Intercept	0.613	0.750
Husband's share	–0.875+	—
Children's share	—	–0.172*
Childhood family:		
Stepfamily I	0.446	0.221
Mother-only family I	0.420	0.160
Stepfather	–0.171	–0.339+
Children in family:		
Child < 4	–0.211	0.250
Child 4–6	–0.449+	0.093
Girl 12–18	2.103**	—
Girl > 18	1.736**	–0.108
Boy 12–18	–0.070	0.080
Boy > 18	–0.177	0.402
Total number	0.700**	0.014
Black	0.666*	–0.092
Size	–0.052	0.017
South	–0.555**	–0.172
Wife's:		
Schooling	–0.024	0.054
Employed	0.018	–0.110
Work hours	0.033*	0.031**
Disabled	0.638	0.567*
Income	0.070*	0.060**
Age	0.085**	0.035*
Sex-role attitudes:		
Family roles	0.314+	0.310**
Job roles	–0.006	0.065
Husband's:		
Schooling	0.072	0.111**
Work hours	—	–0.011*
Income	–0.004	–0.010
Disability	0.817*	0.502*
N = 2572		
R-squared	0.227	0.116
Mean of dependent variable	2.96	3.01

Two-tailed tests of significance:
** = $p \leq .01$
* = $.01 < p \leq .05$
+ = $.05 < p \leq .10$

Table 13.3 Polytomous Logit Models of Sharing with Husband and Children for Separate Chores, Total Population

Dependent	Grocery Shopping		Washing Dishes		Cooking		Child Care	
Variables	*Husband*	*Child*	*Husband*	*Child*	*Husband*	*Child*	*Husband*	*Child*
Dep Mean	0.321	0.040	0.218	0.393	0.247	0.111	0.507	0.058
R-squared	0.069	0.098	0.240	0.353	0.114	0.173	0.212	0.177
N =	2573	2573	2573	2573	2573	2573	2573	2573
Intercept	–1.074**	–4.719	–2.871	–2.203**	–1.658**	–3.378	–0.876**	–3.893*
Childhood family:								
Stepfamily I	0.418+	2.086**	0.270	0.052	0.011	–0.184	0.299	0.296
Mother-only family I	–0.071	0.053	0.140	0.230	0.216	0.274	–0.116	–0.082
Stepfather	0.175+	0.151	0.037	0.427**	–0.029	0.092	0.013	0.508*
Children in family:								
Child < 4	0.274+	–0.124	0.129	–0.396*	–0.086	–0.305	0.106	–0.306
Child 4–6	–0.083	–0.162	0.119	–0.466**	0.035	–0.266	–0.133	0.042
Girl 12–18	0.047	0.652*	–0.065	1.524**	0.081	1.629**	–0.298**	0.611**
Girl > 18	0.106	2.366**	–0.057	0.484*	–0.227	1.070**	–0.286+	1.224**
Boy 12–18	0.036	–0.054	–0.180	–0.039	0.108	–0.123	–0.229*	–0.208
Boy > 18	0.147	–0.305	0.148	–0.474*	–0.082	–0.686**	–0.756**	–1.481**
Total number	–0.014	0.355**	0.117+	0.550**	0.020	0.521**	0.220**	0.966**

Black	0.265*	0.463	–0.094	1.085**	–0.044	0.345+	–0.253*	1.484**
Size	–0.010	–0.019	–0.005	–0.056*	0.031	–0.095**	–0.043+	–0.077+
South	–0.204*	–0.141	–0.125	–0.457**	–0.159	–0.405*	–0.257*	0.312
Wife's:								
Schooling	–0.014	–0.098+	0.063*	–0.026	–0.012	–0.057	0.072**	–0.148**
Employed	–0.258+	–0.811*	0.315+	0.361*	0.092	0.276	0.369*	0.627*
Work hours	0.015**	0.021*	0.010+	0.004	0.019**	0.015*	0.002	–0.007
Disabled	0.540**	0.396	0.450*	0.009	0.057	0.562*	–0.027	0.557
Income	0.020**	0.020	0.030**	0.010	0.030**	–0.010	0.010	0.010
Age	0.001	0.062**	0.006	–0.007	–0.022*	0.014	–0.065**	–0.004
Sex-role attitudes:								
Family roles	0.036	0.209	0.283**	0.224**	0.105+	0.056	0.141**	0.101
Job roles	0.070	–0.050	0.030	–0.100	0.178*	–0.032	0.095	–0.204
Husband's:								
Schooling	0.058**	–0.021	0.060**	–0.000	0.044**	–0.045*	0.046**	–0.053*
Work hours	–0.007*	0.002	–0.006	0.004	–0.005	–0.001	0.000	–0.011
Income	–0.010**	0.000	0.010	0.010	–0.000	0.000	0.000	0.010
Disability	0.074	1.143**	0.099	0.284+	0.386*	0.445*	0.564**	0.393

Two-tailed tests of significance:
** = $p \leq .01$
* = $.01 < p \leq .05$
+ = $.05 < p \leq .10$

Table 13.3 (Continued)

Dependent Variables	*Housecleaning*		*Laundry*		*Yard, Home Maintenance*		*Paperwork*	
	Husband	*Child*	*Husband*	*Child*	*Husband*	*Child*	*Husband*	*Child*
Dep Mean	0.209	0.306	0.116	0.168	0.705	0.133	0.425	0.007
R-squared	0.202	0.303	0.101	0.220	0.396	0.416	0.049	0.036
N =	2573	2573	2573	2573	2573	2573	2573	2573
Intercept	–2.538+	–2.554+	–3.449	–4.384	0.106**	–2.200**	–1.409*	–2.379**
Childhood family:								
Stepfamily I	0.317	0.321	0.000	0.188	0.117	–0.334	0.077	1.362
Mother-only family I	0.032	0.312+	0.159	0.323+	0.019	–0.006	–0.237+	0.525
Stepfather	0.010	0.280*	–0.106	0.066	0.167	–0.039	0.113	–0.939+
Children in family:								
Child < 4	0.099	–0.112	–0.301	–0.430*	0.321+	0.148	0.401**	–0.410
Child 4–6	–0.046	–0.299*	–0.123	–0.348*	0.030	–0.125	0.252*	0.313
Girl 12–18	0.280*	1.689**	–0.118	1.534**	–0.119	0.361+	–0.088	0.519
Girl > 18	–0.145	0.797**	–0.053	1.707**	–0.286	0.016	0.125	1.620+
Boy 12–18	–0.053	–0.067	–0.193	0.097	–0.130	0.928**	0.015	–0.751
Boy > 18	0.039	–0.294	–0.102	–0.371+	0.055	0.410	–0.001	–2.444**
Total number	0.100	0.445**	0.094	0.502**	0.184**	0.425**	0.035	–0.019

Black	0.130	0.685**	0.137	0.511**	–0.149	0.429+	0.459**	1.181+
Size	0.031	–0.062*	0.057+	–0.046	–0.059*	–0.110**	–0.019	–0.258*
South	–0.080	–0.282*	–0.058	–0.074	–0.080	0.216	–0.158+	0.019
Wife's:								
Schooling	0.027	–0.054*	0.054	–0.042	–0.056*	–0.133**	–0.039+	–0.403**
Employed	–0.234	0.055	–0.272	0.155	–0.076	–0.178	0.041	–0.711
Work hours	0.025**	0.008	0.025**	0.010+	0.007	–0.002	–0.002	–0.022
Disabled	0.552**	0.344+	0.378	0.669**	0.203	0.281	–0.172	0.536
Income	0.050**	0.030**	0.060**	0.040**	0.020*	0.020	0.010+	0.100*
Age	–0.019+	0.016	–0.026*	0.028*	0.018+	0.039**	0.023**	0.117**
Sex-role attitudes:								
Family roles	0.239**	0.119+	0.185*	0.133+	0.141*	0.133	0.008	0.272
Job roles	0.076	–0.060	0.111	–0.087	–0.272**	–0.172	–0.005	–0.401
Husband's:								
Schooling	0.045**	–0.007	0.038*	0.003	0.087**	0.040+	0.068**	0.056
Work hours	0.001	0.010**	–0.003	–0.002	0.009*	0.017**	–0.000	–0.010
Income	–0.010+	–0.000	–0.010	0.010	0.010	0.010	0.010**	0.010
Disability	0.383*	0.334*	0.366+	0.120	–0.171	0.589*	0.109	1.426+

Two-tailed tests of significance:
** = $p \leq .01$
* = $.01 < p \leq .05$
+ = $.05 < p \leq .10$

Figure 13.1 The Effects of Sharing by Husbands and Children on the Household Division of Labor

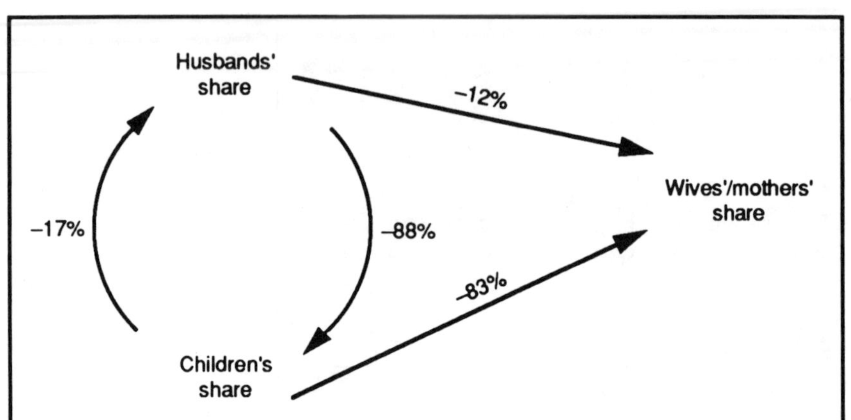

the rest. The factors that lead to high levels of husbands' sharing are likely to lead, therefore, to lower levels of children's sharing.

This is much less the case for factors influencing children's sharing. Each task done by children decreases the husband's participation in domestic chores by only about a sixth of one task; for every six additional tasks children do, husbands do only one fewer. These results suggest that when children take over housework they take over chores that would otherwise be done by their mother, or not get done at all.[11] But the work done by fathers appears to lighten the children's load almost on a one-for-one basis and to reduce the wife's responsibility only very modestly.

This substitution of fathers for children also complicates our understanding of the results we present here. When we examine the effects of, say, a woman's education on the extent her children share in household tasks, we see that the effect can operate through two pathways. It can have a direct effect on how much children share, *controlling for how much husbands share;* and it can affect the husband's share, which in turn affects the children's share as a consequence. We take both pathways into account in presenting our results.

Constraints on Parental Time and Energy

Our analyses indicate that wives do indeed take more responsibility for household chores the fewer hours they work outside the home, but that this is much less the case for husbands. The wife's hours in paid employment increase sharing both with husbands and children; the husband's hours affect his own share (though to a lesser extent than do his wife's hours) and have no direct affect on the extent children share.[12]

However, this result would not have appeared if the entire household economy were not considered, because the effects of women's employment on their family's participation are masked almost entirely by the reciprocal relationship between how much fathers and children share. Part of the pressure on the husband posed by the employment of his wife is *offset* by the response of the children to the employment of their mother, and vice versa. As a result, in simpler models (e.g., Goldscheider and Waite 1991, chap. 7–9), the small substitution of children for fathers weakens the observed impact of women's employment on husbands, and the strong substitution of fathers for children totally wipes out evidence of any effect on children. However, there actually is a strong and very similar effect of the hours of female employment on both children and husbands (although children continue to benefit more from their fathers' participation than fathers from their children's).

When we look at each household task separately, we find that both husbands and children share more grocery shopping, cooking, and laundry the more hours their wife and mother works outside the home;[13] husbands (but not children) are also more likely to share household cleaning and dishwashing. Further, there is a "pure" effect of employment: Net of the number of hours women work, simply being employed leads both their children and husbands to share more in dishwashing, as well as in childcare, even if wives work very few hours. Thus, between the effects of employment, per se, and the effects of the number of hours worked, the only chores for which husbands and children do not increase their responsibility with increases in the women's employment outside the home are yard and household maintainence and paperwork, both tasks that are frequently done by women but are not stereotypically "female."

Resources and Power

Labor-force involvement also produces earnings, and earnings can affect power, allowing spouses to shift some of the housework to others in the family. This is clearly the case for wives' earnings. Sharing with *both* husbands and children increases significantly as the wife's earnings rise, increasing husbands' and children's responsibility both overall and for housecleaning, laundry, and paperwork. Husbands also replace wives in yard work, grocery shopping, dishes, and cooking as her income rises.

These findings suggest that even though families hire help with household cleaning as their income rises (see Goldscheider and Waite 1991, chap. 10, n. 10), they also strongly substitute the labor of husbands and children for that of the wife as her earnings rise, responding to the value of her time outside the home. This implies that the woman's resources are not necessarily used to free the rest of the family from the burden of housework but

Figure 13.2 Effects of Women's Careers on the Household Division of Labor

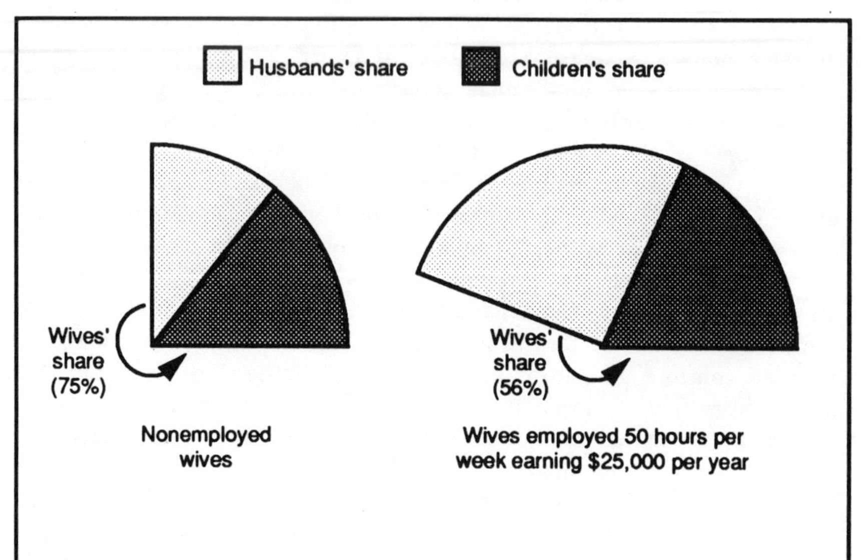

rather to shift it from her to others.[14] Evidently, a wife's power in the family increases with her earnings, providing her with the leverage to shift some responsibility for housework not only to her husband but also to her children. Thus, although many might feel that parents should stand in an authority relationship to children regardless of their earnings, money as a yardstick of worth has entered the family in the most direct way, so that children respect their mother and cooperate more with her when she, too, has earnings in the world outside the family.

To grasp the extent of the combined effects our model predicts for women *with careers,* we estimated husbands' and children's shares in families in which the woman works 50 hours a week and earns $25,000. Figure 13.2 shows that in such families, the wife's share of housework drops from 75 percent to 56 percent of the total, with substantial increases by both husbands and children, compared with nonworking wives.[15] This is an important group, because by 1987 about one out of eight working women earned this much or more (U.S. Bureau of the Census 1989). And if she is sufficiently successful as to earn $50,000 a year, our model predicts that husbands who are working normal hours and earning average salaries join with their children to take on more than half the household tasks measured here, leaving the wife with only about 45 percent.

Although the resources brought into the family by the wife reduce her share of housework, the husband's earnings have no impact on either the share that he does overall or the amount done by the children. For the tasks considered separately, higher-earning husbands are slightly less likely to share grocery shopping and housecleaning.[16] However, they are much more likely to take responsibility for the family paperwork, perhaps because for higher-income men, this function more frequently includes managing investments and savings, tasks they may prefer to retain themselves.

We also examined whether our various indicators of mothers' employment shifted responsibilities *among* children in a more egalitarian direction. We find that mothers who work more hours share slightly but significantly more with both teenage boys and teenage girls relative to younger children, with the greatest increases in boys' sharing of less stereotypically "female" chores and in girls' sharing of washing, cleaning, and cooking. (See Goldscheider and Waite 1991, Table 9.4.)

Given the importance in the current analysis not only of maternal employment but also of mothers' earnings, we looked to see whether children's responses to their mothers' employment differed depending on which dimension of employment was being considered—employment per se, number of employment hours, or earnings. An interesting result emerged. Although both teenage girls and boys increase their participation when their mothers work, as we indicated previously, girls are much more responsive than boys to the *fact* of maternal employment; boys are more responsive to maternal earnings (Goldscheider and Waite 1991, Table 10.6). Children's sharing in shopping, cleaning, and yardwork increases as maternal earnings rise when there are teenage boys in the family; this effect does not appear either for employment or work hours. In contrast, children's sharing in laundry, cooking, and childcare increases when mothers work outside the home and work more hours when there are teenage girls in the family, but the only comparable response to greater maternal earnings is laundry. To the extent, then, that earnings increase mothers' clout in their negotiation with their children, it is primarily felt by sons. Daughters are substituting directly for mothers in their absence.

Attitudes Toward the Division of Household Labor

There are clear differences in the household division of labor by wives' sex-role attitudes (particularly those relating to family roles), and educational level also has a strong effect (particularly that of the wife). The share of husbands and children responds strongly to increases in the family roles scale; however, because the husband's share directly reduces the share children do far more than the children's share reduces that of the husband's, the net result is that husbands in families in which the wife holds more modern attitudes[17] share 44 percent more than husbands in families with traditional wives; children only increase their level of sharing by 5 percent. These increases by both husbands and children relieve women of some of

Figure 13.3 Effect of Wives' Attitudes About Women's Family Roles on the Household Division of Labor

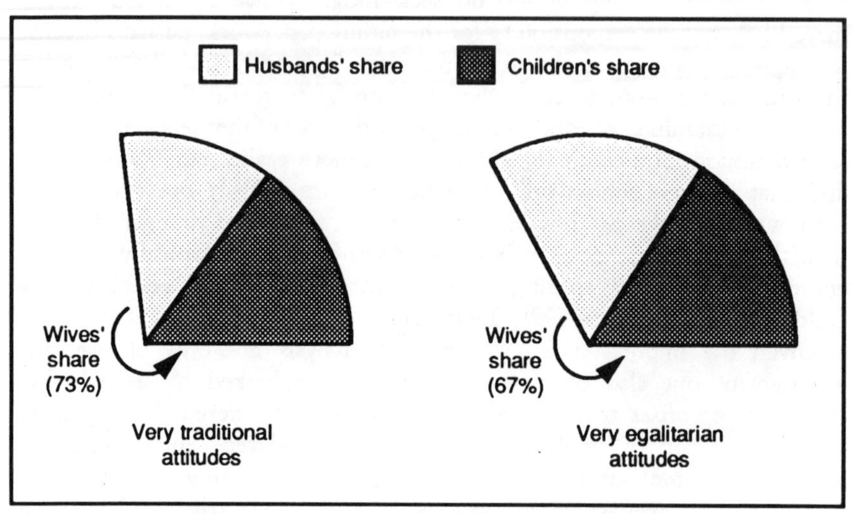

the household burden, but not dramatically—the share of wives with very modern attitudes is 86 percent that of very traditional wives. (See Fig. 13.3.) Nevertheless, the effects on the involvement in housework of both husbands and children are substantial. The chores that are most likely to be shared are laundry, dishwashing, and housecleaning. For other chores—cooking, childcare, and yardwork—it is primarily the husbands that are drawn in by wives with relatively modern attitudes. Only grocery shopping and paperwork remain unaffected by family-related sex-role attitudes.

Holding more modern attitudes about women's role in paid employment (job roles), in contrast, has much less effect. It does not significantly influence KIDSHARE or HUBSHARE in the 2SLS analysis and never leads to increased participation by children in any of the specific chores. Husbands respond more to their wives' attitudes than children do to their mother's, although the response is somewhat equivocal. They increase their responsibility for cooking and childcare but *reduce* their responsibility for yardwork. Evidently, the wife's strong approval of equality for women in the labor market reflects her own job commitment, but it is not coupled with much willingness to pass family tasks on to others.

How do the effects of parental education fit into this picture? Our results show that husbands share more in families in which either the husband or the wife has more education, although the husband's education has a considerably greater effect than the wife's, increasing his participation substantially in all chores. The wife's education further increases her spouse's contribution to washing dishes and to childcare.

Figure 13.4 Effects of Parental Education on the Household Division of Labor

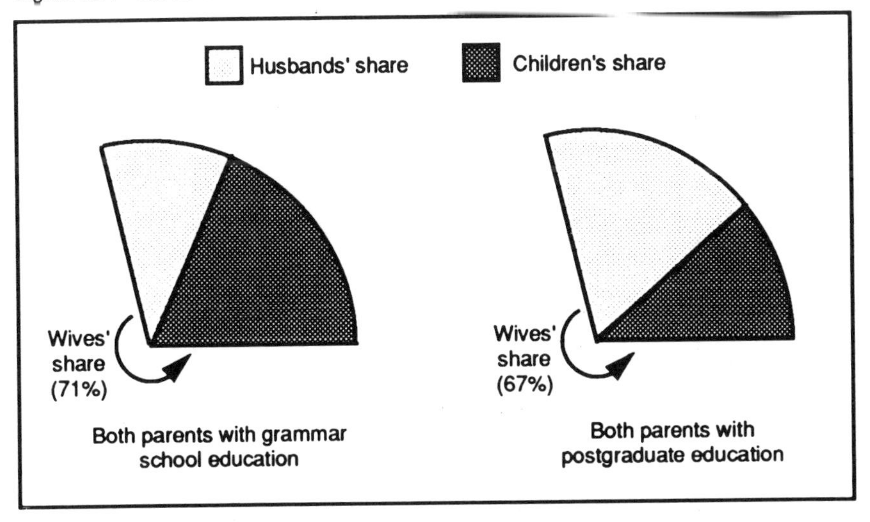

The primary effect of increased male education on the children's share is indirect, because a greater husbands' share reduces the children's share. Highly educated husbands appear particularly to replace their children in cooking and childcare (although their children do take more responsibility for yardwork and home maintenance than do others). Maternal education has a stronger effect on reducing the children's participation: the more schooling the mother has received, the less she shares grocery shopping, childcare, housecleaning, yardwork and paperwork with children (and the less she shares yardwork and paperwork with her *husband*).

In Figure 13.4, we show the power of higher education in trading off the shares of fathers and children. In families in which both parents are highly educated,[18] the husbands' share of household tasks is 80 percent greater than in families in which the parents have only completed grammar school. In contrast, children in highly educated families share at only 68 percent the level of children in poorly educated families. Thus it is clear that most of the effect of increasing education has been to shift *who* is helping the wife and mother; *her* share decreases, but only slightly (from 71 percent to 67 percent of housework responsibility). To the extent that the growth in household sharing exhibited by husbands in recent years is the result of increases in education, then, it is not at all clear that women have gained much relief from their double burden; their husbands have basically substituted for the share previously taken by children.

Thus, children in more educated families *observe* greater sharing in household tasks between men and women. But they *participate* much less in these tasks than children in families in which parents have less education.

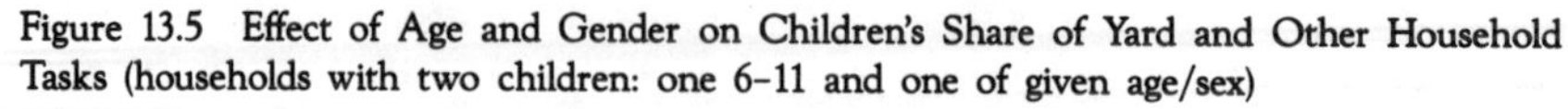

Figure 13.5 Effect of Age and Gender on Children's Share of Yard and Other Household Tasks (households with two children: one 6–11 and one of given age/sex)

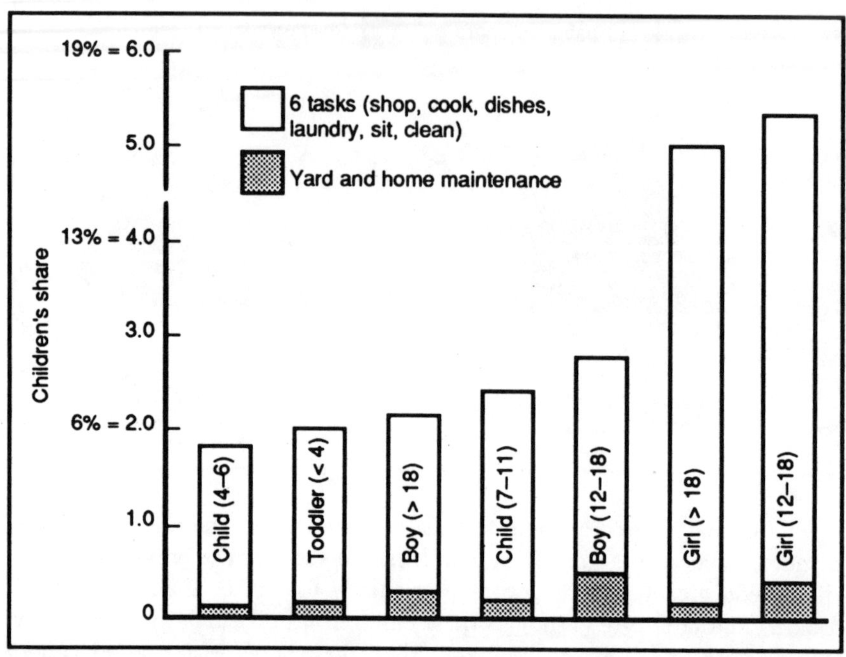

The increase in egalitarianism in more educated families, then, provides children with more positive role models for egalitarian families of their own, but this may also mean that neither gender will come of age with any feeling of competence or pleasure in homemaking.

Children's Age and Sex

The age and sex of the children in the family influence the share of housework that children do and which chores they share. Figure 13.5 presents differences in children's share of household tasks, comparing families with children of different ages, boys and girls. It shows the total amount of sharing for seven of the eight tasks for which information is available (excluding paperwork), distinguishing yard and home maintenance from the others.[19]

The presence of children of different ages, males or females, has no effect on the extent husbands share in household tasks *once the effect on children's share is taken into account.* But the characteristics of the children strongly influence the extent *children* share a great deal. If we consider the younger children first (those younger than 12), there are few differences among families that have only preteenage children, with only a slight tendency to report less sharing if some children are particularly young (toddlers or children 4 to 6). What matters most is the presence of an older daughter, particularly a teenage daughter.

To look at the contribution of older children, we divided families into those with any sons aged 12 to 18 (we call all children of this age teenagers), those with any teenage daughters, those with any adult sons (ages 19 and over) and those with any adult daughters. We then compared the amount of housework done by children in these families to see *which kinds* of children were contributing labor in the family and how much they contributed to "male" as compared with "female" tasks.

As children get older, they clearly become more involved in household chores, in- and out-of-doors. Families with teenage children share substantially more housework with their children than families with only preteens. Teenage children are most particularly helpful with yardwork, with about equal amounts of sharing from teenage boys and girls. But the biggest differences by age and sex are in "female" chores.

Families with teenage girls report sharing *three times more* of these other tasks with children than do families with boys of the same age. In fact, girls ages 12 to 18 seem to carry the largest share of housework. Mothers with a daughter aged 12 to 18 delegate essentially three quarters of an entire task (most of the laundry, say; or most of the dishes) compared with mothers with children ages 6 to 11. Although teenage girls do more of all household tasks (except paperwork) than their younger brothers and sisters, they seem to contribute especially large amounts toward doing dishes and cleaning the house and to share substantially in cooking and laundry. Their teenage brothers, in contrast, share little more than younger siblings overall, with only a significant increase in yardwork.

Of adult sons and daughters, girls seem to continue their contributions to the household economy as they reach young adulthood, sharing only slightly less after age 18 than before. However, young adult males contribute no more overall to housework than do preteen children, and substantially less than their sisters of the same age. In fact, grown sons do significantly less dishwashing, cooking, childcare, and laundry than children 6 to 12 years old. It is not that these young men contribute to the family through their earnings, because most evidence suggests that adult children living at home keep their earnings (Goldscheider and Goldscheider 1991). Hence, grown sons are being subsidized by their parents both financially and in terms of household services, because although they certainly eat and require clean clothes, they rarely contribute to the performance of these tasks; someone has to provide these services to them. Staying at home after age 18 seems to provide much less benefit for daughters than for sons. Although sons provide virtually no help in housework (even in yard and home maintenance), daughters continue to contribute at a very high level after age 18.

Conclusions and Discussion

From our examination of the three-way division of labor within the family that focuses on trade-offs between wives, husbands, and children in performing housework, it is clear that the primary productive interaction in American homes in the 1980s is one that still reflects the time when families were in an economy that only employed men outside the home and that held out opportunities for future paid employment only to sons and not daughters. Wives, even those working as many hours outside the home as their husbands, still take responsibility for most domestic tasks; and parents raising children in the 1980s still share household tasks with them in very traditional ways, giving girls more responsibility than boys and dividing tasks up so that what are considered female adult tasks are shared with daughters and what are considered male adult tasks are primarily shared with sons.

But our evaluation of the effects of time constraints, power, and attitudes suggests that there is likely to be a strong trend toward increased sharing by men in household tasks. As wives increase their time in paid employment, and particularly as their pay for that employment nears parity with men, spouses' responsibility for household tasks is likely to come much closer to equality, although full equality depends on greater acceptance of more egalitarian sex-role attitudes. But household responsibilities may reach equality at extremely low levels of competence in domestic skills if the next generation of adults receives the domestic training that currently is being given to children; the picture of family life that modern, egalitarian parents often present is one in which both parents are picking up after and waiting on their children. As such, they may well be finding that the additional burden of children is too much to impose on a modern, egalitarian marriage.

For children, particularly daughters, seem increasingly to be withdrawing from domestic responsibilities. Not all signs point in this direction: Increases in women's paid employment and in egalitarian sex-role attitudes do increase children's share, but these effects are nearly offset by the increases in the husbands' share and the reduction this causes in children's shares. And other forces seem to lead unequivocally to a decline in children's involvement in the productive work of the household. Over time, as the women in our sample who were educated during the depression and World War II are replaced by younger women who have achieved considerably higher levels of education, children's responsibility for household tasks is likely to decline. Other factors that we did not discuss explicitly, particularly those associated with mothers' age and with rural residence, suggest also that the trend in children's involvement is likely to be negative. Traditional men may soon be as unlikely to find a wife with domestic skills as modern women are to find such skills in their potential husbands.

The study of the domestic economy in the late twentieth century is in its infancy. Clearly, we need to look at the roles of all family members and particularly to take into account the ways husbands and children substitute for each other rather than lightening the burden on their wife and mother. But we also need to more directly examine the home and the ways family relationships are developed there. Is it only a "haven" from the world of work, first for working men, then for studious children, and now for women reaching for full-time employment outside the home? Is it only a place for leisure? Or might not this primary locus of family interaction also be the site for learning how to share, to give, and to interact in positive ways?

For homemaking can be an act of love. Everything people do to help, or cheer, or please one another is showing their love and care. Working overtime to earn a little more to buy a spouse a present, making something at school for a parent, or preparing a favorite dish for a grandchild are all ways people can express their love and warmth and strengthen each other's lives. The home touches people's lives at so many points—at rest, at meals, at play. As such, it is perhaps the richest environment of all for this kind of interaction. The skills required to function there successfully may be the most important training families can give to both their male and female members.

Acknowledgments

This research was supported by Center Grant No. P-50-HD-12639 from the Center for Population Research, NICHD, and Grant No. SES-8609092 from the National Science Foundation. It is a revision of a paper presented at the 1989 meetings of the American Sociological Association, San Francisco, CA. We acknowledge the helpful comments of Calvin Goldscheider, Eileen Miech, Rafe Stolzenberg, and Lynn White, and the invaluable and patient programming assistance of David Rumpel.

Notes

1. An important exception to this generalization is the pathbreaking work of Berk (1985), which looks at the apportionment of work in American households. The study considers the roles of husbands, wives, and teenage children in housework as well as the effects of the volume and apportionment of these tasks on the employment of wives and mothers. Many of our interpretations are buttressed through reference to Berk's findings. However, most of the results we report did

not appear in that study, probably because of the small size of her sample (335 families).

2. So far, no one has asked parents a question parallel to one often asked about husbands: "Is it fair to ask a child who has worked hard all day at school and has homework to do chores around the house?"

3. In our interpretations, we assume that if families with teenagers tend to share more with children than do families with younger children only, then these families probably share more with teens. Similarly, if women in families with girls share more with their children than do women in families with boys, we can reasonably conclude that they are sharing more with their daughters. This allows us to answer in a general way questions about the characteristics of children that increase the extent of their sharing in household tasks. We were able to confirm this inference directly in families with only one child, because the patterns we found by age and gender of child are the same for these families as for all families.

4. Either she has sole responsibility, shares with someone other than children, or has no responsibility and the children also have none.

5. Analysis of the scale characteristics of the household tasks was performed with ANLITH (analysis of item-trait homogeneity). The relationship between each item and the scale was corrected for overlap between the item and the scale, because the scale is the sum of all household tasks. An item-scale correlation corrected for overlap in the correlation between the item score and the sum of the items in the scale other than the item in question. All items needed a corrected correlation of 0.30 or higher to be included in the final scale (Donald and Ware 1982). Using this criterion, childcare and yard and home maintenance could also have been included in the combined scale for sharing with children, but we chose to use the same set as for husbands for clarity of interpretation.

6. Each coefficient shows how a change in the variable affects the log-odds ratio of choosing a given alternative relative to some other alternative. In the equations estimated below, the value of each explanatory variable is the same over all alternatives for each individual; its effect is allowed to differ among the responsibility configurations. These multinomial logistic equations have been estimated by an ordinary least-squares approximation described in Haggstrom (1983). This technique provides unbiased estimates of the multinomial logistic coefficients and their t-statistics but does not provide a summary statistic of goodness of fit.

7. We originally had expected to include a measure of the husband's disability with the husband's hours of paid work as an additional restriction on a man's ability to take responsibility for domestic tasks, but we found that disabled husbands actually increased their responsibility for many chores, even controlling for their hours of paid work and earnings. This suggested to us that the fact of disability has effects beyond the physical and may disproportionately restrict men's hours in public activities such as socializing with friends, encouraging them to spend more time at home and be involved in its domestic activities.

8. We do not discuss here the full set of variables included in our regressions, which also included race, region, city size, mother's age, her experiences of non-traditional family structures in childhood, and whether her husband is the father of the resident children. For a fuller elaboration of the rest of our model and a

discussion of the results of the other variables included in these regressions, see Goldschieder and Waite 1991, Chapter 10.

9. There are, of course, many other sources of marital power. Women who think that they are particularly attractive to men wield greater power over their husbands through their sense of having alternatives (Udry 1981). It is also the case that men in some occupations, such as the ministry, are constrained from leaving their wives because of the remaining stigma of divorce, which is likely to increase wives' power in the marriage.

10. Previous studies have measured the wife's earnings, the husband's earnings, and the ratio between them. Most studies find relatively little impact of relative earnings of spouses on the division of household labor; absolute levels of earnings and education have more effect. See, in particular, Berk and Berk 1979; Coverman 1985; Farkas 1976; Hannan, Tuma, and Groeneveld 1977; Kamo 1988; Maret and Finlay 1984. However, Ross (1987) finds that the smaller the gap between the husband's earnings and those of his wife, the greater his relative contribution to housework.

11. An alternative interpretation is that husbands are much more efficient than children, so their sharing a task reduces the amount of work to be done far more than is the case with children. This could happen if, to earn the response that they "share responsibility" for these tasks, children are only cleaning their rooms, or doing their own laundry. No data are currently available to resolve this puzzle, because what is needed is not only information on housework hours but on the efficiency of housework by various family members.

12. Given the structure of the 2SLS mode, we could only look for a direct effect of husbands' work hours on children's sharing in the individual chores analyses, but, consistent with our hypothesis, husbands' hours have no direct effect on the children's share of individual chores.

13. However, *employed* mothers less often share grocery shopping with either children or husbands. Working women apparently shop on the way home from work.

14. We should note again here that we are not studying housework hours; rather our focus is on sharing responsibility for housework. If families purchase substitutes—dinner at Wendy's, take-out Chinese, order-in pizza—for the wife's labor, then family members could be increasing their share of household chores simply because the wife has reduced her contribution. So the husband and children take responsibility for a large proportion of the chores, but the chores themselves have shrunk. And families may simply be shifting responsibility for arranging for a given chore—rather than for doing it—to children or husband. For example, the husband—or even a 10-year-old child—could call in an order or stop and pick up dinner on the way home.

15. This and the figures to follow show the effect of the factors being considered, not of all the other factors we include in our models. We solved jointly for values of both husbands' and children's shares using iteration, taking the mean values of other variables.

16. In part because their earnings are contributing to hiring outside help.

17. We define modern wives as those with family roles scale values of +1.5; traditional wives as those with scale values of −2.0.

18. We compare families with both parents with some postgraduate education (18 years) with those who did not complete any years of high school (8 years).

19. This figure is based not on Table 13.2 but on Tables 9.1 and 9.2 in Goldscheider and Waite 1991, which do not include the effects of husbands' sharing. However, the pattern of results is similar for the ages and sex of children in the two analyses; and the regressions on specific tasks in these other tables are based on information on the extent of sharing (rather than on the fact of sharing, as is the case in the polytomous logit analysis), allowing us to include the quantitative assessment of the proportion accounted for by "yard and home maintenance."

References

Berk, Sarah Fenstermaker, 1985. *The Gender Factory*, New York: Plenum.

Berk, Richard A., and Sarah Fenstermaker Berk, 1979. *Labor and Leisure at Home: Content and Organization of the Household Day*, Sage Library of Social Research, Vol. 87, Beverly Hills: Sage.

Brody, Charles J., and Lala Carr Steelman, 1985. "Sibling Structure and Parental Sex-typing of Children's Household Tasks," *Journal of Marriage and the Family*, Vol. 47, May, pp. 265–273.

Chodorow, Nancy, 1978. *The Reproduction of Mothering: Psychoanalysis and the Sociology of Gender*, Berkeley: University of California Press.

Cogle, Frances L., and Grace E. Tasker, 1982. "Children and Housework," *Family Relations*, Vol. 31, July, pp. 395–399.

Coverman, Shelley, 1985. "Explaining Husbands' Participation in Domestic Labor," *The Sociological Quarterly*, Vol. 26, No. 1, pp. 81–97.

Coverman, Shelley, and Joseph F. Sheley, 1986. "Change in Men's Housework and Child-Care Time, 1965–1975," *Journal of Marriage and the Family*, Vol. 48, May, pp. 413–422.

Donald, Cathy A., and John E. Ware, Jr., 1982. *The Quantification of Social Contacts and Resources*, R-2937-HHS, Santa Monica: The Rand Corporation.

Duncan, Beverly, and Otis Dudley Duncan, 1978. *Sex Typing and Social Roles: A Research Report*, New York: Academic Press.

Farkas, George, 1976. "Education, Wage Rates, and the Division of Labor Between Husband and Wife," *Journal of Marriage and the Family*, Vol. 38, August, pp. 473–483.

Fuchs, Victor R., 1988. *Women's Quest for Economic Equality*, Cambridge, MA: Harvard University Press.

Gershuny, Jonathan, and John P. Robinson, 1988. "Historical Changes in the Household Division of Labor," *Demography*, Vol. 25, No. 4, November, pp. 537–554.

Goldscheider, Frances, and Calvin Goldscheider, 1991. "The Intergenerational Flow of Income: Family Structure and the Status of Black Americans," *Journal of Marriage and the Family*, Vol. 53, May, pp. 499–508.

Goldscheider, Frances, and Linda J. Waite, 1991. *New Families, No Families? The Transformation of the American Home*, Berkeley: University of California Press.

Greif, Geoffrey L., 1985. "Children and Housework in the Single Father Family," *Family Relations*, Vol. 34, No. 3, pp. 353–357.

Haggstrom, Gus W., 1983. "Logistic Regression and Discriminant Analysis by Ordinary Least Squares," *Journal of Business and Economic Statistics*, Vol. 1, pp. 229–238.

Hannan, Michael T., Nancy Brandon Tuma, and Lyle P. Groeneveld, 1977. "Income and Marital Events: Evidence from an Income-Maintenance Experiment," *American Journal of Sociology*, Vol. 82, No. 6, May, pp. 1186–1211.

Kamo, Yoshinori, 1988. "Determinants of Household Division of Labor: Resources, Power, and Ideology," *Journal of Family Issues*, Vol. 9, No. 2, June, pp. 177–200.

Lasch, Christopher, 1977. *Haven in a Heartless World*, New York: Basic Books.

Light, Harriett K., Doris Hertsgaard, and Ruth E. Martin, 1985. "Farm Children's Work in the Family," *Adolescence*, Vol. 20, No. 78, Summer, pp. 425–432.

Maret, Elizabeth, and Barbara Finlay, 1984. "The Distribution of Household Labor Among Women in Dual-Earner Families," *Journal of Marriage and the Family*, Vol. 46, May, pp. 357–364.

Mason, Karen O., and Larry L. Bumpass, 1975. "U.S. Women's Sex-Role Ideology," *American Journal of Sociology*, Vol. 80, pp. 1212–1219.

Mason, Karen O., John L. Czajka, and Sara Arber, 1976. "Change in U.S. Women's Sex-Role Attitudes, 1964–1974," *American Sociological Review*, Vol. 41, pp. 573–596.

Miller, Joanne, and Howard H. Garrison, 1982. "Sex Roles: The Division of Labor at Home and in the Workplace," *Annual Review of Sociology*, Vol. 8, pp. 237–262.

Propper, Alice Marcella, 1972. "The Relationship of Maternal Employment to Adolescent Roles, Activities, and Parental Relationships," *Journal of Marriage and the Family*, Vol. 34, No. 3, August, pp. 417–421.

Ross, Catherine E., 1987. "The Division of Labor at Home," *Social Forces*, Vol. 65, No. 3, March, pp. 816–833.

Ross, Catherine E., and John Mirowsky, 1989. *The Social Causes of Psychological Distress*, New York: Aldine de Gruyter.

Roy, Prodipto, 1961. "Maternal Employment and Adolescent Roles: Rural-Urban Differentials," *Marriage and Family Living*, November, pp. 340–349.

Sanik, Margaret Mietus, 1981. "Division of Household Work: A Decade Comparison—1967–1977," *Home Economics Research Journal*, Vol. 10, No. 2, December, pp. 175–180.

Shorter, Edward, 1975. *The Making of the Modern Family*, New York: Basic Books.

Spitze, Glenna D., 1986. "The Division of Task Responsibility in U.S. Households: Longitudinal Adjustments to Change," *Social Forces*, Vol. 64, No. 3, March, pp. 689–701.

Thornton, Arland, 1989. "Changing Attitudes Towards Family Issues in the United States," *Journal of Marriage and the Family*, Vol. 51, November, pp. 873–893.

Thrall, Charles A., 1978. "Who Does What: Role Stereotypy, Children's Work, and Continuity Between Generations in the Household Division of Labor," *Human Relations*, Vol. 31, No. 3, pp. 249–265.

Tilly, Louise, and Joan Scott, 1978. *Women, Work, and Society*, New York: Holt, Rinehart & Winston.

Timmer, Susan Goff, Jacquelynne Eccles, and Kerth O'Brien, 1985. "How Children Use Time," pp. 353–382 in F. Thomas Juster and Frank P. Stafford (eds.), *Time, Goods, and Wellbeing*, Ann Arbor: SRC, ISR, University of Michigan.

Udry, Richard, 1981. "Marital Alternatives and Marital Disruption," *Journal of Marriage and the Family*, Vol. 43, pp. 889–897.

U.S. Bureau of the Census, 1989. "Money Income of Households, Families and Persons in the United States: 1987," in Current Population Reports, Series P-60, No. 162. Washington, D.C.: U.S. Government Printing Office.

Walker, Kathryn, and Margaret E. Woods, 1976. *Time Use: A Measure of Household Production of Goods and Services*, Washington, D.C.: American Home Economics Association.

Weiss, Robert S., 1979. "Growing Up a Little Faster: The Experience of Growing Up in a Single-Parent Household," *Journal of Social Issues*, Vol. 35, No. 4, pp. 97–111.

White, Lynn K., 1989. "Comments," remarks prepared for the session "The Family Division of Labor," annual meetings of the American Sociological Association, San Francisco, August.

White, Lynn K., and David B. Brinkerhoff, 1981a. "Children's Work in the Family," *Journal of Marriage and the Family*, Vol. 43, November, pp. 789–798.

———, 1981b. "The Sexual Division of Labor: Evidence from Childhood," *Social Forces*, Vol. 60, No. 1, September, pp. 170–181.

Zelizer, Viviana, 1985. *Pricing the Priceless Child: The Changing Social Value of Children*, New York: Basic Books.

Appendix 13.1: Measuring Sex-Role Attitudes

The NLS is a relatively rich source of information on this subject, containing a series of general questions on sex-role attitudes measured in several years. We used this information to construct two general indices of sex-role attitudes from questions asked in the National Longitudinal Surveys of Young Women and Mature Women. The questions deal primarily with the impact of women's employment on their families and ask respondents for value judgments about the appropriate roles for men and women. These were Likert-type questions coded as five-point scales from "strongly agree" to "strongly disagree." These questions were asked, with some modest variations, in a number of survey years. The analysis reported here uses measures of sex-role attitudes taken from the 1982 mature women's survey and the 1983 young women's survey.

The variables used in our analyses are the composite indices (or factor scores) derived from the coefficient matrix of a factor analysis done with oblique rotation. Our factor analysis of each of the series produced two distinct dimensions. One, which we call family roles, reflects the importance of women's time at home to their children and families. The second dimension, job roles, measures views of the importance of women's employment to their self-esteem and to the economic well-being of their families. A higher score indicates greater acceptance of nonfamilial roles for wives and mothers. These two dimensions had a correlation of .3 with each other. Greater detail on these indices can be found in Goldscheider and Waite (1991).

Finding two distinct dimensions of sex-role attitudes in this series of questions replicates results from a number of other studies. Mason and Bumpass (1975) and Mason, Czajka, and Arber (1976) found, using questions overlapping to some extent with those we use, that respondents answered relatively consistently to all questions on the appropriateness of the traditional division of labor within the family and to those on women's roles in the labor market but apparently saw little need to connect their views across these two dimensions.

About the Book

In this book, leading authorities on the family show how families, parents, and children have been affected by changing patterns of marriage and cohabitation. Taking a long historical perspective, some authors consider trends such as the decline of multigenerational families and group differences in the relationships between economic opportunity and the timing of marriage. But the focus is predominantly on questions of current interest: patterns of union formation, differences between marriage and cohabitation, contact between divorced fathers and their children, the division of household labor, and the transmission of attitudes and behavior across generations. Intended for scholars and advanced students, this book offers essential analysis of the changing dimensions of the American family.

About the Editors and Contributors

Neil G. Bennett is Associate Professor and Director of Graduate Studies in the Sociology Department at Yale University and Research Associate at the National Bureau of Economic Research. Much of his work is concerned with issues related to the sociology of marital formation and dissolution. Other work focuses on out-of-wedlock childbearing, the development of formal demographic models, their application to mortality estimation in the United States and less developed nations, and policy issues surrounding U.S. health care.

David E. Bloom is Professor and Chairman in the Economics Department at Columbia University and Research Associate at the National Bureau of Economic Research. He writes predominantly on problems in demography and labor economics.

Larry L. Bumpass is Norman B. Ryder Professor of Sociology at the University of Wisconsin–Madison and a member of the Center for Demography and Ecology. He and James Sweet are co-directors of the National Survey of Families and Household. His research deals with marriage, marital disruption, cohabitation, fertility, family structure, and intergenerational relations.

Patricia H. Craig is a doctoral candidate in the Sociology Department at Yale University. Her research interests are primarily in political sociology and the family.

Frank F. Furstenberg, Jr., is the Zellerbach Family Professor of Sociology and Research Associate in the Population Studies Center at the University of Pennsylvania. His interest in the American family began at Columbia University where he received his Ph.D. in 1967. His most recent books include *Adolescent Mothers in Later Life* (with J. Brooks-Gunn and S. Philip Morgan) and *Divided Families: What Happens to Children When Parents Part* (with Andy Cherlin).

Ron Goeken is a doctoral candidate in History at the University of Minnesota. He is currently writing a dissertation on unrelated individuals in America since 1880.

Frances K. Goldscheider is Professor of Sociology and Director of the Population Studies and Training Center at Brown University. Her research specialty is household and family demography. She has recently published (with Linda Waite) *New Families, No Families? The Transformation of the American Home.*

Kathleen Mullan Harris is Assistant Professor of Sociology and Fellow of the Carolina Population Center at the University of North Carolina at Chapel Hill.

Her research interests include poverty, family, and social policy. She is completing a book on the life course of teenage mothers and their experience with welfare dependency. Her ongoing research projects focus on the dynamics of work and welfare among single mothers in poverty and the changing role of fathers in the family.

Amy E. Holmes is a Ph.D. candidate in the Department of History at the University of Michigan. She is the author of "'Such Is the Price We Pay': American Widows and the Civil War Pension System," in Maris A. Vinovskis (ed.), *Toward a Social History of the American Civil War: Exploratory Essays.*

Nancy S. Landale is Associate Professor of Sociology at The Pennsylvania State University. Her major research interests pertain to family formation and dissolution processes, especially the influence of contextual factors on family behavior over the life course. She is currently working on a study of the marriage and childbearing behavior of mainland Puerto Ricans and is also engaged in research on assimilation and family formation in the early twentieth-century United States.

Dawn Owens is a doctoral student in the Department of Sociology, University of Illinois at Urbana-Champaign. Her dissertation focuses on the determinants of nonmarital cohabitation after divorce.

Ronald R. Rindfuss is Professor of Sociology and a Fellow of the Carolina Population Center, University of North Carolina at Chapel Hill. His current research includes investigation of patterns of social change in Nang Rong, Thailand, the relationships among activities of young adults in the United States, and changes in patterns of contraceptive and sexual behavior among American adolescents.

Steven Ruggles is Associate Professor of History at the University of Minnesota. He is the author of *Prolonged Connections: The Rise of the Extended Family in Nineteenth Century England and America* (1987) and several articles on historical family structure.

Robert Schoen is a Professor in the Department of Population Dynamics at Johns Hopkins University. His research interests are the changing American family, ethnic demography, and population models.

Scott J. South is Associate Professor of Sociology at the State University of New York at Albany. His research on families deals primarily with the impact of imbalanced marriage markets on women's sociodemographic behavior and with the structural determinants of marriage and divorce rates.

James A. Sweet is Professor and Chair of the Department of Sociology at the University of Wisconsin–Madison and a member of the Center for Demography and Ecology. He and Larry Bumpass are co-directors of the National Survey of Families and Households, a large, comprehensive national survey of American family life. The sample, first interviewed in 1987–1988, is being reinterviewed in 1992–1993. His research deals with marriage, marital disruption, cohabitation, and family structure.

Jay D. Teachman is Professor of Sociology and a member of the Center on Population, Gender and Social Inequality at the University of Maryland. He is interested in family demography and the statistical tools necessary to analyze complex life histories.

Arland Thornton is Professor of Sociology and research scientist at the Institute for Social Research at the University of Michigan. His research focuses on trends, causes, and consequences of marriage, cohabitation, divorce, fertility, gender roles, adolescent sexuality, and intergenerational relations. He conducts research on these topics in Nepal, Taiwan, and the United States.

Stewart E. Tolnay is Associate Professor of Sociology and Director of the Center for Social and Demographic Analysis at the State University of New York at Albany. His research interests include the historical demography of southern blacks and the history of racial violence in the South.

Audrey VandenHeuvel is a research associate at the Australian Institute of Family Studies, Melbourne, Australia. Her research interests center on the intersection of social demography and family sociology.

Maris A. Vinovskis is a Professor in the Department of History and a research scientist in the Institute for Social Research at the University of Michigan. He is the coauthor, with Gerald Moran, of *Religion, Family, and the Life Course: Explorations in the Social History of Early America.*

Linda Waite is Professor of Sociology at The University of Chicago, Research Associate at the National Opinion Research Center, and Research Associate at the RAND Corporation. She is currently working on social exchange networks, the relationship between childbearing and marital disruption, mortality among married couples, the formation and dissolution of cohabiting and marital relationships, and family formation and higher education.